Speaking Face to Face

SUNY SERIES, PRAXIS: THEORY IN ACTION
Nancy A. Naples, editor

Speaking Face to Face

The Visionary Philosophy of María Lugones

Edited by Pedro J. DiPietro, Jennifer McWeeny, and Shireen Roshanravan

Cover image: "Hunger." © e nina jay.

Published by State University of New York Press, Albany

© 2019 State University of New York

All rights reserved

No part of this book may be used or reproduced in any manner whatsoever without written permission. No part of this book may be stored in a retrieval system or transmitted in any form or by any means including electronic, electrostatic, magnetic tape, mechanical, photocopying, recording, or otherwise without the prior permission in writing of the publisher.

For information, contact State University of New York Press, Albany, NY
www.sunypress.edu

Library of Congress Cataloging-in-Publication Data

Names: DiPietro, Pedro J., editor. | McWeeny, Jennifer, editor. | Roshanravan, Shireen, editor.
Title: Speaking face to face : the visionary philosophy of María Lugones / edited by Pedro J. DiPietro, Jennifer McWeeny, and Shireen Roshanravan.
Description: Albany : State University of New York Press, [2019] | Series: SUNY series, praxis: theory in action | Includes bibliographical references and index.
Identifiers: LCCN 2018033268| ISBN 9781438474533 (hardcover : alk. paper) | ISBN 9781438474540 (e-book) | ISBN 9781438474526 (paperback : alk. paper)
Subjects: LCSH: Lugones, Maria, 1944- | Feminist theory.
Classification: LCC HQ1190 .S676 2019 | DDC 305.42—dc23 LC record available at https://lccn.loc.gov/2018033268

10 9 8 7 6 5 4 3 2

To all those who commit to living and loving large against the expectations of a world that relies on our living and loving small. And, of course, to María Lugones, for inspiring us to see, feel, speak, think, cook, sing, dance, create, and enact impossible worlds of verifiable love into existence.

Contents

List of Illustrations — xi

Acknowledgments — ix

List of Abbreviations — xvii

Introduction Like an Earthquake to the Soul: Experiencing the Visionary Philosophy of María Lugones — 1
Pedro J. DiPietro, Jennifer McWeeny, and Shireen Roshanravan

PART I COALITIONAL SELVES, MULTIPLE REALITIES

1 Trash Talks Back — 31
   Elizabeth V. Spelman

2 A Focus on the "I" in the "I → We": Considering the Lived Experience of Self-in-Coalition in Active Subjectivity — 47
   Kelli Zaytoun

3 The Ripple Imagery as a Decolonial Self: Exploring Multiplicity in Theresa Hak Kyung Cha's *Dictée* — 65
   (Brena) Yu-Chen Tai

PART II MOVING WITH AND BEYOND INTERSECTIONALITY

4 Beyond the "Logic of Purity": "Post-Post-Intersectional" Glimpses in Decolonial Feminism — 85
   Anna Carastathis

5 Witnessing Faithfully and the Intimate Politics of Queer South Asian Praxis — 103
   Shireen Roshanravan

PART III GENDER, COLONIALITY, AND DECOLONIAL EMBODIMENTS

6   Border Thinking/Being/Perception: Toward a "Deep Coalition" across the Atlantic   125
    Madina Tlostanova

7   Motion Sickness and the Slipperiness of Irish Racialization   145
    Jennifer McWeeny

8   Toward a Decolonial Ethics   175
    Manuel Chávez Jr.

PART IV KNOWING ON THE EDGE OF WORLDS AND SENSE

9   Beyond Benevolent Violence: Trans* of Color, Ornamental Multiculturalism, and the Decolonization of Affect   197
    Pedro J. DiPietro

10 Travel to Death-Worlds   217
    Joshua M. Price

PART V *HABLANDO CARA A CARA*

11 Deep Coalition and Popular Education Praxis   239
    Cricket Keating

12 Walking Illegitimately: A *Cachapera/Tortillera* and a Dyke   255
    Sarah Lucia Hoagland

13 Carnal Disruptions: Mariana Ortega Interviews María Lugones   273

    Afterword   285
    Paula M. L. Moya

    Chronological List of María Lugones's Publications   291

    Contributors   299

    Index   303

Illustrations

Figure 6.1	*Delinking* by Taus Makhacheva, 2011.	138
Figure 7.1	Frontispiece from *Ireland from One or Two Neglected Points of View*, 1899.	152
Figure 7.2	"The Ignorant Vote: Honors are Easy" by Thomas Nast, 1876.	153
Figure 7.3	"Florence Nightingale and Bridget McBruiser" from *New Physiognomy*, 1866.	154
Figure 7.4	"The Irish Declaration of Independence" by Frederick B. Opper, 1883.	155

Acknowledgments

The kind of thinking that Lugones's praxis calls for necessarily arises out of interpersonal engagements that are in turn situated within and among a variety of communities. This book would not have been possible without the dynamic interactions that we shared with each other and with the diversity of groups and individuals that have sustained us during the time it took to bring this project to fruition.

We acknowledge the College of Arts and Sciences at Syracuse University, the College of Arts and Sciences at Kansas State University, and the College of Arts and Sciences at Worcester Polytechnic Institute, for their generous support of our research and the production of this book. We are also grateful to the National Women's Studies Association for sponsoring two panels relevant to this collection at its annual meetings. This gave the editors and authors opportunities to receive valuable feedback. These events include a roundtable discussion on the book in Milwaukee, Wisconsin, in 2015 and a panel on Lugones's praxical philosophy in Denver, Colorado, in 2010.

We are grateful to two communities for playing an important role in cultivating practice and scholarship on Lugones's work and aiding significantly in our respective developments, albeit in different ways. First, thank you to the Center for Interdisciplinary Studies in Philosophy, Interpretation, and Culture (CPIC) at Binghamton University, and especially its members associated with the Politics of Women of Color Workshop and the Decolonial Thinking Workshop who have inspired many crucial conversations. Among them are Wanda Alarcón, Mazi Allen, Manuel Chávez Jr., Maria Chaves-Daza, Cindy Cruz, Josh Franco, Nelima Gaonkar, Colette Jung, Nikolay Karkov, Jen-Feng Kuo, Hilary Malatino, Xhercis Mendez, Chantal Rodais, Gabriel Soldatenko, Ovidiu Tichindeleanu, Tushabe, and Gabriela Veronelli. Second, the Latina Feminism Roundtable organized by Mariana Ortega at John Carroll University fostered several explorations of Lugones's work. Members, participants, and keynote speakers include Linda Martín Alcoff, Mariana Alessandri, Natalie Cisneros, Veronica Isabel Dahlberg, Brittan Davis, Theresa Delgadillo,

Pedro DiPietro, Carmen Lugo-Lugo, Jacqueline Martinez, Jennifer McWeeny, Cynthia Paccacerqua, Laura Elisa Pérez, Andrea Pitts, Monique Roelofs, Stephanie Rivera Berruz, Alexander Stehn, Gloria Vaquera, Sujay Vega, Ernesto Rosen Velasquez, Elena Ruíz, Chela Sandoval, Ofelia Schutte, Daphne Taylor Garcia, and Kelli Zaytoun.

We express our sincere thanks to the artists who have granted us permission to reproduce their work on the book's cover and in chapter 6, respectively: e. nina jay and Taus Makhacheva. The General Research Division of the New York Public Library generously helped to locate the frontispiece reprinted in chapter 7. We are also appreciative of the careful work of the editorial team at the State University of New York press, including Rebecca Colesworthy, Beth Bouloukos, Jenn Bennett-Genthner, and Michael Campchiaro. Thank you to John Wentworth for copy editing the manuscript with such keen attention, to Kirk Warren for the cover design, to Aimee Harrison for typesetting the manuscript, and to David Martinez for compiling the book's index. Additionally, we are grateful to Nancy A. Naples for including this work in the Praxis: Theory in Action series.

Finally, this book was realized through the hard work, expertise, and care of each of its contributors. We are deeply grateful for their patience, perseverance, and insight through what was a long and demanding editing process. Together, these contributors are crafting and authorizing a field of research that emerges out of a deep engagement with Lugones's ideas, and they are thus bringing her visionary philosophy to more and more circles of people practicing resistance against multiple oppressions. We are grateful to Paula M. L. Moya for writing an afterword that emphasizes the playfulness and complexity of walking with Lugones's thinking. The advice and guidance of M. Jacqui Alexander was crucial for enriching the introduction and its potential for making connections across generations of antiracist feminist movements and across multiple sites of transnational and translocal solidarities.

Pedro: Echoes of many voices resonate in mine. They accompany me on a journey of self-transformation and collective transformation. They have brought me to this page, literally. Among these companions and their voices, I would like to especially acknowledge those I have known since the very beginning of life or whom I encountered in my childhood and have remained with me in a shared affective map: Yamile Dip, Hugo DiPietro, Tía Nené, Cecilia Sanchez DiPietro, Cristian DiPietro, Pachi Sanchez, Agustina Checa, Santiago Checa, Lidia Patagua, and Claudia Mendieta; my beloved companion Brian and the adorable nonhuman animals, Bisel and Inti, who have enriched our life together;

those whose friendship or mentorship I cherish and whose presence sustains me in many ways—Laura Elisa Pérez, Joshua Price, Himika Bhattacharya, John Strohmeier, Gabriela Veronelli, Gloria Bonder, Eunjung Kim, Chandra Talpade Mohanty, Linda Carty, Ariel Monterrubianesi, Suronda Gonzalez, Joe Galante, Peter Fazo, and Maya Strohmeier; those whose political visions inspire my hemispheric sense of belonging to decolonizing collaborations, particularly the mentors, colleagues, and students of the coloniality/modernity/decoloniality network, the Association for Jotería Arts, Activism, and Scholarship, the Democratizing Knowledge Collective at Syracuse University, and the graduate and undergraduate students at the Latin American Graduate School of Social Sciences (FLACSO-PRIGEPP, Buenos Aires), Binghamton University, the University of California, Berkeley, and Syracuse University.

From the networks I've listed, I am truly indebted to the following colleagues, mentors, comrades, and students for their constant support and inspiration: Wanda Alarcón, M. Jacqui Alexander, Eddy Alvarez Jr., Hossein Ayazi, Paola Bachetta, Himika Bhattacharya, Gloria Bonder, Mauro Cabral, William Calvo-Quiros, Linda Carty, Hayley Cavino, Manuel Chávez Jr., Maya Chinchilla, Randy Conner, Cindy Cruz, Laura Dumond-Kerr, Carol Fadda-Conrey, Blas Fernandez, Myrna García-Calderón, Mike Gill, Marcelle Haddix, Michael Hames-García, David Hatfield Sparks, Celia Herrera Rodriguez, Sarah Lucia Hoagland, Lourdes Ibarra, Ariko Ikehara, Dellareese Jackson, Paula Johnson, Cricket Keating, Eunjung Kim, Jen-Feng Kuo, Claudia Laudano, Liliana Louys, Hilary Malatino, Aja Y. Martinez, Ernesto Martinez, Vivian May, Jen McWeeny, José Medina, Cherríe Moraga, Dana Olwan, Jackie Orr, Cinthya Paccacerqua, Laura Elisa Pérez, Suyapa Portillo, Gwendolyn Pough, Seth Quam, Yosimar Reyes, Shireen Roshanravan, Gabriel Soldatenko, Lynn Stephen, Chandra Talpade Mohanty, Emmanuel Theumer, Anita Tijerina Revilla, Silvio Torres-Saillant, Santiago Slabodsky, Cristina Serna, Marisol Silva, Julie Thi Underhill, Gabriela Veronelli, Ashton Wesner, Kelly Zaytoun, Susy Zepeda, and the late Lohana Berkins and Ana Paula Jaramillo.

Jen: I am grateful for the support, love, and patience of my family: Cameron DeMarche, Thomas DeMarche, William McWeeny, Amy Knowlton, Caren Plank, and four-legged companions MacGuinness, Honey, and Buster. Additionally, I am thankful for friends Emily Stowe, Ashby Butnor, Matthew MacKenzie, Claudia Tomsa, Noreen Khawaja, John Kaag, Carol Hay, Matt Allen, and Ture Turnbull, who can always be counted on to bring smiles, encouragement, and meaning. My work grows out of connections with a stimulating and inspiring constellation of scholars spread across various circles and locales for whom I express my sincere appreciation. These individuals include Ruth Smith, Beth Eddy, Roger Gottlieb, John Sanbonmatsu, Geoffrey Pfeifer, Peter Hansen, Kris Boudreau, Michelle Ephraim, Vrinda Dalmiya, Arindam Chakrabarti, Garth Bregman, Li-Hsiang Lisa Rosenlee, Rodney Roberts, Mark Johnson, Naomi Zack, Bonnie Mann, José Jorge Mendoza, Amelia Wirts, Mariana Ortega, Michael Eng, Patrick Mooney, Pedro DiPietro, Shireen Roshanravan, Keya Maitra, Kelli Zaytoun, Samir Haddad, Leonard Lawlor, Dermot Moran, Richard Kearney, James Morley, Gail Weiss, Susanna Siegel, Naomi Scheman, Janine Jones, Iva Apostalova, Abdullah Hajjar, Nicole Garner, and Courtney Miller. My feminist praxis and scholarship has also been shaped by my participation in the Feminist Working Group Initiative, whose members include Celia Bardwell-Jones, Dana Berthold, Kimberly Garchar, Rochelle Green, Chaone Mallory, Amy Story, and Lisa Yount. The International Merleau-Ponty Circle, the International Simone de Beauvoir Society, and the Roundtable on Latina Feminism, as well as collectives resistant to oppression at John Carroll University and Worcester Polytechnic Institute have provided me with fertile ground to grow my praxis and ideas. Rosalie Post, Tomas O'Leary, Sean O'Leary, and Ria Roy have been gracious roommates and interlocutors who helped to create the kind of space where this work can be done. Finally, María Lugones's complex thinking has inspired me to go forward with the honest self-reflection necessary to become a philosopher who speaks face to face with others and engages multiple visions of resistance. Her person and friendship continues to challenge and encourage me beyond these pages, as does the friendship of her students and my co-editors, Pedro DiPietro and Shireen Roshanravan, who held and crafted meaningful relational spaces for this kind of work.

Shireen: Thank you to my co-editors, Jen and Pedro, for the journey that became this book. I have learned much from our collaboration. My family of origin, Mehrban, Bakhtawar, Shayzreen, Matt, Nathan, and Aiden, provided space and nourishment and love during integral moments of working on this collection. I am grateful to my diasporic cousins, Mehernosh Chemi, Shiraz D'Mello, Aspan, and Mehershad Dahmubed, who expanded my sense of familial backup that fed my contribution to this collection in ways I never could have imagined. Melisa Posey, Isabel Millán, Norma Valenzuela, and April Petillo held/hold it down for me in Kansas in ways that make doing work like this possible. Thank you to Larin McLaughlin, Shannon Winnubst, Lynn Fujiwara, Liz Philipose, Ernesto Martínez, and Michael Hames-García for steadfast support, counsel, and encouragement. I am eternally grateful to

María Lugones, Nelima Gaonkar, and Gabriela Veronelli, with whom I began to mobilize Women of Color coalition politics on the ground in Binghamton and weave the consciousness of becoming a politically identified Woman of Color into my embodied ways of living. Members of La Escuela Popular Norteña, especially María Lugones, Laura Dumond-Kerr, and Cricket Keating, accompanied and guided me in the process of learning what it is to become a praxical thinker. The Midwest Society for Women in Philosophy, and especially the Women of Color Caucus, provided an exuberant space of interlocution in my early years of graduate school. I thank those who created and shared that space with me, especially María Lugones, Sarah Hoagland, Anne Leighton, Jackie Anderson, Janine Stone, Alison Bailey, Crista Lebens, and Gabriela Veronelli. Lilith Mahmud, Raja Bhattar, and Sri Sudhira Silva, my L.A. family, offered generous friendship and respite when most needed. My ability to question and push the meaningful ways I live my South Asian American identity is indebted to members of Chicago Desi Youth Rising, Desis Rising Up and Moving, Satrang Los Angeles, South Asian Lesbian and Gay Association in New York City; in particular, I thank Matthew Varghese, Lorna Daniel, Karen Naimool, Raja Bhattar, Suzanne Persard, Mashuq Mushtaq Deen, and all facilitators of the monthly SALGA NYC support groups. Thank you to Manuel Chávez Jr., Jen-Feng Kuo, Jotika Chaudhary, Tina Sinha, Mala Nagarajan, and Vega Subramaniam, Suparna Bhaskaran, Falu Bakrania, Rakshita Koirala, Priya Kandaswamy, Tina Trinh, and the Izzat Collective. Finally, I thank Mugi and Leo Tyree for their intimate support, faithful companionship, and love.

List of Abbreviations

ARTICLES BY MARÍA LUGONES

BLF   "On Borderlands/*La Frontera*: An Interpretive Essay"
BP   "Boomerang Perception and the Colonizing Gaze: Ginger Reflections on Horizontal Hostility"
C   "Community"
CFE   "Competition, Compassion, and Community: Models for a Feminist Ethos" (co-authored with Elizabeth V. Spelman)
CG   "The Coloniality of Gender"
CIC   "Tenuous Connections in Impure Communities"
DC   "Dominant Culture: *El Deseo por un Alma Pobre* (The Desire for an Impoverished Soul)" (co-authored with Joshua M. Price)
DF   "Methodological Notes toward a Decolonial Feminism"
DP   "*El Pasar Discontinuo de la Cachapera/Tortillera del Barrio a la Barra al Movimiento*/The Discontinuous Passing of the *Cachapera/Tortillera* from the Barrio to the Bar to the Movement"
ED   "Enticements and Dangers of Community and Home for a Radical Politics"
FU   "Faith in Unity" (co-authored with Joshua M. Price)
GSM   "Cosmology and Gender in Sylvia Marcos's *Taken from the Lips: Gender and Eros in Mesoamerican Religions*"
HCS   "*Hablando Cara a Cara*/Speaking Face to Face: An Exploration of Ethnocentric Racism"
HGS   "Heterosexualism and the Colonial/Modern Gender System"
HHA   "Hard-to-Handle Anger"
HL   "*Hispaneando y Lesbiando*: On Sarah Hoagland's *Lesbian Ethics*"
HMD   "Hacia Metodologías de la Decolonialidad"
IC   "Impure Communities"
IP   Introduction to *Pilgrimages*/Peregrinajes: *Theorizing Coalition against Multiple Oppressions*
LPF   "On the Logic of Pluralist Feminism"
MC   "Multicultural Cognition" (co-authored with Joshua M. Price)

MMH	"*Milongueando* Macha Homoerotics: Dancing the Tango, Torta Syle (a Performative Testimonio)"
MP	"Multiculturalism and Publicity"
MSR	"Motion, Stasis, and Resistance to Interlocked Oppressions"
ND	"Reading the Nondiasporic from within Diasporas"
OC	"On Complex Communication"
PIS	"Purity, Impurity, and Separation"
PP	Preface to *Pilgrimages*/Peregrinajes: *Theorizing Coalition against Multiple Oppressions*
PRE	"Towards a Practice of Radical Engagement: The Escuela Popular Norteña's 'Politicizing the Everyday' Workshop" (co-authored with the EPN Collective)
QT	"It's All in Having a History: Response to Michael Hames-García's 'Queer Theory Revisited'"
RCG	"The Inseparability of Race, Class, and Gender: Response to Antonia Darder and Rodolfo D. Torres" (co-authored with Joshua M. Price)
RFC	"Multiculturalismo Radical y Feminismos de Color"
RLC	"*Encuentros and Desencuentros*: Reflections on the LatCrit Gathering in Latin America" (co-authored with Joshua M. Price)
RM	"Radical Multiculturalism and Women of Color Feminisms"
RP	"Racism and Pedagogy"
RR	"On Richard Rodriguez's *Hunger of Memory*"
SAS	"Structure, Anti-structure: Agency under Oppression"
SE	"Subjetividad esclava, colonialidad de género, marginalidad y opresiones múltiples"
SF	"Sisterhood and Friendship as Feminist Models" (in collaboration with Pat Alake Rosezelle)
TDF	"Toward a Decolonial Feminism"
TPT	"Problems of Translation in Postcolonial Thinking" (co-authored with Joshua M. Price)
TSC	"Tactical Strategies of the Streetwalker/*Estrategias Tácticas de la Callejera*"
TY	"Have We Got a Theory for You! Feminist Theory, Cultural Imperialism and the Demand for the 'Women's Voice'" (co-authored with Elizabeth V. Spelman)
WC	"Wicked *Caló*: A Matter of Authority of Improper Words"
WGS	"From within Germinative Stasis: Creating Active Subjectivity, Resistant Agency"
WT	"Playfulness, 'World'-Traveling, and Loving Perception"

Introduction

Like an Earthquake to the Soul: Experiencing the Visionary Philosophy of María Lugones

Pedro J. DiPietro, Jennifer McWeeny, and Shireen Roshanravan

I inherit a legacy of colonial mimicry as a South Asian American of Parsi descent. To assimilate the ways of those in power was a key survival mechanism that my family and larger community instilled in me. I came to María and her work through a desire to identify politically as a Woman of Color and found in her the kind of faithful witness who would call me to transform against my disposition to assimilate to power. The call, heard in her writing and in my work with her, was always demanding but unquestioningly loving in its commitment to accompany me in my desire to remake myself against the grain of oppressive familial tradition and communal expectations.

I was in my first semester of graduate school when I first read María's work, and I was immediately taken in by its intricacy, depth, and complexity at the precipice of feminist-antiracist social change. I knew it in my body, but not in my language at the time, that María was giving me a way to articulate a past and a colonial inheritance, a longing and a hurt, that I never thought could be expressed. For me, María's praxis was an opening and an invitation to travel deeper into myself by undertaking the fraught but necessary work of coalition across difference, of finding myself and my fears and desires by listening to others on their terms, by traveling to their comportments and worlds. Here I found something that I had rarely encountered before: an encouragement to go forward in connecting with others.

When I first met María my heart would swell and felt larger, my body felt recognized, and my spirit connected to hers. Her style of moving intentions across sometimes unfriendly terrains made me aware of her determination to ignite insurgent desires. We were both born in Argentina and learned from our families how to negotiate the ties to the country's underside, outsiders, and detractors. Our encounter pushed me to see the world with blurring eyes, revealing porous realities of uncertain and yet thickly resistant meanings. Witnessing her maneuvering of the legacies of colonization across multiple sites of struggle and identification moved me to embrace my resistant positionality as a transnational, Latinx, and feminist practitioner. If the education I received had led me to mistrust my flesh, its aberrant passions and needs, María read me thriving in them. In learning with and from her, I have come to inhabit the illicit dwellings of my soul, heart, and spirit.

Through our different journeys of engaging María Lugones and her commitment to radical political and intellectual formations, the three of us came together to realize a book that entices others to encounter her thinking, enter into it, and be touched by it. The urgency of our desire to share the possibilities of transformation that we each individually found in Lugones's writing both motivated and sustained our collaboration on this collection. Lugones's coalitional approach to praxis, rooted in Women of Color feminist politics, taught us not to take our collaboration as co-editors for granted. Rather, we emphasize the *pull* we feel to Lugones's work that compelled us to generate this collection and to do so with an intimacy that is risky—risky because Lugones's work delivers the possibilities of the self in a way that makes the appeal of individualism too strenuous to the soul. For each of us, engagement with her work has felt like an earthquake to the soul, igniting deep longings for ever-expanding circles of resistant company that require contesting familiar, safe, common-sense boundaries of kin, community, and identity. We offer *Speaking Face to Face* as an invitation to experience Lugones's visionary philosophy, to shift your ground of collective possibility, and to ignite your resistant imagination.[1]

Earthquakes are born of tension points that, when released, shift the ground beneath us. The eruption sets one in motion, fleeing potential death, looking for new footing to build one's self, one's life, one's community anew. Such are the conditions under which Lugones left Argentina in the 1960s and arrived in the United States in the midst of the Civil Rights and Third World Liberation movements. In her words: "My location is that of someone who relocated away from battering, systematic rape, extreme psychological and physical torture, by those closest to me. I relocated in the sense of going for a new geographical place, a new identity, a new set of relations" (IP 19). The pain of enduring violence inflicted by those closest to her, and then entering a new terrain of struggle as a "nondiasporic Latina,"[2] shapes the ground of her insurgent feminist theorizing.[3] It is no surprise, then, that Lugones's work never takes for granted that community, coalition, or solidarity is something given, presumed by blood, law, or even shared interests and identity. Concrete experiences of oppressing / being oppressed ←—→resisting punctuate Lugones's writings, allowing the reader to sense the connection between her negotiations with institutional and interpersonal violence and her praxical theorizing of the obstacles and pathways toward forging company in the face of isolating despair.[4] In her work as feminist philosopher, professor, popular educator, community organizer, and *compañera*, as with the chapters in this book, you come face to face with questions such as: Who do you come to understand as your own people? What constitutes the ground of this claim? Is it solid? Or can you feel it tremble with histories of harm yet to be confronted or repaired? What are the central points of tension in your communal groundings that are on the verge of release?

The notion that one does not find one's own people but rather forges them in a constant process of building deep coalitions of understanding permeates Lugones's body of work, from her doctoral dissertation on the radical potential of friendship, *Morality and Personal Relations*, completed in 1978 at the University of Wisconsin, Madison, to her contemporary elaboration of a decolonial feminism to her grassroots community organizing and popular education work with Chicanas/os, Mexicanas/os, and Hispanas/os in Northern New Mexico, in Pilsen and La Villita in Chicago, and in East Los Angeles, as well as with Indigenous movements in Bolivia and with those working in antiviolence movements and Women of Color organizing across the United States. Guided by the maxim "I won't think what I won't practice," Lugones calls on us to invest in perceptions of ourselves as accomplices in struggles to end violence in all its forms. Important to her development of this maxim is her involvement in the Escuela Popular Norteña, the popular education collective that she cofounded, and other national organizations in antiviolence movements such as Critical Resistance and Incite! Women, Gender NonConforming, and Trans People of Color Against Violence.

Throughout her oeuvre, Lugones reimagines in concrete and practical steps, tactics, and strategies, the untapped and hidden possibilities of subject formation. From within a politics focused on magnifying the everyday, or what happens at the corner, at home, and on the street, and from within what she calls "body-to-body engagement," or the places of intimacy so readily denied insurgent potential, her theorizing begins with the reconstitution of the subject and uncharted ways of interpreting praxis (TSC 207). This book is thus motivated by Lugones's spirit of *playfully* exploring pain and pleasure, suffering and resistance, oppression and liberation, always with an eye to forging expansive coalitions of understanding.[5]

The work of U.S. and Third World Women of Color feminists M. Jacqui Alexander, Gloria Anzaldúa, Audre Lorde, Chandra Talpade Mohanty, Cherríe Moraga, Bernice Johnson Reagon, Chela Sandoval, and Barbara Smith has been important political and intellectual company for Lugones. In *Pilgrimages/*

Peregrinajes: *Theorizing Coalition against Multiple Oppressions*, she describes Women of Color coalition as a "formation against significant and complex odds" that depends on an "epistemological shift to non-dominant differences" (WT 84; see also Lorde 1984, 111). From her early examination of how people of color utilize the dominant logic of "the real and the fake" to police the boundaries of their homegrown resistant seeing-circles (BP) to her rejection of homophobic injunctions within nationalist affirmations of Latina/o community (ED), Lugones elaborates cognitive shifts that expose our complicity with the many faces of domination.

Lugones's analysis of these shifts translates shared feminist yearnings for solidarity into opportunities to trouble the notion of ally-ship at the different sites of contemporary struggles for justice, such as the movement to end sexual violence against women of color or the Black Lives Matter Movement. The National Women's Studies Association conference in 2017 invited scholars, activists, and artists to reflect on the forty-year legacy of the Combahee River Collective (CRC) and its 1977 Black feminist manifesto. The conference discussed the very concerns that Black women writers/activists gathered in the manifesto with regard to multiracial, multigender, and anticapitalist struggles. A year earlier, 2016 marked the thirty-fifth anniversary of the publication of *This Bridge Called My Back*, a foundational anthology of Women of Color writers that weaves their voices and experiences into teachings about the coalitional possibilities of antiracist feminisms. *Speaking Face to Face* offers timely and enriching contributions to the examination of Lugones's body of work within the broader constellation of Women of Color thought that CRC and *This Bridge* embody. This work is important, unprecedented, and crucial in the genealogy of Women of Color feminisms.[6]

Whether this is your first time encountering Lugones's thinking or you are a seasoned reader of her essays, whether you have worked in the kinds of activist circles that Lugones has moved through or you are new to Women of Color political praxis, we offer this book to you as a nexus of multiple points of entry into her work. As co-editors, we foresee readers in classrooms, activist circles, and popular education workshops learning more about Lugones and giving uptake to the originality of her philosophy by exploring, in close company with others, how to interpret the questions she inspires about coalitional praxis: What are the practical and theoretical meanings of joint and bridged struggles and collaborations? What are the body-to-body, coalitional possibilities of practicing solidarity across multiple borders and boundaries?

SPEAKING FACE TO FACE

Speaking face to face, a practice described in Lugones's early essay that bears that title (HCS), calls members of feminist circles to examine our motivations concerning empathy and sympathy toward each other. Primarily, it provides a method for both interpreting and dislodging ethnocentric racism and its shaping of our capacity for communication and interdependence (HCS 43). It makes us confront the ways that colonial legacies inform political friendships. What would happen to one's senses of integrity, of accountability, of being committed to fighting against all forms of injustice if one had the privilege of hearing only one's own voice, or of choosing to silence everyone else's? What would happen if that sense of one's commitment to social justice entailed distortion and appropriation of the lives, thoughts, and dreams belonging to those one deems the closest to one's position and history?

Lugones's questions about distortion, disengagement, and silencing apply, more broadly, to those contexts where any two people come together with the intention of making our world a better place. Gloria Anzaldúa concurs with Lugones's analysis of how racism bears on such collaborations when she states that there is not enough honest talk about racism and that we neglect to acknowledge how much it permeates all aspects of life (1990, xix). More recent scholarship demonstrates that much has yet to be discussed about racism within ethnic, feminist, and women's studies classrooms and movements (Chang 2007; Cruz 2013; Falcón 2015; Hernandez and Rehman 2002; Pough 2007).

Together with an account of the barriers that racism brings to feminist collaborations, Lugones offers creative suggestions about the practice of speaking face to face. Rather than focusing on feminists of color directing all their efforts to changing how they are heard, distorted, or silenced, she invites them instead to devote equal energy to affirming their realities even at the risk of making no sense to the members of a dominant culture (HCS). This is significant when we think about our classrooms, where the tensions among geopolitical, economic, and sociocultural differences are ever starker today. It has been our experience that modeling feminist classrooms centered on women of color thinkers incites feelings of confusion, disorientation, guilt, and anger. In what ways, inside and outside the classroom, can we foster a critical competence that moves us forward, beyond but not necessarily avoiding the political and epistemic value of anger and resentment, beyond the consequences of ignorance and self-delusion or the frustration associated with wanting to do right and being ill-equipped to learn how? In what ways do women of color communicate to each other and with each other by anchoring their sense of who they are in opposition to available languages, histories, and knowledges?

Becoming fluent in speaking face to face entails a willingness to know oneself in unfamiliar ways that may take us to expand our sense of who we are in relations of solidarity. In feminist struggles, speaking face to face animates alternative realities, providing a faithful mirror to those seeking self-affirmation outside dominant culture. The readers of this text may recognize such moments in their own learning environments but also throughout the chapters in this book since they refuse to settle or downplay the tensions that ensue when centering Women of Color epistemologies. As co-editors of this book, we looked to the practice of speaking face to face, of fostering solidarity across differences and divides, as a model for interrogating our own process of becoming feminist collaborators. The three of us have learned to listen to each other "without presupposing unity of expression or experience" (TY 573). Recognizing the difficulty of saying "we" without erasing the multiplicity and tension this "we" holds, we have worked to develop the capacity of "faithfully witnessing" the generative dimension of our differences (IP 7). This faithful hearing does not resolve disagreements as much as mine them for what they reveal about our unexamined assumptions. In what follows, we offer moments where we had to confront selves complicit with domination that we did not realize we animated until we encountered communicative impasses in our collaboration.

Not only do the three of us have dissimilar journeys into the coalitional politics of Women of Color praxis but also diverging connections to activisms, academic appointments, philosophical training, and Lugones's work. We inhabit different social locations: a queer South Asian American-becoming-Woman of Color from Texas; a white, Boston-born, American-Irish woman who carries immigrant and working-class legacies; and a nonbinary transfeminine Latinx originally from the Andes. We each find Lugones's praxical thinking affirming to us in our complexity and ambiguities, and in our shared interest in getting people together beyond our own scope, even though we come to her work differently. And yet, the "physical realities of our lives—our skin color, the land or concrete we grew up on, our sexual longings" place us on historical ground already ridden with deep fissures (Moraga and Anzaldúa 1981, 23). They erupted in our co-editing process, leading to moments of communicative impasse.

One significant tension emerged with respect to how we each are situated within coalition building and Women of Color politics. Although Lugones is trained and known as a philosopher, Shireen never engaged Lugones's work in terms of her being a philosopher, but rather in terms of her commitment to advance a coalitional politics of Women of Color. Terms like *ontological* and *phenomenological* blocked her engagement in conversations that, to her, seemed to be *about* Lugones's philosophical import and not *from within* the practice of coalitional politics. While the three of us recognize that feelings of incompetence in relation to disciplinary language are both raced and gendered, we didn't always succeed in shifting our collective engagement with Lugones.

What gets to be read as fluency in a specialized field, such as women's studies or feminist philosophy, also speaks to broader dynamics within contemporary feminist collaborations, many seeking to close the gap between rural and urban, periphery and center, local and global, and activism and academia. Lugones instead intervenes in the theory/practice divide by praxically placing feminist theorizing "in the midst of people mindful to the tensions, desires, closures, cracks, and openings that make up the social" (IP 5). How then were we supposed to take each other on while being mindful of our tensions in the face of writing and press deadlines? How were we to faithfully take each other on without breaking our spirits?

At times, in our co-writing process, Pedro found that we were missing openness toward each other in the form of disengagement. Speaking face to face also made Pedro confront the image that they may have of themselves as moral or good people. In cases when Pedro disagreed with both Jen and Shireen about an editorial choice, Pedro would painfully read their agreement as a matter of cisgender feminist affinity. Questions of authority and knowledge arose, and Pedro shied away from asking point blank whether Jen and Shireen would have had equally critical views had the contributions at hand been written by a cisgender man of color submitting feminist scholarship for this book. Many readers, as well as students in a women's and gender studies classroom, are likely familiar with the type of discomfort that Pedro experienced—that is, with not asking what everybody else in the room may be thinking. Take, for instance, the situation where a straight-identified cisman of color gets a pass from their women of color classmates on pressing questions about crossgender solidarity just because the cisman was down enough to enroll in a women's studies class. Pedro has seen racially privileged women who, within similar dynamics, asked women of color to explain the reasons behind their choosing to give cismen of color a pass when it comes to sexism. Asking satisfies the need of racially privileged women to be taught and to learn. Their decision places the burden of dispelling their ignorance on those who may intend to remain unintelligible.

In some interactions with Jen and Shireen, Pedro came to pause the impulse to ask, dwelling instead in the possibilities of not knowing.

Some of the most difficult times of the collaborative process for Jen involved receiving the politics of disengagement. She experienced these relational moments as thick and dense in their concreteness, attention-pulling and anxiety-producing insofar as she wished for connection and resolution. At certain points, she found these modes of communicating and her responsive impulses suffocating; it is harrowing to feel missed in who you understand yourself to be at the same time that you long for intellectual and political intimacy. Jen also felt deep confusion both because of her relative lack of practical experience with many of the communicative and political methodologies that we were employing and because even her resistant selves that she had cultivated over a lifetime of feminist and antiracist practice were reflected in unfamiliar, destabilizing ways. We understand that given the systemic nature of multiple oppressions or "the coloniality of gender" (HGS, CG, TDF, DF), the liberatory frames that have been embraced by those who benefit from dominant constructions of reality can often signal complicity with the violent reduction of women of color. Within our collective, Jen sensed the multiple meanings when she thought of the possibility of her expressing vantage points that see from a lower economic class; this way of interacting could be a defense against hearing viewpoints that revealed her racial or gender privilege. Speaking face to face does not always entail looking at each other head-on, being in proximity to one another, verbalizing methods and designs step by step, or knowing what comes next; it also involves sideways glances, turning one's attention elsewhere, learning and listening in the silences, walking away and then returning differently.

Several of the chapters that this book brings together also reflect on some of the tensions we've encountered when speaking face to face. They underscore that doing feminist community is not without painful lessons, most of which are attached to the possibility of fostering interdependence. In our own journey, we have graciously learned to end conversations on disagreement, not so much as a result of relativism but rather as a way of stopping the defense of one's ground of meaning. As co-editors, we have come to realize this book after roughly six years, and we are aware that we still long for a more satisfying kind of conviviality and intimacy. Each chapter in *Speaking Face to Face* offers expressions that are at once personal and outward-moving. In this sense, they are loving gestures of *facing* other people. Resonating with Lugones's determination to think beyond the confines of social fragmentation, ours is a practice of situated writing that asks, "*¿En qué voz*, with which voice, *anclada en qué* *lugar*, anchored in which place, *para qué y porqué*, why and to what purpose, do I trust myself to you … ?" (HCS 45). In what follows, we detail the key concepts and themes introduced in each of the book's sections and describe the ways the chapters extend and apply Lugones's ideas.

COALITIONAL SELVES, MULTIPLE REALITIES

Our collaboration was set in motion through multiple coalitional spaces inspired by Lugones's work in and beyond the classroom. At Binghamton University, Lugones was central for over two decades in the growth of the Philosophy, Interpretation, and Culture Program (PIC), unique for its interdisciplinary approach to philosophy and its emphasis on examining the relation between knowledge and action, aesthetic and political motivation, and culture and ethical practice. Shireen and Pedro met as PIC graduate students in 2003 and became part of a wider community that, inspired by Lugones, engaged in radical and critical theorizing. The Latina Feminism Roundtable organized by Mariana Ortega at John Carroll University was an important node in this community, where Jen and Pedro first met in 2006. One year later, the three of us found ourselves together for the first time as participants in a three-day Politics of Women of Color seminar hosted by the Center for Interdisciplinary Studies in Philosophy, Interpretation and Culture, where Lugones served as director for more than ten years.[7]

As mentioned in the previous section, our collaboration has been a journey of learning to recognize and affirm the multiplicity, complexity, and impurity within and between each of us. One of her earliest articulations of multiplicity and coalition can be found in Lugones's most famous article, "Playfulness, 'World'-Traveling, and Loving Perception." To world-travel is to learn to see yourself and others through the eyes of those who inhabit the different landscapes you (in)voluntarily traverse.[8] World-traveling is one of many methodologies that helps build *deep coalition*, which entails coalitions of understanding that endure beyond short-term, issue-based, collaborations (IP 30). Unity is never the goal of deep coalition insofar as unity relies on the erasure of multiple ways of knowing, being, and desiring. Rather, the goal is to foster skills to navigate the ugliness and discomfort of political collaborations when they are not built to align with one's sense of being at home, or in one's own "barred room" in the world (Johnson Reagon 1983, 359). Deep coalitions reveal the amount of support one needs to cross cultures without killing oneself, to confront the simultaneity of each other's complicities and resistances to multiple oppressions (363–64).

Building deep coalition requires hard work, challenging the fiction of an individualist self and its erasure of the resistant subjectivity of those targeted for exploitation, genocide, enslavement, and other logics of systemic oppression operative in neoliberal capitalist and white supremacist realities. To understand the cultural power of the individualist self, one need only reflect on Western culture's ableist celebration of the "self-made man" whose legibility is dependent on the racist construction of the Black "welfare queen" (Cohen 1997; Clare 1999). Lugones shatters the individualist fiction of the "self-made man" who deserves what he gets and gets what he deserves by putting pressure on the concept of agency it hails. Because notions of agency are inextricably tied to notions of the individualist unified subject, the concept erases the many collectivities and institutionalized circuits of exploitation that enable the fiction of the individualist agentic self. Many of our students come to college with meritocracy ingrained in their value system, particularly if they belong to racially privileged groups, taking for granted that as long as they work hard they will get where they are going with no debts to anyone, either for their failures or successes. In dispelling this myth, Lugones crafts the notion of an "active subject" to illuminate our ability to form intentions against the grain of the hegemonic system that subjects us, and to emphasize how this ability is dependent on socialities that can sustain and intensify resistance (TSC 211; WGS). Using the term *active subjectivity* rather than *agency*, Lugones offers language for marking the collective backup upon which all subjects depend to move their intentions into action and, thus, names the potential of the resistant-oppressed to enact sustained political transformations.

If coalition becomes the possibility for active subjectivity, then our interdependence on each other becomes a source of empowerment rather than the mark of weakness or paralysis. Lugones's account of selves and realities as multiple, without an underlying unity, makes a complicated ontological claim (WT 89; Moya 2006). Following several theorists of oppression, we call this "ontological pluralism" (SAS 55–56). It arises out of this empowering sense of liberatory interdependence that motivates coalition building across "worlds of sense," a concept Lugones introduces to reference the different social landscapes we inhabit throughout our lives. These worlds of sense anchor a unique system of meanings, sensibilities, intentions, and directions. For example, the way a queer Latinx dresses and speaks, their bodily comportment, and their sense of being at ease or on guard, will change as they move from their job at a predominantly white heterosexual male law firm to the queer dance club in the predominantly Latinx neighborhood they go to with their friends every Friday night. This person is both the self animated in the office of the law firm and the self animated at the queer Latinx dance club; neither self, Lugones explains, is the *real* self. In her words, "one inhabits the realities as spatially, historically, and thus materially different: different in possibilities, in the connections among people, and in the relation to power" (IP 17). The multiplicity and heterogeneity present in the experiences of the queer Latinx at the law firm and the dance club is not merely a matter of one's imagination, psychology, perspective, or interpretation. The queer Latinx dance club is a world of sense where the queer Latinx subject may inhabit their queer and Latinx identities playfully, as creative sites of resistance against their stereotypical negative meanings institutionalized by the interlocking of white supremacy, homophobia, sexism, and classism. For Lugones, it is imperative that we travel "playfully," or without a sense of self-importance, to "worlds of sense" where we generate and affirm the resistant meanings of our nondominant differences because it is in seeing each other as resistant that we are motivated to identify with each other without requiring that we become like one another (LPF).

Central to world-traveling is a methodology of sensing oppression and resistance as never existing alone, but instead always emerging in a tense relation: oppressing ←→ resisting. In chapter 1, "Trash Talks Back," Elizabeth V. Spelman analyzes how themes of "trash" illuminate Lugones's challenge to the unidirectional concept of "the oppressed" as only marking victimization because, as Spelman argues, trash talks back in spite of its construction as waste, as inessential, and unproductive. Both Kelli Zaytoun and (Brena) Yu-Chen Tai consider the liberatory potentials of the *plurality of selves* that unfolds from the oppressing ←→ resisting relation. In chapter 2, "A Focus on the 'I' in the 'I → We': Self-in-Coalition and Active Subjectivity," Zaytoun extends Lugones's ontological vision by detailing the mutually constitutive relationships among active subjectivity, complex communication, and deep coalition in her thinking. While Zaytoun emphasizes the social and unifying aspects of this self as it seeks communication and coalition, Tai takes a different route in chapter 3, "The Ripple Imagery as a Decolonial Self." With a close reading of *Dictée*, Theresa Hak Kyung Cha's experimental autobiography, which includes stories about the Japanese colonization of Korea, she expands Lugones's theories of multiplicity and coloniality by showing how the plurality of coalitional selfhood materializes across different bodies, separated by culture and time. Taken together, the chapters in part I provide a unique viewpoint on the various pilgrimages that active subjects undertake and through which they leave no oppressions fully functional. Whereas Lugones's concepts of selfhood and multiplicity anchor the chapters in this section, part II continues to unearth resistant socialities with reference to her key interventions in theorizing intersectional, interlocking, and intermeshed oppressions and identities.

MOVING WITH AND BEYOND INTERSECTIONALITY

When Lugones states that her latest work on the coloniality of gender complicates the understanding of racialized gender and goes "beyond intersectionality," we interpret her claim as an invitation for antiracist feminisms to move with intersectionality to the edge of its contradictions (DF 72). Lugones's focus lies with resistant, decolonizing, active subjectivity at the point of the expansion of oneself, of the search for another with whom to grow competent in each other's struggles. Her project is then about the co-constitution of subjects, from within what lies between them in the myriad incarnations of coalitional politics.

Much in the vein of the Women of Color writers anthologized in *This Bridge* and of the members of the Combahee River Collective, Lugones seeks an analysis that makes sense of both the mechanisms of marginalization that tie together gender, race, and class, and the ways of thinking, learning, and listening of people who do theory in the flesh. She opens one's attention to what people experience, how they experience it, how they resist and think, and how they theorize. Long before there was a field of intersectional studies or the term *intersectionality* was coined, U.S. Third World women created a new politics of solidarity. In doing so, they charted a "differential mode of consciousness" (Sandoval 2000, 54; see also Pérez 2010) and criticized available models for the interpretation of power and how it moves across one's body, life, and identity (Davis 1981; Gunn Allen 1981; hooks 1981; Jayawardena 1986; Joseph and Lewis 1981; Lorde 1980, 1982). With her theories of ontological pluralism and active subjectivity, Lugones has taught us to move with and beyond intersectionality. She helps us understand that women of color engaging in coalition building have kindred and yet different histories in their thinking and learning, that their models for explaining the simultaneity of oppressions are situated, and that they don't share a unified account of the invisibility imposed upon women of color, their experience, knowledge, and methods of resistance.[9]

Lugones's attention to the co-constitution of subjects takes her to the examination of deep friendships, conviviality, and complex dialogue, such as those in women's collective art-working and story-telling (Barkley Brown 1989) and those others where intimacy is earned through the thickness of everyday life (WT, SF, DC, MC, TY). She arrives at an interactive understanding of difference among women, refusing to lump women of color under the umbrella *women*. Most important, her theorizing signals that some women have the lives they do because they are oppressing other women, that white middle-class women holding on to their privileges, or ignoring them, implicates both the subordination of nonwhite women and their invisibility. At a time when critiques of humanism are being co-opted by a trend to move past race and gender (Holland 2012), Lugones's decolonial feminism stands out in light of its opposition to an evacuation of the category woman of color, and in light of how this opposition bears on contemporary deployments of intersectional studies and derivative notions of intersectional identities.[10]

By engaging Lugones's theorizing of multiple oppressions, we invite readers to recognize her visionary journey into the work of feminists of color from the early to mid-1980s. To do so would allow those reading this book to interrogate intersectionality as a nodal point where women of color, co-constituted by multiple oppressions, unveil intertwined logics of marginalization and discrimination. It would also be significant to consider how, in turn, the politics of race and gender shape the production of knowledge about intersectionality and its circulation. What assumptions are we asked to make about the reach of intersectionality and whose voices are authorized to speak on its scope and applicability (Cho, Crenshaw, and McCall 2013, 791)?[11] Do contemporary feminist receptions usually lead us to read certain groups of women of color as the presumed subject position of intersectionality? Do they equally place *intersectionality* within a genealogy that tends to obliterate its roots prior to the term being coined by Kimberlé Crenshaw in 1989? Does Lugones's lack of a diasporic Latina/o community prevent the field from fully recognizing her insightful way of moving with and going beyond intersectionality?

There are shared features between Lugones's account of the co-constitution of subjects and other models of the simultaneity of oppressions that we find among women of color writers: all forms of what she calls "oppressing" reduce a person touched by and coupled with other oppressings (TSC 223); this process of reduction and encasing originates in hierarchical and systemic social structures (SAS 60; WT 84; TSC 231); and the person facing this encasing anticipates their own active response to being oppressed (TSC 223). What usually gets overshadowed by typical interpretations of intersectionality are the following of Lugones's contributions: (a) her theorizing offers a critique of seeing oppressions as disconnected and divisible, which she describes as the "interlocking of oppressions" or a form of domination that operates at the level of cognition; (b) she provides an alternative to the interlocking of oppressions with the notion of "intermeshing of oppressions," of multiple and mutually implicated power lines that give rise to a coalescence, or as distinct and yet not quite divisible substances that can fully dissolve into each other; and (c) she demonstrates, in her formulation of the coloniality of gender, that seeing gender, race, class, and sexuality as interlocked underwrites widespread applications of intersectionality.

Ultimately, at stake in Lugones's proposal is a fierce critique of the notion of the modern individual, or agent, and its iteration in key theories of subjectivity within women of color thinking. One such case is the use of Crenshaw's theory to derive intersectional identities (i.e., Black women) since this use fails to account for the limitations of a method aimed at mapping legal subjectivities. Primarily, Crenshaw examines the violence perpetrated against Black women, the marginalizations, disempowerments, and vulnerabilities that cannot find any relief or uptake precisely because the law does not recognize Black women except as additions of identity categories that do not fit their experiences to begin with (1989).[12] Based on the model of a unitary, stable, and closed individual who is self-determining, the law constructs its subject by marginalizing certain actors or claims whose histories and identities the legal system can't contain (Lacey 1998, 144). In exposing what makes Black women invisible under the law, Crenshaw also observes that they occupy "a location that resists telling" (1991, 1242). When she describes Black women as the collision point, the intersection, where cars driving down separate streets (discriminations) meet (1989, 139), she is mapping such a location in its telling of legal subjectivities. Lugones's intervention in this debate leads us to reflect on whether the demarginalization of Black women on the map of the law prevents us from conflating legal and nonlegal subjectivities, from presuming that a legal subject equally maps what she theorizes as the co-constitution of social subjects.

In chapter 4, "Beyond the 'Logic of Purity': 'Post-Post-Intersectional' Glimpses in Decolonial Feminism," Anna Carastathis argues precisely that categorial thinking—seeing oppressions as interlocked—is one with the logic of the legal, homogeneous subject. Therefore, what many within feminist scholarship and activism call intersectional identities are logically impossible within the law but also, as Lugones and Carastathis contend, within feminist theorizing whenever it leaves the interlocking of oppressions untouched.[13] Together, Carastathis's critique of a post-intersectional paradigm and the remaining chapter in part II, weave praxical dialogues about the psychosocial experience of oppressing ←—→ resisting relations in which selves become both multiple and impure, and where they explore ways of witnessing resistance to colonial histories with and beyond intersectionality. In chapter 5, "Witnessing Faithfully and the Intimate Politics of Queer South Asian Praxis," Shireen Roshanravan turns to love as a transformational praxis, as a way of attending to the communicative barriers and fragmenting logics blocking deep coalition. She shows that the practice of "witnessing faithfully" may operate as a commitment to affirm another's multiplicity through intergenerational, community-defined well-being. Teasing out the nuances of Lugones's contribution within intersectional studies and its application to critical analysis of racialized gender, part II sets the stage to engage the paradigmatic shift that she calls the "coloniality of gender."

GENDER, COLONIALITY, AND DECOLONIAL EMBODIMENTS

Lugones published one of her most impactful articles, "Heterosexualism and the Colonial/Modern Gender System," in *Hypatia* in 2007. Here she articulates a new theory of gender that takes seriously the notion's "deep imbrication" with race and coloniality (HGS 187). She argues that the concept of gender emerged in tandem with the expansion of colonialism in the sixteenth and seventeenth centuries and the consequent advent of the modern concept of race as a means of classifying people, labor pools, subjectivities, and knowledges. For Lugones, gender does not signify the binary categories of either male or female, or even a spectrum of genders between these poles, but a system of relations with light and dark sides. The light side of the colonial/modern gender system is the one most often referred to in mainstream feminist theorizing and activism: it is based on the ideas of biological dimorphism and heterosexuality between men and women, opposing an ideal of the weak, passive, domestically bound, and sexually pure woman to that of a strong, active, self-governing, and sexually aggressive man. The light side is hegemonic in that it establishes the modern meanings of "woman" and "man," and thus of "human"—those who are civilized and evolved enough to warrant the labels "woman" and "man." By contrast, the dark side of the colonial/modern gender system does not organize gender in these terms; colonized/nonwhite females were "understood as animals in the deep sense of 'without gender,' sexually marked as female, but without the characteristics of femininity" (HGS 202–3). This construal of colonized and nonwhite peoples is "thoroughly violent" (206) as it works to justify the hierarchies constitutive of Eurocentered capitalism—the labor exploitation, sexual exploitation, abuse, reduction to animality, and denigration of cosmologies and knowledges of those on the dark side.

Most important, the light side of the colonial/modern gender system is maintained by perpetuating the dark side: the more people of color are dehumanized, the more womanly and manly white bourgeois people become. In this way, the priority given to heterosexuality in the colonial/modern gender system has simultaneously turned "people into animals and [...] white women into reproducers of 'the (white) race' and 'the (middle or upper) class'" (HGS 201). Lugones refers to this reduction of people that "fits them for classification" as *coloniality* (TDF 745). The hallmarks of Lugones's theory of gender are, first, that it recognizes the differential ways that gender is constructed in relation to Europeans/whites and colonized/nonwhite peoples, and, second, that it sees the concept of gender as a colonial/modern imposition developed in the service of consolidating and facilitating the global exercise of power in Eurocentered capitalism.[14]

Lugones's description of the colonial/modern gender system is born out of her struggle with questions that arise in the context of political organizing: Why do men of color often assume a posture of indifference toward "the systematic violences inflicted upon women of color" (HGS 188)? Why do white bourgeois women fail to take the coloniality of power seriously, fail to recognize the constitutive relations between gender, race, class, and colonization in their politics (187)? Lugones observes how these patterns of indifference that inhabit political practice are respectively reflected in the ways that men of color make sense of coloniality and decolonization, on the one hand, and white women make sense of gender, on the other. For example, although Lugones's view builds on Aníbal Quijano's notion of the "coloniality of power," she sees his account as too narrow because it naturalizes gender by conceiving of it as a heterosexual dispute over sexual access and reproduction (HGS 189–90). The heteropatriarchal gender binary of "man/woman" in this framework becomes white supremacist criteria for colonizing definitions of who counts as "human," but also of who counts as the subject of feminist struggles. U.S. Third World liberation, anticolonial, and mainstream feminist movements that employ gender and heteropatriarchal rhetoric in their struggles to be recognized as "human" reinforce the very logics of coloniality justifying violence against them.

The coloniality of gender paradigm positions Lugones's thinking differently than before in relation to feminist theory since it views the concept of gender as violent, a colonial/modern invention that facilitates the racialization and dehumanization of those under colonial rule and its aftermath. Whereas her earliest work, such as "Have We Got a Theory for You!," problematizes any feminism that would take the group "women" as its universal subject, this new phase in Lugones's thinking turns from criticizing this central category of feminism to changing the very terms of the discussion through an original analysis of gender (HGS 188). Moreover, white feminists and lesbian activists who align themselves with Lugones's earlier feminist work, especially in its engaging certain forms of separatism as politically useful, may have difficulty recognizing their embrace of womanhood as a feature of the light side of the gender system and its complicity with coloniality and the dehumanization of people of color.[15]

The colonial/modern gender system not only offers a new way of thinking about gender, it also calls for a corollary form of political praxis—one where the critique of coloniality is enacted in everyday, intersubjective relations (TDF 746–47). Lugones names this praxis "decolonial feminism," which she describes as "the possibility of overcoming the coloniality of gender" (TDF 747). As a practice passed on across generations, the decolonial marks the coexistence of mechanisms of dehumanization over colonized and localized resistances—that is, resistant ways of claiming resources, beliefs, languages, knowledges, and passions. The decolonial, at its most suggestive, delivers a wealth of social arrangements, embodied in ways of speaking, gesturing, praying, cooking, working, being carnally intimate, and so many others. In the unearthing of this wealth, numerous questions about colonizing mechanisms and decolonial possibilities guide our path: What forms of labor, such as indentured servitude, are integral to the subordination of Native and indigenous economies, spiritualities, kinship, and authority? What type of economies, such as sustainable farming, carry with them subaltern legacies in opposition to the colonization of non-Western forms of kinship? What type of spiritual systems, cosmologies, and ways of understanding the nonworldly provide principles of relationality antithetical to sexual dimorphism and its anchoring of the coloniality of gender? Which approaches to sexual violence center women of color and their history of dehumanization vis-à-vis the state's protection of white middle-class femininity? By waking us to the memories that these questions seek, decolonial feminism instills an anticapitalist sentiment in our fashioning of differences, resistances, and coalitions (TDF 754).

Lugones's theory of the colonial/modern gender system has been employed to illuminate a variety of resistant experiences and colonial positions, from those discussed in Donato Ndongo's novel *Shadows of Your Black Memory* (Figueroa 2015) to those that shape marriage practices in Khumasi, Ghana (Nave 2017). Each of the chapters in part III of this book continues these extensions of Lugones's concept by respectively providing a contextualized point of entry into this new paradigm, while also taking up the call to reflect on complicated moments of complicity with the coloniality of gender. In chapter 6, "Border Thinking/Being/Perception," Madina Tlostanova exposes an understanding of colonial oppression that merges Lugones's light and dark sides of the colonial/modern gender system. In her view, Caucasus and Central Asian peoples suffer systemic violence at the same time as they are illegible as colonized peoples—particularly when they are compared to Amerindians and enslaved Africans and their descendants who are readily seen as colonized. In chapter 7, "Motion Sickness and the Slipperiness of Irish Racialization," Jennifer McWeeny describes the phenomenon of "ontological slipperiness," an experience and a disorder that involves moving between at least two distinct or "partitioned" racialized positions in the coloniality of power that alternatively apply to the same person. Closing with a meditation on "Toward a Decolonial Ethics," chapter 8 by Manuel Chávez Jr. responds to a crucial aspect of Lugones's decolonial feminism: her call for men of color to make sense of their indifference to violence against women of color even as they proclaim themselves antiracist and decolonial activists and movement protagonists.

KNOWING ON THE EDGE OF WORLDS AND SENSE

There is a transitional space between worlds of sense that is both empty and fecund because it lacks the hardened meanings of dominant structures. Lugones often refers to this space as the "limen" or "borderland" and conceives of the liminal as that which holds more than one contradictory meaning at the same time, that which falls off the bounds of sense. When seen from the perspective of the coloniality of gender, readers may encounter a fruitful connection between Lugones's notion of active subjectivity and a broader account of liminal beings. The decolonial, as it has been argued, underlines historical possibilities of resistance, of moving to dismantle the coloniality of gender. As Kelli Zaytoun discusses in chapter 2, Lugones follows Victor Turner's account of antistructures to emphasize that liminality is both "the place where one becomes most fully aware of one's multiplicity" and "an interstice from where one can most clearly stand critically toward different structures" (SAS 59). For a praxical thinker such as Lugones, the difficulties of communication among liminal beings are not surprising. She understands too well the risks that women of color face when they engage in the labor of deep coalition. In her more recent work, she explores the ways that the concept of liminal space can falsely implicate a communicative transparency among people whose subjectivity rests outside of dominant constructions (OC). However, insofar as we become active subjects through different journeys and struggles, there will also be multiple limens—that is, multiple spaces of resistance, multiple ways of living creatively outside dominant sense. To expect transparent communication in these spaces is thus to fall back into the structures of sense that Lugones has described as being fueled by the logics of purity and top-down views, of either/or truths, or of knowledge attained through distance and neutrality (PIS, TSC). She reminds us that deep coalition is not necessarily coextensive with liminality; it is something that must be achieved by meeting, hearing, and seeing others face to face in their own liminal spaces, by world-traveling into and across worlds, and by attending to the ways that communication is both opened and foreclosed in these encounters.

Part IV excavates that epistemic, ethical, and affective labor of dwelling in the transformation of selves who are learning to become accountable for each other's liminal possibilities. Pedro DiPietro and Joshua Price respectively engage two concrete examples of liminality: decolonizing cognitive practices in contemporary analysis of trans* embodiments and the death-worlds of the incarcerated. They both suggest that marginalized subjects can't take for granted each other's coalitional or empathic orientations. In chapter 9, "Beyond Benevolent Violence: Trans* of Color, Ornamental Multiculturalism, and the Decolonization of Affect," DiPietro expands the notion of radical multiculturalism from within the affective turn (DC), introducing the notion of benevolent violence to examine how particular epistemic dispositions aimed at suppressing complexity, multiplicity, and opacity impoverish and distort racialized trans* and transing embodiments. Chapter 10, "Travel to Death-Worlds," describes Price's encounter with the legacy of coloniality among those who live on opposite ends of the incarceration divide, troubling deep-seated patterns of apathy toward the condemned, those whom the carceral system denies selfhood, and toward the liminal worlds they inhabit.

Lugones's theorizing of political praxis as a site of deep personal and social transformation, of figuring out how to move from liminal consciousness to practice, makes important contributions to several other debates, including those in religious and Indigenous studies where they explore the limits of modern and postmodern notions of secular subjectivity. More significantly, however, it is the uptake that her teaching on the liminal may receive in queer studies where there is marked emphasis on the examination of art and performance rather than on activism and politics (Floyd 2010; Chávez 2013). Recent scholarship on *queer* social movements provides evidence that what occurs behind the scenes, in the backstage of social protest, is as important for coalitional politics as what takes place in public view (Chávez 2013; DiPietro 2015).[16] Some leading voices in queer studies and queer of color critique attempt to trouble typical notions of temporality with respect to unconventional political and cultural forms (Halberstam 2005; Muñoz 2009). Particularly, they criticize the neoliberal and oftentimes white supremacist pragmatics of LGBTQ rights, one that demands urgent solutions and upholds nationalist, family-centered values. Through this critique, they place the potential of nonnormative ways in the hopes of a different utopia, a constant and reversible new dawn. A notion such as liminality has crucial consequences for that type of queer of color projects where utopianism fuels current debates. Rather than taking us to a temporality of potency, of constantly redefining many futures, liminality in the form of world-traveling or street-walker theorizing threads together multiple timelines, including coexisting constructions of selves and of who we come to be for one another. The limen is a site of concrete, body-to-body possibility rather than potency. It spans over the ongoing or continuous present tense, of learning one another, of getting a feel about one another, and of meeting in solidarity at the edge of both dominant and counterdominant sense.

"I WON'T THINK WHAT I WON'T PRACTICE"

Likely the most distinctive feature of Lugones's philosophy is the extent to which she refuses to separate the theoretical and the practical. Indeed, for those of us who have been trained to categorize interventions and insights as either one or the other, it takes time to learn to read Lugones's works in a way that senses their nooks and crannies—the complexity, thickness, and nuance that constitute her relentless and evolving praxical thinking. This fullness is embodied in the image and experience of the streetwalker / *la callejera*, whose spatiality Lugones invokes to illustrate the importance of navigating the social at "street-level" without the height of abstraction, without allegiance to established social norms, and without the trappings of transparency that communities of choice often evoke (TSC, ED). In her view, theorizing resistance against multiple oppressions involves physically being with one another, hanging out together, traveling to each other's worlds, speaking face to face, playfully risking one's sense of self-importance. The political work implicated in Lugones's notion of praxis is not centered on particular issues or goals, but rather "on the process and on the people involved" (PRE 14).

Many of the communities where Lugones has carried out her unique political praxis have already been mentioned: the Escuela Popular Norteña; Critical Resistance; Incite! Women, Gender Non-Conforming, and Trans People of Color Against Violence; feminist and Indigenous collectives in Argentina, Bolivia, Colombia, and Mexico; the Latina Feminism Roundtable; and the Philosophy, Interpretation, and Culture program (PIC) at Binghamton University. There are still many others, such as the Women of Color Caucus of the Midwest Society for Women in Philosophy (SWIP), Hispano communities of rural Northern New Mexico, and alternative schools for gang members in La Villita. The chapters in part V offer glimpses into ways that Lugones has cultivated coalition in some of these spaces, and, by extension, also help us to envision new coalitional methods for our communities and our present.

In chapter 11, "Deep Coalition and Popular Education Praxis," Cricket Keating illustrates the methodological implications of Lugones's coalitional approach to popular education by analyzing the Escuela Popular Norteña (EPN) workshops and *encuentro* notes used during residential gatherings of community organizers in Latina/o and people of color communities across the nation. Sarah Hoagland's piece, chapter 12, "Walking Illegitimately: A *Cachapera/Tortillera* and a Dyke," is a beautiful testament to the political friendship that Lugones and Hoagland have maintained for over thirty years in Midwest SWIP and other contexts that can be read as an enactment of feminist praxis, especially in regard to the decolonization of language, territoriality, and socialities. The final chapter of *Speaking Face to Face*, titled "Carnal Disruptions," features a rare interview between Mariana Ortega and María Lugones, two Latina philosophers who generate an exchange that deepens our sense of Lugones's political and conceptual terrain, from her deeply influential methodology of world-traveling to her current thinking within Indigenous movements of *Abya Yala* on the insidious violence of the coloniality of gender.[17]

The chapters of part V provide standpoints from which to think Lugones's work differently than others in this book because they expose those central parts of her coalitional practice that lie beyond the boundaries of the written word. They remind us that writing spoken face to face is possible only insofar as we speak face to face in each other's presence at street-level. They give flesh to Lugones's claim that empathetic and sympathetic thinking flourishes not in a theory or maxim, but in "the devotion of friendship" (HCS 43). They lend texture to the ground from which we can engage a question that Hoagland asks at the start of her chapter: "What happens when marginalized others meet?"

It is important to keep open the multiple lines of meaning that live in Lugones's writing, even as we navigate political and institutional landscapes that beckon us to classify her work monologically, as either philosophical or political, either theoretical or practical, either academic or populist, either feminist or decolonial, either feminist or queer. As we work against this ossification of living meanings that we find in our body-to-body and face-to-face relations—those multiple, incisive, and fluid meanings that inhabit Lugones's pen—we invite readers to see the place of her work, her pilgrimages/*peregrinajes*, alongside a living repertoire of resistance that inscribes politics in the flesh. This includes but is not limited to a larger constellation of feminist writings in antiracist and decolonial feminisms: Gloria Anzaldúa's *Borderlands/*La Frontera, Akasha Hull, Patricia Bell-Scott, and Barbara Smith's *But Some of Us Are Brave*,

Audre Lorde's *Sister Outsider*, Cherríe Moraga's *Loving in the War Years*, Moraga and Anzaldúa's *This Bridge Called My Back*, M. Jacqui Alexander's *Pedagogies of Crossing*, Chandra Talpade Mohanty's *Feminism Without Borders*, "A Black Feminist Statement" by the Combahee River Collective, and Angela Davis's *Women, Race, and Class*.

Like the feminist fighters within the fierce cohort mentioned above, María Lugones is a visionary whose insights, praxis, and example give us tools to shape a present we have not yet inhabited. The strength of her vision moves not only through time, but also through the hard shell of categories and knowledges that parse up our worlds. Engaging Lugones's thinking actively involves cultivating ways to "see deeply into the social" (TSC 226), "to see the multiplicity" (TDF 756), "to see the world multiply" (TDF 749), "to see non-white women" (TDF 742; DF 69), and to "[see] the world anew" (TDF 753).

Making irreverent meaning out of the Euro-Western association of knowing with seeing omnipotently, from both nowhere and above, Lugones reconceives vision as that which can sense beyond Western logocentrism and Eurocentric worldviews for building violence-free communities. Seeing each other's resistances is not about gaining clarity or transparency. It is rather about cultivating eyes for the histories of uncharted creativity that equally shape and expand our present possibilities at the point of their opacity, their sometimes not intelligible meaning. Inspired by Marilyn Frye's criticisms of arrogant perception, that type of perception that understands others as for oneself (WT 78), Lugones imagines new forms of perception that foster empathetic and sympathetic coalitions of daring and love. The streetwalker's duplicitous perception notices multiple, contradictory, sometimes unspeakable meanings. The loving perception of the world-traveler sees another's "own sense of herself from within her world," and sees the world-traveler her/him/themselves with the other's eyes.[18] Such methodologies of resistance are kinds of vision that transgress the boundaries of the eyes, instead running through the senses and sensuousness of our intimate, everyday relationships.

We have only just begun to encounter the depth and socially transformative possibilities of Lugones's philosophy. Her most recent notions such as the colonial/modern gender system and decolonial feminism have yet to be developed in detail, and many fields are just starting to take note of the value and prescience of her ideas. This book is an invitation to travel more deeply into the social by way of Lugones's visions and the thirteen chapters that have been inspired by them, to engage *hablando cara a cara* across our varied modes of expression, social locations, and worlds of sense. Hers is a call for you and us to face one another and ourselves, to write to each other face to face, and to witness each other's insurgent and more-than-oppositional creativity. For the three of us and the other authors of this collection, Lugones's methodologies of resistance release seismic shifts in what is possible, shifts that we want so much to open to you.

NOTES

1. When capitalized, the phrase "Women of Color" is meant to denote the feminist coalitional identification. When lowercased, "women of color" references a demographic description of those legally classified in the United States as both "woman" and "nonwhite." This distinction is important to Lugones, as her focus is primarily on the former locution (WT 78).

2. Lugones defines a nondiasporic person of color as someone who does not belong to a U.S. diasporic community of color with a collectively revalorized history (ND 19). See also her account of those missing a solid identity as core women of color in the United States (BP).

3. See Roshanravan (2014) for an in-depth consideration of the relationship between Lugones's locus and her theorizing.

4. Lugones uses the double-sided arrow to signify her understanding of oppression as an ongoing process always met with resistance (IP 12).

5. Lugones understands playfulness as an openness to uncertainty, which includes a vocation not bound by the meanings and norms that constitute one's ground (IP 26).

6. In February 2017, as part of her contribution to a roundtable honoring the legacy of *This Bridge* at Syracuse University, Lugones discussed the incomplete project of U.S. Women of Color coalition building. See https://spark.adobe.com/page/sxHxHhgbWQxzr

7. The Center for Interdisciplinary Studies in Philosophy, Interpretation, and Culture, associated with the PIC program, worked as a node within the modernity/coloniality/decoloniality network. Over a decade of collaborations, it fostered sustained conversations on decoloniality. See the acknowledgments for a representative list of the participants in these conversations.

8. Lugones emphasizes both that the notion of a "world" is intentionally suggestive rather than fixedly defined and that the quotation marks around "world" are important because they disrupt a person's ability to think of worlds as atomistic and impermeable (IP 16; WT 87). Since this construction is implied in this book, we have dropped the quotation marks around "world"-traveling and "world" throughout for clarity and ease of reading.

9. See also Collins (1998) and Mohanty (2003).

10. Along the lines of post-positivist realism, scholars such as Linda Martín Alcoff (2006) and Michael Hames-García (2011) argue that this evacuation of the category woman is prevalent within poststructuralist philosophy (Judith Butler's antirealism is a case in point).

11. On the debate about the post-intersectional imaginary, see Kwan on intersectionality's lack of engagement with identities whose marginalization is not multilayered (1997), Hutchinson on the need to continuously add more axes to the analytic frame (2001), Chang and Culp on suggesting metaphors other than intersectionality to visualize how power operates (2002), and Nash on Black feminisms' nonidentitarian politics of love (2011a, 2011b). See also this book's chapter 4, Carastathis (2016), and McWeeny (2014).

12. On the slippage from Black women to women of color in Crenshaw's theorization of intersectionality, see Holland (2012).

13. See May (2014) for a discussion of feminist distortions of intersectionality. See Hammonds (1994) for a prime account of the logical invisibility of Black women's sexuality.

14. Lugones's decolonial feminism expands on paradigmatic theories of decoloniality, including those of Quijano (1992), Mignolo (1995, 2000), Dussel (1996), and Maldonado-Torres (2013).

15. See this book's chapter 12. For a complex study of separatism, see Hoagland (1989, 1992, 2007a, 2007b), and Lugones's discussion of Hoagland's lesbian ethics (HL).

16. James Scott's work on "hidden transcripts" of resistance has left an imprint on Lugones's thinking and is evident in her theorizing of resistant practices (1985, 1990).

17. This is the term indigenous peoples and decolonial activists/scholars such as Lugones give to what is commonly referenced in English language as "Latin America."

18. This formulation comes from the 1987 version of WT, page 8.

REFERENCES

Alcoff, Linda Martín. 2006. *Visible Identities. Race, Gender, and the Self*. New York: Oxford University Press.

Alexander, M. Jacqui. 2005. *Pedagogies of Crossing: Meditations on Feminism, Sexual Politics, Memory, and the Sacred*. Durham, NC: Duke University Press.

Anzaldúa, Gloria. 1987. *Borderlands/La Frontera: The New Mestiza*. San Francisco: Aunt Lute Books.

———. 1990. "Haciendo Caras, Una Entrada." In *Making Face, Making Soul. Haciendo Caras. Creative and Critical Perspectives by Feminists of Color*, edited by Gloria Anzaldúa, xv–xxviii. San Francisco: Aunt Lute Books.

Barkley Brown, Elsa. 1989. "African-American Women's Quilting." *Signs* 14(4): 921–29.

Carastathis, Anna. 2016. *Intersectionality: Origins, Contestations, Horizons*. Lincoln: University of Nebraska Press.

Chang, Grace. 2007. "Where's the Violence? The Promise and Perils of Teaching Women of Color Studies." *Black Women, Gender + Families* 1(1): 46–73.

Chang, Robert S. and Jerome McCristal Culp. 2002. "After Intersectionality." *UMKC Law Review* 71: 485–92.

Chávez, Karma. 2013. *Queer Migration Politics: Activist Rhetoric and Coalitional Possibilities*. Urbana: University of Illinois Press.

Cho, Sumi, Kimberlé Williams Crenshaw, and Leslie McCall. 2013. "Toward a Field of Intersectionality Studies: Theory, Applications, and Praxis." *Signs* 38(4): 785–810.

Clare, Eli. 1999. *Exile and Pride: Disability, Queerness, and Liberation*. New York: South End Press.

Cohen, Cathy. 1997. "Punks, Bulldaggers, and Welfare Queens: The Radical Potential of Queer Politics?" *GLQ: A Journal of Lesbian and Gay Studies* 3(4): 437–65.

Combahee River Collective. 1978. "A Black Feminist Statement." In *Capitalist Patriarchy and the Case for Socialist Feminism*, edited by Zillah Eisenstein, 362–72. New York: Monthly Review Press.

Collins, Patricia Hill. 1998. "It's All in the Family: Intersections of Gender, Race, and Nation." *Hypatia* 13(3): 62–82.

Crenshaw, Kimberlé. 1989. "Demarginalizing the Intersection of Race and Sex: A Black Feminist Critique of Antidiscrimination Doctrine, Feminist Theory and Antiracist Politics." *University of Chicago Legal Forum* 1(8): 139–67.

———. 1991. "Mapping the Margins: Intersectionality, Identity Politics, and Violence against Women of Color." *Stanford Law Review* 43(6): 1241–99.

Cruz, Cindy. 2013. "LGBTQ Youth of Color Video Making as Radical Curriculum: A Brother Mourning His Brother and a Theory in the Flesh." *Curriculum Inquiry* 43(4): 441–60.

Davis, Angela. 1981. *Women, Race, and Class*. New York: Random House.

DiPietro, Pedro Javier. 2015. "Decolonizing *Travesti* Space in Buenos Aires: Race, Sexuality, and Sideways Relationality." *Gender, Place, and Culture: A Journal of Feminist Geography* 23(5): 677–93.

Dussel, Enrique. 1996. *The Underside of Modernity: Apel, Ricoeur, Rorty, Taylor and the Philosophy of Liberation*. New York: Humanities Press.

Falcón, Sylvia. 2015. "The Globalization of Ferguson: Pedagogical Matters about Racial Violence." *Feminist Studies* 41(1): 218–21.

Figueroa, Yomaira. 2015. "Faithful Witnessing as Practice: Decolonial Readings of *Shadows of Your Black Memory* and *The Brief Wondrous Life of Oscar Wao*." *Hypatia* 30(4): 641–56.

Floyd, Kevin. 2010. "The Importance of Being Childish: Queer Utopias and Historical Contradictions." *Cultural Logics*: 1–19. www.yumpu.com/en/document/view/41289037/importance-of-being-childish-queer-utopians-and-cultural-logic. Accessed January 4, 2018.

Gunn Allen, Paula. 1981. *Grandmothers of the Light: A Medicine Woman's Sourcebook*. Boston: Beacon Press.

Halberstam, Judith. 2005. *In a Queer Time and Place: Transgender Bodies, Subcultural lives*. New York: New York University Press.

Hames-García, Michael. 2011. "Queer Theory Revisited." In *Gay Latino Studies: A Critical Reader*, edited by Michael Hames-García and Ernesto Martinez, 19–45. Durham, NC: Duke University Press.

Hammonds, Evelyn. 1994. "Black (W)holes and the Geometry of Black Female Sexuality." *differences* 6(3): 127–145.

Hernández, Daisy, and Bushra Rehman. 2002. *Colonize This! Young Women of Color on Today's Feminism*. New York: Seal Press.

Hoagland, Sarah Lucia. 1989. *Lesbian Ethics: Toward New Value*. Palo Alto, CA: Institute for Lesbian Studies.

———. 1992. "Why Lesbian Ethics?" *Hypatia* 7(4): 195–206.

———. 2007a. "Heterosexualism and White Supremacy." *Hypatia* 22(1): 166–85.

———. 2007b. "What is Lesbian Philosophy?" In *The Nature of Philosophy: Whose Knowledge? Whose Tradition?* edited by George Yancy, 49–79. Lanham, MD: Rowman & Littlefield.

Holland, Sharon Patricia. 2012. *The Erotic Life of Racism*. Durham, NC: Duke University Press.

hooks, bell. 1981. *Ain't I a Woman: Black Women and Feminism*. Boston: South End Press.

Hull, Akasha (Gloria T.), Patricia Bell Scott, and Barbara Smith. 1982. *All the*

Women Are White, All the Men Are Black, But Some of Us Are Brave. New York: The Feminist Press.

Hutchinson, Darren L. 2001. "Identity Crisis: 'Intersectionality,' 'Multidimensionality,' and the Development of an Adequate Theory of Subordination." *Michigan Journal of Race and the Law* 6(2): 285–317.

Jayawardena, Kumari. 1986. *Feminism and Nationalism in the Third World*. New Delhi: Kali for Women.

Johnson Reagon, Bernice. 1983. "Coalition Politics: Turning the Century." In *Homegirls: A Black Feminist Anthology*, edited by Barbara Smith, 356–68. New York: Kitchen Table Women of Color Press.

Joseph, Gloria, and Jill Lewis. 1981. *Common Differences: Conflicts in Black and White Feminist Perspectives*. Garden City, NY: Doubleday.

Kwan, Peter. 1997. "Intersections of Race, Ethnicity, Class, Gender, and Sexual Orientation: Jeffrey Dahmer and the Cosynthesis of Categories." *Hastings Law Journal* 48: 1257–92.

Lacey, Nicola. 1998. *Unspeakable Subjects: Feminist Essays in Legal and Social Theory*. Evanston, IL: Northwestern University Press.

Lorde, Audre. 1980. *The Cancer Journals*. San Francisco: Spinsters.

———. 1982. *Zami, A New Spelling of My Name*. Trumansburg, NY: Crossing Press.

———. 1984. *Sister Outsider*. Berkeley, CA: Crossing Press.

Maldonado-Torres, Nelson. 2013. "On the Coloniality of Being: Contributions to the Development of a Concept." In *Globalization in the Decolonial Option*, edited by Walter Mignolo and Arturo Escobar, 94–123. New York: Routledge.

May, Vivian. 2014. "Speaking into the Void? Intersectionality Critiques and Epistemic Backlash." *Hypatia* 29(1): 94–112.

McWeeny, Jennifer. 2014. "Topographies of Flesh: Women, Nonhuman Animals, and the Embodiment of Connection and Difference." *Hypatia* 29(2): 269–286.

Mignolo, Walter. 1995. *The Darker Side of the Renaissance: Literacy, Territoriality, and Colonization*. Ann Arbor: University of Michigan Press.

———. 2000. *Local Histories/Global Designs: Coloniality, Subaltern Knowledges, and Border Thinking*. Princeton, NJ: Princeton University Press.

Mohanty, Chandra. 2003. *Feminism without Borders: Decolonizing Theory, Practicing Solidarity*. Durham, NC: Duke University Press.

Moraga, Cherríe, and Gloria Anzaldúa. 1981. *This Bridge Called My Back: Writings by Radical Women of Color*. San Francisco: Aunt Lute Books.

Moraga, Cherríe. 1981. "Entering the Lives of Others." In *This Bridge Called My Back: Writings by Radical Women of Color*, edited by Cherríe Moraga and Gloria Anzaldúa, 25–60. San Francisco: Aunt Lute Books.

———. 1983. *Loving in the War Years: Lo que nunca pasó por sus labios*. Boston: South End Press.

Moya, Paula M. L. 2006. "Review of *Pilgrimages/*Peregrinajes*: Theorizing Coalition against Multiple Oppressions*." *Hypatia* 21(3): 198–202.

Muñoz, José Esteban. 2009. *Cruising Utopia: The Then and There of Queer Futurity*. New York: New York University Press.

Nash, Jennifer. 2011a. "Home Truths on Intersectionality." *Yale Journal of Law and Feminism* 23(3): 455–70.

———. 2011b. "Practicing Love: Black Feminism, Love-Politics, and Post-Intersectionality." *Meridians* 11(2): 1–24.

Nave, Carmen. 2017. "Marriage in Kumasi, Ghana: Locally Emergent Practices in the Colonial/Modern Gender System." *Hypatia* 32(3): 557–73.

Pérez, Laura Elisa. 2010. "Enrique Dussel's *Ética de la liberación*, U.S. Women of Color Decolonizing Practices, and Coalitionary Politics amidst Difference." *Qui Parle: Critical Humanities and Social Sciences* 18(2): 121–46.

Pough, Gwendolyn. 2007. "What It Do, Shorty? Women, Hip-Hop, and a Feminist Agenda. *Black Women, Gender + Families* l(2): 78–99.

Quijano, Aníbal. 1992. "Colonialidad y modernidad/racionalidad." *Perú Indígena* 13(29): 11–20.

Roshanravan, Shireen. 2014. "Motivating Coalition: Women of Color and Epistemic Disobedience." *Hypatia* 29(1): 41–58.

Sandoval, Chela. 2000. *Methodology of the Oppressed*. Minneapolis: University of Minnesota Press.

Scott, James. 1985. *Weapons of the Weak: Everyday Forms of Peasant Resistance*. New Haven, CT: Yale University Press.

———. 1990. *Domination and the Arts of Resistance: Hidden Transcripts*. New Haven, CT: Yale University Press.

Part I Coalitional Selves, Multiple Realities

1 Trash Talks Back

Elizabeth V. Spelman

The subtitle of Lugones's extraordinary collection *Pilgrimages/*Peregrinajes is *Theorizing Coalition against Multiple Oppressions*. Readers of Lugones's work might wonder if she chose this subtitle only with considerable reluctance. Its telescoping conciseness perhaps assures readers who might be puzzled by the title that they will be in familiar conceptual and political territory: "theory," "coalition," and "oppression" are eminently keyword-worthy. But it is a measure of the forces against which Lugones has been in continuous struggle that those concepts—especially oppression—may seem all too inviting: they promise but are unlikely to deliver an opening for resistance and liberation. In what follows I briefly review some of Lugones's reservations about the work performed by the notions of oppression and the oppressed. I then go on to suggest that concepts hinted at but not fully articulated in her work—"trash," "waste," "disposable," and the like—provide a vocabulary that direct us to sources of resistance she takes the language and the structure of oppression to occlude.

"IF YOU SEE OPPRESSION, YOU TEND NOT TO SEE RESISTANCE"[1]

Toward the conclusion of "Tactical Strategies of the Streetwalker/*Estrategias Tácticas de la Callejera*," Lugones remarks:

> I end with a reflection of what pulls us into a frenzy of recognizable political activity, recognizable in dominant terms. Street-level sociality can provide a despairing, demoralizing "picture" of the complexities and depth of oppression and of the barriers to emancipatory change. There is a desire to imbue oneself with a sense of power against this demoralization. Not infrequently, the pedestrian theorist is tempted to favor a mode of comportment that speaks the languages of systems of oppression, seeking within them redress or assistance. This temptation, seduction, is understandable and ubiquitous. We feel a need to

demand equality, respect, and justice within a particular dominant construal of sense, even if that sense—conceptually, materially—requires that equality, respect and justice be mechanisms congruent with fragmentation and domination. (TSC 229)

The very notion of oppression appears to open up a space in which the oppressed are both recognized and attended to: the systemic and suffocating domination, abuse and exploitation to which people are subjected is acknowledged, presumably as part of projects to end such violence. But Lugones worries that attention framed in such terms comes at a high price. Oppressive systems—including the tools they provide for reflexive examination—thrive on truncated, reductive portrayals of the oppressed that obscure their existence as "subjects, lively beings, resisters" (IP 18):

> If we think of people who are oppressed as not consumed or exhausted by oppression, but also as resisting or sabotaging a system aimed at molding, reducing, violating, or erasing them, then we also see at least two realities: one of them has the logic of resistance and transformation; the other has the logic of oppression. (IP 12)

These two "logics" typically are in interplay; it is not as if a person is (or is to be understood as) simply oppressed *or* is (or is to be understood as) simply engaged in resistance. Nonetheless, oppressors intent on enjoying the fruits of oppression have a lot at stake in "not seeing sabotage and resistance," even though in order to get rid of such pushback they'd have to see it (15).[2] To not only take off the blinders that protect them from such awareness, but to come to understand what they then would face, they'd have to learn to "travel" to the world of the resisters, be open to seeing not just how the resister sees the oppressor and the oppressor's world, but how the resister sees her own world.[3]

But even those who acknowledge the oppressed as the oppressed and as unfairly deprived of justice, equality, and respect aren't thereby "traveling" to the worlds of the oppressed. Even those who recognize oppression as a problem and do not boast of it as an achievement may mistakenly think that the solution to that problem is to guarantee justice, equality, and respect. But that is an answer to oppression that is offered in the "logic of oppression." To be seen as unfairly deprived of a certain standing that others enjoy—despite being entitled to that standing in virtue of sharing with them attributes such as reason or personhood—is not the same as being seen as having traits and capacities that allow one to recognize and resist the insidious forces of oppression and the oppressors who keep those forces fueled. Recognition of people simply as deprived of that to which they are entitled doesn't invite recognition of them as beings who are capable, for example, of seeing straight into and mocking the delusion and self-deception adoringly embraced by oppressors in order for the latter to hide their desperate need of and dependence on the very people they lord over. Portraying the oppressed as satisfied by coming at last to enjoy justice, equality, and respect is at odds with entertaining the possibility that the fondest dream of the oppressed may in fact *not* be that they come to be seen as enough like those who oppress them that they are guaranteed a certain shared formal set of rights. There is no reason to be thrilled if the best the oppressors have to offer is a version of something along these lines: "We've changed our minds. First we thought you were rather radically different from us and we wanted to mark such difference by depriving you of what we know ourselves to be entitled to. But now we've come to our senses: we no longer will exclude you or deny you the rights we have. After all, basically you are just like us. So come join us, won't you?"

Lugones doesn't wish to cease using "oppression," "oppressors," and "the oppressed"; they remain a means of bringing attention to the violent relationships resistance to which she is theorizing. But she does not want the conceptual armory therewith deployed to be seen as the only or the best device for undoing that violence and for understanding and giving voice to those subject to it.

ON THE CREATION OF TRASH

I hope to highlight pervasive aspects of Lugones's work in which she employs concepts that capture the texture of oppression but that do not at the same time lend strength to the logic of oppression. Recall her worry: if to be oppressed is simply and only not to enjoy justice, equality, and respect, then to cease to be oppressed is to enjoy them; but this is very thin conceptual and procedural gruel, too much in service to the systems it promises to undo. The fact that oppression does include the denial of justice, equality, and respect doesn't mean that satisfying the demands of justice, equality, and respect carries no seeds of treachery, that it takes care of the problem rather than leaving behind fertile ground for the sprouting and spread of myriad forms of mistreatment.

But what can open up or reveal possibilities shoved out of sight by the star status of "oppression"? I suggest looking at a more colloquial expression than "oppression" or "domination" or "exploitation," one often used by people subject to mistreatment by others in order to capture their experiences of being the object of various forms of aggression and violence: they talk about being "treated like trash." Indeed "trash" and close siblings such as "waste" and "disposable" occur quite commonly in descriptions of abuse. Often such terms are incorporated into titles of books or articles. Recent examples include Ha Jin, *War Trash* (2004); Zygmunt Bauman, *Wasted Lives: Modernity and its Outcasts* (2004); Grace Chang, *Disposable Domestics: Immigrant Women Workers in the Global Economy* (2000); Kevin Bales, *Disposable People: New Slavery in the Global Economy* (2004); and Dorothy Allison, *Trash* (2002).[4] An Amnesty International blog entry by Fotis Philippous on October 18, 2010, sports the headline 'Roma Community in Romania Still Treated Like Waste Six Years On." A blog from July 8, 2009, on the New Zealand organization E2NZ quotes member of Parliament Jim Anderton describing migrants being "treated like waste products."

Though the semantic home of *trash* seems to be in reference to things, focusing on its broader use in reference to people may illuminate important features of common forms of mistreating others—features that more formally developed concepts such as oppression only dimly reveal or in fact occlude. Even more, in light of Lugones's efforts to bring attention to "the oppressed" as "subjects, lively beings, resisters," a notable feature of trash comes to the fore: because of what trash is and how it is created, it can talk back. It does talk back. It resists our attempts to banish it. Perhaps, then—paradoxical as it may at first seem—the description of people as being treated like trash allows or invites us to notice avenues of resistance and refusal.

We focus first on how a thing becomes trash, leaving for the next section an exploration of how trash can talk back.[5] We shall then return to the question of what it means for people to be treated like trash and the exploration of this mode of mistreatment, and resistance to it, in Lugones's work.

Something becomes trash only in virtue of our making it so, through our actions or our words. We toss it out, throw it away, or deign it to be tossable, throw-awayable. However much or little we valued it or used it, we now declare its worthlessness or uselessness (at least for our purposes; we may easily forget that others may find it not at all worthless or useless). We dispose of it. Rendering it no longer in the orbit of our care or concern, we separate ourselves from it, abandon it, disown it, leave it unattended or in any event to be dealt with by others. Our reasons for doing this, and our own feelings and attitudes about doing so, are many and various. Just because we throw something out doesn't necessarily mean we are glad to do so. We might or might not have a sense of loss, or a sense of relief (or both). We might or might not have considered it as something contaminating or polluting. We may have tossed it out accidentally. Or regret having done so on purpose.[6]

TRASH TALKS BACK

Just because we have managed to get something to disappear from our immediate view or concern doesn't mean it has disappeared entirely.

1. Even if we live in neighborhoods where household trash is regularly scooped up and taken away by sanitation workers, we might be aware of the fact that figuring out what to do with all that stuff is at the heart of political battles over the siting of landfills, transfer stations, incinerators, ship containers, and other destinations for our detritus.[7] Indeed it would never occur to anyone to declare "Not In My Backyard"—let alone employ all the political muscle one can marshal to make sure the stuff ends up in the backyards of those with little political pull—if one really thought that for trash to disappear from one's sight is for it to have thoroughly vanished.

2. Catching up on headlines of the gossip glossies while standing in the grocery checkout line, we might be aware of the fact that one of the favorite research tools of tattletale columnists is rifling through the trash bins outside the homes of the objects of their insistent inquiry. A.J. Weberman gained borrowed fame by appointing himself chief investigator of Bob Dylan's garbage—all in the hope of getting the real dirt on Dylan, revealing him to be not at all the hero his fans adored.[8] And in fact combing through trash is a widespread practice. What it can and cannot reveal, should and should not be allowed to reveal, are topics of considerable concern to legal professionals and social scientists. State and federal courts, up to and including the Supreme Court of the United States, have been called on to decide whether or not a person's trash can be seized and pawed through by government agents without a warrant (*California v. Greenwood*). Garbology—the word was blessed for inclusion in the *Oxford English Dictionary* in 1989—is recognized as a subfield within archaeology. One of its foremost practitioners, whose work is cited in the OED entry, is William Rathje. For decades he and teams of his graduate students at the University of Arizona engaged in social science–sanctified snooping. Their research led Rathje to the conclusion that "…what people have owned—and thrown away—can speak more eloquently, informatively, and truthfully about the lives they lead than they themselves ever may" (Rathje and Murphy 2001, 54).[9]

3. Perhaps we are or have met dumpster divers, freegans, or others searching for food in household, supermarket, or restaurant waste receptacles—just a small sample of the many activities that vividly illustrate the familiar saw that one person's trash is another person's treasure.[10] Visitors to art museums or galleries are no longer surprised to learn about the use artists make of the refuse scattered across both urban and rural landscapes or beached unceremoniously at the edge of the sea.[11]

In short, as confident as some of us may be that what we have consigned to the garbage heap or trash bin is safely out of sight and *en route* to the landfill or "wherever that stuff goes," it perhaps has grown harder and harder to ignore the fact that though our trash is no longer here it very likely is somewhere else. (Our worries about material we think we have expunged by putting it in the computer trash bin are not irrelevant in this connection.) Trash talks back: it frustrates attempts to thoroughly dismiss it, shove it out of sight, silence it, send it as if by centrifugal force out of contact with us. On the one hand it may cause problems, especially for those left to deal with the toxic menace it may contain, or for those whose histories it reveals. On the other hand it may provide rich resources for those capable of and interested in divining the treasures within.

ON BEING TREATED LIKE TRASH

So far, then, we've explored some of the features of trash—in particular how something becomes trash, and ways in which trash in a sense talks back, refuses to bury once and for all activities or histories the very vanishing of which it might be thought to achieve. I've suggested that thinking about these features of trash might illuminate and be illuminated by Lugones's work, especially if we focus on people being treated like trash: in light of her concern about the narrowness of the concept of oppression, might it help to consider ways in which oppression, or aspects of it, involve being treated like trash? And given the vagueness of the concept of "being treated like trash," might Lugones's close attention to the experiences of oppressed persons—persons also in resistance to such violence—help give a bit more definition to the notion of being treated like trash?

Certainly the concepts of purity and impurity that Lugones deploys in her descriptions of the forms of mistreatment visited upon the oppressed suggest a possible link to trash. But as we shall see, a great deal else in her working vocabulary also points in that direction.

Erasure. "Erase" and "erasure" appear with some frequency in Lugones's descriptions of the experience of the oppressed. "All oppressive control is violent because it attempts to erase selves that we are that are dangerous to the maintenance of domination over us" (SAS 59). This use of *erase* suggests not an attempt to eradicate the oppressed but a way of trying to mute or obscure or disregard aspects of their lives that oppressors find unwelcome because threatening to the dominating position they do not wish to give up. Of course if there weren't anyone to dominate, that position would be lost. As the proverbial expression would have it, the oppressors don't want to throw out the baby with the bathwater: that is, they want to hold on to what is to their advantage while nonetheless getting rid of what undermines it. They don't want to throw out the baby—oppressed persons that are the embodied site of their domination—with the bathwater of the baby's "dangerous" recalcitrance.[12]

This sense of *erasure* occurs elsewhere as well. Commenting on the impersonality of cultural imperialism, Lugones points out that "there is no person-to-person mistreatment to make it clear that one is about to be erased from the discourse by being asked to speak in or listen to a universal voice" (LPF 70). In such a case, the cultural imperialist has appropriated another's voice, folded it into, for example, the "woman's voice," but in the same breath has disposed of that voice, though not of the person whose voice it is. To some cultural imperialists, such voices are "nonsensical" (PIS 140)—spouters of semantic and conceptual rubbish. The white/Angla feminist theorist cut in the cultural imperialist mode conceives of her theory-making in a way that requires both reference to women different from herself and erasure of the significance of such difference. Here again, there appears to be a worry about not wanting to throw the baby out with the bathwater. In this case the baby is the necessary acknowledgment of differences among women; the bathwater is what exploration of the significance of such differences would reveal.

The concept of erasure also appears in Lugones's explanation of the difference between the loving playfulness she takes to be central to "traveling" to another's world and what she describes as the "agonistic traveling" celebrated in the works of Johan Huizinga and Hans-Georg Gadamer. The playful attitude characteristic of the agonistic traveler, she argues, is not at all a loving one. It is that of someone primed for "conquest, domination, reduction of what they meet to their own sense of order, and erasure of the other 'world'" (WT 95). The agonistic conqueror does not exterminate those he comes in contact with but folds them into his expanding kingdom. However, he has no love, no tenderness for them, and in fact a vested interest in the "erasure of [their] resistant subjectivities" (ED 192). He is in search of subjects whose subjectivity he will disregard.

Still other forms of erasure are articulated in Lugones's discussion of playfulness and world-traveling: "I am interested here in those many cases in which white/Anglo women do one or more of the following to women of color: they ignore us, ostracize us, render us invisible, stereotype us, leave us completely alone, interpret us as crazy. All of this *while we are in their midst*" (WT 83).

Here again it is notable that the women of color referred to have not been tossed out bodily, have not literally disappeared, have not been killed. They exist, and in this case exist in the company of white/Anglo women. But they are not paid attention to; they are kept at the margins, rendered invisible or unintelligible, abandoned. (Lugones isn't saying that such attitudes or actions all appear simultaneously. Some cannot take place at the same time: for example, you can't both thoroughly ignore a person and interpret her as crazy, though interpreting her as crazy involves ignoring certain things about her, or her craziness might be offered as a reason for ignoring her.) The women of color remain present, but they've been rendered worthless or in any event unwelcome as participants in whatever is going on. They've been tossed out in thought if not in deed, banished from the circle of care and attention.

Purity. The various kinds of erasure that Lugones describes appear to reflect oppressors' doubts about the wisdom of actually "rubbing out" the oppressed, eradicating them: the baby is just too valuable to eliminate entirely. But at the same time, the oppressors seem to be anxious about contact with the cultural bathwater with which the very being of the baby is saturated: hence the widespread use by oppressors of the multiple devices by which humans explicitly or implicitly declare the worthlessness and disposability of the thoughts, speech, and cultural life-worlds of others. Such a picture is strongly suggested by Lugones's exploration of the oppressors' need to establish and maintain a purifying order.[13] The order in question is a hierarchical ranking among groups of people, and it is an order established not by the expunging or eradication of the subordinated (which is not to deny that human history is chockfull of attempts to establish such an order) but through structures that differentiate between the purity of the dominating and the impurity of the subordinated.

In her discussions of purity, impurity, and separation, Lugones implies that among the privileges oppressors award themselves is the capacity to know what is and is not trash, the authority to determine what can and cannot be, is and is not to be, disposed of. Only they can tell what's the baby and what's the bathwater; only they can be trusted to keep them separate. The power of the disposers, the trashmakers, lies not only in erasing, tossing out or banishing untoward aspects of the dominated, but also in consigning to the wastebasket aspects of themselves they hope to get rid of.

This capacity to know, and know how to act upon, the distinction between what is worth having or keeping and what is not belongs to the dominators in virtue of their having an uncompromised form of rationality—reason that can be exercised objectively and impartially precisely because those possessing it lie "outside history, outside culture" (PIS 130). On such a view, culture is an encumbrance, a sure carrier of impurity, including though not limited to an adulterated capacity to reason. Quoting Renato Rosaldo, Lugones alludes to the work the notion of "culture" is made to do in marking distinctions between the precious and the worthless, the valuable and the useless: "Full citizens lack culture, and those most culturally endowed lack full citizenship" (125; cf. Rosaldo 1989, 198). The distinction at work here is not between better and worse cultures, between pure and impure cultures, but between the "postcultural" (those who somehow have shed cultural identity altogether) and those still laboring under the restricting weight of cultural baggage—all that impure stuff of human life that centers on human senses, passions, embodied habits and rituals, the contaminating scum from which the postcultural pure reasoner has achieved cleansing.

But how did the "impartial reasoner" peel off the "symbolic and institutionalized inscriptions" that are sure markers of cultural membership (PIS 130)? By arrogating the authority to tell who can and who cannot get rid of one's culture and then declaring oneself "outside of culture" (HCS 46). I can toss aside my culture, disown it, but you can't: after all, "racialization and the having of a culture are what happens to others" (49).

TRASH TALKS BACK, REVISITED

So far, then, I've been reviewing Lugones's work with an eye out for ways in which the idea of being treated like trash does justice to and enhances her description of the mistreatment of the oppressed and of their resistance to it. In the kinds of cases Lugones brings to our attention, oppressors do not wish to get rid of the oppressed entirely, but they do want to mute or obscure or remove from attention features of the oppressed they deem threatening to their domination. They want to keep the baby but throw out the bathwater, and they assume that they can tell the difference. They presume to know what is useful and what is useless about the subordinated, what is valuable and what is worthless. They fancy themselves to be tidy householders, excellent judges of the difference between the pure and the impure, the wheat and the chaff, the keepable and the disposable.

But like run-of-the-mill trash creators, they fail to notice some significant characteristics of trash—in particular its capacity to reveal unflattering facts about its creators and yet also to harbor rich possibilities for its own continued existence and livelihood. Treating something or someone as trash, attempting to get it out of sight, out of mind, can tell us a lot about those who have tossed it out, and about the assumptions they are likely to make, indeed need to make, about those they have treated that way.

1. For example, those who treat others as trash may well make the mistake of assuming that if you treat human beings like trash you turn such people into things—entities of a sort that don't have lives, don't speak, don't fight back. But as we were reminded above, even nonhuman trash talks. Indeed curious gossip columnists, narcotics agents, and meticulous archaeologists can make it squeal. Just as people's histories do not stop with but live on in what they toss out, the fears and anxieties and self-deceptions of the oppressors show up in their apparently nonchalant but in fact studied efforts to hide their need to both depend on and erase the oppressed, the very ones they must render as lacking "agency, autonomy, self-regulating ability" (PIS 130). This becomes particularly clear in Lugones's discussion of the "lover of purity" posing both as someone in whom pristine reason is ever so neatly separated from the contamination of the "confused, worthless remainder—passion, sensuality" (129), and as someone "outside history, outside culture" (130). But however much the pure reasoner wants to slough off markers of impurity, his very treatment of those who he insists are imbued with such flotsam reveals his inability to rid himself of his own contamination. It exposes his failure to ensure "that his remainder become of no consequence to his own sense of himself" as exquisitely and uniquely qualified to control the messy world around him (130). "Thus his needs must be taken care of by others hidden in spaces relegated outside of public view, where he parades himself as pure" (130). His needs don't disappear just because he thinks of them as defiling dross. But he does what he can to hide from himself the fact of their lingering presence. He arranges for the hopelessly impure to keep his own impurity out of sight, out of mind. Similarly, his declaring himself "outside of culture is

self-deceiving" (HCS 46)—he may think, or wish, that he's gotten rid of that pesky pollutant, but it is still right there in the hallway or on the back porch. He just chooses not to notice it. Trash talks back, undermines efforts to make it go away.

2. Those who treat others as trash may be brought up short, even shocked, to be reminded that their judgment about what is to be valued and what is worthless about things and people, what constitutes the appropriate use of them and what does not, is not dispositive. No doubt they are aware of the old saw that one person's trash is another person's treasure, but they seem to have ignored that fact in this case. Indeed, they have tried to ensure that anyone who thought there might be treasure will be ignored, her voice silenced, her capacity to find treasure erased. In this connection, Lugones's exploration of curdling is particularly pertinent:

3. In one of the most vivid and enduring of the many rich images Lugones develops to explain a phenomenon she wants to bring to our attention, she describes what happens when mayonnaise curdles. Mayonnaise, she points out, is an oil-in-water emulsion. In the process of making it, an impatient stirrer may cause it to curdle: instead of being smoothly blended together, "the ingredients [yolk, water and oil] become separated from each other." More accurately, they tend to "coalesce toward oil or toward water," albeit in different degrees. One ends up with variable portions of "yolky oil and oily yolk" (PIS 122).

Lugones brings attention to the difference between the blending effort of making mayonnaise and the detaching effort of separating yolk from white. In the latter case, one's efforts also can go awry, but on account of producing an unwanted blending (of yolk and white) rather than on account of not effecting a desired one (of yolk, oil, and water).

Lugones wants to focus on a form of separation that is tied not to purity but to impurity. The "splitting" separation of yolk from white is part of an "exercise in purity," whereas the "curdling" separation of yolky oil and oily yolk constitutes an "exercise in impurity" (123). Such impurity provides for Lugones a "connection between impurity and resistance" (122) and, in this connection, an image for *mestizaje* "as a central name for impure resistance to interlocked, intermeshed oppressions" (122).

It's crucial for Lugones that embracing the impurity of curdling separation is not the same as affirming the impurity of splitting separation: the latter is "in allegiance to" whereas the former is "in defiance of" the "domination intention" of the exercise of separation (122). The position of the "impure" vis-à-vis their dominators is to be understood not as an eagerness to share the dominators' understanding of and rejection of impurity and thereby to provide evidence of the dominated's own claims to purity, but to emphasize their own impurity understood in terms not set by dominators: "*Mestizaje* defies control through simultaneously asserting the impure, curdled multiple state and rejecting fragmentation into pure parts [that is, purely pure and purely impure]. In this play of assertion and rejection, the mestiza is unclassifiable, unmanageable. She has no pure parts to be 'had,' controlled" (123).

Lugones might be seen as in effect arguing that the not-quite-thoroughly impure condition of "the oppressed"—not so impure as to be totally banished or eliminated, but impure enough to be considered as trash and thus appropriately kept out of the orbit of concern—is in fact a condition in which great treasure is to be found, treasure unimaginable to those confident of their right to declare what is trash and what is treasure. It is in such impurity—albeit understood in a sense beyond the ken of the dominators—that the strength of the multiply oppressed as resisters, as lively subjects, can be found.

Lugones's emphasis on embracing the impurity of curdling is a kind of finding treasure in what others have regarded as trash. The embrace of curdledness is part and parcel of the resisters' mocking the pathetic need of the dominators to establish their purity: of course the dominators aren't pure and it bothers them, so they rely on the "impurity" of those they dominate to try to sustain the illusion. Not only do the dominated see through what the dominators are doing—indeed see the trash in the dominators' alleged treasure of purity—but they see treasure in the trash the dominators allege them to be.

ON THE LOGIC OF RESISTANCE AND THE LOGIC OF TRASH

What have we learned from exploring "being treated like trash" (and close variations thereof) as a means of talking about oppression that avoids strengthening forces of oppression and fortifies resistance to it? And does such an exercise at the same time help trim away any unhelpful vagueness in that widely used phrase?

Thinking about how something or someone comes to be called or treated like trash is quite instructive. The deeming of something or someone as trash tells us nothing about the inherent value of that thing or that person. It does, however, tell us something about what the trash-proclaimer reckons to be worth or not worth having or keeping in her orbit. Though it is true that one might only reluctantly part with an object, might unhappily feel obliged to toss it in the trash, it doesn't seem likely that one will treat a person like trash and have a sense of loss or be pained in doing so. In any event, though the very existence of trash doesn't tell a single or simple story about how something came to be so regarded, it does point to the fact of there being some kind of story about the beliefs and values and judgments of the one who anointed the thing or the person as trash.

Resistance to oppression of the sort Lugones appears to have in mind involves both weakening the oppressors and strengthening the resisters. Focusing on people being treated like trash can work on both fronts: it both aids attempts to reveal features trashmakers may wish to deny about themselves, and supports efforts to highlight features the "trashed" may wish to animate and reveal about themselves. Following Lugones's lead, and suggesting a few additions to her conceptual repertoire, we come to see oppressors/trashmakers as both confident about their ability to distinguish the pure from the impure, the passion-free postcultural from the swinishly enculturated, and at the same time so anxious about just where they themselves belong that they desperately need those they deem contaminated to sustain the illusion of their own purity. Considering the common idea that one person's trash is another person's treasure, we are invited to observe ways in which the oppressed/"trashed" harbor in themselves the treasure the oppressors/trashmakers cannot or will not see. The dominated are indeed impure, Lugones argues, but not in the sense of "impure" so beloved and belabored by the oppressors/trashmakers. The "trashed" not only can come to see the treasure ready at hand in their worlds—they also can smell the stench wafting through the oppressors' proud proclamations of purity.

Two large questions lie behind this chapter: one, just reviewed, is what might be learned by describing the mistreatment of the multiply oppressed and their resistance to it in terms of their being treated like trash, keeping in mind Lugones's desideratum that any such account serve the logic of resistance and not the logic of oppression. The second, to which we now return, is whether along the way we have made any ground in becoming clearer about the meaning of "being treated like trash." Of course it is not necessarily the case that carving out a definition is desirable, that we'd be better off uncovering or stipulating conditions for the proper use of the expression. Perhaps its attractiveness and ready availability depend on the looseness of criteria for its employment, its evident lack of inclusion in the lexicons of political and moral philosophy. Given the apparent rhetorical value of the phrase "being treated like trash" and close relatives such as being treated as if one were "waste" or being "disposable," its political potency might well be reduced by attempts to limit its range. In this connection it is pertinent to point out that in parsing Lugones's account of the particular kinds of abuse to which she brings our attention it seemed necessary to highlight that if such abuse is indeed a way of treating people like trash, then we must think of such treatment as not being the same as exterminating people. And yet there is no rule, implicit or explicit, excluding the use of the phrase in the context of such extermination. Still, the occasion Lugones's work provides to think about what it means to be treated like trash does invite us to consider the difference between efforts to throw out the bathwater but not the baby, and those aimed at getting rid of the baby altogether. It also alerts us to the insidious preparatory work that throwing out the bathwater nevertheless can do for projects of ultimately throwing out the baby.[14]

NOTES

1. IP 13.

2. I understand Lugones to be using "the logic of oppression" and "the logic of resistance" to refer to what more broadly might be called "the logic of the situation." What she seems to have in mind are fairly predictable sets of beliefs and actions that characterize conditions of oppression and those that characterize conditions of resistance. For example, oppressors are not prevented by what we think of as "logical thinking" from imagining those they oppress as being "lively subjects," but "the logic of the situation" in which they are oppressors militates against their entertaining that possibility.

3. I have found it useful and I hope not at odds with the kind of work she wants her notion of "world" to do to think of such worlds as something like theaters in which a certain range of performances are made possible for characters constructed in particular ways. Their vocabularies, activities, attitudes, relations, efforts, and achievements are intelligible to those who are familiar with the theater and the performers, but not to those who are not and who either don't know or don't care about learning how to understand what is going on. It is to be fully expected that actors are constructed in quite different ways and with quite different consequences in different theaters. One important limitation to this reading is that Lugones explicitly says that moving from one world to another "is not a matter of acting. One does not pose as someone else; one does not pretend to be, for example, someone of a different personality or character or someone who uses space or language differently from the other person" (WT 89–90). But the fact that she goes out of her way to distinguish world-travel from moving from one performance into another does suggest that reference to some degree of similarity may be helpful, especially in light of her use of the

notion of inhabitants of worlds being "constructed" in particular ways and "animating" such constructions, sometimes knowingly, sometimes not (WT 88–89).

4. See also Allison (1993), and Wray and Newitz (1997). When used derogatorily, "white trash" alludes to those considered marginal members of and a disgrace to the "white race."

5. It is worth noting that *trash, waste, garbage, junk, rubbish,* and their close semantic siblings are not as interchangeable as they may in some contexts seem to be. Though distinctions among the terms are not hard and fast, different ones are employed to mark what are considered important differences. Instructions from sanitation departments provide familiar examples: though regulations vary over time and place, householders and business owners may be expected to know and to honor the distinctions among various kinds of matter left out for removal by the appointed parties. A charming example from the city of St. Paul in 1912 insists that while a license is required to "remove, transport or carry dust, ashes, manure, grease, offal, rubbish or waste matter," such restrictions do not apply to "the removal of garbage or night soil" ("St. Paul, Minn.: Refuse and Waste Matter. Disposal Of" 1912, 200). It is not uncommon to distinguish between the "junk" in the attic and the "trash" in the can in the kitchen, or for that matter to wonder whether the junk ought to go in the trash. Again, on the whole, there don't seem to be rigid rules about which term is to be used for which kind of substance, but it is clear that we often do want some way to mark distinctions we think are of some significance.

6. Much of the broad framework I employ here for the discussion of trash is developed at length in my book *Trash Talks: Revelations in the Rubbish* (Spelman 2016).

7. See for example Pellow (2002).

8. Robert Mayer, "Dylan's Boswell," *St. Petersburg Times*, April 26, 1971, news.google.com/newspapers?nid=888&dat=19710426&id=CD9SAAAAIBAJ&sjid=tnUDAAAAIBAJ&pg=6848,5781519.

9. This particular conclusion of Rathje's is overdrawn but not without great interest.

10. For a rich account of the remarkable culinary treasures to be found in dumpsters, see Stuart (2009), especially chapter 1.

11. On use of garbage and trash by artists, see for example Scanlan (2005), especially chapter 3.

12. Readers unfamiliar with the phrase "throwing out the baby with the bathwater" may find it not apt here, but in its widespread, ordinary use there is no suggestion that what is referred to as "the baby" is being conceptually or politically infantilized.

13. Citing Mary Douglas's views about the function of the containment of "dirt" and related pollutants in efforts to create and sustain order, Lugones remarks on what she sees as Douglas's lack of attention to the difference between "oppressive and non-oppressive structuring" (PIS 132; cf. Douglas 1989).

14. Many thanks to Monique Roelofs for helpful discussions as I was developing the analysis in this chapter.

REFERENCES

Allison, Dorothy. 2002. *Trash*. New York: Plume.
———. 1993. *Bastard Out of Carolina*. New York: Plume.
Bales, Kevin. 2004. *Disposable People: New Slavery in the Global Economy*. Berkeley: University of California Press.
Bauman, Zygmunt. 2004. *Wasted Lives: Modernity and its Outcasts*. Malden, MA: Polity.
California v. Greenwood. 486 U.S. 35.
Chang, Grace. 2000. *Disposable Domestics: Immigrant Women Workers in the Global Economy*. Cambridge, MA: South End Press.
Douglas, Mary. 1989. *Purity and Danger*. London: Ark Paperbacks.
Jin, Ha. *War Trash: A Novel*. New York: Vintage.
Pellow, David Naguib. 2002. *Garbage Wars: The Struggle for Environmental Justice in Chicago*. Cambridge, MA: MIT Press.
Rathje, William, and Cullen Murphy. 2001. *Rubbish! The Archaeology of Garbage*, 2nd edition. Tucson: University of Arizona Press.
Rosaldo, Renato. 1989. *Culture and Truth*. Boston: Beacon.
Scanlan, John. 2005. *On Garbage*. London: Reaktion Books.
Spelman, Elizabeth V. 2016. *Trash Talks: Revelations in the Rubbish*. New York: Oxford University Press.
"St. Paul, Minn.: Refuse and Waste Matter, Disposal Of." *Public Health Reports* (1896–1970), Vol. 27, No. 6, February 9, 1912, 200.
Stuart, Tristram. 2009. *Waste: Uncovering the Global Food Scandal*. New York: Norton.
Wray, Matt, and Annalee Newitz, eds. 1997. *White Trash: Race and Class in America*. New York: Routledge.

2 A Focus on the "I" in the "I → We"

Considering the Lived Experience of Self-in-Coalition in Active Subjectivity

Kelli Zaytoun

> How much and what sort of "agency" do we need to move with others without falling into a politics of the same, a politics that values or assumes sameness or homogeneity; without mythologizing place; attempting to stand in the cracks and intersections of multiple histories of domination and resistances to dominations?
> —María Lugones, Introduction to *Pilgrimages*/Peregrinajes: *Theorizing Coalition against Multiple Oppressions*

The question above is one Lugones considers in her attempt to "put into words" and "participate in" the sense of agency that works against oppression in its various forms (IP 7). This sense of agency or "active subjectivity" defined by Lugones rejects a modern understanding of self as unitary and of intentionality "as residing in and emanating from the individual or from monolithic collectives" (TSC 210). Instead, intentionalities of the resistant-oppressed are enacted "between rather than in subjects," as well as "between worlds of sense," in "a long-winded intersubjective project" (208–9). My main goal in this chapter is to highlight the significance of and links between Lugones's longstanding theory of active subjectivity and her later work on complex communication in relationship to feminist phenomenological conceptions of selfhood.[1] This discussion illuminates the role of what I call a lived sense of "self-in-coalition" in work across differences.

Informed by Lugones's as well as Gloria Anzaldúa's theories, I define the self-in-coalition as a concrete person's sense of themselves and others as multiply and continuously constructed by social relations, an awareness that prompts a deep listening to the specificities of the testimonies and strategies of others as they participate with them in mutually formed resistance efforts. I will argue that the self-in-coalition is necessarily pluralistic and decolonial, formed by complex communication in coalitional limens as defined by Lugones (OC). I draw from Anzaldúa's theory of self, particularly the aspect of *naguala*, or 'shapeshifting,' to describe the intricate, concrete intersubjective processes in which persons participate as they develop the complex interrelatedness required for coalition (2002, 549). Lugones and Anzaldúa have been at the heart of a body of literature that calls for coalition that does not require its members to share identities or commonalities, but the extent to which active subjectivity, complex communication, and naguala deepen this conversation is profound and under-recognized.[2] Both theorists' nuanced approach to self and conditions for resistance are unparalleled. I contend that active subjectivity and naguala involve capacities enacted by concrete persons, such as empathy and the "cross-referencing" of realities, which are necessary for coalition (IP 14–15). I call the lived sense and enactment of those capacities the self-in-coalition.

My description of the self-in-coalition is prominently informed by Lugones's understanding of selves as pluralistic; however, I argue for attention to "*self*-in-coalition" in order to bring into relief how the concrete, in-the-flesh experiences of selfhood, negotiated in relation to other resisters, structures, and limens, contribute to the effectiveness of the collective.[3] I seek to emphasize (but not privilege) the lived sense of selfhood that identifies a "me" and a sense of remembering across many "selves" and its role in complex communication. To highlight the self-in-coalition is not to argue for its core, or its "trueness" or transcendence, nor is it to deny its social constructedness or diminish the "abstract" self of which Lugones speaks.[4] I contend that my focus on selfhood highlights and develops an aspect of active subjectivity that is already present in Lugones's theorizing, parallel to her "multiplicitous person reasoning practically within and across worlds" (SAS 62) and a "sense of self as an active subject" (OC 78). Another way of explaining my project, more simply, is that I want to explore more deeply, without separating out or assuming unitary, the "I" present in Lugones's concept of "I→we," the "attenuated" active subjectivity that exercises resistant intentionality and agency (IP 6). This is a tricky move, given Lugones's call to "keep a multiple reading of the resistant self in relation" (TDF 748). With this in mind, I introduce a critical conversation on selfhood as an aspect of active subjectivity and complex communication, and propose that a theory of self-in-coalition is important to that discussion, as well as the concrete coalitional practices that ensue.

BEYOND THE "MONOSENSICAL" SELF[5]

> When I do not see plurality in the very structure of a theory, I see the phantom that I am in your eyes take grotesque form and mime crudely and heavily your own image. Don't you?
> —Lugones, "On the Logic of Pluralist Feminism"

Because Lugones's theory of selves as pluralistic is central to my argument for a self-in-coalition, I begin by tracing her thinking on the "self," a concept that pervades her work but has received little critical attention.[6] Throughout her vast body of writing, Lugones maintains that self and reality are manifold; therefore, the plural "selves" and "realities" work best in engaging what Jennifer McWeeny has called Lugones's "pluralistic metaphysics" (2010, 297). McWeeny explains the ontological problem apparent in Lugones's take on "the self that is at the same time both one and many," a problem that, as McWeeny mentions, Lugones not only recognizes but intends (298). According to her analysis, "On the one hand, although Lugones denies the existence of any underlying 'I,' she affirms that a person is somehow able to identify each different self as 'me'" (297). Although McWeeny, like many others, embraces Lugones's "fresh ontological apparatus" (297), Mariana Ortega identifies the need for "a more complete explanation of selfhood" in Lugones's work, one that develops the sense of "me," or "togetherness," that identifies and remembers difference across selves and worlds (2001, 16, 17). Ortega finds Heidegger's "mineness" useful in giving an account of continuity among embodied, multiplicitous selves, what she calls "an active self in the making ... situated in a social and historical milieu," or, with respect to Lugones's work, a "world-traveler self," offering a phenomenological explanation for "what makes a self a self" in Lugones's theorizing (19, 16).

I attempt to take up Ortega's suggestion that we continue to explore in more detail "the ontological element [that] makes it possible for me to be aware of my being," as well as its place in Lugones's theorizing. I contend that this sense of awareness or continuity of selfhood is crucial coalitional work (2001, 18). Moreover, I agree with Ortega that identifying a "sense of togetherness," one that retains multiplicity, ambiguity, and is always in-the-making, can help to answer questions about concrete responsibilities and actions of persons. Attending to selfhood also can help us to explore concrete interactions within coalitional groups in ways that might tell participants something about the functions, failures, and effectiveness of their collective struggle. I will show that the evidence for this type of selfhood described above already exists in Lugones's work; I seek to underscore it. Ortega's article was published in 2001 and focused on Lugones's world-traveling; Lugones's more recent emphasis on complex communication in liminal space and the logic of fusion contribute to my understanding of selfhood present in her theorizing. Although attending to the sense of "me" mentioned earlier is the focus of this essay, I first emphasize the significance of plural selves and "worlds of sense" in Lugones's work and in my own.

Lugones's insistence that self is multiple is, among many things, an attempt to decolonize the modern/colonial *self*. Scholars who have kept up with Lugones's work since *Pilgrimages*/Peregrinajes are familiar with her investment in exposing the vast and pervasive implications of what she calls "the colonial/modern gender system" (HGS). Although this ongoing project is most known for uncovering how gender and sexuality were/are constituted, racialized, and systematically imposed by colonial modernity, Lugones also provides, with this analysis, a framework for exploring how a colonial/modern subjectivity and selfhood were imposed. For Lugones, a resistant, active subjectivity is conceived beyond structure, in the limen, involving "a sense of agency different from the modern sense, both in its not being univocal and unitary, and in its not being recognized institutionally or hegemonically" (DF 72).[7] Active subjectivity is therefore at least twofold: it is necessarily multiple, and it operates beyond modern logic, in liminality.

Lugones's "On Complex Communication" (OC) builds on her theorizing of subjectivity and liminal space, introduced in "Structure/Anti-structure and Agency under Oppression" (SAS). Before moving on to complex communication, I highlight another discussion in "Structure/Anti-structure" important to my argument on selfhood: one on pluralism and memory. Lugones's rejection of the unified self is informed by multicultural people who "are very familiar with experiencing themselves as more than one: ... acting, enacting, animating their bodies, having thoughts, feeling the emotions, in ways that are different in one reality than in the other" (57). These different realities offer different opportunities (and lack of opportunities) for action, because actions, or more specifically "practical syllogisms," have different meanings in different realities.[8] A person might or might not have memories of themselves in particular realities. To make this point, Lugones offers the example of people in positions of power over others not recognizing themselves "in the reality of the dominated," such as when people "act in front of their maids as if there were no one in the room" (58). They do not see themselves as the person the maid sees, nor would they want to. In this example, we can see how the worlds of the dominated are invisible to the dominators and how, for dominating and dominated alike, "self-deception and mystification" affect the memories of all our "selves" (59).

Using Lugones's logic, we can understand realities and selves as pluralistic. We can also see that having the opportunity for one's actions to be seen and understood depends on the reality or "worlds" in which that person is operating. Conversely, one only sees oneself in a world if they understand that world; therefore, "the task of remembering one's many selves is a difficult liberatory task," but an important one nonetheless (SAS 59). If, according to Lugones, cross-referencing various realities and identifying and remembering differences among selves and between those selves and others are important for emancipatory work, attention to those tasks is needed.

I am interested in this task of remembering. The concept of self-in-coalition that I put forth serves this purpose; the task of remembering is an embodied yet socially constructed, epistemic one, not a Lockean one.[9] The location of remembering is liminal space. But as Lugones says, memory is not enough; also necessary are "collective struggle" and "transformation of structures" that are "born of dialogue among multiplicitous persons" (SAS 62). In-the-flesh multiplicitous persons develop recognition and memory of their different selves moving within and between various realities. A certain lived sense of continuity is required for such movement. Multiplicitous persons, as selves-in-coalition, also articulate testimony, listen and respond to the testimonies of others, and struggle for change within a continuously shifting context of relationship to other persons and collectives. Attention to selfhood—how a person experiences being a self-in-coalition—renders important one's narratives and experiences of identities and relationships, which are always and necessarily incomplete. Attention to concrete persons does not diminish Lugones's important rejection of the unified self; instead it helps to offer examples of practical syllogisms and a deep look at the concrete, complex realities, psychologies, and articulations of multiple selfhood in the spaces where multiplicity is understood, respected, and engaged.

SELF IN CONCRETE COALITIONAL CONTEXT

One specific, praxical way in which attention to lived sense of selfhood is useful in coalition can be seen in Cricket Keating's model of coalitional consciousness-building (2005). Inspired by Lugones, among others, Keating takes participants through three steps: (1) locating experience, (2) seeing resistance to multiple oppressions, and (3) coalitional risk taking. In stage one, participants explore how experiences are marked by socially constructed contexts in forms that "illuminat[e] different ways that each participant is raced/classed/

gendered" (95). Stage two invokes Lugones's "faithful witnessing," where participants explore "multiple relations of power" and "resistances" at play. Last, participants engage in coalitional risk taking, where they look at possibilities, barriers, and actions, including "power relations among the group" (Keating 97–98). Posing questions to be discussed in each stage, Keating offers a concrete alternative to the consciousness-raising of second-wave feminism that was criticized for assuming unanimity among women. Her alternative involves the operating of two mutually constructed levels of consciousness—one at the level of the inner life of the multiplicitous person, and the other at the collective, coalitional level. The model Keating offers is one that fits Lugones's call for "collective practice" that is "born of dialogue among multiplicitous persons who are faithful witnesses of themselves and also testify to, and uncover the multiplicity of, their oppressors and the techniques of oppression afforded by ignoring that multiplicity" (SAS 62). The self-in-coalition offers a testimony to how one's identities, socially constructed at particular moments in times and places, are conceived and experienced. But testifying works two ways: a providing of an account of one's own experience, and a witnessing that requires a reading of how others are marked as different and have also practiced resistance. Further, in Keating's model, resistances can be explored for how they support or undermine the larger coalition, and persons can help take responsibility for and be held accountable to the resistant collective.

The types of conversations that Keating's model demands are necessarily difficult and require a complicated decolonial understanding of identity and selfhood, as well as a movement beyond structure. In the next two sections, I explore in more depth how Lugones's theorizing about coalitional context—liminality—provides a foundation for such conversations—foundations, in part, mediated by the self-in-coalition.

SELF IN COALITIONAL CONTEXT: MEETING AT THE LIMENS

Because of the tendency in the United States toward treating identity as fixed and singular, "liberal conversations" and organizing against oppression are problematic (OC 84). According to Lugones, such "categorial seeing" is a socially constructed tool of oppression; however, such categories are still "real" and experienced in concrete ways (RM 75). Categorial seeing becomes most problematic in the denial of multiplicity, for it dismisses people at the intersections of oppressions (75). Recognizing the intersections, we begin to meet others in liminal space, where "one becomes most fully aware of one's multiplicity" (SAS 59). Beyond structure, liminal spaces are where relational selves are created by acknowledging others' "opacity" and by the refusal of the assumption of transparency or sameness (OC 75). Resistances are forged in such spaces as communicative achievements. Lugones identifies "complex communication" as a "dialogical, collective creation" among differently oppressed, multiplicitous persons (82). Such coalition "requires recognition of the intersectionality of oppressions as real and important for struggle and it requires a movement outward toward other affiliative groups recognized as resistant" (76). What Lugones offers in her theory of complex communication cannot be overlooked in coalition theory and practice; effective resistance to oppression cannot take place without concrete, liminal spaces, spaces that occur geographically, epistemologically, and communicatively, spaces in which concrete selves-in-coalition collectively participate.

SELF-IN-COALITION AS FUSION

More recently, Lugones's discussions of self are within her projects of building decolonial feminisms and radical multiculturalisms that emphasize a "move from the logic of intersectionality to the logic of fusion, intermeshing, coalescence" (RM 73). I read this discussion as, in part, a development of her theory of curdling/impurity put forth in "Purity, Impurity, and Separation" (PIS). In her early work, Lugones found the term *intermeshed*, though not perfect, a better metaphor than interlocking or intersecting for indicating the *inseparability* of oppressions (TSC 231). Later, she turns to *fusion* and explains that although intersectionality importantly exposes the lived realities of oppressive social order, the concept is insufficient because it suggests identities intersect as separate categories to begin with. In considering the concrete actions of the self-in-coalition, I want to take up Lugones's suggestion that we move to a logic of fusion.

The logic of oppression, including that revealed by Lugones's theory of intersectionality, has had profound implications for coalition; it created for white women a blindness to understanding their own privileged positions and a binary construction of womanhood with a "light and a dark side," leading them to enact a false or "ornamental" multiculturalism and sisterhood (HGS 187; RM 69). The logic of fusion first "unmasks" white feminism's collusion with the colonial/modern gender system; the logic of intersectionality, which exposes the relationship between white women's privilege and women of color's oppression, is important to this unmasking (RM 73). The second unmasking in the logic of fusion exposes the logic of intersectionality as a conceptual trap. In other words, the logic of fusion "corrupts" the logic of categories on which the theory of intersectionality depends, a logic that does not take us far enough in the move toward coalition (73). As Lugones states, "seeing the violence while trapped in its logic does not awaken one to resistance to it" (75). Intersectionality exposes "combined fragments" of categories; Lugones urges us to resist seeing ourselves as fragments (76). Instead, she encourages "a superimposing of the recognition that oppressions intermesh"; they not only interlock, they are inextricable (76). The logic of fusion demonstrates what intersectionality hides: oppressions do not interlock as separate categories; they all relate to and depend on each other. Therefore, we are more likely to seek out coalition across differences when we understand our situations from the logic of fusion.

According to Lugones, intersectionality should not be seen as an identity or a move toward coalition. A different logic is required, one that discloses how all oppressions are fused and interdependent, and how a variety of resistant strategies can be explored for how they support or diminish one another. Lugones is arguing, therefore, that active subjectivity is a fusion, and although we may live in both the realities of categories and the realities of fusions, the fusion is where resistance is possible. The logic of intersections/categories does not allow for the same liberatory, coalitional possibilities as fusions. Adding Lugones's logic of fusion to her discussion of complex communication helps us to see clearly that subjects and selfhoods and selves in coalition are always relational and incomplete. Such an understanding of self is necessary in coalition.

Throughout Lugones's work we see the language of *self*, but her use of the term is always cautious. Not to use caution in the discourse on self would risk denying the depth and severity of violence inflicted on colonized peoples, violence that decimated human possibilities for living/being at every possible level (physical, material, social, psychic, cosmic). According to Lugones, when the coloniality of the Americas began in the sixteenth century, it

> encountered complex cultural, political, economic, religious beings: selves in complex relations to the cosmos, to other selves, to generation, to the earth, to living beings, to the inorganic, to production; selves whose erotic, aesthetic, and linguistic expressivity, whose knowledges, sense of space, longings, practices, institutions, and forms of government were not to be simply replaced but met, understood, and engaged in crossings and dialogues and negotiations. (DF 77)

They were not thus engaged. Lugones honors the possibility of constructions of selfhood beyond colonial epistemologies and ontologies by insisting on its multiplicity. This is a stance I take seriously. I proceed with my attention to self-in-coalition with the caveat that the sense of self I put forward, like active subjectivity, cannot be understood within a modern construction of self as fixed, autonomous, and independent.

Working from Lugones's self as plural and the logic of fusion, I now seek to bring into relief some functions of the lived experience of selfhood in movements toward coalition. Lugones states that "[s]ince the fusion is a resistance to multiple oppressions, one can also appreciate the ways in which others have conceived, given cultural form to, theorized, expressed, embodied their resistance to multiple oppressions. One can also come to understand how and to what extent these resistances support or undermine each other" (RM 77). The appreciation and understanding of which Lugones speaks here seems to me to be, on a concrete level, the embodied, epistemological, and communicative work of persons. The type of "knowing" and communicating required for the work involves memory or the capacity to *recognize difference*, the capacity to *recognize a (shifting) self* across selves and worlds, and the capacity to *recognize resistance* as well. The recognizing occurs at bodily, epistemic levels, in social context, and may have many forms. Communication also takes many forms, oral and written narration, and nonverbal expression, for example. In liminal space, the type of "knowing" I describe above is most acute, and complex communication and fusion is most possible. At this point I will invoke Gloria Anzaldúa's concept of "knower" to provide theoretical grounding for my claims about selfhood, and to add to our understanding of Lugones's active subjectivity and the logic of fusion.

THE KNOWING SELF-IN-COALITION

Throughout her body of work, from the first *Bridge* to the last, Anzaldúa's discussion of selfhood is not cautious like Lugones's; in fact, she refers to herself as having "preoccupations with the inner life of the Self…" in the preface of the first edition of *Borderlands/La Frontera: The New Mestiza*.[10] This investment in the experience of self is evident in a statement she made in an interview with Christine Weiland: "You make the inner changes first, and then you make the outer changes. I've always believed that. Sometimes you can do both at the same time: work to create outer change, through political movement, at the same time you're… developing yourself" (Keating 2000, 101). That interview was in 1983, and over the next twenty years Anzaldúa's thinking about "do[ing] both at the same time" evolved into her theory of *conocimiento*. Similar to Lugones, Anzaldúa also understood the self to be multiplicitous. In fact, Lugones draws on Anzaldúa's theories of subjectivity, especially those developed in *Borderlands/La Frontera:*

The New Mestiza (for example, new *mestiza*, *mestiza* consciousness, *mestizaje*, *atravezados*), in her own work. Lugones points out that "the new mestiza is a scavenger of collective memories, memories that she [Anzaldúa] does not see as completely discontinuous with her own... It is the coalitional gesture; it begins to provide an understanding of complex communication" (OC 80). Anzaldúa's thick description of her own journey to the borderlands serves, for Lugones, as a specific example of how complex communication takes place. Lugones's theories offer an intricate exploration of the location and conditions for such communication in ways that deepen not only Anzaldúa's explanation of borderland subjectivity, but also her theory of *conocimiento*. First, I propose that Anzaldúa's later work, especially, offers not only a specific narrative of an *atravezado*, but also a theory of selfhood that adds to Lugones's theory of active subjectivity. This time, Anzaldúa writes in second person, which suggests that she wants her project to be understood as more than one narrative; I read it as an invitation into a complex multiple selfhood that includes the reader and the resistant oppressed in general.

Like Lugones's work, Anzaldúa's is a decolonial project. Norma Alarcón states that Anzaldúa's "telos was a quest for personal and political decolonization, a project that begins with processes entailed in a self-reconstruction of a damaged self due to trauma suffered" (2013, 189). For Anzaldúa, the process of *conocimiento*, of transformation and decolonization on personal and collective levels, starts with inner work. For this reason she offers a rich and complex description of a sense of selfhood, much of which I will not mention in this chapter.[11] However, I attempt to provide some overview of the work as it relates to self-in-coalition. Anzaldúa's concepts of *nepantla*, knower, and *naguala* relate most specifically to my goals.

In Anzaldúa's "now let us shift... the path of conocimiento... inner work, public acts," the last of her most substantial published essays, she describes a complex journey of physical, emotional, spiritual selfhood in relationship to the difficult work of collective struggle to end oppression. According to Anzaldúa, that journey, *conocimiento*, or "reflective consciousness," begins with *el arrebato*, or a disruption or "pull[ing] [of the] linchpin that held your reality/story together" (2002, 542, 546). From "el arrebato... rupture, fragmentation... an ending, a beginning," Anzaldúa describes six more stages of consciousness, a process through which self and collective knowing are achieved but not in static or definitive ways (note that stage one is labeled "an ending, a beginning"). In stage two, *nepantla*, one is aware that they can't live "according to the old terms" (549). To Anzaldúa, *nepantla* is "the site of transformation" or "zone between changes" (548). I see a lot of similarity between *nepantla* and the liminal space described by Lugones, but Anzaldúa focuses on the experience of a self in the in-between. Because of Anzaldúa's attention to selfhood, what she says about self in *nepantla* might be read as self-work in the limens.

Martina Koegeler-Abdi offers a fresh analysis of Anzaldúa's move from mestiza to *nepantlera* subjectivity in "now let us shift," and suggests that "while a mestiza locates herself in the synthesis of many sites at once, a *nepantlera* affiliates herself with no side at all," or experiences "non-affiliation with any conventional identity category," which "is never a stable state of being" (2013, 72–73). Koegeler-Abdi offers a detailed shift in Anzaldúa's thinking about nepantleran subjectivity as a neutral position, one that, I propose, can be read with Lugones's request that we move from the logic of intersectionality to the logic of fusion. I argue that *nepantleras* move into the "superimposed site," the fusion, where resistance takes place, according to Lugones, because they see themselves as always relational, not categorial or static (RM 76). Although I agree with Koegeler-Abdi's analysis, I want to add to it the overlooked yet important role that Anzaldúa's "knower" and la naguala, an aspect or "function" of the knower, play in becoming *nepantlera*.[12]

For Anzaldúa, la naguala, or shapeshifting, represents the function of selfhood that makes the move toward new ways of knowing that precipitate coalition work.[13] The shift is embodied and epistemological. Although la naguala might be interpreted as a metaphor, I argue that it is more than a metaphor because Anzaldúa, following her Nagualismo-informed beliefs, held that individual and collective transformation begins *with the imagination*, which she saw as material, a vehicle for extending intention into the physical world. For this reason, I believe Anzaldúa unapologetically stayed preoccupied with the experience of selfhood; she saw its transformative possibility on large-scale levels. I propose adding to Lugones's theories of self a consideration of Anzaldúa's later thinking on nepantleran subjectivity, aided by la naguala.

Anzaldúa's most substantial description of naguala and the epistemic shift in selfhood is in stage seven of *conocimiento*, "shifting realities." In discussing "transformation," which I argue is parallel to the sense of self in the process of enacting active subjectivity, Anzaldúa states:

> When a change occurs your consciousness (awareness of your sense of self and your response to self, others, and surroundings) becomes cognizant that it has a point of view and the ability to act from choice. This knowing/knower is always with you but it is displaced by the ego and its perspective. This knower has several functions. You call the function that arouses the awareness that beneath individual separateness lies a deeper interrelatedness, "la naguala." (568–69)

The sense of *knower* of which Anzaldúa speaks suggests a certain continuity of selfhood that I argue does not presuppose a unitary self, especially understood within the context of the entire essay and Anzaldúa's larger body of work. The "knower," an embodied capacity, not a transcendent one, senses the self as having multiple parts and functions. Anzaldúa says in an interview with Inés Hernández-Ávila, "When you watch yourself… you find that behind your acts and your temporary sense of self (identities) is a state of awareness that, if you allow it, keeps you from getting completely caught up in that particular identity or emotional state" (Keating 2000, 177). According to Anzaldúa, the knower can observe identities in which the self takes part; this capacity "gives you the flexibility to swing from your intense feelings to those of the other without being hijacked by either" (2002, 569). She goes on to say that "when [you are] confronted with the other's fear, you note her emotional arousal, allow her feelings/words to enter your body… you detach so those feelings won't inhabit your body for long. You… attend to the other as a whole being, not an object, even when she opposes you" (569). This passage reflects a phenomenological relationality in Anzaldúa's description of selfhood. The "ego," or sense of self-importance/singularity, gets in the way of the self's ability to function in a more multiple way.[14] This complex experience of self has a capacity for what Anzaldúa calls "neutral perception," or not being consumed by the logic of narrow identity or by the falsehood of complete, individual autonomy; the capacity is enacted relationally (569). I propose that we consider this capacity as part of resistant intentionality within the fusion, within the active subjectivity defined by Lugones.

I now return to the last part of the blocked quote above, to Anzaldúa's attention to naguala, the function of knowing that is vital to the self's move to coalition. In stage seven, Anzaldúa says the following:

> When you shift attention from your customary point of view (the ego) to that of la naguala, and from there move your awareness to an inner held representation of an experience, person, thing, or world, la naguala and the object merge. When you include the complexity of feeling two or more ways about a person/issue, when you … try to see her circumstances from her position, you accommodate the other's perspective, achieving un conocimiento that allows you to shift toward a less defensive, more inclusive identity. When you relate to others, not as parts, problems, or useful commodities, but from a connectionist view, compassion triggers transformation.… When you are in a place between worldviews (nepantla) you're able to slip between realities to a neutral perception. A decision made in the in-between place becomes a turning point initiating psychological and spiritual transformations. (569)

In this paragraph, we see what Anzaldúa believes is the concrete power of the imagination to enact change. The imagination she describes here and in much of "now let us shift" is the imagination of self, a "knower" informed and moved by naguala, who continuously shifts the subjectivity of personhood from "inner preoccupations" to neutrality (nepantla/liminal space) to what she calls a "'nos/otras' position—an alliance between 'us' and 'others'" (570). Anzaldúa offers a detailed description of the self's process of recognizing deep interconnectivity, but under what conditions and contexts is the self motivated to make such shifts in knowing? Lugones's work helps to answer this question.

I have argued that Lugones's "On Complex Communication" strengthens Anzaldúa's theory of *conocimiento* by (1) offering an analysis, and a calling for the dismantling, of the "logic of narrow identity" and (2) describing how liminal encounters and forms of resistance are enacted by active subjects (Zaytoun 2013). The reconstruction of selfhood of which Anzaldúa speaks can occur only in the types of coalitional limens described by Lugones, where one's multiplicity is most vivid, and the opacity of others—the different histories, realities, and resistant strategies that are enacted at the colonial difference—are read, respected, and seen as integral to coalitional aims. Lugones's recent discussion of the coloniality of gender and the logic of fusion also add to our understanding of Anzaldúan selfhood as a decolonial project, a decolonizing of modern selfhood, consciousness, and resistance. Because Anzaldúa focuses on an inner (psychological, spiritual) process, and Lugones's emphasis is sociality and the plurality of subjectivity, reading the two together provides a thicker description of and contribution to theories of coalition.

SELF-IN-COALITION IN SUMMARY

I now return to my argument for the self-in-coalition as an aspect of active subjectivity. Although Lugones insists that the self is multiple, part of my task in this chapter is to demonstrate that she does not deny the role of "sense of selfhood" in the activities of the resistant-oppressed. My understanding of Lugones's take on self is that within collectives that reject the construction of the oppressed as inferior, a person can enact a "resistant agency," but always and only within the company of others (DF 71). That said, Lugones does recognize the role of persons participating in active subjectivity and in complex communication, which she says is exercised through "a change in one's own vocabulary, one's sense of self, one's way of living, in the extension of one's collective memory, through developing forms of communication that signal disruption of the reduction attempted by the oppressor" (OC 84). What she asks us not to forget in our theorizing about "one's sense of self" is that resistant identities, individual and collective, and selves, are created in relationship and in liminality. Identities and selves do not precede the contexts in which they are operating. Anzaldúa offers a way of theorizing a self with multiple parts, such as the "knower" that senses difference and naguala that alerts the self to recognize deep interrelatedness among difference. Anzaldúa, summoning Nahua mythos and epistemologies, provides a theorizing about a selfhood that is constructed in complex communication, outside the colonized, modern sense of self.

Theorizing the sense of self-in-coalition is important in understanding and enacting the possibilities for a decolonial selfhood in relation as well as for collective struggles. Self-in-coalition is not active subjectivity, but it plays a role in it. In-the-flesh persons participate in the "cross-referencing of different realities" they experience in order to engage in liberatory work (IP 15). The self-in-coalition, always and continuously constructed in relationship, serves several functions within the coalition, including recognizing difference, recognizing a multiple self across selves, and recognizing resistant tactics and movements of oppressed others. The type of "recognizing" or memory to which I refer here is an embodied consciousness, a sense outside modern epistemology that occurs in the sociality of liminal space, and in the neutral consciousness of *nepantla* where one understands identities as real and multiple, but impermanent and socially constructed, in the self and others. I contend that the "neutral perception" of *nepantla* (Anzaldúa 2002, 569) responds to what Lugones means by "not ... maintaining a hybrid" and instead "maintaining multiplicity" (DF 85). In liminal space/*nepantla*, identities, and selfhood are not categorical, reductive amalgamations but instead multiple, inseparable fusions that resist oppression. As Lugones says, "These (fusions) are not just theorized but lived possibilities. That is why we seek coalition" (RM 77).

I close with language from Lugones that points to the significance of selfhood in coalition maintained throughout her work. In the final pages of *Pilgrimages/*Peregrinajes, Lugones refers to "two sides of resistance," a movement "between the solitary and the collectively social," a process that sounds much like Anzaldúa's *conocimiento*—inner work/public acts (TSC 226). She is referring here to the consideration and enacting of "tactical strategies" in the intersubjective journey to liberation (226). Indeed, Lugones's writing, teaching, and activism are all a part of this lifelong project. Over ten years later, Lugones writes: "As we live as fusions resistant to multiple oppressions we can appreciate the ways in which others have conceived, given cultural form to, theorized, expressed, embodied, the resistance to multiple oppressions" (RM 80). I seek to remind us that although recognition, appreciation, testimony, and communication are relationally achieved, they are also embodied and experienced at the level of self-in-coalition. I assert that attention must be paid to how a lived sense of selfhood, negotiated in solidarity with others, contributes to the identity and effectiveness of the collective. In effect, awareness of the intricacies of interactions between self and collective can contribute to the success of social movements.

NOTES

I wish to thank the editors of this volume and Mariana Ortega for their invaluable feedback on drafts of this chapter.

1. My definition of *selfhood* corresponds with feminist phenomenological accounts of self, what Linda Martín Alcoff has described as "lived subjectivity" or "how we experience being ourselves" in particular moments in time and place (2006, 93). Bodily/emotional/cognitive/spiritual experiences of selfhood are continuously in the making through concrete, in-the-flesh, lived relationships to other beings, matter, social structures and situations, and particularly to power. My position on selfhood is primarily informed by scholars such as Gloria Anzaldúa, Susan Brison (2003), Robert Kegan (1998), Mariana Ortega (2001, 2006, 2008), Alexis Shotwell and Trevor Sangrey (2009), Erin Tarver (2011), and of course, Lugones.

2. For example, see M. Jacqui Alexander (2007), Elizabeth Cole and Zakiya Luna (2010), AnaLouise Keating (2000, 2005), and Iris Young (1997).

3. I use the term *structures* here in the way that Lugones, in reference to Victor Turner's 1974 work, sees them as "systematic, complete, coherent, closed socio-political institutions or normative systems that construe persons" (SAS 60). In contrast to structures are anti-structures or liminality, that which is beyond "structural descriptions" (61).

4. According to Lugones, the abstract self or "you" is "a person spatially and thus relationally conceived through your functionality in terms of power" (IP 9). The abstract "you" is distinct from the you (without quotations), which is "sensing, recognizing, and moving through the spatiality of your everydayness" (IP 8–9).

5. Because of my focus on "sense" of selfhood, I borrow the term "monosensical" from Lugones's discussion of "faithful witnessing," a "multiple sensing" of resistance "against the grain of oppression" (IP 7).

6. For discussions of Lugones's work in relation to selfhood, see Ortega (2001, 2006, 2008), McWeeny (2010, 2014), and Lowe (2011).

7. According to Lugones the limen is "the place in between realities, a gap 'between and betwixt' universes of sense that construe social life and persons differently, an interstice from where one can most clearly stand critically toward different structures" (OC 59).

8. Lugones borrows "practical syllogism" from Aristotle; it is "reasoning that ends in action, not as propositions that entail other propositions" (SAS 56).

9. Ortega reminds us that memory is Locke's "main criteria for personhood"; therefore, he dismisses the role of the body in identity and selfhood (2001, 16).

10. Anzaldúa's first major publication (edited with Cherríe Moraga) was the collection of essays, *This Bridge Called My Back: Writings by Radical Women of Color* (1981) and last publication, edited with AnaLouise Keating, was *This Bridge We Call Home: Radical Visions for Transformation* (2002), which was a twenty-year follow-up to the first *Bridge*. "now let us shift" is the final essay of the last *Bridge*.

11. For more detailed description of how Anzaldúa's work relates to literature on selfhood, see Zaytoun (2005a, 2005b, 2010, 2013).

12. I use the term *function* here, as Anzaldúa does, to refer to concrete action and purpose, which is distinct from the use of *function* in the mechanical sense.

13. La naguala, the feminine form of the shapeshifter, is one of many concepts that Anzaldúa invokes from the Nahua tradition. The *nagual* has, generally, three meanings: *nagual* as shapeshifter (usually humans to animal forms), *nagual* as an animal that serves as a spirit guide, and *nagual* as 'knower.'

14. Anzaldúa doesn't say much more about "the ego" or what she means by it in the essay, but I read *ego* here to mean "self-importance," although Anzaldúa could have also meant *ego* in the psychoanalytic sense as the intellectual or cognitive mechanism that seeks to regulate the self, curbing its desires and needs to fit into society in an appropriate way.

REFERENCES

Alexander, M. Jacqui. 2005. *Pedagogies of Crossing: Meditations on Feminism, Sexual Politics, Memory, and the Sacred.* Durham, NC: Duke University Press.

Alarcón, Norma. 2013. "Anzaldúan Textualities: A Hermeneutic of the Self and the Coyolxauhqui Imperative." In *El Mundo Zurdo 3*, edited by Larissa Mercado-López, Sonia Saldívar-Hall, and Antonia Castañeda, 189–208. San Francisco: Aunt Lute Books.

Alcoff, Linda Martín. 2006. *Visible Identities: Race, Gender, and the Self.* New York: Oxford University Press.

Anzaldúa, Gloria E. 1987. *Borderlands/La Frontera: The New Mestiza*. San Francisco: Aunt Lute Books.

———. 2002. "now let us shift ... the path of conocimiento ... inner work, public acts." In *This Bridge We Call Home: Radical Visions for Transformation*, edited by AnaLouise Keating and Gloria E. Anzaldúa, 540–78. New York: Routledge.

Brison, Susan. 2003. *Aftermath: Violence and the Remaking of a Self*. Princeton, NJ: Princeton University Press.

Cole, Elizabeth, and Zakiya Luna. 2010. "Making Coalitions Work: Solidarity across Difference within U.S. Feminism." *Feminist Studies* 36(10): 71–97.

Keating, Cricket. 2005. "Building Coalitional Consciousness." *Hypatia* 17(2): 86–103.

Keating, AnaLouise. 2000. *Gloria E. Anzaldúa: Interviews/Entrevistas*. New York: Routledge.

———. 2007. *Teaching Transformation: Transcultural Classroom Dialogues*. New York: Palgrave Macmillan.

Kegan, Robert. 1998. *In Over Our Heads: The Mental Demands of Modern Life*. Cambridge, MA: Harvard University Press.

Koegeler-Abdi, Martina. 2013. "Shifting Subjectivities: Mestizas, Nepantleras, and Gloria Anzaldúa's Legacy." *MELUS* 38(2): 71–88.

Lowe, Barbara J. 2011. "Ethereal Identities and Ethereal Subjectivity: An American Pragmatist Appreciation of María Lugones's Theory of Oppression and Resistance." *Inter-American Journal of Philosophy* 2(1): 11–25.

McWeeny. Jennifer. 2010. "Liberating Anger, Embodying Knowledge: A Comparative Study of María Lugones and Zen Master Hakuin." *Hypatia* 25(2): 295–315.

———. 2014. "Topographies of Flesh: Women, Nonhuman Animals, and the Embodiment of Connection and Difference." *Hypatia* 29(2): 269–86.

Moraga, Cherríe, and Gloria Anzaldúa, eds. 1981. *This Bridge Called My Back: Writings by Radical Women of Color*. New York: Kitchen Table Press.

Ortega, Mariana. 2001. "'New Mestizas,' "'World'-Travelers," and '*Dasein*': Phenomenology and the Multi-Voiced, Multi-Cultural Self." *Hypatia* 16(3): 1–29.

———. 2006. "Being Lovingly, Knowingly Ignorant: White Feminism and Women of Color." *Hypatia* 21(3): 56–74.

———. 2008. "Multiplicity, Inbetweeness, and the Question of Assimilation." *The Southern Journal of Philosophy* XLVI: 65–80.

Shotwell, Alexis, and Trevor Sangrey. 2009. "Resisting Definition: Gendering through Interaction and Relational Selfhood." *Hypatia* 24(3): 56–76.

Tarver, Erin. 2011. "New Forms of Subjectivity: Theorizing the Relational Self with Foucault and Alcoff." *Hypatia* 26(4): 804–25.

Turner, Victor. 1974. *Dramas, Fields, and Metaphors*. Ithaca, NY: Cornell University Press.

Young, Iris. 1997. "The Complexities of Coalition." *Dissent: A Quarterly of Politics and Culture* 44: 64–69. www.dissentmagazine.org/article/the-complexities-of-coalition.

Zaytoun, Kelli. 2005a. "Theorizing at the Borders: Considering Social Location in Rethinking Self and Psychological Development." *NWSAJ* 18(2): 52–72.

———. 2005b. "New Pathways toward Understanding Self-in-Relation: Anzaldúan (Re)Visions for Developmental Psychology." In *EntreMundos/Among Worlds: New Perspectives on Gloria Anzaldúa*, edited by AnaLouise Keating, 147–59. New York: Palgrave Macmillan.

———. 2010. "Beyond Self-Authorship: Fifth Order and the Capacity for Social Consciousness." In *Development and Assessment of Self-Authorship: Exploring the Concept across Cultures*, edited by Marcia Baxter Magolda, Elizabeth Creamer, and Peggy Meszaros, 151–66. Sterling, VA: Stylus.

———. 2013. "A Case for the Self-in-Coalition: Exploring Anzaldúa's Legacy of La Naguala with Lugones' Complex Communication." In *El Mundo Zurdo 3*, edited by Larissa Mercado-López, Sonia Saldívar-Hull, and Antonia Castañeda, 209–24. San Francisco: Aunt Lute Books.

3 The Ripple Imagery as a Decolonial Self

Exploring Multiplicity in Theresa Hak Kyung Cha's *Dictée*

(Brena) Yu-Chen Tai

María Lugones's decolonial feminism is characterized by a methodology of multiplicity that emphasizes the irreducibility of the histories, epistemologies, memories, and cosmologies of the colonized in their contact with colonial power. Lugones argues that coloniality names not only the "classification of people in terms of the coloniality of power and gender, but also the process of active reduction of people, the dehumanization that fits them for the classification, the process of subjectification, the attempt to turn the colonized into less than human beings" (TDF 745). To address the dehumanization that occurs within the subjectivity of the colonized under coloniality, Lugones calls for "decolonizing ourselves."[1] However, because the construction of the modern subject is problematic for Lugones, the project of decolonizing ourselves does not aim to render the self into the rational, unified individual that is the subject of colonial modernity. Whereas the mechanisms of categorization, reduction, and dehumanization buttress coloniality, recognizing, maintaining, and creating multiplicity in us and in others are crucial steps toward the project of decolonizing ourselves.

In Lugones's decolonial feminist thought, the irreducible multiplicity in the subjectivity of the colonized shows that the coloniality of gender is never a successful enterprise. As Lugones contends, "Without the tense multiplicity we only see either the coloniality of gender as accomplishment, or a freezing of memory, an ossified understanding of self in relation from a precolonial sense of the social" (DF 84). The coloniality of gender is not an accomplished product because resisting forces exist simultaneously with oppressing forces, as in Lugones's visual expression of "resisting ←→ oppressing" (TSC 223). Resistance disrupts the fantasy of coloniality as accomplishment by undermining oppressive forces. Alternatives always exist in the borders of oppressive spatiality because we are ontologically multiple.² In Lugones's words, "You are concrete. Your spatiality, constructed as an intersection following the designs of power, isn't. This discrepancy already tells you that you are more than one" (IP 10). The spatiality drawn by those in power is only one possibility for our concrete bodies to inhabit. In addition to excavating the multiple spatialities in which we reside, Lugones's vision of decolonizing ourselves requires us to learn about each other "to encompass in our imagination the multiplicity of the powerfully oppressive constructions of the social and of the infrapolitically resistant collectives" (DF 71). The decolonial possibility therefore lies in the praxis of transformation at both individual and collective levels. The colonized self becomes a decolonial self by recognizing and insisting on one's own multiplicity and that of others when trespassing the spatiality of oppression. Decolonial selves thereby invent a liberatory and coalitional spatiality from the bottom up.

To illuminate the contours of the decolonial self that emerges from Lugones's theory of multiplicity, this chapter turns to Theresa Hak Kyung Cha's experimental autobiography, *Dictée*, for inspiration. *Dictée* can be read as a decolonial feminist text in which a decolonial self who is both multiplicitous and coalitional is created. Whereas Lugones mostly conceives of the multiple selves of the oppressed-resistant subject as occurring in one body (Ortega 2001), this chapter seeks to expand Lugones's theory of multiplicity by showing that the multiplicity of a decolonial self also exists across different bodies, separated by culture and time. As a means to elaborating Lugones's vision of "decolonizing ourselves" through Cha's *Dictée*, this chapter proposes a ripple imagery as a metaphor to conceptualize a self that is simultaneously connected to and separated from other people. The ripple imagery will help us envision the construction of a decolonial self that can maintain multiplicity both *within* a body and *across* bodies in the process of remembering resistance to oppressive powers at different temporal and spatial moments.

DICTÉE AND MULTIPLICITY

Theresa Hak Kyung Cha was a diasporic Korean American writer and performer. Her autobiography, *Dictée*, is an anomaly within Asian American literary criticism and cultural studies due to its distinctive narrative style and structure as well as its lack of a central narrating voice. This text cannot be easily categorized into any specific literary or artistic genre because it uses a variety of representational forms including prose, poetry, letters, and photos. Moreover,

Dictée consists of Chinese calligraphic characters, clinical diagrams, and multiple seemingly discrete narratives, such as stories about the Japanese colonization of Korea, Asian American diasporic experiences, and several known and unknown women's stories across time and space. Cha thwarts readers' desires for a transparent, unified story because her book offers no clear storyline to weave the visual and written elements of the text into a linear and developmental narrative. It is therefore difficult to pinpoint what *Dictée* is with certainty. It could be a collection of some marginalized histories of women fighters against the matrix of colonial power; an Asian American woman's diasporic story; a narrative about mother-daughter relations; a story of a colonized woman's struggle to come to voice; and so on.

Besides its nonlinear structure and ambiguous storyline, *Dictée* causes even more confusion for readers due to its diverse narrative voices. Even though the University of California Press labeled *Dictée* an autobiography, its autobiographical elements are debatable.[3] Cha's *Dictée* poses a challenge to the liberal notion of the self that is fully enclosed and autonomous; the dominant presumption of unity in subject formation is undermined and the boundaries between speaking subjects are interrogated by mixing the pronouns of "I," "we," "she," and "you." Multiplying the voice of the narrating self and making these voices ambiguous, Cha renders the formation of a unified identity, and thus an "autobiography," unattainable. As Shelly Sunn Wong argues, *Dictée* refuses "the dominant culture's demand to represent (and, by implication, to establish a formal identity with), and thereby legitimate, an ideology of cultural assimilation" (1994, 45). Similarly, Hyo Kim points out that *Dictée* is a "critique of this very desire to name, anchor and fix the identity of a subject according to an arbitrarily constructed criterion" (2008, 470).

Cha refuses to delineate a unified identity for the subject in *Dictée* in order to explore the multiplicity of both oppressors and the oppressed, which reveals Cha's decolonial feminist politics. *Dictée* can be read as a decolonial feminist text because it not only exposes the active reduction of the colonized under the matrix of coloniality but also gives accounts of multiple women's practices of resistance across time and space. The self delineated in *Dictée* is not a unified self, but a decolonial self who insists on the stickiness of multiplicity without collapsing differences into a hybrid and without seeing multiplicity as self-fragmentation. This self therefore enacts Lugones's emphasis on "maintaining multiplicity at the point of reduction—not in maintaining a hybrid 'product,' which hides the colonial difference—in the tense workings of more than one logic, not to be synthesized but transcended" (TDF 755). According to Lugones, if we collapse the differences produced by colonial power into a hybrid, or worse, a unity, we will fail to discern the fractured point between oppressing and resisting forces, which will lead us to believe that the differences embodied by the colonized are consistent with dominant power rather than a contestation against it.

Both Cha and Lugones highlight, in different ways, the irreducibility of differences in the construction of a decolonial self, but they also do not foreclose the possibility of a coalitional self formed by multiple decolonial selves whose differences are likewise not collapsible or synthesizable. I suggest that two levels of a decolonial self can be discerned in *Dictée*. On the one hand, Cha emphasizes a decolonial self at an individual level whose multiplicity resides in one body within the liminal space between oppressing and resisting forces. On the other hand, Cha draws a contour of a coalitional decolonial self, the autobiographical "I" of *Dictée*, whose multiplicity is located across bodies. The coalitional decolonial self situates itself across several women's lives that collectively resist a shared colonial logic characterized by dichotomies, categories, and domination. Fusion, Lugones tells us, is "a resistance to multiple oppressions" (RM 77). In recognizing our resistance to multiple oppressions, we can also "appreciate the ways in which others have conceived, given cultural form to, theorized, expressed, embodied, their resistance to multiple oppressions" (77). Fusion is not an abstract concept but it is a series of lived possibilities that can unfold an alternative future if we are able to share resistant tactics against multiple oppressions with each other. The logic of fusion is what makes the individual and collective dimensions of a decolonial self interconnected.

COLONIALITY AS ACTIVE REDUCTION OF MULTIPLICITY

Cha's refusal to delineate a unified subject can be contextualized within Lugones's criticisms of the modern subject that follows the logic of purity and fragmentation. Lugones contends that the modern subject as a unified self is only a fictitious construct because, in reality, each person is multiple in nature (SAS 57); even the modern subject is multiple. She argues that a unified self is conceivable only through a split-separation imagination that "generates the fictional construction of a vantage point from which unified wholes, totalities, can be captured... The series of fictions hides the training of the multiple into unity as well as the survival of the multiple" (PIS 128). A unified self is possible only from a particular vantage point reserved for those in power. What appears unified is produced through active reduction of multiplicity; unification is not originally given.

Lugones's revelation of the active construction of the modern subject also hints at the production of hierarchical difference. As Lugones argues:

> To the extent that he is fictional, the tainting is fictional: seeing us as tainted depends on a need for purity that requires that we become "parts," "addenda" of the bodies of modern subjects—Christian white bourgeois men—and make their purity possible. We become sides of fictitious dichotomies. To the extent that we are ambiguous—non-dichotomous—we threaten the fiction and can be rendered unfit only by decrying ambiguity as nonexistent—that is, by halving us, splitting us. Thus, we exist only as incomplete, unfit beings, and they exist as complete only to the extent that what we are, and what is absolutely necessary for them, is declared worthless. (PIS 131)

The difference produced by split-separation is hierarchical in the sense that only one difference is important, namely, the dominant difference. In the passage above, the dominant difference is the difference embodied by the modern subject who claims to be unified in an illusory whole while hiding his *difference* as neutrality. In contrast, subordinate differences are viewed as fragmented parts that make the dominant difference complete. From the perspective of the modern subject, those differences viewed as deviation from the dominant difference have neither value nor wholeness; they are only supplementary and subordinate to the dominant difference. Those ambiguous differences suffer violent dichotomization and categorization in order to serve the dominant difference that clings to purity and that assumes the possibility of fragmentation. Those differences that fail to make the dominant difference complete or that threaten the wholeness of it are viewed as anomalies in need of forgetting, suppression, or erasure.

In *Dictée*, Cha uses the production of whiteness as a symbol of the active reduction of multiplicity under colonial powers. In the following poetic passage from the book, we can see that the assumption of whiteness follows the logic of purity, demands transparency and control, and asserts itself as the dominant, yet neutral, difference:

> Ever since the whiteness.
> It retains itself, white,
> unsurpassing, absent of hue, absolute, utmost
> pure, unattainably pure.
> If within its white shadow-shroud, all stain should

> vanish, all past all memory of having been cast,
> left, through the absolution and power of
> these words.
> Covering. Draping. Clothing. Sheathe. Shroud.
> Superimpose. Overlay. Screen.
> Conceal. Ambush.
> Disguise. Cache. Mask. Veil.
> Obscure. Cloud. Shade. Eclipse. Covert. (2001, 132)

Cha's words highlight that whiteness is never self-evident. It retains itself as absolutely pure only through various mechanisms that actively hide the multiplicity that constitutes whiteness itself. Whiteness is never pure but a mixture of multiple hues. In order to expose that multiplicity within whiteness, Cha uses a series of verbs that allude to hiding something from being discovered, such as *shroud*, *conceal*, *obscure*, and *eclipse*. Through these words, Cha exposes the various acts that are actually operative but downplayed in the construction of unquestionable whiteness. Only when "all stain" and "all past all memory" are suppressed or cast out can whiteness appear to be pure. But as Cha notices, pure whiteness is "unattainable"; it is only imaginable from a vantage point that conceals its own production.

In the context of the Japanese colonization of Korea represented in *Dictée*, anyone who embodies the differences that cannot make the dominant difference of the colonizers complete or that threaten its legitimacy will be eliminated in order to maintain colonial power. Cha features a photo taken from a distance that depicts oppressors who are about to execute three blindfolded people in white who are tied up in a cross-shape posture (2001, 39). In this image, Cha exposes the interrelations between coloniality, dehumanization, and violence in the subjection and subjectification of the colonized. Although Cha does not specify the context of the photo, it is likely a photo taken during the Japanese colonization of Korea because the photo is included at the end of a section on the story of female Korean nationalist Yu Guan Soon, who lived from 1903 to 1920 (lunar calendar). The photo shows the power of coloniality at work: colonizers subjugate the colonized to manifest their colonial power. The impaired mobility of those facing execution is indicated in the photograph by their bound bodies. The anonymous figures of the colonized were not allowed to look back at their colonizers during the execution, so they were blindfolded. This photo refers to the anonymity of causalities under the matrix of colonial power. I use the term *anonymity* to highlight that those in power do not distinguish the individuality of those who transgress the norms but only view them as homogenous faceless agitators who threaten to challenge the status quo. Their anonymity results from the active dehumanization and reduction of the colonized through the deprivation of their individuality and identity. Once the colonized are stripped of individuality, their bodies become exchangeable.[4]

The notion of exchangeability is articulated more explicitly in the section where Cha offers an account of Yu Guan Soon's life. Yu Guan Soon, who was a daughter of patriot parents, organized the Korean people to protest Japanese colonization in 1919. Cha sees Yu Guan Soon as "Child revolutionary child patriot woman soldier deliverer of nation" (2001, 37). When Yu Guan Soon was arrested as a leader of the revolution at the young age of seventeen, she was stabbed in the chest and tortured to death by Japanese oppressors. Cha evaluates her life in the following way: "Actions prescribed separate her path from the others. The identity of such a path is exchangeable with any other heroine in history, their names, dates, actions which require not definition in their devotion to generosity and self-sacrifice" (30). In the contact zone between colonizers and the colonized, the bodies of the colonized are ready to be killed and stripped of their individuality whenever they trespass the colonial spatiality from the bird's eye view perspective of the colonizers. The bodies to be killed mark the physical limit of oppressive spatiality wherein the life and movement of the colonized is permitted. Anyone who challenges colonial rules will be punished or eliminated because their rebelliousness exposes the boundary of the spatiality of oppression delineated by colonial powers.

In the case of the Japanese colonization of Korea, crushing those who transgress colonial spatiality to maintain authority is imperative because Japanese occupation also results from Japanese infringement of an agreement between the two countries. In *Dictée*, Cha includes a document titled "Petition from the Koreans of Hawaii to President Roosevelt" written on July 12, 1905.[5] The document tells that the object of the Japan-Korea Protectorate Treaty between Japan and Korea was to "preserve the independence of Korea and Japan and to protect Eastern Asia from Russia's aggression" (2001, 34). However, rather than preserving the independence of Korea during the time when Korea allowed Japan to use its territory as a military base to resist Russia, Japan expanded its imperialism and broke the promise by "forcibly obtaining all the special privileges and concessions" from the Korean government (35). The annexation of Korea by Japan between 1910 and 1945 can be viewed as a violation of Korea's sovereign body by Japanese imperial power (Choi 1993). Facing the uprising of Korean nationalists, Japanese colonizers attempted to erase the colonized who rebelliously transgressed the border of colonial power. The oppressive act reveals the colonizers' deep fears that their authority will be undermined if they remember their previous encroachment on Korean sovereign territory.

Interestingly, although execution is about reduction, the multiplicity of both the colonizers and the colonized is emphasized in the very act of killing. The multiplicity of the colonizers is revealed through their insecurity about not being what they think they are when seen from the eyes of the colonized. In other words, from the perspective of Japanese colonizers, they view themselves as rightful rule-enforcers. But in the eyes of colonized Koreans, Japanese colonizers are lawbreakers and exploiters. The intense threat Japanese colonizers face from Korean nationalists results from the colonizers' refusal to see themselves in dual ways, as both law enforcers and law violators. Japanese colonizers represented in *Dictée* stick to the logic of purity to maintain illusory unified selves in the act of killing. Japanese colonizers are, to borrow Lugones's phrase, "self-deceiving multiple [selves]" (IP 14). Lugones insightfully argues that oppressors self-deceive themselves about their own multiplicity through "disconnection of memory," which entails the failure of "cross-referencing, without first person memories of him- or herself in more than one reality" (14–15). Killing the transgressors of colonial power aims to help the colonizers to forget their own violation; colonizers rely on self-deception to secure the legitimacy of their dominance and the success of their practice.

Although forgetfulness helps colonizers suppress their multiplicity, remembering is a crucial aspect of survival for the colonized. As Cha writes:

> Why resurrect it all now. From the Past. History, the old wound. The past emotions all over again. To confess to relive the same folly. To name it now so as not to repeat history in oblivion. To extract each fragment by each fragment from the word from the image another word another image the reply that will not repeat history in oblivion. (2001, 33)

To revisit the past and to reclaim memory as a "[w]ould-be-said remnant" (38) is to re-live the liminal space between the two arrows in Lugones's articulation of "oppressing ←→ resisting" forces; it is to remember the multiplicity of the colonized. As Lugones says, "The limen is the place where one becomes most fully aware of one's multiplicity" (SAS 59). Lugones calls the liminal space in the colonial context a "fractured locus" (TDF 748). The colonial fractured locus results from ongoing negotiation and resistance between the colonial imposition of systems of oppression on the colonized and the fluency and memory that the colonized have of their native cultures. The fractured locus allows the colonized to conceive of themselves as "not exhausted by domination" (OC 77).

While the colonizers strive to create unified selves to sustain their authority, the colonized aim at maintaining their multiplicity for survival and emancipation. In the colonial fractured locus, the colonized adopt what Lugones calls a streetwalker's perspective, which defies the bird's-eye view sight of the colonizers (TSC). The colonized resist the power of coloniality at every turn of contact in both small and large scales, which renders coloniality an impossible accomplishment. Remembering, maintaining, and deploying multiplicity at the colonial fractured locus is imperative for the colonized to transform their reduced, colonial selves into *decolonial* selves who insist on their own irreducible multiplicity.

DECOLONIAL SELVES IN *DICTÉE*

Cha's decolonial feminist strategies mainly include challenging the anonymity and exchangeability of people enacted by colonizers and created by the logic of oppression. In several sections of *Dictée*, Cha humanizes resisters by including photos of woman warriors before she narrates their lives.[6] For example, the section "Calliope-Epic Poetry" begins with a photo of Cha's mother in her youth. The section ends with another photo of her mother at an older age, which appears just after Cha tells her mother's struggle in the process of immigrating to the United States. Cha's mother's identity and history is constantly questioned at U.S. immigration checkpoints: "Every ten feet they demand to know who and what you are, who is represented" (2001, 57). In order to decolonize the colonial gaze that freezes the colonized as ahistorical objects, Cha includes two close-up photos of her mother at different ages in the same section to highlight the change of the corporeal body in the passage of time.[7] This decolonial strategy makes her mother visible as an historical subject and as multiple across time. Elizabeth Frost also notices that the photos of Cha's mother "provide a point of reference and signify both the concrete effects of time's passage and a historical frame" (2002, 184).

In addition to putting faces back on resisters to challenge the anonymity that the oppressive power actively produces, Cha defiantly subverts the notion of exchangeability that operates in the logic of oppression with an alternative concept of interchangeability guided by the logic of resistance. Cha's particular idea of resistant interchangeability emphasizes the continuity of resistance across time and space. In her close reading of *Dictée*, Michelle Black Wester notices that the interchangeability of women is emphasized through Cha's mother, Hyung Soon Huo, whose story follows that of Yu Guan Soon. While the story of Yu Guan Soon focuses on her sacrifice at the age of seventeen, Cha's mother's story begins when she is eighteen years old. Wester argues that "the numbering is significant because it implies that Hyung Soon Huo's story can be read as a continuation of Yu Guan Soon's" (2007, 184). Wester's insightful observation suggests that whenever colonial forces cannot be successfully combated, resisting forces always emerge as embodied and manifested in particular women's lives. The shared colonial forces that Yu Guan Soon, Cha's mother, and Cha resist at different temporal moments and spatial locations are those of the Japanese colonization of Korea in reality and in memory.

Yu Guan Soon's resistance is outward, direct, and large scale in her organization of a massive demonstration against Japanese colonizers. Although Yu Guan Soon's cry for Korean liberation from Japanese colonization in her native land is stifled when she is violently killed, Cha's mother continues Yu Guan Soon's resisting force in a more private and small-scale fashion by speaking Korean in the foreign land of China while it was forbidden under Japanese occupation.[8] Cha writes: "The tongue that is forbidden is your own mother tongue. You speak in the dark. In the secret. The one that is yours. Your own. You speak very softly, you speak in a whisper. In the dark, in secret. Mother tongue is your refuge" (2001, 45).[9] While Cha's mother speaks a resistant language in private in China, Cha makes her mother's Korean whisper in China and Yu Guan Soon's outcry in Korea heard once again in English in the United States through her writing in *Dictée*. The multilayered echo of resistant voices among Yu Guan Soon, Cha's mother, and Cha at different temporal moments and spatial locations suggests a particular construction of the self that McDaniel identifies as "an episodic, serialized version of self" (2009, 73). McDaniel argues that the main characteristic of a serial and relational strategy of self-construction lies in "the desire to expose the significance of others on our own self-imaging" (84). According to McDaniel, simply collecting and repeating the stories and histories of others is not enough to form a serial self. Instead, a serial construction of the self must encompass the notion that "seeing the self through the bodies of others allows their stories to continue beyond their physical existence. This continuation beyond death is a driving force behind seriality and serial self-representation, as objects that are lost may also be found" (84). Cha's construction of a serial self reveals a particular form of interchangeability with difference guided by the logic of resistance that does not fall into the pitfall of anonymity. Interchangeability with difference involves an overlapping of lives and experiences without substitution or exchange but with ongoing interaction.[10] I argue that Cha's resistant notion of interchangeability is a kind of *intersubjectivity* in Lugones's sense of the term; it results from our fluency in each other's resistant histories and strategies in order to make each other legible subjects in different "worlds."

For Lugones, intersubjectivity is the basis on which others recognize us as resisters and we recognize others as resisters: "there is a need and an excitement to being understood in intersubjective encounters" because intersubjectivity makes resisters who are invisible in the matrix of oppression legible to each other (TSC 219). Intersubjectivity is not only what resisters desire but also what they must achieve in order to make sense of their own existences because resisters are not individuals affirmed by institutions; resisters are "active subjects" who require each other's backing at every turn in order to make sense of their words, gestures, and movements, all of which lack institutional support (219).

To facilitate intersubjective encounters among resisters that would make their subjectivities sensible, complex communication is required. Complex communication enables us to communicate across differences through a playful attitude in a liminal space, even though we may arrive at that liminal space through different journeys.[11] What makes complex communication successful is recognizing each other as resisters to intermeshed oppressions, as well as our willingness to decipher each other's resistant strategies in order to imagine, nurture, and create liberatory possibilities collectively. Complex communication demands our openness to uncertainty without "assimilating the text of others to our own" (OC 84). It is a manner of interaction that is "enacted through a change in one's own vocabulary, one's sense of self, one's way of living, in the extension of one's collective memory, through developing forms of communication that signal disruption of the reduction attempted by the oppressor" (84). Complex communication is not only a linguistic practice but also a spatial one. Lugones's world-traveling is a strategy that facilitates complex communication and points to a spatial dimension where intersubjectivity and multiplicity can be supported. World-traveling requires its travelers to "[trespass] against the spatiality of oppressions" that are guided by a categorial and dichotomous logic (IP 11). The epistemic shift catalyzed by traveling to others' worlds to recognize "*what it is to be them and what it is to be ourselves in their eyes*" requires us to rechart the relationality of space not only to reconceive our sociality with people in different worlds anew but also to try out alternative interactions with them to create decolonial options collectively (WT 97; original emphasis).

While world-traveling helps us shift perspectives, a politics of memory also plays a crucial role in the process of complex communication. Lugones argues that

> the liberatory experience lies in this memory, on these many people one is who have intentions one understands because one is fluent in several "cultures," "worlds," realities. The liberatory possibility lies in resistant readings of history that reveal unified historical lines as enacting dominations through both linearity and erasure. (SAS 58–59)

We need to remember our other selves in different worlds in order to cross-reference different realities for the purpose of retaining our multiplicitous self. However, merely remembering ourselves in other worlds and understanding ourselves as multiplicitous is not sufficient to achieve liberation, as Lugones tells us (SAS 62). What leads to emancipatory possibilities is a collective practice "born of dialogue among multiplicitous persons who are faithful witnesses of themselves and also testify to, and uncover the multiplicity of, their oppressors and the techniques of oppression afforded by ignoring that multiplicity" (62). Remembering is both individual and collective rebellion with a transformative and subversive potential. Through the strategies of world-traveling and remembrance, intersubjectivity achieved through complex communication begins from a coalitional starting point. If we are satisfied in our own compartmentalized space delineated by the oppressors, we will not be able to recognize other resisters as active subjects and will not begin to imagine emancipatory spatialities. In *Dictée*, Cha performs complex communication to read women warriors across time and space alongside each other; she fosters the intersubjectivity between them without collapsing their differences. The interchangeability with difference between Yu Guan Soon and Cha's mother embodies complex communication in this sense.

THE RIPPLE IMAGERY

> Tenth, a circle within a circle, a series of concentric circles.
> —Theresa Hak Kyung Cha, *Dictée*

In *Dictée*, Cha unfolds two levels of a decolonial self: on the one hand, the decolonial self is embodied in each woman warrior who maintains her multiplicity at the fractured locus in the matrix of oppressive power. Cha highlights their resistances at the point of reduction of their lives, languages, and politics in different narrative segments such as the respective stories of Yu Guan Soon and Cha's mother. On the other hand, reading *Dictée* as a whole, Cha constructs a decolonial self who is also a coalitional self by creating a community of women warriors across time and space, as is the case with Cha's situating herself in the serial lives of Yu Guan Soon and her mother. Cha creates this alternative genealogy of resistance through memory, cross-reference, and a sense of belonging. In recognizing differences, intersubjectivity is achieved in the construction of the coalitional dimension of the decolonial self through complex communication.

The two levels of a decolonial self are interconnected. To conceptualize the two levels of a decolonial self at once, I propose a ripple imagery to illuminate Lugones's concept of multiplicity as it relates to her notion of a decolonial self. I theorize the ripple imagery by detailing the forces and spatialities that facilitate the emergence of a decolonial self. These include the simultaneously distinguishable and connected relation between nondominant differences in the decolonial self and its underlying coalitional politics.

The ripple imagery is an energy field that consists of a series of concentric circles or partial circles. A set of visible circles in the ripple imagery is created by the intensification of both the oppressive force moving from the inside out and the resistant force moving from the outside in. The oppressive force is the energy accumulated when an outside object drops into a collective body of water. The outside object alone does not create the ripple itself. Instead, it is the energy gathered at the moment when the object violently collides with one point of the body of water that creates multiple layers of the ripple. Therefore, the ripple is the effect of the oppressing ←→ resisting forces in Lugones's articulation rather than of a single direction in itself. The visible layers of the ripple show that the oppressive force does not precede the resistant force; rather, the two exist simultaneously. The particular movement in the ripple imagery is well captured by Cha's words: "You are moving accordingly never ahead of the movement never behind the movement you are carrying the weight from outside being the weight inside. You move. You are being moved. You are movement. Inseparably. Indefinably. Not isolatable terms" (2001, 51). What connects the layers of the ripple together is the tension between the continuous resisting force and the dispersed oppressing force, just as the lives of Yu Guan Soon, Cha's mother, and Cha are concentric circles in their shared resistance to Japanese colonization in reality and in memory.

Each visible ripple layer can be viewed as the emergence of a decolonial self who maintains its multiplicity at the fractured locus of opposing forces. The fractured locus allows the self to see "a double image of herself" when shifting perspectives between different realities, and this in turn leads the self to recognize her incompatible attributes in different worlds (WT 92).

The incompatible attributes make the self multiplicitous rather than unified. Furthermore, in the ripple imagery, each circle of the ripple field is a nondominant difference with its own value and wholeness; there is no hierarchical relationship between layers in a horizontal field of the ripple. Unlike the hierarchical difference that privileges one dominant difference and views other differences as deviation from the dominant difference, nondominant differences are recognized in virtue of their own value without hierarchical evaluation. Communicating between nondominant differences can nurture the repertoire for emancipation as well as extend the collective memory between resisters without privileging one difference over others.

Conceptualizing each layer of the ripple as a whole in itself does not mean that it is isolated from other layers and self-enclosed. While layers of the ripple have distinguishable boundaries, a set of circles can also be mapped onto the same field of the ripple without a clear-cut separation from other layers of the ripple. In the ripple imagery, there is no possibility to separate one layer of the ripple entirely from another because the boundary between layers is permeable to the others. As Lugones writes, "worlds are indeed permeable," while also being multiple (IP 16). Therefore, each discernible layer of the ripple is in itself whole but is also a part of the larger whole of the ripple field. The creation of a whole field of the ripple does not erase the differences between its layers. Visualizing differences through the ripple imagery shows how the coexistence of the dual nature of individuality and interconnectivity in Lugones's theory of difference is possible.

Shifting the focus from individual layers of the ripple to the entire ripple field is to move from the first level of an individual decolonial self whose multiplicity is located in the liminal space between the oppressing and resisting forces to the second level of a decolonial self who is a coalitional self situated in a resistant community of difference. It is also a shift from "I" to "we" in Lugones's expression of "I → we," where the arrow signifies "the transitional quality and dispersed intentionality of the subject" (TSC 227). Lugones uses the term *active subjectivity* to refer to the dispersed intentionality of resisters. What characterizes active subjectivity is its intersubjective nature. As Lugones argues: "Resistant intentions are given form necessarily intersubjectively" (216). Lugones understands the intentionality of resisters as "lying *between rather than in subjects*" (208; original emphasis). Further, Lugones explains:

> Active subjectivity is alive in the activity of dispersed intending in complex, heterogeneous collectivities, within and between worlds of complex sense. The activity is not subservient or servile but in

transgression of dominant sense. The dispersion includes a dispersion of meaning through a translation that does not rest on equivalences between words but on worldly connections in living in transgression of reduction of life to the monosense of domination. (217)

Lugones moves away from the notion of agency to that of active subjectivity whose backing comes, not from institutional recognition, but from other resisters who are aware of both the reduction of their lives and their multiplicity. Active subjects are not only oppressed but also resistant against the spatiality of domination. The intersubjective nature of active subjectivity in the movement of "I → we" makes conceivable a decolonial self whose multiplicity resides not only in one body but also across bodies and times to form a coalitional self. But the move from "I" to "we" does not erase the differences between bodies that consist of the "we." Similar to the relation between layers in a ripple field, the differences constituting the coalitional decolonial self are simultaneously individually distinguishable and collectively interconnected. In the example of *Dictée*, Cha retains the individual differences among women warriors but emphasizes the continuity of their resistant forces across time and space.

The ripple imagery is a metaphor of being as well as doing. It illuminates two levels of Lugones's theory of multiplicity in relation to her decolonial feminist thought: the ontological and the coalitional. Each discernable layer of the ripple manifests the ontological dimension of multiplicity that makes visible the fractured locus between oppressing and resisting forces where the colonized are situated. The entire field of the ripple helps us grasp the coalitional aspect of multiplicity that renders seemingly discrete colonial differences into a sticky field of nondominant differences with inseparable interconnectivity due to memory and complex communication. Lugones's project of decolonizing ourselves requires understanding and praxis in regard to both levels of multiplicity at the same time. The decolonial self conceptualized in the ripple imagery is infinite, open, and always in the making. The decolonial self can be expanded, condensed, or multiplied depending on whether the interaction between the oppressive forces and the resistant forces that drive the ripple imagery of the decolonial self is weak, strong, or multiple.

NOTES

1. María Lugones, "Resisting Gender: Toward a Decolonial Feminism" (lecture, The Ohio State University, Columbus, Ohio, March 14, 2014).

2. I use the term *border* with reference to Walter Mignolo's concept. Mignolo argues that decolonial thinking dwells in the border, a space of "exteriority" that is "not the outside, but the outside built from the inside in the process of building itself as inside" (2012, 26). The border is the space where those who do not conform to Western modernity reside; it is also the space where we have the potential to cast off our previous epistemic baggage by "learning to unlearn in order to relearn and to rebuild" (26).

3. For example, Nicole McDaniel calls for reading *Dictée* as a memoir rather than as an autobiography (2009).

4. I use the concept of exchangeability to reflect a particular intracorporal relationship that Jennifer McWeeny identifies when she states that "bodies are 'exchangeable' with one another when they are alternately used to serve the same function" (2014, 280).

5. The Japan-Korea Protectorate Treaty, signed in 1905, ended Korean diplomatic sovereignty and made Korea a protectorate of Japan.

6. A woman warrior is "a female figure—historic, literary, or mythical—who performs male tasks or social roles with the aim of avenging a family, village, nation, or a group of people oppressed by war, poverty, or colonial rule" (Lee 2010, 64). The phrase "women warriors" also recalls Asian American writer Maxine Hong Kingston's famous novel about immigration, *The Woman Warrior*. With the use of this phrase, I also hope to situate *Dictée* within the genealogy of Asian American women's writings on immigration that feature women resisters.

7. I use the term *colonial* here because it is important to emphasize that the U.S.-Korea relationship is also a colonial one, despite the role of "liberator" that the United States assumed after World War II by removing the Japanese from Korea. As Chungmoo Choi argues, "(post)colonial South Koreans have continued to mimic Western hegemonic culture and have reproduced a colonial pathology of self-denigration and self-marginalization, which have [*sic*] long blinded the South Koreans from critically assessing their 'liberator-benefactor' as a colonizing hegemon" (1993, 83).

8. Cha's mother is a Korean born in Manchuria to first-generation Korean exiles.

9. In *Borderlands*/La Frontera, Chicana feminist philosopher and writer Gloria Anzaldúa also states that speaking one's mother tongue is an act of home (re)creation: "For some of us, language is a homeland closer than the Southwest—for many Chicanos today live in the Midwest and the East" (2007, 77). In addition, Anzaldúa proclaims that mother tongues are integral to one's identity formation when she writes, "Ethnic identity is twin skin to linguistic identity—I am my language" (81).

10. Lugones emphasizes the interactive dimension in forming self-knowledge and catalyzing self-change when she writes: "self-knowledge is interactive" and "self-change is interactive" (LPF 74).

11. According to Lugones, a playful attitude refers to an "openness to uncertainty, which includes a vocation not bound by the meanings and norms that constitute one's ground"; it "enables one to find in others one's own possibilities and theirs" (IP 26).

REFERENCES

Anzaldúa, Gloria. 2007. *Borderlands/*La Frontera*: The New Mestiza*. 3rd ed. San Francisco: Aunt Lute Books.

Cha, Theresa Hak Kyung. 2001. *Dictée*. Los Angeles: University of California Press.

Choi, Chungmoo. 1993. "The Discourse of Decolonization and Popular Memory: South Korea." *Positions* 1(1): 77–102.

Frost, Elizabeth A. 2002. " 'In Another Tongue': Body, Image, Text in Theresa Hak Kyung Cha's *Dictée*." In *We Who Love to Be Astonished: Experimental Women's Writing and Performance Poetics*, edited by Laura Hinton and Cynthia Hogue, 181–92. Tuscaloosa: University of Alabama Press.

Kim, Hyo. 2008. "Depoliticising Politics: Readings of Theresa Hak Kyung Cha's *Dictée*." *Changing English* 15(4): 467–75.

Kingston, Maxine Hong. 1976. *The Woman Warrior: Memoirs of a Girlhood among Ghosts*. New York: Random House.

Lee, Karen An-Hwei. 2010. "From Female Self-Sacrifice to Korean Freedom Fighter: Yu Guan Soon in Theresa Cha's *Dictée*." In *Transnationalism and the Asian American Heroine: Essays on Literature, Film, Myth and Media*, edited by Lan Dong, 63–81. Jefferson, NC: McFarland.

McDaniel, Nicole. 2009. "'The Remnant Is the Whole': Collage, Serial Self-Representation, and Recovering Fragments in Theresa Hak Kyung Cha's *Dictée*." *ARIEL* 40(4): 69–88.

McWeeny, Jennifer. 2014. "Topographies of Flesh: Women, Nonhuman Animals, and the Embodiment of Connection and Difference." *Hypatia* 29(2): 269–86.

Mignolo, Walter D. 2012. "Decolonizing Western Epistemology/Building Decolonial Epistemologies." In *Decolonizing Epistemologies: Latina/o Theology and Philosophy*, edited by Ada María Isasi-Díaz and Eduardo Mendieta, 19–43. New York: Fordham University Press.

Ortega, Mariana. 2001. "'New Mestizas,' 'World'-Travelers,' and '*Dasein*': Phenomenology and the Multi-Voiced, Multi-Cultural Self." *Hypatia* 16(3): 1–29.

Wester, Michelle Black. 2007. "The Concentric Circles of *Dictée*: Reclaiming Women's Voices Through Mothers and Daughters' Stories." *Journal of Asian American Studies* 10(2): 169–91.

Wong, Shelly Sunn. 1994. "Unnaming the Same: Theresa Hak Kyung Cha's *Dictée*." In *Feminist Measures: Soundings in Poetry and Theory*, edited by Lynn Keller and Cristanne Miller, 43–68. Ann Arbor: University of Michigan Press.

Part II Moving with and beyond Intersectionality

4   Beyond the "Logic of Purity"

"Post-Post-Intersectional" Glimpses
in Decolonial Feminism

Anna Carastathis

This chapter examines Lugones's germane and insightful attempt to theorize "intermeshed oppressions," which, she argues, have been (mis)represented in women of color feminisms by the concepts of "interlocking systems of oppression" and, more recently, "intersectionality." The latter, intersectionality, introduced by Black feminist legal scholar Kimberlé Crenshaw as a metaphor (1989) and as a "provisional concept" (1991), has become the predominant way of referencing the mutual constitution of what have been theorized as multiple systems of oppression, constructing the multiplicity of social identities. But Lugones's analysis, which maintains subtle but important distinctions among the concepts of "intermeshed," "interlocking," and "intersecting" oppressions, shows that intersectionality theory often conflates fragmentation with multiplicity, and—by reifying "intersectional identities"—reproduces social-ontological fragmentation at the political and perceptual-cognitive levels of representation. Intersectional accounts redeploy unitary categories (e.g., race, gender, class, sexuality, disability) that are defined to the exclusion of each other by privileging the identities of normative group members. Consequently, they remain within what Lugones calls the "logic of purity," which erases "curdled," impure, category-transgressive, border-dwelling, mestiza subjects. Although, according to Lugones, intersectionality enables us to discern how the logic of purity produces "women of color" as impossible beings, she argues that the liminal identities of subjects dwelling in categorial interstices can be made visible only by conceptualizing oppressions as fused or "intermeshed." However, as I interpret her, Lugones is not merely criticizing intersectionality or seeking to transcend its conceptual limitations by proposing an alternate concept. Rather, the concepts of "intermeshed," "interlocking," and "intersecting" oppressions do significantly different work in her account and illuminate different aspects of the social ontology, phenomenology, and epistemology of resistance to oppression.

First, I situate Lugones with respect to the current conjuncture in intersectionality studies, in which some scholars are calling for a post-intersectional turn. Then, I reconstruct Lugones's complex account of intermeshed oppressions, interlocking oppressions, and intersectionality. Finally, I discuss the status of intersectionality in the shift in Lugones's work from "women of color feminisms" to "decolonial feminism." Intersectionality is now routinely invoked as a representational theory of multiple identities, but Lugones's heterodox interpretation helps us to see that it is best understood as a *critique* of representations based on the logic of purity: specifically, of how categorial axes of oppression (mis)represent intermeshed oppressions. Lugones's triadic distinction (intersecting/interlocking/intermeshed) points toward a provisional usage of intersectionality, namely, to diagnose the fragmentation of social experiences of multiplicity (which, I would argue, is more consistent with the concept's original aims). In her visionary philosophy, which attempts to theorize resistance against the grain of fragmentation from a conceptual space outside of the "logic of purity," we find "glimpses" of a nonfragmented account of oppression, and praxical possibilities for liberatory, decolonial feminist coalitions.

POST-POST-INTERSECTIONALITY

In the quarter-century since the publication of Crenshaw's work, intersectionality has been "mainstreamed" and "institutionalized" in the interdisciplinary field of "intersectionality studies" and in international human rights and state discourses (Dhamoon 2011; Nash 2014). While intersectionality's ascendancy has been celebrated, a recent wave of critical engagement offers reasons to regard the institutionalization of intersectionality with a dose of "analytic skepticism" (Bilge 2013; Nash 2010). Increasingly, calls to "go beyond intersectionality" question the adequacy of the metaphor to the complexities of lived experiences; critique the concept's reliance on and reproduction of ossified identity categories; and problematize the epistemic violence inherent in the appropriation and commodification of Black feminists' intellectual labor in the simultaneous fetishization and erasure of Black women within "intersectionality studies" (Kwan 2002; Nash 2008, 2010, 2011, 2014; Puar 2007).[1]

While some criticisms of intersectionality's deployments are well taken, the post-intersectional move arguably makes a critical error: it reduces intersectionality to the predominant, positivist interpretation of the concept, evading a close reading of Crenshaw's work. Specifically, most proponents of intersectionality *and* many post-intersectional critics routinely ignore that Crenshaw proposed intersectionality as a "provisional concept," conceding, at the outset, its inherent limitations. While intersectionality admittedly engages dominant assumptions that race and gender are essentially separate categories, its ultimate goal is to disrupt the cognitive habit of seeing them as mutually exclusive or even separable (Crenshaw 1991, 1244–45n9). However, as intersectionality was mainstreamed and institutionalized, it was heralded as *just that* methodology which, by theorizing the co-synthesis of multiple axes of oppression, overcomes unitary models that falsely separate them. Indeed, Robyn Wiegman characterizes intersectionality as "*the* primary figure of political completion in U.S. identity knowledge domains" (2012, 240). Celebrants of intersectionality evacuate the provisionality of the concept while extolling the "arrival" of feminism at a postracial, inclusionary telos. Critical attempts to "go beyond intersectionality" fail to grapple with its role in effecting the *conceptual transition* between essentialist, analytically discrete categories and a nonfragmented account.

In a recent lecture, Crenshaw expressed a "hope and an aspiration" for "a neo-intersectionality, a post-post-intersectionality, an erasure-of-the-'post'-intersectionality," based on a recognition of the fact that, "if anything, we are pre-intersectional" (2014). In this chapter, I attempt to read Lugones's work in relation to the present conjuncture in intersectionality theory, showing how her deflationary approach to intersectionality that critically assesses the scope of the concept—as opposed to mobilizing the term (often anachronistically) as a "catch-all" for *any* integrative theory of multiple oppressions—will yield greater analytical clarity and open a broader epistemic space for the articulation and appreciation of the diversity of historical and contemporary Black feminisms, women of color feminisms, and decolonial feminisms.

INTERMESHING/INTERLOCKING/INTERSECTING

It is surprising that Lugones's layered contributions to intersectionality scholarship have not been thoroughly analyzed.[2] I say that her thought is "layered" because, surveying Lugones's oeuvre, I discern at least three levels to her efforts to conceptually and practically transcend the fragmenting effects of what she calls "the logic of purity." First, Lugones proposes a distinction between intermeshed and interlocking oppressions, which corresponds to the ontological difference between multiplicity and fragmentation in her account. Lugones argues (particularly in her later work) that the concept of interlocking oppressions—an antecedent concept to "intersectionality" introduced (at least in print) by the Combahee River Collective in *A Black Feminist Statement* (1978)—disguises multiplicity and fragments oppressed groups and individuals (TSC 223–24). However, this does not mean that "interlocking oppressions" is a "bad concept": Lugones clarifies that it is "not merely an ideological mechanism, but the training of human beings into homogeneous fragments" (224). In other words, "interlocking" does capture one aspect of the functioning of oppression—the categorial fragmentation of multiplicitous heterogeneity into discrete, homogenized social groups, which entails the simultaneous erasure, reduction, and hypostatization of difference as a threat to unity, sameness, and identity. If the interlocking of oppressions names a material process based on a logic of purity through which multiplicity is reduced to fragmentation, it also conceals the functioning of intermeshed oppressions that are concretely, simultaneously experienced by "curdled beings" but that are cognitively distorted through categorial politics that divide, select, and prioritize among them.

At the second level of her analysis, Lugones argues that "interlocking oppressions" and "intermeshed oppressions" function jointly, creating "a conceptual maze that is very difficult to navigate" (TSC 224). Intermeshed oppressions are misrepresented as interlocking, both by systems of domination and by social movements that "contest univocally along one axis of domination" (222); "everywhere we turn we find the interlocking of oppressions disabling us from perceiving and resisting oppressions as intermeshed" (224), mystifying the fact that oppressed people's lives and struggles are interconnected.

Finally, at the third level of the analysis, Lugones offers a "theory of resistance to both the interlocking of oppressions and to intermeshed oppressions" (TSC 208). Lugones refuses to "mythify territorial enclosures and purities of peoples, languages, traditions" (220); rather, she traces dwellings in heterogeneous, subaltern, "resistant worlds of sense" and crossings back and forth from these to dominant worlds. In Lugones's view, oppressions function materially in a dual way: on the one hand, oppressions are intermeshed—through a historical process of "persistently violent domination that marks the flesh multiply by accessing the bodies of the unfree in differential patterns devised to constitute them as the tortured materiality of power" (HGS 188). On the other hand, this multiplicity itself is suppressed or fractured through unitary if interlocking systems which fix, isolate, and determine subjects through objectifying processes. It is important to notice that interlocking oppressions constitute both a process of systemic fragmentation and antisystemic resistance; the fragmentation and dissimulation of intermeshed oppressions by analyses and activisms that rely on the concept of interlocking (or, for that matter, unitary) oppressions is part of the process through which curdled beings are relegated to margins, to intersections or interstices, to spaces of social invisibility.

If intermeshed oppressions and interlocking oppressions collaborate to fix, reduce, and injure, what is the role of intersectionality in Lugones's theory of resistance? Interestingly, in many places, the word *intersection* appears to signify the "crossings between worlds of sense" (ED 197, 201; TSC 220). For instance, Lugones writes: "sometimes it is levels in the sense of meanings that erase other meanings, which, in turn, seek an intersection to find a worldly voice" (IP 3). The intersection—constituted by the logic of purity, of domination—enables the (mis)communication of meanings generated in resistant worlds of sense, but not without distortion, erasure, and reduction. In another usage that invokes the spatial terrain of Crenshaw's intersection metaphor (1989, 149), Lugones asks us to "visualize … a map that has been drawn by power in its many guises. Your life has been spatially mapped by power. Your spot lies at the intersection of all the spatial venues where you may, must, or cannot live or move" (IP 8). Lugones is clear that at the intersection constituting one's social location there is "no 'you' there" except "as thoroughly constructed by power"; accordingly, "you may not go there in resistance to domination" (9). This spatially mapped intersection cognizes and admits only the ascriptive dimensions of identity as understood through the dominant logic. In Crenshaw's original use of the intersection metaphor, this logic was embodied in juridical frameworks that precluded the remedying of discrimination in cases where the plaintiff's identity was not marked by the relative privileges of whiteness and masculinity. In other words, the categories deployed in antidiscrimination law reproduce rather than undermine privilege, precisely through fragmenting the "multidimensionality of Black women's experiences" of discrimination using mutually exclusive categories which rely on whiteness and maleness to define "normative" experiences of discrimination that exclude Black women by design (Crenshaw 1989, 140, 148).

Lugones's interpretation of the "intersection" metaphor seems to restore it to its original meaning in Crenshaw's 1989 essay, liberating it from the positivist significations that it has subsequently acquired. Lugones rejects a positivist, identitarian deployment of *intersectionality* that reifies axes of identity, constructing the intersection as the site of a politics of location for multiply oppressed subjects. Black women, on this view, are purported to have "intersectional identities" made visible by an intersectional politics. However, Lugones argues that their intersection does not *represent* women of color; rather, given the logic of purity informing the categorial construction of axes of "race" and "gender," the intersection functions as an index of their *invisibility*. She concludes, "once intersectionality shows us what is missing, we have ahead of us the task of reconceptualizing the logic of the intersection," to "perceive gender and race as intermeshed or fused" so "that we actually see women of color" (ED 193). Intersectionality is not the theoretical solution to intermeshed and interlocking oppressions (as it is generally re-presented), the arrival of an inclusive feminism, or the paradigm case of political completion; rather, in showing us what is missing, it constitutes the point of departure for a liberatory, coalitional project of decolonizing gender (HGS, TDF). Lugones reads the intersection as a space of violent reduction, of invisibility, and of desubjectification. However, this categorial invisibility is made visible through the intersection of "pure" categories; in that sense, intersectionality constitutes an important intervention.

MULTIPLICITY/FRAGMENTATION

To better understand Lugones's intervention in intersectionality theory, we must briefly explain her ontological concepts of multiplicity, impurity, and "curdling." Lugones articulates a critique of the logic of purity from the perspective of being (and being among and aligned with) "mestizaje, of curdled beings" (PIS 126). Rejecting a holist ontology based on a logic of purity that assumes that, fundamentally, "there is unity underlying multiplicity" (126), Lugones offers an impure logic of curdling, according to which "the social world is complex and heterogeneous and each person is multiple, nonfragmented, embodied" (127). While holism is often taken to entail a commitment to anti-reductionism, or to nonseparability, Lugones argues that "fragmentation is another guise of unity," so that "according to the logic of purity, the social world is both unified and fragmented, homogeneous, hierarchically ordered" (127). For something to be fragmented it has to be unified, one. Think of a pane of mirrored glass shattered into broken shards, which reflects an object in front of it only partially, distorting and occluding it. By contrast, think of a prism, which is inherently multiplicitous, but which diffracts light into its different constituent colors in a nonfragmented way.[3] Crucially, Lugones distinguishes between fragmentation and multiplicity as ontological conditions, and argues that while "fragmentation follows the logic of purity, multiplicity follows the logic of curdling" (PIS 126).

While "each person is multiple, nonfragmented, embodied," multiplicity is "trained" "into fragmented unities" (128). To say that one is "fragmented" means that one's "parts" lie in "pieces," and that these "parts ... do not fit well together," or are "taken for wholes," so that one becomes a "composite, composed of parts of other beings, composed of imagined parts, composed of parts produced by a splitting imagination, composed of parts produced by subordinates enacting their dominators' fantasies" (127). The fragmentation of oppressed individuals and groups results from the "politics of marginalization," which through the erasure of nonnormative members of social groups falsely homogenize and universalize the essentialized experiences of normative members (140). From the point of view of the logic of purity that presupposes unity as a naturalized ontological condition, multiplicity and fragmentation are often conflated; but Lugones argues that multiplicity—the existence of multiple realities—is *erased* through social fragmentation. This is crucial to the distinction Lugones draws between interlocking and intermeshed oppressions, and to the possibilities for collective resistance intimated by each concept. Lugones relates purity/fragmentation and impurity/multiplicity to two distinct kinds of separation, which we can understand both in ontological (descriptive) and political (normative) terms: these are split-separation (maintaining the boundaries of a pure category) and curdle-separation (coalescence in and through differentiation). The distinction between these two meanings of separation came to Lugones in a dream of "mayonnaise curdling," which recalled a childhood memory of her gender "ambiguity," her "standing in the middle of either/or" (IP 34). She explains that "mayonnaise is an oil-in-water emulsion," inherently "unstable":

> When an emulsion curdles, the ingredients become separate from each other. But that is not altogether an accurate description: rather, they coalesce toward oil or toward water, most of the water becomes separate from most of the oil—it is, instead, a matter of different degrees of coalescence. The same with mayonnaise; when it separates you are left with yolky oil and oily yolk. (PIS 122)

The impure, curdle-separation that results in "different degrees of coalescence" of "yolky oil and oily yolk" differs in kind from that mode of separation that aims at splitting something into discrete, pure parts (for instance, separating the white from the yolk of an egg). Educated into categorial thinking, we are habituated into thinking of separation in the latter sense of split-separation, but Lugones offers the concept of "curdling separation," or "mestizaje" (mixing) as a form of impure resistance to social fragmentation (122–23). Rejecting an ontology in which sameness precedes difference, and unity precedes fragmentation, Lugones argues that the impure, curdled state of multiplicity is the original state; yet multiplicity is not conceptualized in terms of "pure parts" (123). Rather, Lugones enjoins her readers to "superimpose" the "world of *mestizaje*, of curdled beings" onto "the conceptual world of purity" in order "to see ambiguity," to "see that the split-separated are also and simultaneously curdled-separated" (PIS 126).

(MIS)REPRESENTATION

If "multiplicitous subjects are rendered anomalous by unity" (PIS 133), they are "trained" by the logic of purity into fragmented, distorted versions of themselves, "altered to fit within the logic of unification"—or, what amounts to the same thing, they are "split over and over in accordance with the relevant dichotomies of the logic of unity" (133). According to Lugones, "the interlocking of oppressions is a central feature of the process of social fragmentation," which "requires not just shards or fragments of the social, but that each fragment be unified, fixed, atomistic, hard-edged, internally homogeneous, bounded, repellent of other equally bounded and homogeneous shards" (TSC 232n1). Intermeshed oppressions are misrepresented as interlocking—as constituted through pure categories of identity that define one in terms of race, gender, sexuality, nation, class, disability, and species—but "representation" is not merely an ideological process. Intermeshed oppressions are socially, discursively constructed—by systems of dominance and by single-axis social movements—as separable, distinct phenomena, affecting discrete groups with divergent political agendas. In other words, the interlocking of oppressions obscures the simultaneity of experiences of multiple, intermeshed oppressions, and dissimulates the necessity of contesting and resisting multiple oppressions simultaneously. The very fact that we conceptualize oppressions as interlocking presupposes the fragmentation of simultaneous experiences of "multiple oppressions." In "Tactical Strategies of the Streetwalker/ *Estrategias Tácticas de la Callejera*," Lugones more fully develops the qualitative distinction between intermeshed and interlocking oppressions:

> [O]ppressions interlock when the social mechanisms of oppression fragment the oppressed both as individuals and collectivities. Social fragmentation in its individual and collective inhabitations is the accomplishment of the interlocking of oppressions. Interlocking is conceptually possible only if oppressions are understood as separable, as discrete, pure. Intermeshed oppressions cannot be cogently understood as fragmenting subjects either as individuals or as collectivities. Thus, the interlocking of oppressions is a mechanism of control, reduction, immobilization, disconnection that goes beyond intermeshed oppressions. It is not merely an ideological mechanism, but the categorial training of human beings into homogeneous fragments is grounded in a categorial mind frame. Interlocking is possible only if the inseparability of oppressions is disguised. The politics of disguising intermeshed oppressions through interlocking discrete fragments of subjected subjects, are disabling. (TSC 223–24)

Lugones's point is not just the semantic objection to the prefix "inter-" in *interlocking* which, as Marilyn Frye apparently insisted to Lugones, implies "two entirely discrete things... that articulate with each other" (PIS 146n1), but whose articulation "does not alter the monadic nature of the things interlocked" (TSC 231–32n1).[4] After all, Lugones concedes that *intermeshed*—which shares the same prefix—implies "still too much separability" (TSC 231–32n1). By offering *intermeshed oppressions* as a new term, Lugones is not trying to "one-up" the existing concept of "interlocking oppressions" and the theorists who invoke them. On the contrary, Lugones describes her reluctance "to give up the term because it is used by other women of color theorists who write in a liberatory vein about enmeshed oppressions" (PIS 146n1). Although in her earlier work she is searching for "better images" to render the simultaneity of multiple oppressions, as her thought progresses, I think she diagnoses different political conditions requiring different conceptualizations and resistances, to be signified by different terms. Otherwise, a sentence conveying the "recognition of the obscuring of oppressions as intermeshed by the interlocking of oppressions" would carry no semantic weight (IP 32). It is not just that "intermeshed oppressions" is a better concept for the same phenomenon that "interlocking oppressions" names; rather, "intermeshed oppressions" signifies an ontological, existential, and social condition of multiplicity that has been discursively and materially obscured through a systematic social process of material and conceptual fragmentation—that is, through the interlocking of oppressions.

In a sense, this is not a new claim; it could be interpreted as a heterodox elucidation of the Combahee River Collective's concept of "interlocking oppressions," the impetus for which was the contestation of social fragmentation in political movements through a radical act of curdle-separation as Black feminists. They write: "[I]t was our experience and disillusionment within these liberation movements, as well as experience on the periphery of the white male left, that led to the need to develop a politics that was antiracist, unlike those of white women, and antisexist, unlike those of Black and white men" (1978, 363). Oppressions were fragmented through their split-separation in mutually exclusive liberation movements that understood their political tasks as distinct and discrete of one another. Famously, in response to this fragmentation, the Combahee River Collective articulated as their "particular task the development of integrated analysis and practice based upon the fact that the major systems of oppression are interlocking. The synthesis of these oppressions creates the conditions of our lives" (362). The question is: Is the Collective's claim that oppressions interlock just the same claim as the experience of the simultaneity and synthesis of oppressions?[5] Does the concept of "interlocking oppressions" *reveal* or *conceal* the knowledge of "racial-sexual oppression which is neither solely racial nor solely sexual, such as, the history of rape of Black women by white men as a weapon of political repression" (365)? Could it be that in order to give this "integrated analysis" a proper name and a proper object, it was conflated with the claim that oppressions "interlock" (or, later, that they "intersect")?

As the project of developing "multi-axial" theories of oppression has been institutionalized under the banner of "intersectionality," the distinctions in the threefold definition of the concept that Crenshaw offers, not to mention the differences between concepts bearing the prefix "inter," have been flattened. Crenshaw distinguishes between "structural," "political" and "representational" intersectionality. *Structural intersectionality* refers to the qualitative differences in experiences produced by the structural location of women of color, "the ways in which the location of women of color at the intersection of race and gender makes our actual experience of domestic violence, rape, and remedial reform qualitatively different than that of white women" (1991, 1245). *Political intersectionality* describes the fact that, historically, feminist and antiracist politics in the United States "have functioned in tandem to marginalize issues facing Black women" (1245). Consequently, political struggles against oppression are fragmented: "women of color are situated within at least two subordinated groups that frequently pursue conflicting political agendas" (1252). Neither agenda is constructed around the experiences, needs, or political vision of women of color; to the extent that antiracism reproduces patriarchy, and feminism reproduces racism, women of color are asked to choose between two inadequate analyses, each of which "constitutes a denial of a fundamental dimension of our subordination" (1252). Finally, *representational intersectionality* concerns the production of images of women of color drawing on sexist and racist narratives, as well as the ways that critiques of these representations marginalize or reproduce the objectification of women of color (1283). The most frequently invoked aspect of Crenshaw's threefold definition of intersectionality is structural intersectionality, which is generally construed as a descriptive claim about social location at the convergence of various systemic axes of oppression and is assumed (in true positivist fashion) to have causal priority over political and representational dimensions of intersectionality. However, one implication of Lugones's unique use of the term *interlocking* in contrast to *intermeshed* to describe oppressions is that the phenomenon that Crenshaw terms "political intersectionality"—the fact that liberation movements have functioned in tandem to exclude women of color—is not just an epiphenomenal manifestation of "structural intersectionality," or of identities too "complex" to be represented by extant political discourses. Instead, political intersectionality constitutes part of the causal history of structural intersectionality, a location of social invisibility that we might characterize as "liminal." In other words, although it is usually assumed that political intersectionality follows from structural intersectionality—that the multiple identities of women of color are too "complex" to be adequately represented by the available political discourses—Lugones's distinction between fragmentation and multiplicity helps us see that anti-oppressive discourses that contest only one form of oppression fragment multiplicity at the individual and at the group level, and in the process produce "intersectional" identities.

> If oppressions intermesh but are represented as interlocking, oppressed people are categorically lumped together and categorically broken from each other. Then, if the resistances are not going to follow the logic of representation—a logic tied to purity as an instrument of social control—the resisters must be ready to intervene in the categorial separations and the categorial lumping together of peoples in a struggle to connect with each other. (IP 3)

The theory of representation that underlies this claim is not a correspondence theory, in which reality exists outside representation and is variously well or badly reflected in it. Instead, Lugones's account offers a richly materialist conception of representation that enables us to make sense of the claim that group and individual identities are historically formed through the discursive production of what are represented as discrete social groups. Thus, since interlocking oppressions *both* perceptually/cognitively *and* materially fragment social reality, identities, and experiences of intermeshed oppressions, the concept of "interlocking oppressions" *both* adequately describes certain material phenomena of oppression *and* misrepresents oppression, in its intermeshedness.

A further distinction Lugones makes between "transparent" and "thick" members of groups helps us understand and intervene in the processes of "categorial lumping and breaking" that result in social fragmentation. "Transparent" group members are those who perceive themselves as paradigmatic of the group, a perception that is generally confirmed and "becomes dominant or hegemonical in the group" (PIS 140). By contrast, "thick" group members are those who are made aware of their "otherness," of being outsiders within a group, and who are continually relegated to the margins in intragroup politics (140). The false universalization of "transparent" members' interests as representative of the entire group marginalizes "thick" members "through erasure." The consequence is that "thick members of several oppressed groups become composites of the transparent members of those groups" (140). Thus, Lugones identifies an "insidious dialectic" (141) between the fragmentation of individuals and groups:

persons are fragmented because society is fragmented into homogenized groups that are constructed as pure. Every group is structured through a normative affiliation to its transparent members. This structure of affiliation fragments persons who are torn in several different directions to separate groups; importantly, however, identification with curdled, thick members is foreclosed through this process of collective and individual identity formation. The exclusions of thick members based on the logic of purity "cross-fertilize" the disconnection of oppressions (141). In other words, a dialectic process of fragmentation at the individual and group level results in the material phenomenon of interlocking oppressions and disjointed resistances, precisely because groups are imagined as the homogeneous, collective personifications of the identities of their normative, "transparent" members. To the extent that monistic oppressions based on race, class, gender, disability, nation, citizenship, religion, sexuality, or species are viewed as the reflections of the experiences of "transparent" subjects, their interlocking dissimulates the intermeshed oppressions based on the "prismatic identities" (López 2014) of "thick" subjects. Lugones reaches a very important normative conclusion about the politics of representation: unless we reconceptualize groups as "embracing a non-fragmented multiplicity" the representation of ostensible "group interests" will not actually benefit most group members, since these interests reflect only "transparent" members, whose very identities "embody the marginalization of thick members and contain their fragmentation" (PIS 141).

INTERSECTIONALITY AND DECOLONIAL FEMINISM

Lugones's explicit critique of the prevailing understanding of intersectionality is that it reproduces the "categorial separation" of categories based on the invisibility of women of color (HGS 192–93). Rather than making our experiences visible, as has been widely imputed to intersectionality, the intersection of these categories reveals the failure of representation—the absence of concepts adequate to the lived experience of simultaneous oppression(s).[6] In "Heterosexualism and the Colonial/Modern Gender System," Lugones continues to insist on the distinction between the intersection and the intermeshing of oppressions and writes,

> Intersectionality reveals *what is not seen* when categories such as gender and race are conceptualized as separate from each other ... the logic of categorial separation distorts what exists at the intersection, such as violence against women of color.... So, once intersectionality shows us what

is missing, we have ahead of us the task of reconceptualizing the logic of the intersection so as to avoid separability. It is only when we perceive gender and race as intermeshed or fused that we actually see women of color. (HGS 192–93; emphasis added)

While this may be read simply as a critique of intersectionality, I think it is more productive to view it as a heterodox interpretation, which delimits the scope and intent of the concept to reveal the theoretical and political work that still lies ahead, an interpretation not inconsistent with Crenshaw's own characterization of intersectionality as a provisional concept in her early work. In this respect, my reading of Lugones differs from Ann Garry's and Kathryn Gines's respective assessments of her analysis of intersectionality. Garry places intersectionality on a spectrum with Lugones's concept of the colonial/modern gender system, arguing that, as conceptualizations that aim to "make women of color visible," they each participate to different extents in the logics of purity and impurity (2012, 508–10). Garry seems to reject Lugones's critique that intersectionality commits categorial separations that render visible the *invisibility* of women of color because, Garry contends, intersectionality's intervention into categorial thinking has changed the nature of the categories in question (510). Specifically, she argues intersectionality has decisively undermined an "essentialist" understanding of categories of oppression, even if they are not quite "as impure as Lugones desires" (510). In fact, Garry disputes any necessary connection between intersectionality and the logic of purity. Since it can simultaneously be useful "within both curdled and pure logics," paired with a family resemblance theory of categories, Garry advocates preserving intersectionality. Given Lugones's abiding concern with fragmentation, it seems a bit odd that Garry indicts her decolonial account of intermeshed oppressions on these grounds, arguing that the thesis that the colonial/modern gender system produces multiple (as opposed to binary) racialized genders "promotes fragmentation" (513). I think that Garry's interpretation—apparently motivated by a desire for a singular, unified (if heterogeneous) category of "women" who "share a gender" as the ground for feminist politics (516)—conflates multiplicity with fragmentation, and for the same reason, does not fully appreciate the distinction between intermeshed and interlocking oppressions.

Something similar could be said about Gines's analysis, who concedes that "some may interpret Lugones to be taking a position against intersectionality," but contends that "her uses of concepts like multiplicity, mestizaje, curdled, impure, and intermeshed" are "compatible with concepts like intersectionality, matrices of domination, and interlocking systems of oppression"

(2012, 11). Like Garry, Gines attempts to recuperate the concept of intersectionality against criticisms that have been levied against it; but in the process, she flattens important theoretical differences between the concepts of interlocking, intersecting, and intermeshing oppressions that, particularly in her later work, Lugones is careful to differentiate and deploy with specific purpose. For Lugones, as I read her, intersectionality fails precisely at giving an account of the concrete, interstitial social location that women of color occupy, and of the intermeshed oppressions that construct this location—but this "failure" is precisely its function as a provisional concept.

The question, it seems to me, is whether intersectionality—for Lugones, but also for Crenshaw—constitutes a representational theory of identity, or whether it functions as a critique of representations using categorial axes of oppression. In "Toward a Decolonial Feminism," Lugones indicates the latter, arguing that

> modernity organizes the world ontologically in terms of atomic, homogeneous, separable categories. If *woman* and *black* are terms for homogeneous, atomic, separable categories, then their intersection shows us the absence of black women rather than their presence. (TDF 742)

The intersection of unitary categories fashioned through the logic of purity reveals that they render multiplicity invisible. Insofar as it preserves these categories, intersectionality anticipates and illuminates the task of conceptual transformation and "impure resistance"; but it does not entirely transcend colonial/modern cognitive limitations. Nevertheless, intersectionality reveals something important: inasmuch as we are trained into perceiving and thinking through the logic of purity, we are not habituated into seeing race and gender as "intermeshed or fused." To the extent that multiple oppressions are understood through "pure" concepts and resisted through interventions that "contest univocally along one axis of domination" (TSC 222), social movements contribute to social fragmentation at least as much as they combat it. A "dichotomizing imagination" is "one impelled by the need to control or by the internalization of domination" (ED 196). By contrast, "impure" perception resists the effects of domination on the imagination by disrupting dichotomies (196).

Identifications, affinities, and alliances are neither natural nor inevitable, but have to be forged through coalitional, curdled, impure resistance (198). For curdled beings, thick members of fragmented groups, who are vulnerable to erasure, it is particularly important to reimagine their affiliations that are normatively directed toward transparent members, and away from other curdled subjects, both within and outside their ascribed identity groups (PIS 143). "The fragmentation of perception disempowers our resistance by making deep coalitions logically impossible," writes Lugones (BP 160). She interprets coalition as a horizon of meaning that orients us toward possible alignments, identifications, and solidarities (IP ix). Lugones's methodological shift from women of color feminisms to a decolonial feminism in her recent work radicalizes her insights about curdled, coalitional, impure resistance to the violences of fragmentation and multiple oppressions that she articulates throughout her oeuvre (TDF 746). Defining decolonial feminism as "the possibility of overcoming the coloniality of gender," that is, "racialized, capitalist gender oppression" (747), Lugones describes it as a "movement toward coalition that impels us to know each other as selves that are thick, in relation, in alternative socialites, and grounded in tense, creative inhabitations of the colonial difference" (748).

If women of color feminisms have become nearly synonymous with an identitarian project of intersectionality, decolonial feminism unravels the historical production of racialized gendered identities. Lugones argues for a synthesis of an intersectional awareness of multiplicity that the colonial/modern logic of purity renders invisible through categorial fragmentation with a theorization of the coloniality of power (ED 188–89). Intersectionality, writes Lugones, remains useful "when showing the failures of institutions to include discrimination or oppression against women of color" (TDF 757n9). But the emphasis of a decolonial feminism shifts from explicating the logic of domination to perceiving both oppression ("the coloniality of gender") and resistance ("the colonial difference at the fractured locus") that women of color, indigenous women "fluent in native cultures," and colonized women embody (758n9). In this respect, decolonial feminism advances Lugones's abiding concern with the generative tension between oppressing ←→ resisting that conditions active subjectivity, as well as her epistemological commitment to liberatory theory—for even when we "unravel... the logic of the oppressor's gaze" and "discover its irrationality we are not on our way towards a resistant subjectivity. That requires a different logic" (BP 156). If intersectionality reveals an absence constructed in and through the logic of purity, the concept of intermeshed oppressions seeks to make visible those liminal existences violently disarticulated by the dominant logic.

One of the challenges that Lugones issues to her readers in "worlds of resistance" is that we must "get ready to intervene at the level of meaning" (IP 3). She writes that "the question of inter- and intraworld communication is central" and made difficult by domination, which "fragments the social" and undermines resistance through the enactment of "power differentials, collaborations and betrayals" in the process of "resistant sense-making" (IP 26). One of the most courageous aspects of Lugones's thought, to my mind, is that in intervening at the level of meaning, she has "little expectation of being understood": her creative practices of meaning-making are deliberatively "tentative," exceed a "common language" and "common expectations," and refuse refuge in a "comfortable womb-warm sense of safety and of having come home" (TSC 229). Uncertainty, risk, and tentativeness form part of the terrain of conceptual and social transformation, which offers no guarantees of legibility, reciprocity, or safety; for a curdled being looking for company, it can be an epistemologically lonely road.

Until fairly recently, few sustained critiques of intersectionality existed, and arguably those that were raised were unconvincing from the point(s) of view of women of color feminisms (assuming, for instance, the genericity of whiteness and other bases of privilege in the construction of gendered identity).[7] The relative absence of critiques of intersectionality was, in my view, symptomatic of a superficial, if celebratory engagement. However, given the paucity of antiracist commitment within mainstream feminism, it is not clear how one ought to critique intersectionality, or whether it is timely to seek to go "beyond" it. Indeed, if intersectionality signals the need for a *conceptual transition* between essentialist, categorially discrete concepts that fragment oppressions, then the call to "go beyond" intersectionality is premature. For this reason, it seems to me that there is something utopian about "post-intersectionality," and Lugones advises us not to think what we "cannot practice" (IP 5), but rather to "live differently in the present, to think and act against the grain of oppression" (5). Honing our resistant perception against our being tortured "into simple fragmented identities" opens up a space for "rearranging one's own identity, for making the complexity of one's own subjectivity explicit, for articulating it, for making it public" (MSR 50–52). Intermeshed oppressions, violently forged through a colonial/modern gender system, are interlocked through categorial and social fragmentation, a process that the multiply oppressed, curdled being, the "streetwalker theorist" concretely "comes to understand through a jarring vivid awareness of being broken into fragments" (TSC 231). Lived experience also discloses "that the encasing by particular oppressive systems of meaning is a process one can consciously and critically resist with uncertainty," through a collective, decolonial coalitional praxis, or one "to which one can passively abandon oneself" (231), dwelling invisibly in a deadly intersection.

NOTES

1. On this last point also see Alexander-Floyd, who does not position herself as a "post-intersectional" theorist, but diagnoses a "post-black feminist approach... on intersectionality within the social sciences... that disappears or re-marginalizes black women" and argues for a disruption of the "(neo)colonization of intersectionality by centering the voices of black women and other women of color" (2012, 9, 1, 19).

2. Two important exceptions are Garry (2012, 504–10) and Gines (2012, 11–14).

3. I borrow the terms of this example from Leonard López (2014) who uses the metaphors of the mirror and the prism to describe Lugones's account of the fragmentation of identity into identities, and offers the notion of "prismatic identity" to capture the inherent multiplicity of the gay Chicano subject who is categorially fragmented through hate crimes law that cannot cognize the dimensions of injuries "based" on his multiplicitous identity.

4. In these two notes, Lugones paraphrases Frye's objection to the term *interlocking*, presumably made in personal communication.

5. "We also often find it difficult to separate race from class from sex oppression because in our lives they are most often experienced simultaneously" (Combahee River Collective 1978, 365).

6. Interestingly, Lugones writes that she was alerted to the need to address the "categorial separation" reproduced by intersectionality in part by its apparent inadequacy to "arouse in those men who have themselves been targets of violent domination and exploitation any recognition of their complicity or collaboration with the violent domination of women of color" (HGS 188).

7. The false universalization of relatively privileged ("transparent") group members' experiences of oppression as definitive of the entire group proceeds through the construction of such experiences as "generic," "essential," or "unmodified," and of subordinated ("thick") members as "specific," "nuanced," "complex." This purported genericity or "invisibility" of privilege may come into relief, but is not displaced, through the intersection of categories of oppression and privilege that, in an important sense, through their mutual exclusion already negatively construct each other.

REFERENCES

Alexander-Floyd, Nikol G. 2012. "Disappearing Acts: Reclaiming Intersectionality in the Social Sciences in a Post-Black Feminist Era." *Feminist Formations* 24(1): 1–25.

Bilge, Sirma. 2013. "Intersectionality Undone: Saving Intersectionality from Intersectionality Studies." *Du Bois Review* 10(2): 405–24.

Combahee River Collective. 1978. "A Black Feminist Statement." In *Capitalist Patriarchy and the Case for Socialist Feminism*, edited by Zillah Eisenstein, 362–72. New York: Monthly Review Press.

Crenshaw, Kimberlé. 1989. "Demarginalizing the Intersection of Race and Sex: A Black Feminist Critique of Antidiscrimination Doctrine, Feminist Theory and Antiracist Politics." *University of Chicago Legal Forum* 140: 139–67.

———.1991. "Mapping the Margins: Intersectionality, Identity Politics, and Violence against Women of Color." *Stanford Law Review* 43(6): 1241–99.

Dhamoon, Rita Kaur. 2011. "Considerations on Mainstreaming Intersectionality." *Political Research Quarterly* 64(1): 230–43.

Garry, Ann. 2012. "Who Is Included? Intersectionality, Metaphors, and the Multiplicity of Gender." In *Out from the Shadows: Analytic Feminist Contributions to Traditional Philosophy*, edited by Sharon Crasnow and Anita Superson, 493–530. Cambridge: Oxford University Press.

Gines, Kathryn T. 2012. "The Politics of Intersectionality and the Import of Transnational and Decolonial Feminisms." Paper presented at the workshop on "Women's Movements and the Politics of Intersectionality: Colonial Legacies" XXII World Congress of the International Political Science Association, Madrid, July 8–12. Accessed June 2, 2014. paperroom.ipsa.org/papers/paper_21667.pdf

Kwan, Peter. 2002. "The Metaphysics of Metaphors: Symbiosis and the Quest for Meaning." *UMKC Law Review* 71: 325–30.

López, Leonard P. 2014. "Chicano *Mens*: Hate Crime, Coloniality, and the Critique of Rights." Master's Thesis, California State University, Los Angeles.

Nash, Jennifer C. 2014. "Institutionalizing the Margins." *Social Text* 32(1): 45–65.

———. 2011. "Practicing Love: Black Feminism, Love-Politics and Post-Intersectionality." *Meridians* 11(2): 1–24.

———. 2010. "On Difficulty: Intersectionality as Feminist Labor." *The Scholar and the Feminist Online* 8(3).

———. 2008. "Re-thinking Intersectionality." *Feminist Review* 89: 1–15.

Puar, Jasbir. 2007. *Terrorist Assemblages: Homonationalism in Queer Times*. Durham, NC: Duke University Press.

Wiegman, Robyn. 2012. *Object Lessons*. Durham, NC: Duke University Press.

5 Witnessing Faithfully and the Intimate Politics of Queer South Asian Praxis

Shireen Roshanravan

"You don't have to tell them," María explained to me, as I struggled at the edge of belonging to a family and community of origin who would read my political and sexual becomings as failure and betrayal. I felt a deep relief. I knew she did not mean that my family was not evolved enough to accept my queerness and that I needed to "hide" it for my own well-being. I heard María, instead, as I had come to know her as a faithful witness to the complexities constitutive of the worlds of meaning-making from which we each emerge and encounter others. No one is disposable in her visionary philosophy of liberation, and nothing can be presumed transparent in its presentation. In response to my worries about painful confrontations with family during obligatory journeys home, she encouraged me to "pay attention to how interesting they are" and bear witness to their modes of resisting daily lived oppressions. To love, in Lugones's deep coalitional praxis, is to commit to faithfully witnessing each other in our struggles and to identify each other as inextricable from our possibilities for liberation. This chapter is born of the many intimate conversations with María, as mentor, friend, and compañera, that allowed me to navigate what has often felt like the contradictory longing for both personal and political integrity.

Efforts to transform familial home places into sites of queer affirmation are central to queer South Asian diasporic cultural work.[1] Alok Vaid-Menon, former member of the now disbanded DarkMatter, a queer South Asian performance duo, describes "[o]ur turn toward our families of origin [as] part of a strategy of intimate organizing—a type of political work that ... suggests a commitment to a type of collective liberation and a practice of solidarity where we refuse to allow our people to be disposable in our movement work." Yet queer South Asian outreach efforts tend to emphasize a celebration of the "accepting" family who embraces their queer-identified children without giving equal attention to developing tools to help those with "unaccepting" family members preserve relationships with our families of origin.² For those with "unaccepting" families of origin, the message is often to take solace in our queer South Asian communities of choice. When juxtaposed against the narratives of "accepting" parents who have embraced their queer-identified children, painful testimonies of parental rejection can intensify the (internalized) hegemonic Western public perspective of the "unaccepting" South Asian parent as shameful, backward, or even monstrous. The focus on seeking and celebrating familial "acceptance" can thus unwittingly reproduce the colonial/modern framing of the "accepting/progressive/modern" versus the "unaccepting/backward/traditional" South Asian family. And this reproduction limits our work, contradicting the stated commitment of queer South Asian praxis to not leave our people behind in our movement work.

Addressing this limit in queer South Asian diasporic cultural work requires heeding Lugones's call for theorists, activists, and popular educators to attend more carefully to the communicative barriers to deep coalition (OC 76). The communicative work of deep coalition involves a commitment to "witness faithfully" (to hone our perception of) the unfamiliar resistant codes and constructions of those we presume to be familiar to us (IP 7). Lugones explains that "to witness faithfully, one must be able to sense resistance, to witness behavior as resistant, *even when it is dangerous, when that interpretation places one psychologically against common sense, or when one is moved to act against common sense, against oppression*" (7; emphasis added). Because it is about refusing to see others as wholly consumed by oppression, witnessing faithfully enables a way of loving rooted in and routed through identification with different journeys of resistance rather than identification with the shared misery of oppression. Witnessing faithfully our "unaccepting" parents thus requires an openness to reading them as enacting resistance to oppression, however ambiguously, *in their rejection of our queer/LGBT-identification*. Doing so disables the unwitting colonial/modern narrative that frames "unaccepting" parents as not-yet-evolved to love unconditionally in ways promoted among "accepting parents" who, in turn, are featured and celebrated by queer South Asian cultural and organizational work.³ The goal of witnessing faithfully rather than "seeking acceptance" shifts the focus of queer South Asian praxis away from a unidirectional finite project of changing our parents' attitudes. Instead, witnessing faithfully encourages a lifelong project of forging loving connections in a way that animates the interdependence of our (queer- and nonqueer-identified) collective well-being.

Witnessing faithfully, methodologically, relies on Lugones's central tenet of "complex communication." She identifies a misconception common among theorists of coalition that occludes rather than resolves communicative difficulties, namely, the assumption that all who are being oppressed ←→ resisting will be semiotically transparent to each other (OC 76–77). Suspending assumptions of semiotic transparency between the resistant codes of our elders and of our own, we can realize that the communicative efforts between us may carry more meaning than the content of what is actually said. For example, many queer South Asian organizations state that "seeking acceptance" is one of their primary goals. However, this goal of "seeking acceptance" interrupts complex communication because it presumes the transparency of an obvious "acceptability" of that for which one seeks acceptance (in this case queerness) as it becomes translated across worlds of sense. As Brinda Mehta theorizes, the Western emphasis on personal (individualist) choice readily translates as "fostering an amoral individualism that is at odds with the collective ethos" of South Asian diasporic worldviews (2004, 38–39). Presuming semiotic transparency of our resistant understandings of "queerness" rests on the assumption that our South Asian immigrant elders share our linguistic and historical domains of distinction to understand queer/LGBT-identification beyond its hegemonic celebration of individualist self-fashioning and personal choice.

Beyond elaborating the communicative obstacles inherent in the "acceptance" discourse, then, I attempt to illustrate potential avenues of complex communication illuminated in the shift to witnessing faithfully our "unaccepting" families of origin. I do so by witnessing faithfully my own mother's recurrent lamentation that she "raised a *hijra!*" This requires refusing colonial distortions of Indigenous *hijra* cosmologies that remain an occluded part of my mother's Indian English world of sense-making. Doing so allows me to hear her insulting use of *hijra* as inextricably tied to her sense that an emotional rejection of same-sex sexuality is essential to upholding respectable Indian diasporic womanhood and, relatedly, to preventing familial disintegration. This resistant connection between "respect" and a communally constituted self, in turn, enables a resistant understanding of Vega Subranamian's seemingly assimilative claim, "I'm not queer, I'm ordinary."[4] Known for her role as part of the first nonwhite couple to sue for same-sex marital rights, Subranamian reveals the communicative limits of *queer* to articulate her self-understanding as a same-sex-loving South Asian American woman committed to remaining a central participant in her own, and her wife's, family of origin. Finally, by threading an analysis of Subranamian's communicative strategies with those illustrated in the *Izzat* Collective's book, *Heartbeats: The Izzat Project* (2014), and Aparajeeta 'Sasha' Duttchoudhury and Rukie Hartman's collection, *Moving Truth(s): Queer and Transgender Desi Writings on Family* (2015), I suggest that complex communication in the queer South Asian diaspora reveals a culturally specific politics of love and respect conditional on what Gayatri Reddy (2007, 151) identifies in her study of hijra community formations in Hyderabad, India as a politics of "being there." This politics of love and respect counters Western/U.S. colonial-racial codes of liberal individualist (self-)respect and unconditional (self-)love and is inextricable from a queer South Asian praxis committed to not leaving our communities behind in our movement work.

MOVING BEYOND A SHARED SENSE OF ANGST AND GRIEF

In the summer of 2013, I attended the story-telling performance "Coming Out Muslim: Radical Acts of Love," which narrated the negotiations of two women's struggle of being both queer-identified and Muslim within their ethno-religious family and the pains and triumphs of learning to love themselves during these negotiations. Most of the audience members (if not the entire audience) were queer-identified South Asians. As the performance drew to a close, I found myself sobbing uncontrollably. I was not alone. The tearful wailing that gripped the room seemed to unsettle the performers who urged us to remember that *Allah* loves us for being queer and that being queer and Muslim is a gift. Two years later, I experienced a similar collective outpouring of grief during my participation in a workshop that included a performance by the *Izzat* Collective on South Asian daughters resisting familial pressures to conform to gender/sexual codes of honor and respect (what some South Asian communities refer to as "*izzat*"). The daughterly resistance performed in a brief skit intimated that leaving home, however painful, may be our only recourse and that the leaving did not preclude loving our families but rather affirmed our right to self-care and self-determination. Again, the audience, South Asian women of various ethno-religious backgrounds, many of whom were queer-identified, found ourselves tearfully sharing stories of familial loss after the performance. During a short question-and-answer session stifled by tears, one woman asked what strategies any of us had for helping our parents deal with their own traumas. No one had any to offer. The upshot, it seemed, was to take relief in the cathartic release of our shared grief.

Although comforted by those who could understand my tears and offer empathetic recognition of my pain, seeing my grief mirrored by other queer-identified and gender disobedient South Asians amplified the pain of our shared condition of familial loss to an almost unbearable level. Lugones helps make sense of this response when she cautions that, "to the extent that we face each other as oppressed ... we repel each other as we are seeing each other in the same mirror" (WT 85). Leaving familial home places, whether via expulsion/ostracism or the decision to flee under duress, did not resonate in either workshop space as a pathway to self-determination insofar as the freedom it offered did not alleviate the haunting of familial loss. Without uptake within our communities of place, individual queer re-signification of our ethno-religious familial home place (for example, the message that "being queer and Muslim is a gift") existed only in our imaginations or in the elsewhere of a queer South Asian counterpublic. In Lugones's terms, *community of choice* could not replace *community of place* in our yearnings for communally constituted selves, and identification with each other's grief, as victims of familial pressures, did not motivate further connection beyond the space of mourning.[5]

The expressions of grief I experienced with other queer-identified South Asians can also be witnessed in the testimonies describing the severe emotional and physical reactions of South Asian parents to the possibility of their children's nonheterosexual sexual identifications: threatening suicide, having heart attacks, experiencing nervous breakdowns, or even expressing preference for their child to be in an abusive marriage rather than in a same-sex relationship.[6] During ten years of participating in queer South Asian support groups, conferences, networks and organizational events, I have been consistently pained by the frequency of such testimonies and struck by the ways the descriptions of these parental reactions often echo the grief and pain experienced by their queer-identified children. If we take seriously these parental threats of suicide, we can question the communicative efficacy of mainstream U.S. celebrity-anchored public service announcements that implore nonqueer-identified family to accept queer-identified youth for who they are.[7]

Queer South Asian organizations that adopt the rhetoric of "accept us for who we are" tend to reproduce this unidirectional logic in which our "unaccepting" families of origin become the primary ones in need of emotional growth and shift in perspective. This framing legitimates the pains of the queer-identified as appropriate responses to their struggle with familial loss while concomitantly registering parents' severe responses to queer ruptures of family as condemnable cultural conservatism. The above anecdotes suggest that the communicative impasse between queer/LGBT-identified South Asians and our "unaccepting" families of origin emerges from a shared source of angst: fear that queer/LGBT-identification can disintegrate one's communal constitution of self. Fear of losing family can motivate queer-identified South Asians to retreat to queer (South Asian) communities of choice, to emphasize helplessness to change one's gender/sexual nonconformity and appeal to parental mercy, and/or to adopt a confrontational accept-me-or-fuck-you approach.[8]

These approaches, in turn, can reinforce parental fears of losing the participation of their children in modes of family-making that give them cultural meaning as dutiful South Asian mothers and fathers. Both queer-identified and non-queer-identified family share angst over the ways gender/sexual nonconformity can result in a loss of family and thus of a "self in community."[9] Understanding the different resistant orientations motivated by this shared angst of losing family can better prepare the communicative groundwork imperative to forging deep coalitional ties with our families of origin. We must therefore witness faithfully our families of origin in their emotionally charged rejections of our gender and sexual nonconformity. This requires suspending Eurocentric and liberal individualist assumptions permeating hegemonic translations of queer/LGBT-identification. Doing so allows us to explore culturally and historically specific conceptions of "self," "family," and "love" that can better illuminate resistant meaning-making among "unaccepting" families of origin.

CUTTING MOTHER TONGUES: HETEROPATRIARCHY IN (NEO)COLONIAL WORLDS OF INDIAN ENGLISH

Sonali Gulati's documentary film, *I Am*, foregrounds interviews with Indian parents who have come to accept their LGBT-identified children. The film also includes glimpses of Indian mothers' commonly phrased negative reactions to their LGBT-identified children. These reactions include statements like: "What will happen to all my marriage plans?" "It's not normal. It's not natural," "I don't want to hear anything about it," and "What's made you gay?" While these responses may not seem culturally specific, we cannot presume a monological translation across distinct cultural contexts just because the English wording of these statements is familiar to queer-identified Anglo children in an Anglo context. Indeed, it is significant that the majority of these responses are made in Indian English because, as Alton Becker makes clear, language shapes domains of distinction through which we make meaning and orient affectively in relation to others and the worlds we inhabit (1991).[10] The ethnocentric imperialist logics of U.S. homonationalism infuse the English world of sense from which *gay* and *lesbian* communicates inherent dissonance with one's family of origin and understands *freedom* in terms of a *freedom from* family, a literal coming out against the traditions, rituals, and codes of respect that ground its formation. If identification as gay or lesbian orients one toward the forgetting of a sexual self that is integrated with families and communities of origin, we can begin to hear the Indian mothers' "unaccepting" responses featured in Gulati's documentary as more than homophobic rejection or heteronormative denial. We can begin to hear them as animating a fear of communal disintegration, a refusal to tolerate queer rupture of their sense of self in community.

Let's begin with the frustrated maternal response to gay or lesbian identification that, as featured in Gulati's documentary, exclaims, "What will happen to my marriage plans?!" Rochona Majumdar has shown that the institution of "arranged marriage" endures, with variation, in India and its diaspora (2009, 240). She notes that the "joint family" remains the primary component of the institution of "arranged marriage" and, despite the modernizing focus on the couple, "subordinates the individual to the family" (240). While heteronormativity of white/Anglo culture also generates parental dreams and plans for their child's presumed marriage, the collectivist ethos of Indian cultural worldviews renders parental investment in the child's marriage more about maintaining the self in community via familial well-being and endurance. This is not an uncommon sentiment as revealed by the growth of Indian same-sex wedding ceremonies performed in ethno-specific religious traditions gaining publicity since the federal legalization of same-sex marriage. Within this specific cultural domain of Indian arranged marriage, the Indian mother (and other family) is supposed to be fully involved in the planning of her child's marriage and has as much at stake in fulfilling this familial obligation. Hearing that one's child is gay or lesbian in this context can translate readily to a loss of these marriage plans and, consequently, to a dismemberment of the family and her collective sense of self in relation to the family. In this regard, the exclamation, "What will happen to my marriage plans?!" can be understood as more than a selfish investment in seeing one's own heteronormative dreams fulfilled or homophobic disregard of one's child's desires.[11] We can also hear it as a decolonial yearning to hold on to one's collective sense of self as it emerges through fulfilling familial obligations and strengthening/growing the family (and self in community) itself.

The contradiction in a South Asian mother's decolonial yearning for a communally constituted self that manifests in the rejection of her queer/LGBT-identified child is born of colonial redefinitions of "civilized" family formation in heteropatriarchal terms. This redefinition reroutes decolonial yearnings for a self in community toward an investment in caste/race boundaries. These caste/race boundaries dismember community in the name of ethno-religious purity. Shefali Chandra's work demonstrates how English-language education and the production of properly consenting heterosexual subjects converged in colonial India to universalize caste restrictions and heteronormative definitions of Indian culture/nationalism. She explains how upper-caste Brahmans and commercially successful Parsis sought to discipline English (prevent its access to the lower-caste and lower-class or "other" Indian communities) by imbuing it with sexual mores suitable only to their women. By teaching/restricting English to their "idealized women" (chaste, married, devoted, conjugal), they were able to Indianize and secularize English without disturbing caste exclusivity. The Indian male elite justified restricting Indian English as the exclusive realm of upper-caste/class Indians, in part, by characterizing other Indian communities as lacking the heteropatriarchal sexual virtues to handle the individualist agency English language acquisition afforded.

Because the "civilizing" practice of companionate conjugal marriage at the heart of Indian English languaging must be circumscribed within heteropatriarchal endogamy, only those women deemed *civilized* enough to handle the power of choice endowed by English language acquisition could be trusted to *choose* within the appropriate caste/class and sexual boundaries.[12] According to this logic, queer-identified Indians would rupture the presumed evolutionary civilized discipline necessary to realize proper heteropatriarchal subjectivity because their queerness evidences a failure to choose sexual companions that are properly conjugal and reproductive of caste/race purity. Within the (neo)colonial worlds of Indian English, then, claiming and enacting same-sex romantic love throws into question one's "civilized capacity" to choose properly one's conjugal companion. Given this, we can witness faithfully the Indian mother's responses of "It's not normal. It's not natural," "What made you gay?" and "I don't want to hear anything about it," beyond homophobic hostility and incapacity to love unconditionally. Instead, we can attend to the ways her Indian English domains of distinction bestow a caste/class and racial civilizational superiority vis-à-vis the rest of the colonized that makes gay identification, in her world of sense-making, definitively unnatural (against biological destiny). As such, gay-identification is registered as an intentional individualist choice to disregard familial well-being and the fulfillment of one's obligations to the family (self in community).

MODEL-MINORITY INVESTMENTS IN "RELATIVE CULTURAL SUPERIORITY"

Colonial ideologies that seduce investment in fictions of relative superiority prepare upper-caste/upper-class Indian immigrants for uptake of the U.S. model-minority racial ideology. The model-minority racial project seduces Asians in the United States to invest in their state construction as culturally superior to other people of color while acquiescing to their relative subordination and vulnerability to white supremacy. Anannya Bhattacharjee especially reveals the gendered seduction of the logic of this racial project that defines the *relative* "cultural superiority" of Asians in terms of their tight-knit heteropatriarchal families (1999). As she explains, the model-minority racial project defines maleness, in addition to whiteness, as a marker for access to power. For upper-caste/class South Asian immigrant men for whom race/caste or class is not a marker of dehumanization in their postcolonial country of origin, the model-minority racial project offers a salve to the pains of their subordinating exclusion from whiteness in the United States. Because the model-minority racial project defines the *modelness* of Asians in terms of their tight-knit heteropatriarchal families, South Asian immigrant men who invest in model-minority racial ideologies can cope with their racial subordination vis-à-vis white peoples by affirming their power to exercise maleness over and against their own women. Such patriarchal collaborations can be understood not only as a complicit response to the pained sense of racial dehumanization endured in the white/Anglo dominated public domain, but also the consequent yearning to belong to a domestic/communal circle where one's humanity is unquestionably recognized and valued. Bhattacharjee explains how in the South Asian immigrant community, family and home space becomes this circle of belonging, and the figure of the "woman," especially the properly married wife/mother, becomes symbolic of its reproduction and preservation as a cultural refuge (1999, 234).

As erin Khuê Ninh notes, "subjects can and commonly do act as guardians of systems which do them fundamental disservice, and a mother may energetically support a patriarchy which oppresses all women in order that she herself or her own daughters may thrive within its rules, relative to other women" (2011, 129). Protecting the home space as cultural refuge is a tremendous weight to bear for the Indian immigrant woman. This cultural pressure, shaped by the model-minority racial project, offers important insight into how we might faithfully hear a mother's disbelief or refusal to hear of her child's sexual and gender disobedience. As the family member responsible for the reproduction of proper cultural etiquette, the mother is implicated in the potential collapse of the communal and familial refuge now, presumably, threatened by her child's gender and sexual disobedience.

Bhattacharjee thus offers an important amplification to Ninh's literary analysis of the model-minority racial project's psychic cost to Asian immigrant families in the United States. Ninh centers the second-generation Asian American daughter as the primary bearer of the psychic cost of this racial project while framing the immigrant parents as consumed by its capitalist logics. The parents' internalization of their racial positioning as model minorities, she suggests, moves them to participate in producing their daughters as the unfilial subject under constant threat of disownment and condemned to fail her immigrant parents' always-growing expectations of repayment for their sacrifice on her behalf. These parental expectations include the daughter's role in upholding familial honor. Upholding familial honor often requires obeying strict boundaries of "respectable" gender and sexual behavior that protect the daughter's marriageability against the inevitable community gossip mills (Ninh 2011, 142). Like Bhattacharjee, Ninh emphasizes the model-minority racial project as a heteropatriarchal mechanism of social control, but she attends less to the ways this social control enacts psychic violence on the entire family, however differentially, including the parents who participate in the mechanisms of control over their daughters. Bhattacharjee reminds us that immigrant parents from high caste/class positions in their home country also experience a psychic cost in their racialized naming as subordinate (becoming "not white" in the United States) and their yearning to heal their racial dehumanization within the space of family and community of origin.

Neither psychic cost is more worthy of attention, nor am I suggesting that psychic violence of racism justifies familial violence enacted against Asian American daughters. Rather, I am highlighting distinct wounds of racial/colonial dismemberment that shape differential journeys of resistance in which (neo)colonial and racial projects often reroute decolonial yearnings via promises of superficial relief in exchange for complicity in their oppressive logics. For the Indian immigrant bourgeoisie, Bhattacharjee explains, the yearning for an affirmed sense of self in community can reroute through an investment in the false invitation to become "model" or "almost-civilized" racialized subjects via "respectable" traditions of heteropatriarchal family formation. For the gender and sexually disobedient (and perhaps queer-identified) daughter, on the other hand, the decolonial yearning for wholeness can reroute through an investment in neoliberal individualist logics of agential self-fashioning as the freedom (and moral obligation) to love without conditions. The concepts of "respect/*izzat*" and "love" thus become contested terrain in their lack of semiotic transparency between queer-identified South Asians and their parents' worlds of sense-making forged through differential journeys of resistance.

Remembering these historical journeys of navigating oppression enables us to understand both immigrant elders and their children as "liminal subjects," active subjects who enact "resistance to particular forms of oppression at particular times in particular spaces" (OC 77). "Since," Lugones explains, "our journeys to the limen are different, often at odds, often in great tension given that we are among each other's oppressors, the freeing spaces where we attempt to chisel our own faces are not readily accessible to each other" (77). So, while the gender and sexually nonconforming children of immigrant South Asian parents may journey through worlds of understanding where they inhabit *queer* or *lesbian* as a liberatory space of community, it does not mean that our immigrant elders have access to this same world of resistant sense-making. Their resistant journeys are likely quite different; moreover, all journeys risk seduction into complicity with oppressive logics. However, as Lugones teaches us, complicity does not erase resistance even as it compromises its liberatory possibility. Without heeding Lugones's fundamental insight that we enact epistemic travel to each other's worlds of resistant sense-making, we cannot but hear/understand each other as antagonistic to our attempts at becoming whole integrated selves *in community*. Let's turn now to these differential journeys of resistance routed through cultural codes of (self-)respect/*izzat* and (un)conditional love.

HIJRA COSMOLOGIES AND OPAQUE CULTURAL CODES OF RESPECT/*IZZAT* AND LOVE

My mother's recurrent exasperation that she "raised a *hijra*!" to express her hurt and frustration at my failed heterosexuality invites an exploration of Indian ways of being that exceed Western modes of meaning-making. While these excess ways of being may be inarticulate beyond their disparaging colonial reductions, they can nevertheless provide insight into the affective modes of communication that relay meaning beyond what is actually said. The British colonial signification of *hijra* as an "uncivilized" indigenous *queer* (read: repulsively nonnormative and nonhuman) caste of unassimilable Indians occludes knowledge of hijra identity that can clarify the notions of respect informing South Asian immigrant familial responses to queer-identified family members. As "a potent and enduring cultural identity in the Indian universe" (Reddy 2006, 5), hijra worlds of sense-making become central to the act of complex communication between queer-identified South Asians and our ethno-religious communities to which we remain affectively tied.

Gayatri Reddy's delineation of "family" in hijra community formations of Hyderabad "complicate[s] our cultural understandings of 'choice' in the context of kin relations" and centers on a "notion of caring, indexed principally through a temporal (and spatial) dimension of 'being there'" (2005, 151). She explains this claim by comparing hijra kin relations with those described in Kath Weston's study of gay kinship ideologies in the United States, where "chosen family" is privileged over "blood family," with the latter a biogenetic given and the former generated through one's individual choosing/desire. While hijra kin relations, like Western LGBT formulations of family, are also not constructed through "blood" and marriage, "the central and only prescriptive bond in hijra conceptualizations of their family—the guru-cela bond—[is] not purely idiosyncratic, being more often assigned rather than chosen, and involve[s] far more structured obligatory responsibilities than the gay familial relationships described by Kath Weston" (151). A hijra becomes recognized as a "real" hijra after putting a *rit* in the house, or *gharana*, of a particular guru. As Reddy explains, "[t]he guru-cela relationship is the most important bond among hijras and is necessarily central to hijra conceptions of family. It is a mutually beneficial, reciprocal relationship, entailing both social and economic obligations and responsibilities for both parties" (156). Putting a *rit* in a *gharana* establishes hijra belonging to a family and larger community of hijras, and this belonging requires a commitment to fulfill obligations in an interdependent, reciprocal, and hierarchical kin relation that is fundamental to achieving *izzat*. Reddy illustrates the centrality of familial belonging in hijra subject formation, in part, through examples of hijras who suffered under their gurus yet, if given the option, would not elect the seeming freedoms of living with a marital partner beyond the obligations of hijra kinship structure (143).

While my mother's use of *hijra* as an insult invokes her implication in these worlds of British colonial distortion, the incredulous tone with which she would declare that she had "raised a *hijra*!" intimates an investment in the concept of "respect" that Reddy elaborates as central to Hyderabadi hijra identity. That is, she suggests that, despite her own efforts at raising a respectable daughter (read: dutiful in one's commitment to familial expectations/obligations over individualist desire), my mother nevertheless failed to yield the proper returns, making me an exemplar of Ninh's "unfilial subject" doomed to fall short of repaying her immigrant parents' self-sacrifice. My failed heterosexuality thus exhibits disrespect to a hierarchical and interdependent kinship structure that, in the middle-class immigrant Indian diasporic world, requires becoming a wife/mother in a commitment to intergenerational care and familial duty. The colonial distortion that puts *hijra* on my mother's tongue as an insult (with *hijra* signifying my disrespect for family) belies her emotional investment in an understanding of respect anchoring an organic definition of hijra identity in India. Because, as Lugones instructs, if I recognize my mother in a limen, a space outside dominant constructions of who she is, I have to assume that she means more than what she says and that her meanings exceed those inscribed by dominant structures like colonialism, homophobia, and white/Anglo cultural imperialism.

The *Izzat* Collective, "a group of young South Asian women [who seek] to challenge how *izzat* or honour has been used to rationalize violence against us," powerfully illustrates the ways differing intergenerational conceptions of respect/*izzat* and love generate communicative impasses between South Asian daughters and our immigrant families of origin (2014, back cover). *Heartbeats: The Izzat Project* is an illustrated popular-education-style book that tells stories about South Asian American women's struggles to negotiate love for their families of origin and self-preservation. The stories center themes of familial silence in the face of incest, forced marriage, familial rejection because of queer-identification, and the cycle of shaming "bad" daughters to limit their social movement, political beliefs, and career choices. At the same time, the authors issue a call for "unconditional love" from their parents and families: "More than anything we want unconditional love. We want support, hope, happiness, and to have a say in our future" (7). The call for unconditional love as interwoven with their call to redefine *izzat* in violence-free terms gives rise to a contradiction that can help illuminate part of the communicative impasse between gender/sexually disobedient daughters and our parents. On the one hand, the authors include a section, "Signs of Violence," clarifying the difference between "abuse" and "love," listing various actions such as "us[ing] anger to intimidate or control you" and "forc[ing] you to marry someone you do not want to" as actions that do not communicate love but rather abuse (32). This section suggests that the authors understand the act of loving *as conditional on not causing psychic or physical harm to those one loves*. Love, then, is understood primarily as *freedom from* harm. Loving another unconditionally would thus require an understanding of what harms this other person and refraining from those actions that compromise their well-being. The authors indicate that unconditional loving requires support for allowing them the freedom to choose who they want to be(come), letting South Asian daughters "have a say in our future" (7).

If the redefinition of *izzat* is the enactment of "unconditional love" that turns on the principle of noninterference in the life paths charted by South Asian daughters, we may begin to glimpse the opacity of *izzat* as it shapes the ground of cultural resistance for both South Asian Americans and our immigrant elders. As mentioned earlier, a collective ethos shapes most South Asian worldviews in which individuals are understood as interdependent in the collectivist mission of familial and communal well-being. Notions of *izzat* thus cannot entertain the support of individualist choice or desire that is not accountable to the well-being of the collective.

Brian Gilley's analysis of autonomy in Native American worlds of sense is particularly useful in elaborating non-Western understandings of self-determination that are tied to the well-being of the community. Gilley explains that for Native Americans, "[a]utonomy is an orientation of respect for other individuals' right to live as they wish insofar as it supports the community and does not disrupt the social order" (2014, 24). Gilley's analysis of Native American conceptions of "autonomy" is a useful guide in rethinking the codes of *izzat* that may shape South Asian immigrant elders' worlds of sense. Here the "freedom to be one's self" is not a "freedom from communal order," but rather a collectivist project of thinking how one's action impacts or disrupts the communal understanding of well-being and social order. When language and identity become more of an impasse than a vehicle to communication, the action of "being there" can be most effective in forging bridges where none seem possible.

FROM A QUEER POLITICS OF RUPTURE TO A QUEER SOUTH ASIAN PRAXIS OF "BEING THERE"

Keeping both the understandings of *respect* elaborated in hijra worlds and the worlds of Indian English meaning-making that inform South Asian diasporic communication, let's now turn to Mala Nagarajan and Vega Subranamian. In their narrative of how they came to be re-integrated into their ethno-religious families of origin, Mala Nagarajan and Vega Subranamian, well-known for their participation in the lawsuit to sue Washington State for the right to marry, detail a long process of "being there" for their families in order to combat their initial ostracism. This included showing up to take care of, attend to, or otherwise participate in collective familial events. Other communicative acts of "being there" included not displaying physical affection publicly, and being persistent, even in the face of silence, about their commitment to fulfill familial obligations commonly expected of South Asian children in the name of respect. Identifying as "queer" was something that Vega clearly expressed as detrimental to the communication process as it signified a departure from the codes of interdependent care that registered as respect within hers and Mala's ethno-religious familial structure. As Vega put it during a conversation with me, "I'm not *queer*, I'm *ordinary*."[13] Her rejection of the term *queer* can be understood both in terms of the identity's individualist associations and her parents' inability to register *queer* as anything but dehumanizing within the worlds of meaning-making among her family of origin.

The identification with ordinariness that Mala and Vega enact invokes understandings of *respect* detailed by Reddy as central to hijra identity in Hyderabad. Here the "ordinariness" becomes radically non-Western in its enactment of a collectivist commitment to care that counters assimilation to Western individualism that queerness often represents. As such, they expose the life ecologies of sustainability colonized into silence or insult when hijra is used to disparage nonheterosexual and gender disobedient South Asians. By excavating worlds of sense-making silenced by colonial massaging of history, we can situate my own mother's exasperation that she raised a "*hijra*" in terms of how queerness signifies to her the prevention of a commitment to grow the self in community. In these terms, her calling me a "*hijra*" could be a calling out my perceived disrespect for a commitment of "being there."

Aparajeeta "Sasha" Duttchoudhury and Rukie Hartman's anthology, *Moving Truth(s): Queer and Transgender Writings on Family*, include stories that illustrate what I am suggesting is a complex communicative act of "being there." This communicative act respects the opacity of resistant worlds of sense by dwelling in the inarticulate, the inchoate, the nonverbal and sensory modes of meaning-making forged between queer/transgender South Asians and their families of origin. The contributors to *Moving Truth(s)* illustrate this communicative act by emphasizing modes of nonverbal communication that can better signify their gender/sexual difference as consonant with a collective sense of self inclusive of one's commitment to one's family of origin (2015, 28, 44, 160).

In the opening chapter, Rajat S. Singh sets the tone for the anthology by detailing intimate perceptions and sensory experiences that communicate a connection to his parents that remain inarticulate. As he acknowledges the "well-accepted notion that South Asian diasporic families don't talk," he also suggests the significance of excavating worlds of meaning-making that are not rooted in verbal expression (2015, 19). He writes: "[W]hat would it look like to question a culture of silence, and examine less visible forms of communication, openness, and ally-ship within Indian families, which may perhaps be couched in the shadows? At what point do faint glimmers of ally-ship emerge, and how do we know how and when to spot the inchoate?" (19). Lugones's strategy of complex communication can be glimpsed in Singh's suggestion that an avenue toward "allyship" between queer/LGBT-identified South Asians and our families requires attending carefully to the meanings generated in nonverbal and nonvisual forms of communication. Instead of dismissing the "accepted notion that South Asian diasporic families don't talk" as evidence of a conservative (read: backward) cultural disposition, he suggests that we mine the silence for culturally specific codes of loving attempts to stay connected. These codes do not map seamlessly onto Western understandings of love as individualist "freedom from interference" in one's life choices. Several iterations of this politics of love and respect, grounded in a "determination to stay," emerge throughout the collection and point to avenues of complex communication between queer/LGBT identified South Asians and our families of origin (Bagri 2015, 99).

Raju Singh, a transgender diasporic South Asian based in London, elaborates his strategy of "being there" as an avenue toward communicating his gender disobedience to his mother that counters colonial translations that equate being transgender with being monstrous. He writes: "I had made a promise with myself when my mother found out that I was transgender, that I would be patient and make sure that any changes happened while she was around, and also that we would always be in contact no matter how hard it was" (2015, 166). A commitment to physical proximity to his mother through his transition was integral to his mother's capacity to "realize I was not turning into a freakish monster" (166). Recognizing the limits of verbal linguistic codes, especially in English, to communicate the ways his mode of being exceeds gender labels, especially the Western gender binary, Raju turns to cooking and creating recipes with his mother as a communicative strategy. By considering the centrality of food as a culturally specific mode of forging loving ties with family of origin, he explains:

> Losing most of my family has made me realize why *spending time together is much more important than any word or label*. We have been meeting up regularly, after a necessary break, coming up with recipes which we make together, mostly so we don't have to talk. No awkwardness, just distraction in a shared interest. That works. *Talking would be too much*, so we cook, a maternal legacy. I somehow subconsciously instigated this pattern *so that we could spend time together* in a way that isn't stressful or uncomfortable for us both. (160; emphasis added)

Although, as Raju explains earlier, his mother expressed her inability to use the correct gender pronouns as her daughter became her son, Raju refuses to let words and labels become more important than spending time with his mother. The act of generating recipes and cooking together, Raju explains, honors a "maternal legacy" often devalued in heteropatriarchal revisions of South Asian cultural histories. In doing so, Raju's transgender identification signifies a commitment to honor and participate in his mother's ways of living and contributing to the family's well-being. This nonverbal action communicates the complexity of Raju's disobedience to South Asian gender norms that English or South Asian verbal languages cannot hold.

A LOVE THAT CAN BE VERIFIED

Forging loving connections dependent on learning to read resistance across worlds of sense, rather than seeking acceptance via "unconditional love," is a central method(ology) and political goal in Lugones's call for deep coalition. Instead of "accepting what is" in an affirmation of unconditional love, which presumes one should love even those who harm them, the project of not disposing of our families of origin in our movement work becomes an ongoing project of mutually enacting and communicating a love that, in the words of June Jordan, can be *verified* among those doing and receiving the loving (WT 85; Jordan 1990, 175). The common goal in queer South Asian organizational outreach efforts to promote "acceptance"[14] presumes a unidirectional effort (with evolutionary undertones) of getting parents and other blood/legal family of queer and LGBT South Asians to grow (educate themselves) into acceptance. Those parents who do come to accept their queer/LGBT-identified children become celebrated examples of model South Asian parents who evidence an unconditional love for their children. The plea for understanding is tied to a plea that South Asian immigrant parents relate to their sexual and gender non-conforming children, an act presumed to be dependent on, and evidence of, loving one's children without conditions. To love without conditions is to love an other *no matter what they do*. Such love is not based on actions but rather an attitude of acceptance and cannot be verified as a commitment to nourishing a collective well-being of consciously interdependent selves. Unconditional love involves the removal of agency from both parties, hence the removal of choice. And hence, the erasure of resistance.

Asking our families of origin to "accept us for who we are" because we are helpless to change our sexual and gender identifications asks them to identify with our pain of isolation and helplessness and frames them as oppressors should they not do so. This leads us back to a logic of disposability with the "accepting" parents as worthy of inclusion and the "unaccepting" (read: unloving) as not-(yet-)acceptable. Shifting the focus of queer South Asian praxis to witnessing faithfully our families of origin also shifts our understanding of love to one that is, indeed, conditional. Specifically, this is a love conditional on our ability to identify with each other's inhabitations and enactments of resistance against oppressions and our commitment to nourish and amplify this resistant ground toward our collective and mutual well-being. As such, witnessing faithfully becomes a project of preparing the ground for communicating a love that can be verified across different worlds of sense.

NOTES

I am grateful to Sarah Hoagland, Nelima Gaonkar, Norma Valenzuela, and Leora Tyree for their generous engagement with earlier drafts of this chapter. Thank you, as well, to Mala Nagarajan and Vega Subramanian and all the queer South Asian collectives, networks, theorists, activists, friendships, and support groups who have sustained me through my multiple becomings.

1. Queer South Asian organizational events that bring together queer South Asians and their families of origin like "Loving Ties: Honoring South Asian Queer Women's Families" (Khush DC 2008), "Desi Family Pride" (South Asian Lesbian and Gay Association NYC 2012), and "We are Family" (Queer South Asian National Network 2015) highlight a recognized need and desire for queer and LGBT-identified South Asians to remain meaningfully tied to their families of origin. Similarly, queer South Asian theorists Gayatri Gopinath (2005) and Jasbir Puar (2007) offer reading strategies to identify familial home spaces and ethno-religious South Asian communities of place as integral to queer South Asian liberation in the face of racist and (neo)colonial state violence.

2. I put the qualifiers "accepting" and "unaccepting" in quotation marks throughout the text to register their colonial/modern categorial logics when used by queer South Asian organizations to celebrate "accepting" South Asians families who embrace their queer-identified relative and, implicitly, to condemn those "unaccepting" families who have not evolved into queer acceptance and, instead, may coerce, ostracize, or disown their queer-identified relative.

3. Asian Pacific Islander American (APIA) "Parents Who Love their LGBT Kids" Campaign. See www.autostraddle.com/this-powerful-multilingual-campaign-features-asian-parents-who-love-their-lgbt-kids-295968. Accessed January 16, 2016.

4. Vega Subranamian, in conversation with the author, October 14, 2012.

5. Chandan Reddy (1998) clarifies the inability for communities or families of choice to replace communities and families of origin associated with "home."

6. These are parental reactions that queer-identified South Asians discussed in queer South Asian support groups and workshops in which I participated as part of my own struggle for over ten years.

7. See, for example, *Give a Damn! True Colors Fund Project*. www.wegiveadamn.org/issues/youth-suicide. Accessed August 28, 2015.

8. During a session focusing on narrating the coming-out experience to family, one participant stated adamantly that his approach to his family has been, "if you don't accept me, then you're a bigot!" This approach is echoed in the slogan appearing on a protest sign during a Queer *Azaadi* (freedom) march in Mumbai, India: "Not Gay as in Happy, But Queer as in Fuck You!"

9. M. Jacqui Alexander invokes the phrase "self in community" to reference a collectivist sense of self that actively recognizes and inhabits one's interdependence and connections to others (2005, 282).

10. I am defining "Indian English" as English domesticated by patriarchal Indian elites in collaboration with British colonials.

11. In the documentary *Jihad for Love*, one of the gay Muslim men explains that his mother was less upset about his being gay than his lack of marriage-ability.

12. Alton Becker (1991) uses the term *languaging* to reference the embodied ways of relating, feeling, and being within a particular language and its specific domain of distinctions.

13. Vega Subranamian, in discussion with the author, October 14, 2012.

14. Queer South Asian organizations in Los Angeles (Santrang), Chicago (Trikone), and Washington DC (Khush DC) explicitly state on their websites that promoting "acceptance" of LGBT South Asians is one of their goals.

REFERENCES

Alexander, Jacqui M. 2005. *Pedagogies of Crossing: Meditations on Feminism, Sexual Politics, Memory, and the Sacred*. Durham, NC: Duke University Press.

Bagri, Harsimran Kaur. 2015. "Deconstructing Desi." In *Moving Truth(s): Queer and Transgender Desi Writings on Family*, edited by Aparajeeta 'Sasha' Duttchoudhury and Rukie Hartman, 87–102. Seattle: Flying Chickadee.

Becker, Alton. 1991. "A Short Essay on Languaging." In *Research and Reflexivity*, edited by Frederick Streier, 226–34. Thousand Oaks, CA: Sage Publications.

Bhattacharjee, Anannya. 1999. "The Habit of Ex-Nomination: Nation, Woman and the Indian Immigrant Bourgeoisie." In *Emerging Voices: South Asian American Women Redefine Self, Family, and Community*, edited by Sangeeta R. Gupta, 231–52. Thousand Oaks, CA: Sage Publications.

Chandra, Shefali. 2012. *The Sexual Life of English: Languages of Caste and Desire in Colonial Desire*. Durham, NC: Duke University Press.

Duttchoudhury, Aparajeeta 'Sasha,' and Rukie Hartman, eds. 2015. *Moving Truth(s): Queer and Transgender Writings on Family*. Seattle: Flying Chickadee.

Gilley, Brian. 2014. "Joyous Discipline." *American Indian Culture and Research Journal* 38(2): 17–39.

Gopinath, Gayatri. 2005. *Impossible Desires: Queer Diasporas and South Asian Public Cultures*. Durham, NC: Duke University Press.

Gulati, Sonali, dir. 2011. *I Am: When Being One's Self is Enough*. Documentary Film. India: 20th Century Fox Entertainment. DVD.

Izzat Collective. 2014. *Heartbeats: The Izzat Collective*. The Pomegranate Tree Group Press.

Jordan, June. 1990. "Where is the Love?" In *Making Face/Making Soul*: Haciendo Caras, edited by Gloría Anzaldúa, 174–76. San Francisco: Aunt Lute Books.

Majumdar, Rochona. 2009. *Marriage and Modernity: Family Values in Colonial Bengal*. Durham, NC: Duke University Press.

Mehta, Brinda. 2004. *Diasporic (Dis)Locations: Indo-Caribbean Women Writers Negotiate the* Kala Pani. University of the West Indies Press.

Ninh, erin Khuê. 2011. *(In)Gratitude: The Debt-Bound Daughter in Asian American Literature*. New York: New York University Press.

Puar, Jasbir. 2007. *Terrorist Assemblages: Homonationalism in Queer Times*. Durham, NC: Duke University Press.

Reddy, Chandan. 1998. "Home, House, Non-Identity: Paris is Burning." In *Burning Down the House: Recycling Domesticity*, edited by Rosemary Marangoly George, 355–79. Westview Press.

Reddy, Gayatri. 2010. *With Respect to Sex: Negotiating* Hijra *Identity in South India*. Durham, NC: Duke University Press.

Sharma, Parvez. dir. 2007. *A Jihad for Love*. Documentary Film. UK: Channel Four Films. DVD.

Singh, Rajat. 2015. "The Picture Beyond the Frame." In *Moving Truth(s): Queer and Transgender Desi Writings on Family*, edited by Aparajeeta 'Sasha' Duttchoudhury and Rukie Hartman, 11–20. Seattle: Flying Chickadee.

Singh, Raju S. 2015. "Recipes and Rites." In *Moving Truth(s): Queer and Transgender Desi Writings on Family*, edited by Aparajeeta "Sasha" Duttchoudhury and Rukie Hartman, 152–57. Seattle: Flying Chickadee.

Vaid-Menon, Alok. "Coming Home: Queer South Asians and the Politics of Family," *returnthegayze* (blog) returnthegayze.com/2014/07/28/coming-home-queer-south-asians-and-the-politics. Accessed July 28, 2014.

Part III Gender, Coloniality, and Decolonial Embodiments

6 Border Thinking/Being/Perception
Toward a "Deep Coalition" across the Atlantic

Madina Tlostanova

Lugones's work offers paradigmatic examples of border being, thinking, and perception within the decolonial thought—an international collective of scholars who, for the last two decades, have been conceptualizing the underside of modernity—that of coloniality. Together, we understand coloniality as a consistent cultivation and maintenance of the economic, social, cultural, ethical, epistemic, and ontological dependency on Western norms and assumptions presented as universal and good for all. The decolonial option is also about possible ways out of coloniality in spheres of power, being, knowledge, perception, and certainly gender, all of which triggered the formulation of Lugones's concept of the colonial/modern gender system (HGS). I believe that the combination of the border way of being in the world and communicating with others, offered by Lugones under the name of world-traveling with a loving perception, and her model of the coloniality of gender and a coalitional opposition to it from the colonial difference are relevant not only for the sphere of coloniality of the Western empires of modernity and their gendered others, but also for the colonial difference of Russia (WT, CG). Previously, I have theorized Russia as a second-class, subaltern empire, whose former and present, particularly non-European, colonies (mainly the Caucasus and Central Asia), have been marked by a complex intersection of gender, race/ethnicity, class, religion, language, and geopolitical positioning (Tlostanova 2010a). This Eurasian configuration complicates Lugones's original ideas and must be considered in dialogue with them yet also as a separate model.

Such a dialogue is possible because Lugones's work on gender does not investigate concrete cases of discrimination or offer a descriptive historical analysis of gender in othered cultures; instead, it operates on the level of epistemic de-linking. This means undermining the very epistemic and logical

125

principles of modernity/coloniality with its universally accepted scholarly myths and grand narratives of progress, development, democracy, human rights, gender difference, and equality. Such a "learning to unlearn in order to relearn" (Tlostanova and Mignolo 2012, 7) often leaves us with meager conceptual instruments and a necessity of elaborating new concepts or digging out the marginalized and forgotten ones by tracing alternative genealogies and trajectories of local histories where, in Lewis Gordon's formulation, the modern ratio-dicea becomes inapt (2010).

In what follows I will try to demonstrate—through a decolonial stance—the potentially fruitful spheres for a dialogue between Lugones's ideas and resistant gender discourses of and in the Caucasus and Central Asia. The Caucasus and Central Asia constitute the two main spheres of coloniality within the former Russian/Soviet empire. They share a number of common elements found in other decolonial border positions of exteriority—a philosophic synonym of border thinking and existence, the outside created from the inside—from the totality of the dominant discourse (Dussel 1985). Such an exteriority, grounded in the experience of being born and educated in the entanglement of the Western invention of modernity/tradition, is not calling for a return to some primordialist state, but, rather, draws our attention to how and why modernity invented the negative image of tradition in the first place. The exteriority of living and thinking in hostile environments while reinstating one's epistemic rights leads to an itinerant, forever open, and multiple discourse marked by transformations, shifting identifications, and a rejection of either-or binarity. In this trajectory, one turns, instead, to a nonexclusive duality and un-sublated contradictions, which are to be found both in the contemporary models of conjunctive logic and in many Indigenous epistemologies, including the better investigated global South as well as the lesser-known Caucasus and Central Asian models.

The first intersectional node between Lugones's thinking and Central Asian and Caucasian resistant discourses of gender is questioning the binary of modernity versus tradition that permeates all cultural, social, political, and religious relations, academic disciplines, and knowledge production. In the sphere of gender, this is expressed in questioning the assumed patriarchal nature of any traditional society and in revealing the (hetero)sexist limits of colonization/modernization grounded in the dichotomy of the same and the other, subject and object, man and woman. Decolonization of gender, then, presupposes questioning the invention of secular modernity and its dark other—tradition—associated with backwardness, patriarchy, humiliation, violence, filth, ignorance, and so on. Other falsely universal ideas of Western feminism questioned in decolonial feminist thought include egalitarianism, fragmentation of identity, linguistic sexism, naturalizing of sexual differences, and the visual (masculine) nature of any culture (Tlostanova 2010a).

The coloniality of gender takes different guises yet always retains its main features of the heteronormative and patriarchal division of humanity and the main vectors of discrimination, resistance, and empowerment of those who have been systematically dehumanized. From such experience emerges a new trans-aesthesis connecting people throughout the world who have suffered Anzaldúa's open (colonial) wound between the lighter and the darker sides of modernity (1999, 25), but who have also learned to build a positive "resisting and re-existing sensibility" and agency out of this trauma (Albán Achinte 2009). Lugones's decolonizing of gender as a false imperial concept is a crucial step on this path. She shows that the concept of gender legitimates modern pseudo-scientific human taxonomies such as the division of people into humans and subhumans (sexually and racially marked) or, in Nelson Maldonado-Torres's idea, the enactment of "misanthropic skepticism" questioning the humanity of the other, and is grounded not in ontological but in epistemic and artificially constructed differences (2007). Lugones's attempt to get rid of the biologicalization of gender is thus linked with a wider decolonial impulse of uncovering the role of particular situated knowledges in any ontology.

It is crucial to examine what mechanism lies in the basis of the discursive decolonization of gender. And there are several intersections between Lugones's method and those nascent positions that we find in the zone of the colonial difference of the Russian/Soviet empire. Of particular significance is her nuanced and truly dynamic intersectional approach, generating multiple shifting positionalities and an optics of complex stereoscopic and pluritopic (that is, multispatial) vision, opposed to structuralist, Marxist, and standpoint intersectional approaches. Such a stance is grounded in the body-politics and the geo-politics of knowledge, being, gender, and perception, marked by the colonial difference instead of the Western, deliberately delocalized vantage point.

Geo- and body-politics represent epistemic and political projects from historical agents, experiences, and memories that were erased in the capacity of epistemic subjects. Lugones calls these politics "the peopled ground" on which one stands and which also run through one (TDF 746). The geo-politics of knowledge, being, and perception refers to the local historical (temporal) and spatial grounds of knowledge and existence. The body-politics can be defined as the individual and collective biographical grounds of understanding, thinking, being, and perception rooted in our local histories and trajectories of origination and dispersion. Such an intersectionality, grounded in a coalitional logic of fusion, intermeshing, and coalescence is *pluriversal* in the decolonial sense (RM 73), meaning a coexistence of many interacting and intersecting non-abstract universals based on the geo-politics and body-politics of knowledge, being, and perception (Tlostanova and Mignolo 2012, 65). The *pluriversal* involves a conscious effort to reconnect theory and theorists with experience and with those who experience discrimination; in other words, it seeks to reinstate the experiential nature of knowledge and the origin of any theory in the human life-world. In the *pluriversal* world, many worlds coexist and interact, and countless options communicate with each other instead of promoting one abstract universal good for all. These options intersect, sometimes inside our bodies and selves, and each locus of intersection is another option. Decolonial *pluriversality* is parallel to intersectionality, but its target is not the constellation of race, gender, class, and other power asymmetries, but rather the aberration of the universal as such, the stress on the epistemic (not ontological) nature of othering. This allows for looking at different locales, including the Caucasus and Central Asia, through a dialectic of transition from intersectionality to fusion as a much better ground for a potentiated coalitional resistance (RM 76).

THE JANUS-FACED EMPIRE AND ITS NON-EUROPEAN COLONIES

If Lugones's trajectory grows out of her geo- and body-politics of knowledge, being, gender, and perception, grounded in the colonial difference with the Western capitalist empires of modernity and a diasporic existence in the United States, the local history of peripheral Eurasia demonstrates a much more blurred and complicated case due to the external imperial difference and its darker counterpart—a secondary colonial difference. The imperial difference refers to various losers, which failed to fulfill, or were prevented by different circumstances and powers from fulfilling, their imperial mission in modernity. They were intellectually, epistemologically, or culturally colonized by the winners. Imperial difference can be divided into internal and external kinds. The former refers to the European losers of the secular phase of modernity, which became the South of Europe (Spain, Italy, Portugal), while the latter refers to the non-Western, noncapitalist, non-Catholic/Protestant, alphabetically non-Latin empires of modernity, for instance the Ottoman Sultanate or Russia. The latter is a paradigmatic case of a second-class non-European empire with a long and unsuccessful history of borrowing and superfluous appropriation of certain elements of modernity, and a chronic mental coloniality vis-à-vis the West.

The first phase of the Russian imperial expansionism was largely directed to Siberia, and its logic generally corresponded to the Western logic of the first

Christian colonial modernity within which the central dichotomy was the hierarchy between the human and the nonhuman (TDF 743). From this major division, other binaries emerged such as men versus women, and white versus nonwhite. From the sixteenth century on, Russia has gradually internalized the European interpretation of non-European people as under-humans and has worked to forge the European roots of noble ethnic Russians (as opposed to peasantry), accentuating the often-problematic Asiatic lineage of its colonial non-European others. In doing so, Russia constructs the colonial difference (which, in the Russian case, has always been vague, due, in part, to the lack of an ocean between the poorly defined metropolis and the colonies). The conquest of Siberia in the late sixteenth century corresponds to the European model of identifying the Indigenous people (in this case, the numerous tribes of Itelmen, Yukagir, Nivkh, Tuvans, Siberian Tatars, Selkups, and others, in many ways similar to Amerindians) with nature. This familiar logic liberated the Russian colonizers from any responsibility for the equally marauding attitude to both nature (as peltry, not oil, was the main commodity Siberia provided then for the international markets) and the Indigenous people. The social-military groups of the so-called Cossacks conquering Siberia often married the Indigenous women. This resulted in a significant number of Russian "Creoles," later completely assimilated and today considering themselves ethnically Russian. However, in the mid–nineteenth century, progeny of this Siberian Russian-Indigenous mixing already made a number of decolonially charged statements denouncing the bloody imperial acts while using this local history to build a political platform for the struggle of regional independence from Moscow. This sentiment is actively revived today. Thus, half-Russian and half-Buryat historian Afanassy Schapov criticized the Russian *zoological economy* that is the parallel annihilation of fur-providing animals and Indigenous people who were forced to hunt them under pain of death (1906). At this early point, all women (both Russian and Indigenous, legal wives and concubines) were regarded by the Siberian conquerors as commodity and property, subject to slave trade and lease (it was common to rent one of one's several wives—no matter Russian or Indigenous—while embarking on the next colonization campaign) (Scheglov 1993). There was yet no gender involved here, only biological sex, and gender was not used as a social and cultural marker of belonging to humanity. As a social concept gender appeared much later and was largely determined by class rather than race/ethnicity (Etkind 2011; Tlostanova 2010a).

If the conquering of Siberia more or less corresponded to the Spanish and Portuguese expansion in the New World, the Caucasus (southward) and Central Asia (eastward) annexation took place in post-enlightenment modernity, when racial and gender divisions were already codified and ossified through the rhetoric of secular Western modernity that the Russians, once again, internalized as their own. Moreover, Russia's own subaltern status in the world-imperial ranking and its catching-up modernizing pace was also firmly naturalized starting from Peter the Great, and confirmed the paradoxical situation of the empire-colony that has generated its own secondary colonial difference. The colonial difference is secondary because of the subaltern and mimicking nature of the empire in question—a Janus-faced empire with different faces turned eastward and westward. It has always felt itself inferior to the West—an out-of-place Tatar dressed as a Frenchman (Kluchevsky 2009). Russia has compensated for this inferiority complex in its non-European colonies (and mainly in the Caucasus and Central Asia) by projecting the image of the Russian/Soviet colonizer as a true European and a champion of civilization, modernity, socialism, and so on. As a result, these colonies were doubly subordinated to Western modernity and to its distorted Russian version, which has still retained, in mutant forms, the main features of modernity, such as Eurocentrism, progressivism, Orientalism, and racism. The Caucasus and Central Asia thus became the colonies of the culturally and mentally colonized empire.

The local histories of the non-European ex-colonies of the Russian empire and the USSR generate multilayered identifications, ways of survival and re-existence and intersectional tangents growing out of the multiple dependencies from modernity/coloniality in its Western, and also insecure Russian and Soviet, forms, as well as from complex and often contradictory religious and ethnocultural configurations. They disturb the simple binary of the colonial/modern gender matrix as they multiply, destabilize, and problematize many familiar categories of decolonial thought. This refers to a redoubling of Orientalism and Eurocentrism, to an increasingly symbolic nature of racism, to a complication of imperial and colonial masculinity and femininity, as well as colonial gender tricksterism.

Secondary Orientalism in the Russian/Soviet empire is a direct result of secondary Eurocentrism—a nonoriginal derivative discourse, borrowed from Western modernity and appropriated and distorted by the Russian imperial consciousness, to be later imposed onto the colonial others. Moreover, this appropriation of the Western modernity's discourses is done by the Russians who, themselves, have always been seen by the West as Asiatic, Oriental, and savage and, therefore, have developed an inferiority complex compensated at times by exaggerated jingoism, as it happens today. Therefore, Russian Orientalism, Eurocentrism, and racism are grounded in a peculiar transfer:

they attempt a redemption, getting rid of the non-White man's burden through an artificial and exaggerated appropriation of Whiteness and belonging to Europe, but always with a hovering realization of the dubious Russian status under Western eyes. Orientalist constructs, in the case of Russian empire and its non-European colonies, are built on the principle of double mirror reflections, on copying Western Orientalism with a deviation and, necessarily, with a carefully hidden, often unconscious, feeling that Russia itself is a form of a mystic and mythic Orient for the West (Sahni 1997; Tlostanova 2010a). As a result, both mirrors—the one turned in the direction of the colonies and the one turned by Europe in the direction of Russia itself—appear to be distorting mirrors that create a specific unstable sensibility, expressed in Victor Yerofeyev's ironic dictum: "If I want, I can go from Moscow to Asia, or—to Europe. It is clear where I am going to. But it is unclear where I am coming from" (2000, 56). It is a balancing between the role of the object and that of the subject in the epistemic and existential sense.

Race as a universal classification in modernity/coloniality has been masked in the Russian and Soviet history by ethnicity and/or religion and later by class or ideology, leading to a highly symbolic nature of racism disconnected from the purity of blood or the color of skin. This made it difficult for outsiders to understand the rules of Russian imperial racist taxonomies and its colonial self-racializing (Central Asia) or self-Whitening (the Caucasus) versions. Once again, as in the case of Siberia, which consists of many tribes and emergent nations belonging to quite different linguistic groups, religions, and cultures, the conquered people of the Caucasus were coded subhuman and therefore had to be seen as non-White savages, even if in the European and North American imaginary of the time the Caucasian race—that is, originating in the Caucasus, according to an early (pseudo)anthropologist Johann Friedrich Blumenbach, was (and still is) a synonym of Whiteness. The purity of blood could not save the Caucasus women from being raped, killed, or sold into slavery (usually to the Ottoman Sultanate).

In the Czarist empire, religion was translated into racial/ethnic categories. For example, Muslims became Tatars (nineteenth century), then bourgeois nationalists (USSR), and today—simply "Blacks." In the Soviet Union class and ideological characteristics were often translated into racial and ethnic ones. Racializing had one face in the metropolis (when the "enemies of the people" of any ethnic and religious belonging were rendered subhuman), and a different face in the colonies where the discourses of the civilizing mission, development, progressivism, and Soviet Orientalism clearly demonstrated their links with the Western colonialist macronarrative. The lighter side of Soviet modernity was grounded in ideological and social differences, whereas its darker side reiterated the nineteenth-century racist clichés and human taxonomies mixed with hastily adapted historical materialist dogmas. Soviet efforts to create its own image of the New Woman in her metropolitan and colonial versions grounded in the typically Soviet double standards and reticence place contemporary gendered subjects from the ex-colonies of Russia/USSR into a complex and undertheorized intersectional zone between postcolonial and postsocialist realms (Navailh 1996; Tekuyeva 2006; Tokhtakhodzhayeva 1999). In the post-Soviet decades, the ruins of the USSR have become, for the rest of the world, a homogenized problematic region in a post-Duboisean collective sense of the people with delayed or questioned humanity and no place in the new global architecture. In the cases of the ethnic Russians themselves and the ex-colonies with European claims (such as Ukraine, Belarus, the Baltic states, Moldova), it is not a clearly racialized division, but, instead, a poorly representable semi-alterity, the realm of the off-White Blacks of global coloniality, looking and behaving too similar to the same, yet remaining essentially others. A border case is the Caucasus, which is actively demonized and blackened by Russia and excessively preoccupied with its self-Europeanization as a compensatory gesture. As for Central Asia, whose ethnic, linguistic, and religious belonging to the Orient cannot be disputed, it managed to take an honorary place in the second world due to Soviet modernity. Today, Central Asia is not ready to agree with its clear belonging to the global South or to work for the development of coalitions and praxis in that direction. By this I mean the local intellectuals infected by secondary Eurocentrism and not the mute subalterns for whom their physical survival is the only goal. All of these are signs of the continuing coloniality of thinking and coloniality of knowledge, which, in the Central Asian case, redoubles in the fawning both before the Russians and the West.

DISTORTION OF THE COLONIAL/MODERN GENDER PARADOX IN THE CAUCASUS AND CENTRAL ASIA

The Russians appropriated the modern gendered and racialized human taxonomies and shaped their own, more complicated, version of the paradox of colonial femininity and masculinity in which the main element of taking humanity away from the colonized has stayed intact. Russian imperial double-consciousness, briefly outlined above, leads to a distortion of most modernity discourses, including those about gender. The colonial gender paradox is based on blaming the colonial others for mutually exclusive vices at once, and is closely linked with the major modern division of humanity into *humanitas* and *anthropos*, the latter being locked in the realm of nature, not culture (Nishitani 2006). Gender is obviously a construct of the *humanitas* invented in order to differentiate its constituents from those that belong to nature and therefore have only biological sex. The definition of colonial femininity and masculinity is self-denying and preventing the colonial subject from building a positive identity. Racialization works, then, through gender, and colonization itself comes to be symbolized as an act of rape or violence. However, this well-known story is typical of the confident empires with a positive masculine identity, whereas Russia has always been an unconfident second-class empire, itself codified as feminine by the West. Its attitude toward colonized people has been marked by a suppressed diffidence and an exaggerated self-assertion linked with a realization of its insufficient (for the empire) superiority over the colonized, particularly in gendered/sexual spheres. Due to the coloniality of gender enmeshed in contradictory impulses, the colonial man in the colonies of the Western empires can be easily feminized (particularly in Orientalist versions) as he lacks any real authority or power. And yet, any hint of his possible will or agency is immediately interpreted as a threat to White society, which presents the colonized male as an essential rapist and an aggressive animal, threatening the chaste White lady (especially in African and some Amerindian stereotypes) and his own women, seen by the Western society as being in need of rescuing from their own males. The non-White woman is regarded as sexually available, voracious, and willing to be raped, a seductress of the White man and a threat to the happiness and well-being of the decent White lady, lacking chastity or honor as such and thus liberating the White rapist from any guilt or responsibility.

In the Russian colonization of the Caucasus and Central Asia, this naturalized ethics was recast in particular ways, connected not with race but with essentialized ethnicity and, later, with Islam, which was early translated into racial terms when the Muslim of any origin equaled "non-White" and hence "subhuman" (Tlostanova 2010b). The paradox of colonial masculinity and femininity differed from the West because the gap between the Orientalist European fantasy and the reality of the Caucasus and Turkistan (the Czarist name of Central Asia) conquest was too obvious and based on the secondary Orientalist ideologies, always poisoning any victory for the subaltern empire.

Muslim and local ethnocultural custom protected the Central Asian Muslim women from the Russian colonizers. They could not act in the role of non-White women in the European colonial imaginary. The Caucasus women, for a while, played the part of exotic sexual slaves and were a profitable commodity, habitually compared by the Russians to animals and associated with familiar characteristics of early puberty, heightened sexuality, and wanton morals (Tlostanova 2010a, 73). However, there were no Black slaves or Amerindians in the Russian colonial spaces (save for the earlier conquests of Siberia and the Far East, which resulted in the extermination or assimilation of the local equivalents of Amerindians). Besides, as stated above, the boundary between the metropolis and the colonies has been always blurred in the Russian case, so European racial classifications had to be transformed and eventually divided between the two human groups. On the one hand, there are the ethnically same (that is, Russian) but socially and culturally inferior serfs (peasants bound by the feudal system to work on their master's estate) who were ruthlessly exploited and dehumanized by the Russian nobility and the state, and who resided mainly in central Russia (and not in the colonies). On the other, there are the inhabitants of the newly colonized spaces of the Caucasus and especially Central Asia who were hardly ever subdued into serfdom yet were still dehumanized, robbed of their lands and other property, and generally deprived of most civil and human rights on the basis of racial/religious taxonomies.

The local men in the Caucasus could not be interpreted within the Orientalist docile stereotype, and any comparison with them was not to the advantage of the much more tepid Russian masculinity, which used the Caucasus male archetype as an attractive sexual model—noble savages who had fallen out of modernity and progress. The erotic element of Russian imperialism—contrary to its European versions—was expressed in the male form and extrapolated into the Russian male anxiety and fear of the Caucasus machismo in war and sex (Sahni 1997, 33–69; Tekuyeva 2006). Therefore, in Russian gender stereotyping of the Caucasus, the local colonial men were associated with violence but never feminized. In Soviet modernity, the light (modern) and the dark (colonial) sides merged in the interpretation of the colonial periphery so that the Caucasian people were racialized and presented as unreformable. Yet, it was paradoxically assumed that, under the influence of Russian/Soviet civilizing efforts, the mountaineers would gradually turn into a different sort of people (Jersild 2002, 9–125). The post-Soviet society retains the gender stereotype of the dangerous Caucasus man, which is used today as the basis of standard racist accusations—from his desire to possess a Russian woman and humiliate Russian men, to his dangerous tendencies of reckless courage. The latter impulse is often seen as a readiness to sacrifice lives—his own and other people's, including women—the so-called black widows, the suicide bombers of the Caucasus Islamic separatist movements.

Several decades after the colonization of the Caucasus, the Russian conquering of Central Asia was already a pale and distorted copy of the British and French march to the Orient, coding the local population as subhuman and, once again, almost animal—this time within the frame of the newly emerged pseudo-scientific anthropology. As late as the 1920s, Soviet "experts" interpreted the Central Asian women with the help of almost zoological visual comparative charts, completely ignoring their humanity. But colonized Central Asian females were substantially different from the African slaves or Amerindians. Central Asian women were not turned into an important part of the economy of sexual and labor exploitation until the Soviet colonial cotton industry emerged in Central Asia, with its racist and misogynist division of labor. Because there was no system of direct colonial slavery in Czarist times in the Caucasus or in Central Asia, it was impossible to create a unified, systematic, and coherent system of labor and sexual exploitation for colonized women. The ethnically Russian serf woman, who resided in the Russian version of the metropolis, performed the role of the sexually, economically, and psychologically exploited female, often seen as an animal and taken out of the realm of the human and feminine (Etkind 2011, 124–28).

In post-Soviet decades, global coloniality started to affect the post-Soviet space directly and not through a mediation of Russian or Soviet imperial difference any more. This has sadly led to a revival of gendered—and this time clearly racialized—slavery. The Central Asians are still seen in modern-day Russia as dirt poor and placed at the bottom of the scale of humanity, to the point of erasing gender markers altogether and seeing so-called illegal women migrants as animals: these women are regarded as biologically female yet culturally and socially subhuman. They are Agambenian bare lives (ab)used in forced overwork and sexual trafficking, and as producers of children sold in the capacity of live goods (1998). There is no future for such ex-slaves. They cannot go back home where the slave trade mafia is going to punish them, or they will simply perish of hunger and unemployment. These people were born and made to exist in the grip of global coloniality, both in the neocolonial world of Central Asia and the postimperial (and also neocolonial) world of the ex-metropolitan Moscow.

The trajectory of these Central Asian migrant bare lives is different from African American women or Latinas in the United States, as it was complicated by dubious Soviet gender discourses and practices. The ancestors of the future post-Soviet downtrodden migrants from Central Asia experienced double standards, racism, othering, forceful emancipation, and low glass ceilings along with all other non-Russians in the USSR, but they also had access to such socialist advantages as universal education (even if Russified and not always of good quality), minimal social guarantees within the colonial monoeconomic model, restricted social lifts for national minorities in accordance with Soviet multiculturalism, and an honorary belonging to the second world that the Central Asians have lost today. It is crucial to keep this in mind when tracing the trajectory of Central Asian women toward their contemporary condition of neo-slavery and Central Asia's firm belonging to the global South without the benefit of sharing its political agency and epistemology.

There are several reasons for this failed solidarity between post-Soviet/postcolonial and global South women. These reasons include the lack of information or access to any relevant texts and the lack of mutual communication in the conditions of persistent isolation of such locales as Central Asia and the Caucasus. This is compounded by a continuing sharp division into the thin layer of intellectuals who could potentially act in the capacity of decolonial agents yet choose not to because of their coloniality of knowledge, and those who obediently follow the old logic. It consists in Russian/Soviet and, today, more often, Western thinkers producing high theory, which then is quoted, repeated, and simply applied to concrete examples from their own experience by the local Central Asian or Caucasian intellectuals. Part of the problem lies in the fact that a newfound gender sensitivity has come to post-Soviet postcolonial spaces from the West, assisted by various grants and institutions that often require a very particular interpretation of gender issues and tend to erase the previous history of gender struggles and models, thereby forcing postcolonial, post-Soviet women to start from scratch in the mode of mainstream Western feminism.

This mode alienates mainstream theorists from the majority of Central Asian and Caucasian women living and struggling in their locales. For these women, Judith Butler's work, likely known by heart among the local scholars indoctrinated by Western feminism, does not mean much. Central Asian and Caucasian women would probably find much more in common with Lugones's project, which remains untranslated and unknown due to the specific preferences of local gender scholars who have been marked by intellectual coloniality. Another reason for the absence of Central Asian and Caucasian voices in gender discourses of the global South today is linked to a persistent agonistic model and an unwillingness to cede one's status as "second world" and be associated with the global South. Third, there is a phenomenon of negative victimhood rivalry expressed among some ex-third world cases where people tend to monopolize their position as victims of modernity, refusing to make room for obscure Caucasians or Central Asians. Overcoming these difficulties requires goodwill from all sides, which is, at times, problematic.

A POTENTIATED ANTIAGONISTIC BORDER THINKING IN THE EURASIAN BORDERLANDS

Parallels and divergences between Lugones's decolonial feminist categories and that of the external imperial difference and its secondary colonial difference bring us to the issue of praxis, or a lack of it, in the post-Soviet case. In a number of her recent texts, Lugones elaborates on such relational oppositional praxis and the emergence of flexible, nonossified, deep coalitions of resistance, crucial for any decolonial gendered efforts aimed at the creation of the transmodern as an other-than-modern world. Such an oppositional praxis is grounded in a nomadic traveling mode of existence, which sees culture itself as a journey and a process of social construction. This brings us back to Lugones's idea of making a journey between worlds of meaning with a loving perception. This is the gist of decolonial border epistemology and ethics grounded in the idea of being the border, having the border cutting across one's own self, not merely crossing borders and observing them from a detached pseudo-objective vantage point (Mignolo and Tlostanova 2006). Growing out of the situation of ontological othering, and resulting in re-existence, this position allows building a specific intersubjective model beyond the well-known ways of dealing with difference and diversity that could potentially lead to future deep coalitions of interrelated others.

Rejecting the Western concept of *agon* and playing, based on aggressive competitiveness as the main principle of social, cultural, political, and economic relations of winners and losers in modernity, Lugones formulates the nonaggressive "loving perception" of a playful world-traveler uninterested in who wins and who loses and who is, instead, forever ready to change. It is a decolonial counterbalance for the official failed forms of boutique multiculturalism and for the impasse of both absolute and opaque otherness and the convenient erasure of differences (WT 96). This recipe is crucial for post-Soviet space because it allows us to de-link from the coloniality of being and knowledge that prescribes the slaves of modernity to aspire for a solidification of a particular space for themselves in its hierarchy, being afraid of losing it, and, thus, ruthlessly competing with other others for the proximity to the same. All of this has been expressed in the complex of catching-up modernization and its accompanying psychological failures of external imperial difference and double

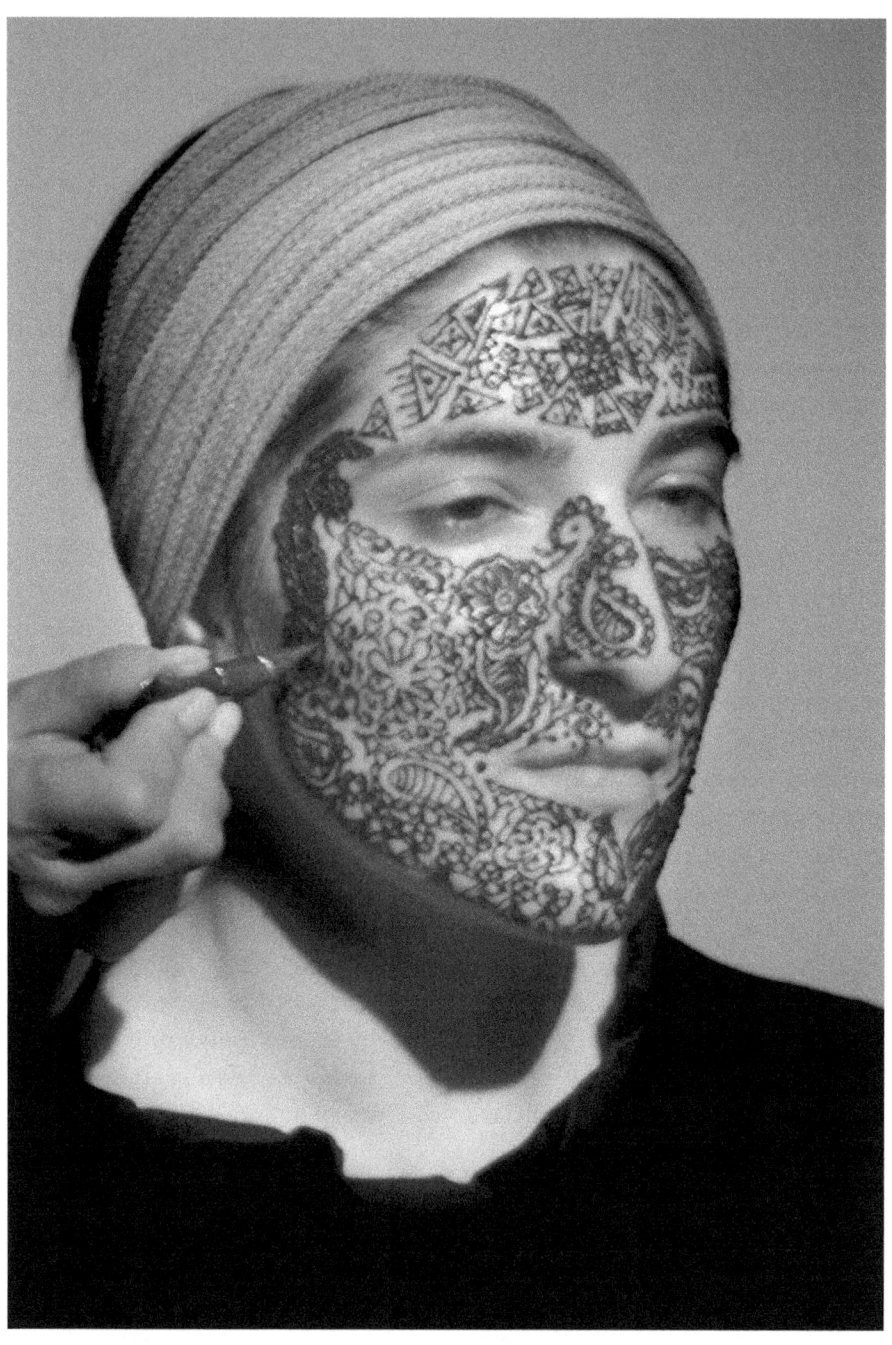

Figure 6.1. *Delinking* by Taus Makhacheva, 2011. Photograph, 45 cm x 30 cm. © Taus Makhacheva.

colonial difference in the Russian empire and in the USSR, as well as in today's collapsing Russian Federation.

In the (post)colonial side of post-Soviet space, the rejection of agonistics finds its parallels, marked by a specific ethics of intersubjective encounters, resonating with Lugones's loving world-traveler's stance. It is grounded in the idea of all-encompassing interconnection of people, nature, cosmos, where each of us represents the other. As an Uzbek Sufi healer *tabiba* Habiba states, quoting her teacher Bahauddin Nakshbandi, "take a hand—we can concentrate on the differences between each of the fingers, marveling how dissimilar they are, but then we risk not noticing the movement of the hand as a whole" (Allione 1997). In Lugones's terms, we then risk cutting off the possibility of deep coalitions-in-the-making.

These ideas intersect with Lugones's concept of communal infrapolitical and body-political resistant praxis (TDF 755). I see it ideally as grounded in the grassroots embodied and historically contextualized level of mutually communicating women's movements within the global colonial difference. This is a good recipe for the Eurasian colonial difference that needs to get rid of its multiple complexes connected with a doubly colonized status, stop looking in the direction of imperial sameness or imperial difference, and start looking in the direction of global colonial difference with different, but intersecting, faces and local histories woven together by global coloniality and *pluriversal* resistance to it.

A young Avarian (Northern Caucasus) diasporic artist, Taus Makhacheva, offers an interesting example of such a position as an intersection of being and knowledge. A playful trying on of various alien roles does not rule out her remaining a part of the symbolic Indigenous reality in dialogue with modernity, which she investigates. Through the prism of a specific negotiating stance, the artist examines the unstable boundary between acceptance and rejection, drawing attention to human efforts to merge, mimic, assimilate, or leak into the other, no matter if it is another person or a community—natural or social, rural or urban, real or imagined. In *Delinking* (fig. 1), Makhacheva is attracted by the idea of de-linking from European ways of receiving knowledge and stresses that all cultures have their own practices of transmitting knowledge, while the world uses only the sanctified Western system. Makhacheva's face was intricately painted with henna using Indian, African, and Middle Eastern ornaments.

Soon the whole face was covered with superimposed inscriptions. After the dry green mass was washed off, the visage changed its color to orange-brownish and stayed so for a week—a new mask, a new mocking identity—tentative yet leaving an obvious trace. The artist manages to graphically represent the decolonial principle of irreducible multiplicity that Lugones discusses in many of her works, the many logics never synthesized or hybridized, and never transcended. The changing face color, as a place for multispatial overlay of different epistemic and aesthetic systems, becomes a complex metaphor for a decolonial shift in the geography of reasoning and a recreation of a fluid decolonial community of sense, to paraphrase Jacques Rancière's dictum, merging the ideational and the visceral meanings of the word *sense* (2009).

A DEEP COALITION AFTER ALL?

Lugones formulates the goal of decolonial feminism as "constructing a new subject of a new feminist geopolitics of knowing and loving" (TDF 756). But if and how can we—the inhabitants of Eurasian borderlands—join this global gendered decolonial community of sense? In the Caucasus and Central Asia, Soviet modernity is replaced with either the Western progressive model or the national(ist) discourses characteristic of young postcolonial nations, allowing for only specific propagandistic models of national culture, creativity, and religiosity. Even the works of many local scholars, who are forced to buy their way into the academic sphere by conforming to mainstream Western gender research, erase or negatively code the complex Indigenous cosmologies, epistemologies, ethics, and gender models discordant with modernity/coloniality. It is therefore important for ex-colonial postsocialist gendered others to get acquainted with non-Western approaches to gender. These approaches are coming from theorists/activists of the global South who are seeking deep coalitions grounded in the intersections of our experience and sensibilities. Moreover, these theorists/activists of the global South are hoping to (re)create a flexible gender discourse, one that would answer the local logic and specific conditions while also correlating with other decolonial voices in the world.

To do this it is necessary to take a border position, negotiating between modernity and its internal and external others, between the frozen categorial thinking and the fusion of intermeshing realities. This would allow de-essentialized, flexible, and dynamic groups to understand each other in their/our mutual struggles. At work here is a horizontalized transversal networking of different local histories and sensibilities mobilized through a number of common, yet pluriversal and open, categories, such as coloniality or the postsocialist imaginary. Such networking would enable us to replace the categorial and negative intersectionality that entraps women in situations of sealed otherness and victimhood and merely diagnoses their multiple oppressions, with a more positive re-existent stance of building an alternative world with no others.

This would lead to a shift toward a more conscious praxis, building a ground for a future solidarity. Transversal crossings of activism, theorizing, and contemporary art are some of the most effective tools in social and political struggles against multiple oppressions and in the creation of an other world where many different worlds would coexist co-relationally and communicate with each other in positive and life-asserting ways, aimed at restoring the right to be different but equal. It is necessary to work further on a critical language that would take into account existing parallels between various echoing concepts and epistemic grounds of different (post)gender oppositional discourses. Then post-Soviet non-European gendered others can hope to find their/our own voices in the global chorus against the many faces of coloniality.

Lugones's architectonically complex and nonlinear mode of argumentation balances on the verge of theory, verbal art, and prophecy while reflecting local histories and subjectivities marked by coloniality and grounded in centuries-old oblivion, appropriation, and distortion and an existence always in defiance to modernity. As such, her decolonial feminist work can act as a beacon for the Eurasian borderlands, facilitating its belated joining in the decolonization of gender as a strategy that liberates being, knowledge, and perception from the constraints of modernity/coloniality. This joining in the decoloniality of gender will enable the Eurasian borderlands to become part of those emerging alter-global coalitions of solidarity in difference and multiplicity which, rooted in oppositional consciousness, may foster *pluriversality* and creativity as essential elements of our existence.

REFERENCES

Agamben, Giorgio. 1998. *Homo Sacer: Sovereign Power and Bare Life*. Stanford, CA: Stanford University Press.

Albán Achinte, Adolfo. 2009. "Artistas Indígenas y Afrocolombianos: Entre las Memorias y las Cosmovisiones: Estéticas de la Re-Existencia." In *Arte y Estética en la Encrucijada Descolonial*, edited by Walter Mignolo, 83–112. Buenos Aires: Del Siglo.

Allione, Constanzo, dir. 1997. *Habiba: A Sufi Saint from Uzbekistan*. Film. New York: Mystic Fire Video.

Anzaldúa, Gloria. 1999. *Borderlands/*La Frontera*: The New Mestiza*. 2nd ed. San Francisco: Aunt Lute Books.

Dussel, Enrique. 1985. *Philosophy of Liberation*. Translated by Aquilina Martinez and Christine Morkovsky. Eugene, OR: Wipf & Stock.
Etkind, Alexander. 2011. *Internal Colonization: Russia's Imperial Experience*. Cambridge: Polity.
Gordon, Lewis. 2010. "Philosophy, Science, and the Geography of Africana Reason." *Lichnost. Kultura. Obschestvo* (Personality, Culture, Society) 12(3): 46–56.
Jersild, Austin. 2002. *Orientalism and Empire*. Montreal: McGill-Queen's University Press.
Kluchevsky, Vassily. 2009. *Kurs Russkoy Istorii* (A Course in Russian History). Moscow: Alfa-Kniga.
sharjahart.org/sharjah-art-foundation/people/makhacheva-taus
Maldonado-Torres, Nelson. 2007. "On the Coloniality of Being." *Cultural Studies* 21(2–3): 240–69.
Mignolo, Walter D., and Madina Tlostanova. 2006. "Theorizing from the Borders: Shifting to Geo- and Body-Politics of Knowledge." *European Journal of Social Theory* 9(2): 205–21.
Navailh, Françoise. 1996. "The Soviet Model." In *A History of Women in the West: Towards a Cultural Identity in the Twentieth Century*, edited by Françoise Thebaud, 226–54. Cambridge, MA: Belknap Press.
Nishitani, Osamu. 2006. "*Anthropos* and *Humanitas*: Two Western Concepts of Human Being." In *Translation, Biopolitics, Colonial Difference*, edited by Naoki Sakai and John Solomon, 259–73. Hong Kong: Hong Kong University Press.
Rancière, Jacques. 2009. "Contemporary Art and the Politics of Aesthetics." In *Communities of Sense: Rethinking Aesthetics and Politics*, edited by Beth Hinderliter, William Kaizen, Vered Maimon, Jaleh Mansoor, and Seth McCormick, 31–50. Durham, NC: Duke University Press.
Sahni, Kalpana. 1997. *Crucifying the Orient: Russian Orientalism and the Colonization of Caucasus and Central Asia*. Oslo: White Orchid Press.
Schapov, Afanassy. 1906. *Sochineniya* (Writings). Saint-Petersburg: M.V. Pirozhkov.
Scheglov, Ivan. 1993. *Khronologichesky perechen vazhneishikh dannykh iz istorii Sibiri: 1032–1882* (Chronological List of the Most Important Data of Siberian History: 1032–1882). Surgut: Severny Dom.
Tekuyeva, Madina. 2006. *Muzhchina i Zhenshchina v Adygskoi Kulture* (Man and Woman in the Adygean Culture). Nalchik: El-Fa.

Tlostanova, Madina. 2010a. *Gender Epistemologies and Eurasian Borderlands*. New York: Palgrave Macmillan.

———. 2010b. "A Short Genealogy of Russian Islamophobia." In *Thinking through Islamophobia: Global Perspectives*, edited by S. Sayyid and Abdoolkarim Vakil, 165–84. London: Hurst & Co.

Tlostanova, Madina, and Walter D. Mignolo. 2012. *Learning to Unlearn: Decolonial Reflections from Eurasia and the Americas*. Columbus, OH: The Ohio State University Press.

Tokhtakhodzhayeva, Marfua. 1999. *Mezhdu Lozungami Kommunizma i Zakonami Islama* (Between the Communist Slogans and the Islamic Laws). Tashkent: Women's Resource Center.

Yerofeyev, Victor. 2000. *Pjat Rek Zhizni* (Five Rivers of Life). Moscow: Podkova.

7   Motion Sickness and the Slipperiness of Irish Racialization

Jennifer McWeeny

I have a sickness—a *motion* sickness. I'm addicted to moving, physically, intellectually, socially, temporally. My sleep is deep and unbroken on planes, trains, buses, boats, and all other vehicles. I have traveled to more countries than I am years old. My favorite hobby is long-distance running because it is an unleashing, the possibility of pursuing any direction that moves me. As a scholar, I find it unduly restrictive to limit my thinking to one discipline, philosophical tradition, or perspective. In my social and personal life, I seek friends, lovers, and intellectual companions who promise to change, move, and grow with me, and who do not expect me to stay put for too long. It's no wonder my grandmother would often refer to me as "the vagabond" when she was alive.

There's something more. My motion sickness is not politically neutral. The manner and frequency with which I move have to do with (my) racial location and (my position in) what María Lugones describes as "the coloniality of gender" (HGS, CG, TDF). In certain social and geographical contexts, despite my political convictions, I move toward the seductions of whiteness, womanliness, and their systemic complicities with the racial state—their (my) participation in the subjection of people of color. In others, I turn away from people like my family who remind me of my own Irishness. These are not necessarily movements that follow the same direction, but both reflect a kind of sickness. Perhaps you know someone who lives with an illness like mine? Perhaps you have it too?

I'm pretty sure my motion sickness is a "post-colonial stress disorder" that comes from navigating the *slipperiness* of my Irishness (O'Connor 1995, 127). Slipperiness is an ontological condition that follows upon being subject to two *contradictory* processes of racialization. Feminist geographer Bronwen Walter's description of Irish racialization in the diaspora is suggestive of this situation:

> Outside Ireland, a key aspect of constructions of Irishness is the paradox by which the Irish are represented by dominant Western groups simultaneously as "other," that is racialised as *essentially* different in stereotypical ways, and also the "same" because "white" people share a similar timeless essence.... These constructions depend on an unstated gendering for their effects. (2001, 22; emphasis added)

Rather than fitting squarely and exclusively within either a humanizing process of racialization or a dehumanizing one, slippery identities inhabit a confusion best expressed by the following paradox: they are treated as nonhuman while they are told they are fully human, and they are treated as fully human while they are told they could never be human. Those who are racially slippery learn quickly that by twisting and turning themselves (foregrounding their white parts and backgrounding their nonwhite parts or vice versa), they can change how they are grasped by others. Curiously, slippery racializations tend to become even more slippery the further they get from the direct experience of colonization, when they travel spatially through emigration and immigration into the diaspora, and temporally through colonized psychologies and cosmologies inherited from one generation to the next.

My own experience of ontological slipperiness is linked to the multiple ways that American Irish racialization can be conceived depending on who is looking, what their political aims are, what the surrounding geographical and municipal context is, and where they are looking from.[1] Within this variability, racializing frames for American Irish persons fall along a spectrum from "white" (that is, just as white as an upper-class Anglo-Saxon protestant or Irish in a way that could only be coincident with whiteness) to what I call "Irish*." The addition of the asterisk indicates that in this usage *Irish* does not signify merely a national, ethnic, or cultural identity, but rather a racial physiognomic perception of Irishness that was forged historically to justify colonization of the Irish. This racializing perception cannot be separated from a colonized psychology marked by severe dissociation, codependency, self-hatred, inferiority complexes, horizontal hostility, and violence (Lee 1994; McGoldrick 2005; Moane 1994, 2000; O'Connor 1995). I learned how to perceive and embody Irishness*, and how to perceive when others have the capacity to perceive Irishness*, from the women in my family and within American Irish communities around Boston, Massachusetts, where I grew up. I learned how to perceive and embody whiteness, and how to perceive when others have the capacity to perceive whiteness, from almost everywhere else, most especially from the academy and the profession of philosophy.

I experience the racializations of white and Irish* that alternatively and simultaneously apply to me as I move through different contexts and spaces as *partitioned* like present-day Ireland itself—ontologically separated and violently incompatible, each a betrayal of the other even though they are both constructions of the same body. Living an ambiguous racialization like this affords high expertise in duplicity and subversion ("shiftiness") even if you don't want such proficiencies, as well as a certain facility with nonlinear, nonliteral, and polysemous uses of the colonizer's (English) language such as those exemplified by a James Joyce or a Mary Daly (WC). When I move socially and geographically, I shapeshift like a selkie from the humanness and womanliness of my white racialization to a different, older sense of my self who exists "beyond the pale" and back again, circling, as if I am becoming another being in the act of shedding and donning a wet and furry skin. Sometimes the turn between the two happens intentionally, as a survival strategy or an act of resistance, or as a deliberate impulse to flee what faces me like a snake gliding into a deep hole. Other times the shift catches me unawares, like a big fall on a shiny patch of ice. Still other times I do nothing to summon the change, but I know it is coming.

I have difficulty locating my experience of ontological slipperiness within the dominant scholarly account of Irish American racialization, which maintains that "the Irish became white" in America in the twentieth century or sometime before (Ignatiev 1995; Jacobson 1998; Garner 2004, 2007; Roediger 2006, 2007; Alcoff 2006). Such views resolve the ambiguities of Irish American racialization by appealing to a linear temporality expressed in the following timeline: nonwhite (pre-1924), in-between/transitioning (1924–1965), and white (post-1965) (Jacobson 1998, 91).[2] According to this schema, the conversion process—Irish American racial assimilation to whiteness—could only ever be completed in its entirety; like the transubstantiation of the Eucharist, this transformation leaves no ontological remainder (Ignatiev 1995, 72–105).

A virtue of "Irish became white" approaches is that they emphasize objective determinants of race such as legal status over and above subjective ones like self-ascription. Conceiving of Irish American racialization in this way thus wards against racist rhetorics that seek to implicate a false and politically charged equivalency between the experiences of Irish Americans and those of minorities like African Americans, Latina/os, Arab Americans, and Asians. By seamlessly equating Irishness with whiteness, the political risks of invoking an equivalency with nonwhites are avoided. However, so too are the personal risks of facing and reflecting on the complicit self who is tempted to do so. When examined in depth, the underlying logic of "Irish became white" views shows cause for feminist concern. To maintain their thesis they often downplay or exclude first-person descriptions of Irish American experiences of racialization (especially women's experiences);[3] deploy a decidedly nonintersectional framework that cleanly separates racialization from colonial status, economic class, religion, nationality, sexuality, and gender post-1924; and affirm the ontological fantasy of the civilizing mission, namely, that everyone would become white as soon as they could (TDF 745). That this idea became widely embraced in academia at the same time that the Irish Republican Army (IRA) and other groups fighting for a nonpartitioned, independent Ireland were under pressure to sign the Good Friday Agreement of 1998 and lay down arms against England *for good* is also suggestive of the account's rhetorical role in furthering England's continued colonization of Ireland.

These worries about "Irish became white" views give me pause and spur me to ask whether or not a more complex account of American Irish racialization is possible—one that can accommodate present-day American Irish whiteness without evacuating an ambiguous racial history tied to colonization. I seek a theory capable of holding rather than reducing the identity's phenomenological tensions, contradictions, and dangers while also facilitating self-scrutiny about the seductions and complicities inherent in claiming equivalency or even similarity with people of color. Lugones's concepts of the colonial/modern gender system and decolonial feminism, as well her calls to become self-conscious about one's own racial location and to practice speaking face to face with others as a means of building coalition (HCS), provide apt resources for articulating this alternative description.

It is not the case that the ontological slipperiness that characterizes my experience of American Irish racialization refers to a movement between the light and dark sides of the colonial/modern gender system, from white to nonwhite.[4] Being subject to a dehumanization that is *irrevocable rather than contingent* is part of what it means to be nonwhite in colonial modernity. Lugones does, however, invite further consideration of social locations that do not fit within either the light or dark sides, that are *neither* white *nor* nonwhite (which is not the same as being *both* white *and* nonwhite). She writes: "I am clear now that there is an ambiguous in-between zone between the light and the dark side that conceives/imagines/constructs white women servants, miners, washerwomen, prostitutes as not necessarily caught through the lens of the sexual or gender binary and as racialized ambiguously, but not as white" (HGS 208n19). In this passage, Lugones is referencing a claim that Anne McClintock makes about Irish women, although this context does not come through in the transcription (McClintock 1995, 56).

In this chapter, I give flesh to the notion of an ambiguous third zone within the colonial/modern gender system by articulating a phenomenology of an ontological slipperiness that seeps through the cross-generational spaces of American Irish womanhood. My intention is that in staying with the specificity of my own experience—an experience that is geographically situated and therefore likely not applicable to all or even most Irish Americans—I can reveal an ontological structure that speaks to others who live at the colonial difference in multiple ways, and that could eventually lead to a treatment for my motion sickness and other postcolonial behavioral syndromes that frustrate possibilities for friendship and coalition between the differently and multiply oppressed. I want to know: Is my motion sickness terminal? What are its complications? Is it contagious? Can I/we be cured?

EARLY COLONIZATIONS OF IRELAND

To my knowledge, no scholar has considered the colonization of Ireland in light of Aníbal Quijano's notion of "the coloniality of power" (2000) or Lugones's "coloniality of gender," nor have these concepts been developed with reference to the Irish case.[5] However, when race is understood as a function of "coloniality" (that is, as a system of labor classification that originated in the colonization of the Americas and that continues to justify and facilitate the global and systemic exercise of power through a capitalist market), Irish racialization becomes much more visible than it is when race is conceived merely in terms of phenotypical designations or geographically and temporally localized social constructions. In turn, because England has been engaged in projects of colonization and conquest in Ireland since the twelfth century and explicitly used such projects as a template for strategies of empire deployed centuries later in the Americas, and because this colonization still continues today in a qualified, "devolved" form in Northern Ireland, Irish racialization is not inconsequential to the development of the coloniality of power and the coloniality of gender. Although a thorough account of the evolving racial/gender classification of Irish peoples across the many phases of the coloniality of power and in relation to other racialized groups warrants a book-length study at the very least, in what follows I discuss certain moments in Irish history that have cultivated ontological slipperiness.

We find the beginnings of a colonial-racial "portrait" (Memmi 2013, 79–89) of the Irish in the writings of the monk Geraldus Cambrensis, which include *The History and Topography of Ireland* published in 1187 and *The Vaticinal*

History of the Conquest of Ireland published in 1189. Cambrensis repeatedly explains that the notable characteristics of the Irish race are hostility, rebelliousness, savagery, treachery, idleness, agility, and lack of faith (1968, 122–25, 136–37, 154, 317, 321–23). He remarks that Irish males are literally "barbarous," letting their hair and beards grow in an "uncouth manner" (125), and that Irish females are barbaric because, unlike English women, they urinate standing up and ride a horse by straddling it (140). Critical of the Irish farming practice of transhumance, Cambrensis believes this semi-nomadism is proof that the Irish are ignorant, lazy, and wasteful. He writes: "The Irish are a rude people, subsisting on the produce of their cattle only, and living themselves like beasts—a people that has not yet departed from the primitive habits of pastoral life. In the common course of things, mankind progresses from forest to the field, from the field to the town, and to the social condition of citizens…" (124). On the one hand, Cambrensis's criticisms of Irish primitivism suggest that the Irish are stuck in an early stage of human development and could therefore transform from barbarians to humans if sufficiently civilized (colonized). On the other, he asserts that the duplicity of the Irish character, made manifest by their tendency to lie, swindle, and break laws, "seems to be innate" and is even "contagious," quickly infecting settlers who live in proximity with the natives (138). He therefore recommends that the Irish be "ruled with great discretion" because they will still be given to crime and rebellion even when fully "reduced to submission" (323).

In response to the "incomplete" conquest of Ireland in the twelfth century that allowed for what is commonly known as the "Gaelic resurgence" in the fourteenth, the English of the sixteenth and seventeenth centuries devoted considerable energy to designing and executing a plan for Ireland that would enable total colonization of its land and people (Bardon 2011, ch. 7). In his 1612 treatise on the subject, *A Discovery of the True Causes of Why Ireland Was Never Entirely Subdued*, Sir John Davies laments that the Irish people seem to have remained unchanged since the time of Cambrensis, even though the English have been colonizing the Irish and exposing them to English customs for four hundred years (Davies 1988, 69, 163). He argues that, despite their recalcitrant character, the Irish are likely to be transformed with a more rigorous and "perfect" strategy of colonization based in English governance, settler colonialism, a plantation system of property, and a program of English language education.[6]

As Davies's plantation system began to take root in the province of Ulster in the North of Ireland, oppositional comparisons between English and Scottish settlers and the native Irish fueled suspicion about the humanity of the Irish, racializing the former as enterprising, governable, and civilized, and the latter as lazy, wild, primitive, and lawless (McVeigh and Rolston 2009). The success of Davies's vision was later ensured by a series of laws passed by a settler Parliament in the eighteenth century designed to restrict native Catholics in most areas of public life, dispossess them of their land, and prevent native uprisings.[7] Although not all Catholics in Ireland were Irish, and not all Irish were living in poverty, these Penal Laws worked to further racialize the Irish by cementing religion and class as ontologically constitutive aspects of Irish racial identity and proof of their primitivism and barbarism (22). As a result of these combined strategies, England controlled most of Ireland by 1776: even though Catholics made up 75 percent of the population in Ireland at the time, they owned less than 5 percent of its land (Foster 1989, 211).

With the expansion of England's colonial labor market to the Americas in the seventeenth century, Irish racialization began to assume a different form. One aspect of this colonial economy involved selling Irish (principally women and children) as indentured servants in England's Caribbean colonies, most notably Barbados.[8] This flow of Irish to Barbados was a crucial strategy for building empire, since it decreased the Irish and Catholic populations vis-à-vis Protestants in Ireland, thus furthering conquest there, while also providing labor to the sugar and tobacco plantations in the West Indies, which lacked an indigenous population large enough for that purpose. And yet, the fact that Irish labor was controlled under the rubric of "indentured servitude" (a property for lease) rather than "slavery" (a property for ownership) as was the case with African labor, for example, suggests that the two groups were differentially positioned in relation to ascriptions of humanness, animality, and gender, even as they were experiencing similarly dehumanizing treatment from owners such as being auctioned, weighed on scales, beaten, starved, and so on (Beckles 1989, 2, 71–72).

Whereas Irish racial ambiguity during the twelfth century derived from the ascription of a racial character that was simultaneously natural and amenable to modification, this new seventeenth-century form was grounded in tensions between word and deed, such as being called "free" while being treated as property, or being called "white" while being subject to legislation that limits the number of Irish admitted to the colony due to the violent, untrustworthy, and lawless character of the race (Beckles 1989, 38, 98). Such contradictory designations were produced through comparisons between the Irish and other racial groups and helped to emphasize the whiteness of the English colonizers vis-à-vis Africans, whose labor was quickly becoming the linchpin of the colonial economy (Garner 2007, 80–98). Irish racial ambiguity at this time thus emerged as a consequence of their moving between two spatially and temporally distinct colonial systems of racial classification (England-Ireland and England-Africa-Caribbean) that had not yet integrated with one another under a global scheme.

IRISH RACIALIZATION AND DIASPORA (1800–1998)

During the famine years of 1845 to 1851, more than one million Irish died of starvation, fever, or disease, and approximately two million Irish emigrated overseas to escape these horrors and the colonialist economic policies that supported them (Foster 1989, 323–24; Howe 2000, 38; Moody et al. 2012, 241). This amounts to a 40 percent loss in Ireland's population within six years. British officials and newspapers frequently invoked a familiar colonial-racial portrait to justify England's policy of *laissez faire* in regard to the Irish famine: it was after all the primitive character of the Irish race that solicited such monumental devastation (Howe 2000, 39; Foster 1989, 325). The appeal to Irish racial traits to explain their poverty, misfortune, disposability, and suitability for servitude and manual labor was also operative in the United States, where huge waves of Irish immigrants lived in overcrowded and unsanitary slums while filling the lowest paid and least desirable jobs.

We should not underestimate the ways that the racialization of the Irish has historically operated through a "visual registry" of physical features thought to be indicative of biological inferiority.[9] Matthew Jacobson explains: "As in the case of other racial categories, the social meanings and distinctions surrounding the Celt [in America] were so ideologically thick as to translate into an immediate

Figure 7.1. Reprinted from H. S. Constable, *Ireland from One or Two Neglected Points of View* (London: The Liberty Review Publishing Co., 1899), frontispiece.

Motion Sickness and the Slipperiness of Irish Racialization   153

Figure 7.2. Cartoon by Thomas Nast. "The Ignorant Vote: Honors are Easy," *Harper's Weekly*, December 9, 1876. Cover.

perception of discernible physicality" (1998, 50). Historically, this cultivated perception has found Irishness in facial angle, width, and shape; type of nose and lips; coloring of skin, eyes, and hair; styles of dress and comportment; indications of types of employment; first and last names; and where and with whom a person can be found. The further association of these traits with an inferior racial character was facilitated by an emerging epistemic-scientific apparatus that included physiognomy, ethnology, comparative zoology, and evolutionary theory. That the chimpanzee at the London zoo in the 1890s was named "Paddy" succinctly illustrates this convergence of colonialism and epistemology (Curtis 1971, 1–22, 101). Cartoons and pictures depicting Irish people published in the United States and

England during the nineteenth century make manifest these types of racializing perceptions that were framing and constituting Irish bodies as simian and that may otherwise remain invisible when imagined from a contemporary lens that sees whiteness as synonymous with humanization (Curtis 1971; Murphy 2000).

The images in figures 7.1 and 7.2 illustrate how the ambiguity of Irish racialization is fueled by their juxtaposition with both white people and Black people. In figure 7.2, the Irishman, whose identity is confirmed by the clay pipe in his hat, is at the same time equal to the Black man (a fact made clear by the evenness of the scales and their common classification as "the ignorant vote"), and the opposite of the Black man because he is labeled "white." The Irishman's shoes and city dress in contrast to the Black man's bare feet and field clothes proclaim his civility. And yet, the Irishman's ape-like face and bestial aggression imply that his whiteness is only skin deep, his undeserving inclusion in the nation-state a necessary evil to counterbalance the Black vote—his status is that of a "begrudged majority" rather than a "model minority." Labels common at this time such as "inside-out-niggers," "white slaves," and "white chimpanzees" (conferred on Irish), and "smoked Irish" (conferred on Blacks) likewise imply that the underlying ontologies of both groups was the same: lazy, rebellious, barbaric, primitive, animal, simian. The copy published below figure 7.1 says as much: "The Iberians are believed to have been originally an African race" (Wells 1866). However, the very necessity of the qualifiers in these labels such as "white" and "inside-out"

Fig. 747. - Florence Nightingale.   Fig. 748.—Bridget McBruiser.

Figure 7.3. Reprinted from Samuel R. Wells, *New Physiognomy* (New York: Fowler and Wells, 1866), 537.

THE IRISH DECLARATION OF INDEPENDENCE THAT WE ARE ALL FAMILIAR WITH.

Figure 7.4. Cartoon by Frederick B. Opper. "The Irish Declaration of Independence," *Puck*, May 9, 1883. Cover.

points to differential kinds of dehumanization and other asymmetries between the racialization of the two groups. Similar to the system of racial classification that developed in Barbados in the seventeenth century, the animality of the Irish in nineteenth-century America was contingent on whom the Irish are being compared to in the moment. In contrast, the animality attributed to Blacks was constructed as indelible and, as such, rendered Blackness as a fixed pole by which the degrees of everyone else's humanity could be dialectically measured.

It follows from Lugones's concept of the colonial/modern gender system that the historical racialization of the Irish relies on differential attributions of womanhood between colonizers and colonized that respectively codes them as human and nonhuman. This gender system is starkly evident in figures 7.3 and 7.4.

Not only does the depiction of the Irish woman in figure 7.3 (which is not a cartoon but a textbook illustration) display the typical simian features ascribed to the Irish race at the time, but her name signals that she is a "bruiser": strong, tough, aggressive, primal, given to conflict, and capable of bearing heavy burdens. The narrative in *New Physiognomy* further clarifies the difference between the English woman/human and the Irish female/animal:

> Florence Nightingale... is developed in the "upper story," while the feminine "McBruiser"... lives in the basement mentally as well as bodily. The former would be governed by high moral principles, the latter by the lower or animal passions; the one is a natural friend and philanthropist; the other is at war with everybody; the one is forgiving, the other is vindictive; the one is, by sympathy, attracted toward the heavenly and the good; the other is of the earth, earthy, seeking her chief pleasure from things physical and animal;... the one is esthetical and refined; the other is gross in taste, and sees no beauty in that which can not be eaten or used for the gratification of the bodily appetites or passions. (Wells 1866, 537–38)

Figure 7.4 paints just this racial portrait of the Irish woman in full body. The Irishwoman's imposing hips and bosom mark her ability to labor, both as a servant and as the bearer of (endless) children; the widespread racial stereotype that Irish women, like hens or "biddies," possess "an exceptional degree of fertility" is at play here (Foster 1989, 331). Finally, her demand for independence is portrayed as an ignorant, misguided result of the very brutishness that justifies both the fact of her station and the continuation of Ireland's colonization. During this period, this image of the Irish female as a virago co-existed with another that emphasized her potential to become a woman through expressions of youth, prettiness, passivity, sexual repression, and stupidity (Murphy 2000). Such constructions of the passive, angelic Irish lass in need of protection was jointly facilitated by expressions of a hypermasculinity on the part of Irish men who were countering the colonizer's feminization of them in struggles for Irish Independence (Nash 2002; Curtis 1971, 68–88).[10] This ambiguous gendering of Irish females and males thus reflected and heightened their ambiguous racialization.

David Roediger and other historians have stressed how in the United States of the late nineteenth and early twentieth centuries, working-class Irish immigrants gained a psychological "wage" by exploiting their ambiguous racialization and aligning themselves with whites at the expense of Blacks, Chinese immigrants, and other people of color (Roediger 2007; Jacobson 1998, 17–19). For the Irish, becoming American entailed becoming white, and becoming white in turn entailed distancing themselves from the people of color with whom they shared neighborhoods, communities, and job ranks at the lowest ends of social and economic ladders. Historical events that evidence such alignments are numerous and include the Philadelphia race riots of 1842 and 1844 (Ignatiev 1995, 159, 174); the New York draft riots of 1863 (Jacobson 1998, 52–56); widespread support of the Democratic Party and its proslavery platform (Jacobson 1998, 46); participation in the Order of Caucasians in San Francisco (Garner 2007, 124); and other horrific instances of racism and violence toward people of color carried out by Irish Americans.[11] This history grounds the distrust that many people of color intuitively feel toward Irish Americans today, as well as widespread expectations that Irish Americans are inevitably racist and possibly even more white supremacist than other whites.[12]

While the racism inherent in these events in Irish American history is undeniable, inexcusable, and shameful, the conclusions that historians like Roediger draw from them about the way that Irish Americans experience and embrace their relationship to whiteness are less clear-cut. At the same time that American Irish were becoming racialized as white within the dynamics of the black–white binary, they were also recognizing and affirming their racial classification as Irish* vis-à-vis the movement for Irish independence and collective resistance to anti-Irish prejudice in the United States (Jacobson 1998, 49–52). For example, of her childhood in New Hampshire in the 1890s, Elizabeth Gurley Flynn writes: "There had been an uprising in each generation in Ireland, and forefathers of mine were reputed to be in every one of them. The awareness of being Irish came to us as small children through plaintive song and heroic story.... As children we drew in a burning hatred of British rule with our mother's milk" (1973, 23). My own experience growing up in Boston a century later involved similar sentiments; all Irish eyes were focused on "The Troubles" in Northern Ireland in the 1970s and 1980s and the subsequent Peace Process of the 1990s, which involved witnessing British officials invoke racial tropes about the Irish like the bestial Fenian and the simian terrorist as justification for their continued intervention in Ireland (McVeigh and Rolston 2009, 20).[13] In a number of cases, the anticolonial, antiracist, and anti-imperialist consciousness held by many American Irish as a result of their histories has led to coalitions with people of color, such as the abolitionist rally attended by 5,000 Irish in Boston in 1842 (Osofsky 1975), the Saint Patrick's Battalion of the Mexican-American War (Ignatiev 1995, 186), Ireland's stance of neutrality during World War II in protest of colonial empires who claim to fight for democracy (Moody et al. 2012, 289), and Ireland's support of Argentina in the Falkland Islands dispute of 1982 (316). There is thus a political ambiguity that follows the ambiguous racialization/gendering of Irish Americans and renders them shifty and suspicious: they can fall on the side of racism and white supremacy at one moment and then on the side of antiracist and anticolonial movement in the next, or even at the very same time.

THE SHADOW OF COLONIAL INHERITANCES

Although most people in the United States no longer possess the perceptive faculties to see Irishness* (physically, racially) and therefore to differentiate it from whiteness, the concentration of those who can in certain locations such as Boston, whose population has the highest percentage of Irish Americans of any major U.S. city, creates geographic spaces within the country that racialize their inhabitants differently than others. Walter remarks on the unique character of my hometown as follows: "Anti-Irish attitudes were particularly strong in Boston, where the intellectual elite had close ties with England and there was a less diversified economic and social structure" (2001, 40). In contrast to cities like New York and Philadelphia where the "upward mobility" of whiteness heavily altered the constitution of their Irish populations, in Boston the Irish remained both working class and "a larger and more disadvantaged minority far longer than elsewhere" (49). Perhaps as a result, Boston's Irish neighborhoods did not follow the trends of dissolution and dispersal common to those in other major cities throughout the 1960s and still persist to this day (60). Lawrence J. McCaffrey's characterization of the Boston Irish as "victims of a frozen historical experience" and therefore not prosperous, well educated, or influential like Irish Americans elsewhere is both fitting and hard to hear (1980, 87).

The ways that Boston's Irish communities call for alternative conceptions of diasporic space and time indicate the need for mapping *where* and *when* a given process of racialization is operative or inoperative in relation to Irish Americans in order to shed light on contemporary experiences of ambiguous racialization. We should consider a process of racialization *operative* in a given locale insofar as there are people (and/or institutions) there who have the capacity to perceive another in terms of that process, and *inoperative* when perceivers are lacking. National borders, colonial epochs, and state and federal legislation pool processes of racialization in relation to certain groups, but they do not exclusively contain them. Leaks may arise and ambiguities may intensify in certain diasporic configurations and through psychologies and ontologies passed on from one generation to the next, among both Irish people and those who hold prejudicial views against them.

Whenever racializing perceptions of Irishness* are operative in a given locale *and* they find resonance in the psychology or self-image of the American Irish individual who is subject to them, a kind of subjectivity that I call "the shadow" is called forth. The shadow involves the literal re-membering of a prior moment in the coloniality of power by inhabiting a habitual bodily comportment and perspective—a subjectivity—that was produced in that moment and has since been inherited through the intimate spaces of everyday, familial life and local community relations.[14] Shadow-subjectivity traces a spiraling and reversible temporality that doubles back between past and present, never to be erased, but also never to be repeated in exactly the same way as before.[15] When I move into the shadow, when I cross the border of this hand-me-down colonial partition, I shift from Florence Nightingale (or at least someone who is almost always mistaken for her) to Bridget McBruiser. Slipping into Bridget's subjectivity, as familiar as it may be, entails being Irish*, that is, being determined by a violent past rife with colonial legacies; it involves experiencing myself as a workhorse who is inescapably gross in taste and spiteful, physically unfeminine, essentially unintelligent no matter my level of education, and forever vulnerable to the immediate and long-term effects of shaming, family dysfunction, and violence. The only way out of this pain and its inevitability is to not be Irish* anymore.[16] Not only does this inherited subjectivity follow you the more that you try to run away from it, it is also a blurred and inexact (and therefore less legible) repetition of the historical subjectivity originally forged in colonization because of its distance from the political relationships constitutive of its origin. The shadow is therefore not the same as the colonial-racial portrait that casts it, but it is not a fantasy either; shadow-subjectivity is an intersubjective phenomenon that must be keyed into a space that racializes and dehumanizes in order to persist in an individual's psychology.

The shadow does not live equally among all Irish in the diaspora, nor is it a subjectivity that can apply to any Irish American just in virtue of being Irish American; it is geographically specific and community specific. The shadow exists differently in people who are differently visible as Irish* due to physical appearance, name, facility with English, levels of education and wealth, skin color, and so on. It is most often conjured when one is living in a way that is immersed in Irish culture and tradition, which could include residing in American Irish neighborhoods, attending Catholic parochial schools, thinking and speaking through Irish Gaelic words and cosmologies, being in regular contact with Irish nationals and undocumented Irish living in the United States, living with grandparents or relatives who experienced anti-Irish prejudice in the 1930s, 1940s, and 1950s, or having a political consciousness connected with anticolonial and anti-imperialist movements for Irish independence. Importantly, the shadow is never far off when the material conditions of one's life reflect legacies of colonialism like poverty, alcoholism, child abuse, domestic violence, incarceration, mental illness, sickness, severe dissociation, depression, and suicide, many of which afflict Irish American populations today at exceptionally high rates.[17]

O'Connor's concept of a "post-colonial character syndrome" evident in Irish populations throughout the diaspora provides one way of envisioning how colonial psychologies circle from past to present, bringing the shadow with them (1995). This syndrome is characterized by high levels of irrational shame and guilt for being Irish* that are inherited cross-generationally. As O'Connor writes:

> In the same way that the caricature or false persona of an abused child can be regarded as a behavioral adaptation to the threat of parental abuse, the "Irish Catholic Character" can perhaps best be seen as a caricature of itself, a cultural false persona based on massive misperceptions of inferiority which evolved as a survival mechanism in the struggle against prolonged abuse by British governments and their representatives in Ireland. (139–40)

When parents are afflicted with "the hidden shame of being Irish," they pass this racialized shame, along with the sense of possessing an essentially inferior identity, on to their children through verbal and nonverbal practices (144). A postcolonial syndrome can be further exacerbated due to the presence of inherited traumas in the family system that originated in events such as famine, genocide, rape, and other forms of colonial violence. Traumas are transmitted from generation to generation by "learning to experience an intense fear, helplessness, or horror through viewing another's experience of trauma (e.g., anger, depression, alcohol/drug abuse) and learning to react/act in similar fashion" (Coll et al. 2012, 95). Colonial processes of racialization and their shadows are also inscribed in the bodies and everyday cultural practices of (post)colonial subjects and their descendants (DF 84, TDF 754). Food choices, household rituals, occupations, ways of speaking to and conceiving of one another, postures, glances, and the facility with which violence, alcoholism, depression, and shame are exercised are all capable of feeding the shadow and circling a colonial-racial portrait from the past to the present. The shadows of colonial inheritances and repetitions thrive here, in the commonplace, in the sensuous, cultural flesh.

Inheriting shame or trauma is not the same as inheriting membership in a racial group or the experience of being subject to a dehumanizing process of racialization.[18] Colonial inheritances do, however, provide fertile ground for the shadow of a historical racial portrait to take seed in one's present-day subjectivity and remain poised to pierce the soil in geographical spaces and family systems where racializing perceptions of Irishness* are operative. Thus unearthed, the shadow-self can follow you to other places where these perceptions are *inoperative*—when you go to apply for a job, when you spend money that your parents never had, when you attempt to speak with intellectual authority, when you make friends and intimates who aren't Irish*, when you attempt to realize your life's dreams. Indeed, the shadow often becomes more pronounced (more menacing) the more you step into the light of success and happiness. Over and over, I've seen the women in my family be suffocated by the shadow, their unshakeable conviction in their own original inferiority and in the inevitability of a tragic future closing off most possibilities for self-expression, success, and happiness. In this dense and humid space, the existential question of "Why go on?" pounds and nauseates (Maldonado-Torres 2007). Connecting with the women in my family thus means connecting with my own shadow and my own pain.

A PHENOMENOLOGY OF SLIPPERINESS

Having frustrated the assumptions of linear temporality and fixed space with the notion of shadow-subjectivity, we are now in a position to elucidate the experience of ontological slipperiness. Considering ontological slipperiness together with a concept that I call "the immediate grasp" will enable us to see how the personal experience of slipperiness—of slipping in and out of the shadow—is always already social and spatial, necessarily tied to intersubjective relationships, locally shaped perceptions, and specific processes of racialization that are variably operative across different geographic places. The visibility of one's shadow is, after all, dependent on the angle from which one is seen. Slipperiness is about twisting and turning within the cognitive grasp of another, writhing and undulating within the heterogeneous spatiality of the social, so as to continuously change the parts of your multiplicity that are visible and accessible to others through their situating epistemic frames. Those who slip bank on the fact that, more often than not, the part will be mistaken for the whole.

The immediate grasp is an intuitive and spontaneous impression of an aspect of another's identity that occurs at the level of sensuous perception and therefore often without conscious reflection, although reflection is frequently used to confirm or deny the original grasp retrospectively. Such perceptions as

"She's Latina too!" "He has a foreign accent," "She's working-class, but trying to hide it," "They're gay," or "I can't believe I never noticed that he's trans" express the kind of epistemic moment at stake in the immediate grasp. In some cases, this grasp is facilitated by a fine-grained cultural skill and practical logic that is built on repeated experiences, whether first or second hand, with the identity in question ("She's Latina too!"). In other situations, the immediate grasp emerges out of a *lack* of familiarity with an identity such as when an Indian man is perceived as "Black" in contexts where the black/white binary is the dominant racializing frame. Although the immediate grasp can be inspired by multiple kinds of perceptions, including loving perceptions or arrogant ones (WT 78), or homogenizing perceptions or "duplicitous" ones that see multiple meanings (TSC 225), *it is always the case that the immediate grasp is not necessarily veridical.* Though accompanied by a feeling of intuitive certainty, the immediate grasp can get things wrong as easily as it can get things right.

The immediate grasp is a self-relation as well as a relation between self and other. This part of the grasp involves the way a person experiences herself when others are trying to hold her, which likely includes a lived sense of her own racialized, gendered, and classed identity at a particular point in time. Like the immediate grasps of others, one's own capacity for different grasps of oneself can be operative or inoperative in relation to the situating context.

In my own case, slipperiness is a function of the range of possibilities afforded by various combinations of the following four factors: (a) whether or not the epistemological frames of white and Irish* are operative in a given geographical location or social structure, (b) which racializing frame others employ to grasp me, (c) which frame I perceive them to be using, and (d) which frame I use to grasp myself. This schema yields a set of eight possible racializing configurations in spaces where both white and Irish* epistemological frames (grasps) are *operative*:

I Grasp Myself as Irish* Configurations

1. I grasp myself as Irish*, am grasped by others as Irish*, and perceive that they grasp me as Irish*.
2. I grasp myself as Irish*, am grasped by others as Irish*, but perceive that they grasp me as white.
3. I grasp myself as Irish*, but am grasped by others as white, but perceive that they grasp me as Irish*.
4. I grasp myself as Irish*, but am grasped by others as white, and perceive that they grasp me as white.

I Grasp Myself as White Configurations

5. I grasp myself as white, but am grasped by others as Irish*, and perceive that they grasp me as Irish*.
6. I grasp myself as white, but am grasped by others as Irish*, but perceive that they grasp me as white.
7. I grasp myself as white, am grasped by others as white, but perceive that they grasp me as Irish*.
8. I grasp myself as white, am grasped by others as white, and perceive that they grasp me as white.

In contexts where the Irish* epistemological frame is *inoperative*, which is to say that there is no other person or institution in that context capable of grasping me as Irish*, the possible grasp-portrait configurations reduce to four: 3, 4, 7 and 8, the set of all possibilities where I am grasped by others as white. Insofar as I *know* that the Irish* racial portrait is inoperative in these contexts, there will be a different, narrower, set of possibilities: 4 and 8.

Slipperiness arises when a person not only moves between different racializing configurations, but also between different *sets* of configurations, such as the set where the capacity to grasp others as Irish* is inoperative (3, 4, 7, 8) to the set where both Irish* and white grasps are operative (1–8). Adding up the configurations in all possible sets and treating each configuration in a different set as a new configuration, we arrive at a total of *seven* sets and *thirty-two* racializing configurations that are ontologically possible for an American Irish female like myself. And yet, slipping entails the *realization* of multiple configurations, not their mere possibility. An American Irishwoman who spends the majority of her time in an Irish community may realize only two of the above grasp-portrait configurations (number 1 when she is home and number 3 when she travels to a place where the Irish* frame is inoperative). Likewise, an Irishwoman who has assimilated completely to whiteness and lives in a place where Irish* racialization is inoperative is represented by number 8: "white" is the only epistemological frame available in other's perceptions and in her own consciousness. For this reason, *motion is crucial to slipperiness*: the more an American Irishwoman moves between contexts where different racializing frames are possible, the more she will slip in and out of the shadows of Irishness*, the more slippery she will *be*. Let us consider the nature of slipperiness with reference to the following examples from my experience, where symptoms of a sickness that comes with living a slippery racialization may already be evident.

Example A

Upon moving back to Boston after having been away for eighteen years, a friend of mine arranged a meet-up event for people interested in classical music where none of the attendees knew each other in advance. At her house, I began to converse with the man standing next to me, who turned out to be a wealthy businessman. He started by saying he was a little nervous to go to an open party where anyone could show up. He then made a joke by imagining what he took to be the worst possible scenario: "You could even get one of those criminal-types from Southland." Locals call the traditionally Irish neighborhood of South Boston "Southie." I knew right away what this man meant and that he was invoking the Irish* rather than the Irish. His offer to connect over *our* obvious difference from those poor, unlawful people left me paralyzed and confused.

Later at the party, I met a couple, he a poet and she an artist, whom I clicked with right away. The man and I immediately recognized each other as Irish* and told all kinds of stories, Irish-style, on the way home once we had left the space. (I learned later he was, like many Boston Irish, a dual-citizen even though he was second generation.) I am struck by how the two men's respective grasps of my identity—at the very same time and in the very same context—could be so different. I am also aware of how I grasped the men's respective identities in relation to the kinds of subjectivity their behavior called forth in me. I slipped into white subjectivity with the classical music connoisseurs, but, relieved when the poet recognized me as Irish*, I stepped into the shadow and even began to exaggerate Irish styles of speech, posture, and interaction. In the course of a few hours, I experienced at least five different grasp-portrait configurations: numbers 4 and 8 with the businessman and 1, 2, and 5 with the poet.

Example B

It's more than ten years ago and I'm sitting on the perimeter at the Roundtable for Latina Feminism. There is a big table in the middle of the room that seats about twenty people. It did not cross my mind to sit at the table. I'm not Latina, and I know the value of separatist politics because of how and where I grew up. As I listen to the conversations, I sometimes imagine myself at the table, speaking from a place of experiential authority about topics like anticolonial political movement, decolonization, and coalitional organizing. In this space I oscillate between numbers 4 and 8 (assuming that no one in the room grasps me as Irish*). From the former configuration, I feel the pull of slipping into a space at the table where my experience is with company. But I also wonder if the desire to make my experience central and pretend otherwise is really a manifestation of number 8, where I grasp myself as white. Out on the perimeter and staying silent, I avoid the risks of engagement—the possibilities that I would be differentiated from Latinas, identified with white women, or left alone in the illegibility of my Irishness*.

Example C

Recently, I participated in a panel on my co-edited book *Asian and Feminist Philosophies in Dialogue* at the annual meeting of a prominent academic society in California. There was a male graduate student in the audience who was contributing regularly to the discussion and seemed to have working command of many of the languages engaged in the book, such as classical Chinese, Sanskrit, Hindi, and Pāli. When the discussion began to address the theme of translation and incommensurability between cultures, he offered the example of the Boston Irish community and explained how, as someone pursuing his linguistics degree at Harvard University, he found their language incomprehensible even though they were speaking in "English." His comment about the Boston Irish shifted my grasp of myself quickly, shockingly, from white to Irish*, and thus the configuration as a whole from number 8 to 3. In the aftermath of this situation, I felt a strong urge to be only white—to rush back to number 8; outed and ashamed, and not expecting the Irish* frame to be operative in this space, I kept angling to hide the shadow right behind me.

Example D

My mother and I are placing baskets of flowers on all of the family graves for Memorial Day. This annual ritual involves driving to four different cemeteries and inevitably walking up and down several rows of headstones reading the names until we find our relatives. My mother does not write down any of the locations; she has where they are in her memory and in the practical habits of her body ("It's up on that hill" or "It's to the right of the bend in the road"). She talks to each person we encounter, touches the warmth of the stones above them, and affirms an ancient cosmology that she learned from my grandfather where there is easy continuity between life and death. Identifying with my mother means identifying with being Irish*. Inversely, any signs that I am slipping away from Irishness* are read as indications that I don't want to be like her, so she eyes me with suspicion intermittently, especially when I talk about worlds that she does not know. We stick to the gossip from the flower shop and everything goes smoothly. It's a good day for us. The usual tensions that we carry for each other are in the background, as are the wider family dynamics and traumas that have shaped us, held by the dead as much as the living. Despite the simplicity of our interaction, the racializing possibilities are exceedingly complex. Since she is fluent with both white and Irish* frames and I can animate both subjectivities (and she's not sure what I am, and I'm not sure what she thinks I am), all eight grasp-portrait configurations are in play.

At first glance, it may seem that ontological slipperiness is a paradigm that can accommodate any kind of racial ambiguity, hybridity, or multiplicity. But slipping is not world-traveling (WT); it can be used to close off meaning, uphold the presumed fungibility of people of color, and forget one's own racial location at the same time that it can be deployed resistantly as anticolonial and decolonial feminist movement. Slipping also exploits *mismatches* rather than congruities between subjectivities and worlds/structures/times. In these respects, the idea of slipperiness is specifically tied to the kind of ambiguous racialization that is characteristic of Irish and Irish American experience. Moreover, slipperiness has been a hallmark of Irish barbarism since the time of Cambrensis, who writes: "This race is inconstant, changeable, wily, and cunning. It is an unstable race, stable only in its instability, faithful only in its unfaithfulness" (1968, 136). At the same time that ontological slipperiness is particular to American Irish experience, the notions of slipperiness, shadow-subjectivity, and the immediate grasp provide a conceptual apparatus that may (with some adjustments) be useful for articulating other experiences of racialization and gendering within the coloniality of power.[19]

Perhaps the most important consequence of the phenomenology of slipperiness developed here is that it encourages us to be attentive to those sites where the coloniality of power desiccates the slipperiness of some racialized identities while it saturates others. Ontological slipperiness is possible whenever there are at least two contradictory ways that a person is (or has been) grasped by herself and others. By contrast, desiccation involves the petrification of meanings such that a person has only one or very few grasp-portrait configurations that she could inhabit. For example, Frantz Fanon describes his experience of being a Black man in terms of "an absolute density" that is perceived monolithically to such an extent that he can't shake the frame of meaning he is seen through no matter what he does or how he moves (Fanon 2008, 113). White supremacist perception fixes the way that Black people are grasped and rings out any fluidity inherent in processes of racialization. It also ossifies whiteness as humanness so that whites are inherently protected from other meanings and designations; their humanity becomes unquestionable, taken for granted, natural law. Nevertheless, degrees of slipperiness do not always map cleanly onto group constructions; within any group there will be variable levels of ontological slipperiness and desiccation among its individual members, even if general patterns are recognizable across groups. Noticing whose identities are dried out and whose are soaking within a given racial group and among groups can reveal vital clues as to where the coloniality of power is headed and which forms of resistance and coalition can best frustrate its course.

AN EPIDEMIOLOGY OF MOTION SICKNESS

In situations of ambiguous racialization, continuous movement across different racializing spaces intensifies slipperiness. However, it is not necessarily the case that ontological stasis is an oppressive condition while ontological mobility is a liberating and resistant one. Lugones reminds us that mobility is itself multidirectional and multivalent (MSR 49). In order to see the political work that movement does, we must examine the particularity of our own movement closely, from multiple perspectives and from the eyes of other resistant beings pressing against, fracturing, the coloniality of power. Lugones encourages us to ask:

> Why are we moving, who is moving, who's moving where, who is she when she gets there, does she recognize them, does she recognize herself, why does she want to go there, what does she bring with her on her trip, what does she hope to gain by going there, is she going there to stay or is she going there to visit? The answers will not be the same for women located differently. Why is it that I, for example, would go to places inhabited by other women of color? (49)

As I direct these questions toward my own slips, slides, and twists within the coloniality of power, I begin to see motivations that fuel my addiction to motion and deepen my motion sickness.

The original impulse for my movement away from those grasp-portrait configurations that recognize me as Irish* was survival. Like Moraga, "I instinctively made choices which I thought would allow me greater freedom of movement in the future" (2000, 91). I wanted education and opportunity. I wanted to transcend the colonial-racial portrait that framed me as "living in the basement mentally." And so I slipped resistantly, to escape different manifestations of coloniality, sexism, heterosexism, and racism. I also slipped away from the shadow of my colonial inheritances—alcoholism, co-dependency, sexual abuse, violence, depression, and poverty—and its promise to tether me to the Irish* portrait for the rest of my life. I knew I exceeded the subjectivity and life anchored in the colonial legacies surrounding me, so I cut the line.

The next stage of my illness began when this survival strategy that I used in rare moments became habitual. I was less intentional about my slipping and less interested in the destination: it was the slipping itself that I needed, that gave me respite from the pressures of being Irish*, of being white, of not being Irish*, of not being white, of being culturally overdetermined, of being culturally indeterminate, of having a family and a history, of starting over on my own. When I slip, I feel like I could be anything: *I inhabit a temporality of potential.* When I stay, I feel like I'm living a life that is wanting in some or many ways. This is when the queasiness sets in. The only cure is to cast off and set my sights on a new destination. And so I quickly became addicted to movement. I started slipping among configurations not only in regard to processes of racialization, but also in respect to ideas, perspectives, friends and intimates, temporalities, geographies, and any other frame that I could oscillate myself into or out of. Slipping became my way of life and my subjectivity; I could not imagine myself located anywhere else but in the movement, in the slip.

This constant slipping progressed further to an emptying of my identity, an "evacuation of [my] locus" (Roshanravan 2010, 15). In this condition, I am unable to meet others from a place of my own specific, cultural history; I am unable to bring the particularity of my location to decolonial feminism and Women of Color coalition. Similar to the phenomenon that Shireen Roshanravan calls "passing-as-if a woman of color," I slip out of my skins and leave a ghostly shell to the intimate and demanding work of political coalition (8). But where Roshanravan's "passing-as-if" is a move motivated by the desire for resistant company, the impetus for my slipping comes from an inverse direction: I want to outrun my past, my future, and my fears of being pinned down, grasped, touched for all of who I am. Unlike when I am with other Irish women or upper-class white women, when I am with women of color I am almost always grasped as ontologically white rather than ontologically Irish*. In these spaces, I can therefore consider the relation between Catholicism and the coloniality of power with Latinas, or mechanisms of British imperialism with Indian women, without placing these aspects of coloniality within my own ambiguous history, my own duplicitous body.

By continuously exploiting the slipperiness of Irish racialization, squirming and writhing from grasp-portrait configuration to grasp-portrait configuration, I evade, however momentarily or superficially, both the shadow-subjectivity that I have inherited and the pain of the wound at the fractured locus, where I am multiple, complex, and complicit in others' oppressions (TDF 754). I also forgo the invitation to stay and cultivate intimacy through the work of love and coalition. My motion sickness is thus a "disorder of belonging" that surfaces "in the intimate narrows of face-to-face relationships" (O'Connor 1995, 140). The symptoms of motion sickness are an intense nausea from perpetual, circular movement; a heartache that follows upon leaving just before being touched by others tenderly, deeply; and amnesia that comes with every twist and turn that alternatively displays my white underbelly and my shadowy pelt.

Paradoxically, however, in my early moves to leave my Irishness* behind, I was also becoming more Irish*. From pre-conquest Indigenous cultures to the ages of conquest, famine, and land dispossession, the Irish have always deployed movement—emigrating, immigrating, pilgrimage, peregrination, exile—as acts of resistance against the horrors of invasion, colonization, and political persecution. The English colonizers and American nativists saw this movement as politically dangerous because it heightened the ungovernability of the Irish and facilitated rebellion. For example, religious pilgrimages were forbidden by law in the seventeenth-century Penal Codes in an expression of the colonizing logic that respectively equates nomadism with barbarism and Catholicism with primitivism (Moody et al. 2012, 191). Decolonial feminism has helped me to see that at the same time that the shadow can pull me down, staying with my Irishness* can also open me to lineages of creative resistance.

It was not until I started to recognize my Irishness* and think it through with depth and complexity that I began to understand how racism and white supremacy work against women of color with depth and complexity—that is, with a genuine capacity to hear their own constructions of themselves and their own constructions of me, even as these constructions are painful to recognize because they reflect me as complicit, less than what I wish I was. Lugones's words resonate with me now viscerally, strumming through my flesh: "You do not see me because you do not see yourself and you do not see yourself because you declare yourself outside culture" (HCS 46). Decolonial feminism has brought me to the reality that I am something more than either a being exhausted by domination (Irish*) or a being exhausted by her complicities with the subjection of people of color (white). I am beginning to grasp the women in my family as something more than these too. Lugones's philosophy teaches me that slips and shadows are always double-edged. It's no coincidence that someone shifty like me would find affirmation and company, but also pain and difficulty, in her praxis.

Once or twice my father has told me a story about a time that precedes my own memories. He said that when I was about two years old we visited the local shopping mall. We were at one end of the mall and I began walking in the direction of the other end. He said he wanted to see how far I would go by myself before I turned around and looked for him, so he followed me from a distance, leaving me room to explore. As he tells it, I motored steadily to the other end of the mall and never once looked back.

But I don't want this story to end here. I don't want the selkie's slippery motion from animal to human to lead inevitably to her isolation, to her living in the world on the other side of intimacy, as it always does in Celtic folklore. I sense the possibility of a different future in this inherited past. After all, the seal skin is both the selkie's most vulnerable aspect and the site of her power and agency, her very capacity for love and transformation. In the version I would write now, I keep going and going out into the world, but then I circle back in search of touch, companionship, and love. And in the place I left, which is now somehow different, I find a grasp that holds and comforts me in virtue of its inability to hold all of me, in virtue of its capacity to sense the ways that I slip through. I meet an embrace that is wide enough to hold each of us in our respective complexities yet fine-grained enough that we just might stay long enough to acknowledge our historical and racialized legacies but not be determined by them, to love and be loved, to move in friendship and connection with you.

NOTES

This chapter would not have been possible without the honest, considered, and direct feedback that I received from several individuals who gave their time and generosity to read earlier drafts. I am deeply grateful for comments from Vrinda Dalmiya, Janine Jones, Noreen Khawaja, José Jorge Mendoza, Courtney Miller, James Morley, Kelli Zaytoun, Pedro DiPietro, and Shireen Roshanravan.

    1. In my own community of predominantly U.S. citizens, we have always referred to ourselves as "Irish" (or, less frequently, "American Irish") rather than "Irish American." Because this essay is attentive to the first-personal experiences of Irish people, I use "Irish American" when I am discussing an outsider's perspective on the culture and "American Irish" when I am emphasizing an insider's perspective.

    2. Garner draws the timeline earlier: nonwhite (pre-1830), in-between/transitioning (1830–1890), and white (post-1890) (2004, 112).

3. Noel Ignatiev, for example, looks at Irish Americans from the outside and divines a collective Irish American (male) subjectivity or will from historical records and documents that, in his words, "aim[s] not so much at facsimilitude as plausibility" (1995, 205).

4. See the introduction to this volume for a summary description of the colonial/modern gender system (p. 15-17).

5. Mignolo mentions Ireland specifically but does not explore the suggestion in any detail (2011, 110).

6. Several scholars have drawn a link between strategies of empire developed to subdue Ireland and their subsequent deployment in the Americas. See Marx (1971), Liggio (1976), Beckles (1989, 71), Jacobson (1998, 38).

7. For descriptions of the Penal Laws, see Moody et al. (2012, 187–200), Ignatiev (1995, 40–41), Howe (2000, 33–35), and Foster (1989, 205–7).

8. Peter Ellis estimates that 50,000 Irish came to Barbados during this period (1975, 154) while Stephen Howe suggests 40,000 (2000, 33).

9. This is Alcoff's phrase (2006, 191–94).

10. Cf. Lugones (TDF 744), Maldonado-Torres (2007, 248).

11. For a recent example involving a policeman called "Big Irish," see Evan Allen and Andrea Estes, "Trooper Involved in Shooting Has History of Racist Online Posts," *The Boston Globe*, March 1, 2018, www.bostonglobe.com/metro/2018/03/01/state-trooper-involved-shooting-has-history-racist-online-posts/0l1bJhMSvNM69RBN30R6RJ/story.html.

12. Cherríe Moraga's story of helping an Irish woman take out the garbage poignantly illustrates this widespread distrust (2000, 125).

13. More recently, discussions of Brexit have provided fertile ground for Irish racial tropes. For example, see Henry McDonald, "Brexit Border 'Would Make Sitting Ducks of Northern Ireland Police,'" *The Guardian*, January 15, 2017, www.theguardian.com/uk-news/2017/jan/15/brexit-border-would-make-sitting-ducks-of-northern-ireland-police.

14. The idea of a shadow-subjectivity or a body-memory of prior intersubjective relations resonates with Fanon's concept of a historical-racial schema that exists beneath the body schema (2008, 91).

15. I am grateful to Rosalie Post for encouraging me to explore this theme of circularity in relation to Irish culture and narrative.

16. Cf. Smith (2005, 8).

17. Coll et al. (2012, 96–97), McGoldrick (2005), and Galvan and Caetano (2003).

18. I am grateful to José Mendoza for stressing this point to me.

19. For examples of other subjectivities that show signs of slipperiness, see Lugones (ND, DC 125), Zack (1996), Weiss (2014), and Mendoza (2017).

REFERENCES

Alcoff, Linda Martín. 2006. *Visible Identities: Race, Gender, and the Self.* New York: Oxford University Press.

Bardon, Jonathan. 2011. *The Plantation of Ulster: The British Colonisation of the North of Ireland in the Seventeenth Century.* Dublin: Gill & Macmillan.

Beckles, Hilary McD. 1989. *White Servitude and Black Slavery in Barbados, 1627–1715.* Knoxville: The University of Tennessee Press.

Cambrensis, Giraldus Silvester. 1968. *The Historical Works of Giraldus Cambrensis.* Translated by Thomas Forester. New York: AMS.

Coll, Kenneth M., Brenda Freeman, Paul Robertson, Eileen Iron Cloud, Ethleen Iron Cloud Two Dogs, and Rick Two Dogs. 2012. "Exploring Irish Multi-Generational Trauma and Its Healing: Lessons from the Oglala Lakota (Sioux)." *Advances in Applied Sociology* 2(2): 95–101.

Curtis, L. Perry Jr., 1971. *Apes and Angels: The Irishman in Victorian Caricature.* Washington: Smithsonian Institution Press.

Davies, Sir John. 1988. *A Discovery of the True Causes of Why Ireland Was Never Entirely Subdued...*, edited by James P. Myers, Jr. Washington, DC: The Catholic University Press of America.

Ellis, Peter Berresford. 1975. *Hell or Connaught! The Cromwellian Colonisation of Ireland 1652–1660.* New York: St. Martin's Press.

Fanon, Frantz. 2008. *Black Skin, White Masks.* Translated by Richard Philcox. New York: Grove Press.

Flynn, Elizabeth Gurley. 1973. *The Rebel Girl, An Autobiography, My First Life (1906–1926).* New York: International Publishers.

Foster, R. F. 1989. *Modern Ireland: 1600–1972.* New York: Penguin Books.

Galvan, F.H., and R. Caetano. 2003. "Alcohol Use and Related Problems among Ethnic Minorities in the United States." *Alcohol Research and Health* 27: 87–94.

Garner, Steve. 2004. *Racism in the Irish Experience.* London: Pluto Press.

———. 2007. *Whiteness: An Introduction.* New York: Routledge.

Howe, Stephen. 2000. *Ireland and Empire: Colonial Legacies in Irish History and Culture.* Oxford: Oxford University Press.

Ignatiev, Noel. 1995. *How the Irish Became White.* New York: Routledge.

Jacobson, Matthew Frye. 1998. *Whiteness of a Different Color: European Immigrants and the Alchemy of Race.* Cambridge, MA: Harvard University Press.

Lee, Joseph. 1994. "The Irish Psyche." *Journal of Irish Psychology* 33: 1–20.

Liggio, Leonard. 1976. "The English Origins of Early American Racism." *Radical History Review* 3(1): 1–36.

Maldonado-Torres, Nelson. 2007. "The Coloniality of Being." *Cultural Studies* 21(2): 240–70.
Marx, Karl. 1971. "Outline of a Report on the Irish Question." In *Ireland and the Irish Question* by Karl Marx and Friedrich Engels, 126–42. Moscow: Progress Publishers.
McCaffrey, Lawrence J. 1980. "A Profile of Irish America." In *America and Ireland 1776–1976*, edited by David Doyle and Owen Edwards, 81–91. London: Greenwood.
McClintock, Anne. 1995. *Imperial Leather: Race, Gender, and Sexuality in the Colonial Conquest.* New York: Routledge.
McGoldrick, Monica. 2005. "Irish Families." In *Ethnicity and Family Therapy*, edited by Monica McGoldrick, Joe Giordano, and Nydia Garcia-Preto, 595–615. New York: Guilford Press.
McVeigh, Robbie, and Bill Rolston. 2009. "Civilising the Irish." *Race & Class* 51(1): 2–28.
Memmi, Albert. 2013. *The Colonizer and the Colonized.* Plunkett: Lake Press.
Mendoza, José Jorge. 2017. "Latinx and the Future of Whiteness in American Democracy." *American Philosophical Association Newsletter on Hispanic/Latino Issues in Philosophy* 16(2): 6–10.
Mignolo, Walter D. 2011. *The Darker Side of Western Modernity: Global Futures, Decolonial Options.* Durham, NC: Duke University Press.
Moane, Geraldine. 1994. "A Psychological Analysis of Colonialism in an Irish Context." *The Irish Journal of Psychology* 15(2–3): 250–65.
———. 2000. "Psychic Liberation: Feminist Practices of Transformation among Irish Women." In *Feminist Interpretations of Mary Daly*, edited by Sarah Lucia Hoagland and Marilyn Frye, 389–417. State College, PA: Pennsylvania State University Press.
Moody, T.W., F.X. Martin, and Dermot Keogh with Patrick Kelly, eds. 2012. *The Course of Irish History.* Lanham, MD: Roberts Rinehart.
Moraga, Cherríe L. 2000. *Loving in the War Years:* lo que nunca pasó por sus labios. 2nd ed. Cambridge, MA: South End Press.
Murphy, Maureen. 2000. "Bridget and Biddy: Images of the Irish Servant Girl in Puck Cartoons, 1880–1890." In *New Perspectives on the Irish Diaspora*, edited by Charles Fanning, 152–73. Edwardsville: Southern Illinois University Press.
Nash, Catherine. 2002. "Embodied Irishness: Gender, Sexuality, and Irish Identities." In *In Search of Ireland: A Cultural Geography*, edited by Brian Graham, 108–27. New York: Routledge.

O'Connor, Garrett. 1995. "Recognising and Healing Malignant Shame: A Statement about the Urgent Need for Psychological and Spiritual Recovery from the Effects of Colonialism in Ireland." In *Distant Relations = Cercanías Distantes = Clann I gCéin*, edited by Trisha Ziff, 126–45. Santa Monica: Smart Art Press.

Osofsky, Gilbert. 1975. "Abolitionists, Irish Immigrants, and the Dilemmas of Romantic Nationalism." *The American Historical Review* 80(4): 889–912.

Quijano, Aníbal. 2000. "Coloniality of Power, Eurocentrism, and Latin America. *Nepantla: Views from the South* 1 (3): 533–80.

Roediger, David R. 2006. *Working toward Whiteness: How America's Immigrants Became White*. New York: Basic Books.

———. 2007. *The Wages of Whiteness: Race and the Making of the American Working Class*. Revised edition. New York: Verso.

Roshanravan, Shireen M. 2010. "Passing-as-if: Model-Minority Subjectivity and Women of Color Identification." *Meridians* 10(1): 1–31.

Smith, Andrea. 2005. *Conquest: Sexual Violence and American Indian Genocide*. Cambridge, MA: South End Press.

Walter, Bronwen. 2001. *Outsiders Inside: Whiteness, Place and Irish Women*. New York: Routledge.

Weiss, Gail. 2014. "Pride and Prejudice: Ambiguous Racial, Religious, and Ethnic Identities of Jewish Bodies." In *Living Alterities: Phenomenology, Embodiment, and Race*, edited by Emily S. Lee, 213–32. Albany: State University of New York Press.

Wells, Samuel R. 1866. *New Physiognomy, Or, Signs of Character, As Manifested through Temperament and External Forms, and Especially in "The Human Face Divine."* New York: Fowler and Wells.

Zack, Naomi. 1996. "On Being and Not Being Black and Jewish." In *The Multiracial Experience: Racial Borders as the New Frontier*, edited by Maria P.P. Root, 140–52. Thousand Oaks, CA: Sage.

8   Toward a Decolonial Ethics

Manuel Chávez Jr.

I write this essay thinking of those who commit themselves—to think, act, live—against White supremacy.¹ In particular, I have in mind straight-identified men of color, who may be committed politically in different ways and at different levels, but nevertheless possess a sensibility critical of Whiteness that resists the internalization of racial self-hatred (personal and communal). I am thinking of men of color who may have become politicized through situations similar to my own. In my case, reading Chicana/o literature served as a starting point to understand anew my own sense of self and the reality in which I live. This new sense of self, informed by the histories and memories of survivors of colonization, motivates me to live consciously in ways resistant to racism. Yet, with the company of Chicana feminist theorists, I also became aware that a gender-binary grounds the "antiracism" of Chicano politics and limits publicly recognized activist and intellectual leadership primarily to straight-identified men of color.² These men of color, in turn, institutionalize the masculinist definition of what it means to be an antiracist. As Kimberlé Crenshaw's (1989) now widely cited analysis of "intersectionality" reveals, a consequence of this form of antiracist politics is the failure to understand how racial oppression differentially affects women of color. This chapter interrogates Chicano investments in a masculinist form of antiracism in response to what María Lugones identifies as "the indifference that men ... who have been racialized as inferior, exhibit to the systematic violences inflicted upon women of color" (HGS 188). Specifically, I examine how a modernist ethics anchors this hegemonic politics of antiracism and perpetuates the gendered logic of colonial domination.³ Given this, the politics of antiracism, often advocated by straight-identified men of color, requires a decolonial shift in our ethical approach in order to confront the violence directed at women of color.

Central to this project is what María Lugones names the "coloniality of gender," a concept she develops through the work of both Aníbal Quijano and

Kimberlé Crenshaw. Expanding Qujiano's (2000) notion of the "coloniality of power," Lugones articulates connections between systems of colonialism and Crenshaw's theoretical framework for the intersectionality of oppression. In so doing, Lugones exposes that, in spite of his anticolonial stance, Quijano's way of thinking "accepts the global, Eurocentered, capitalist understanding of what gender is about" (HGS 190). As a result, his Eurocentered assumption of sex/gender hides colonial forms of violence. He assumes all men are competing for women, ignoring both men of color who may not be erotically interested in women and men of color who are also perceived and treated as objects of sexual domination. Lugones argues that Quijano makes these assumptions because he does not consider how the construction of gender marked the division between humans and nonhumans. Within the Eurocentric perspective, Lugones explains, the gender difference between masculine and feminine traits are relevant to humans, and therefore only Europeans are clearly gendered. In this scheme, non-Europeans are "without gender." Consequently, Quijano's notion of the coloniality of power "serve[s] to veil the ways in which nonwhite colonized women have been subjected and disempowered" (190). In effect, Quijano's elaboration of the coloniality of power does not recognize how our contemporary conception of gender itself is a product and instrument of colonialism, with particularly violent effects for women of color. Lugones understands heteropatriarchal constructions of sex/gender as integral to the racialized apparatus of violence in the service of colonialism. She refers to this as the coloniality of gender. Her insight makes clear that men of color politicized against racism who still uphold heteropatriarchal gender/sex norms are thus complicit in the mechanisms of coloniality. If gender is a colonial construct, Lugones infers it is vital for straight-identified men of color who are committed to antiracism to call on each other to resist colonial heterosexualist and patriarchal masculinities. In this chapter, I unpack the role modern ethics plays in seducing men of color away from this charge. Specifically, I elaborate the link between the politics of antiracism and its investments in individualist conceptions of agency that erase historical relations of power upholding White supremacy.

I begin with how the Chicano Movement is an antiracist project entangled within the coloniality of gender. As Adalijza Sosa-Riddell points out, through their ignorance of "the condition of double oppression under which Chicanas suffer, [Chicanos] are not only perpetuating the stereotypes and the conditions that those stereotypes support, but they are also guilty of intensifying those conditions and their negative results" (1974, 163). Cherríe Moraga argues that it is not simple neglect of gender oppression by Chicanos, but that Chicanos take advantage of heterosexualism:

> Living under Capitalist Patriarchy, what is true for "the man" in terms of misogyny is, to a great extent, true for the Chicano. He, too, like any other man, wants to be able to determine how, when, and with whom his women—mother, wife, and daughter—are sexual.... The control of women begins through the institution of heterosexuality. (2000, 102)

In their focused opposition to White supremacy, Chicano cismen who are complicit with heterosexuality tend to reinforce the coloniality of gender by the indifference they exhibit toward the well-being of Chicanas and nonheterosexual members of the Chicana/o community. As a result, Chicano politics manifests itself as what Elizabeth Martínez calls "Chingón politics" (1998, 172). This form of politics promotes a male-centered hierarchical leadership that "encourages the association of machismo with domination" (175). Chingón politics stifles dialogue and marginalizes women. So instead of informing a movement toward liberation for all, it serves to perpetuate oppression. Moraga laments: "Any movement built on the fear and loathing of anyone is a failed movement. The Chicano movement is no different" (130). Lugones's notion of coloniality of gender helps illuminate the self-delusions necessary to ignore the contradictions and hypocrisy of a movement committed to end White supremacist violence against communities of color that, in its enactment of this commitment, reinforces the oppression of the women and nonheterosexual members within these very communities.

If we, politicized antiracist straight-identified men of color, want to maintain political integrity in our struggles for liberation, we must examine our attachments to the coloniality of gender. An important aspect in this antiracist politics is our ethical stance. The antiracism of Chingón politics is located within modern ethics, which offers politicized straight-identified men of color a positive moral standing denied to them by White supremacy. Modern ethics presumes a universal framework based on a masculinist model (Hoagland 1988).[4] By posing moral actors as self-sufficient, reasonable, and independent, modern ethics offers a strongly individualist stance for fighting racial oppression. However, for straight-identified men of color committed to antiracism, subscribing to modern ethics is a form of self-colonization that serves to reproduce the coloniality of gender. The colonizing logic of modern ethics lives in its masquerade as a universal model that normalizes reality framed by White masculinity. Accordingly, men of color who embrace a modern ethical attitude in their political commitments against racism must remain blind to historical relations of power that produce White male supremacist social reality. The internalization of the assumption that colonial oppression does not impact non-White agency necessarily involves the adoption of a masculinist disposition to assume individualist agency as priority over coalitional work against racism. Men of color seduced by the masculinist construction of individual moral agency offered by modern ethics invest in the very Eurocentric logics that justify their own community's subordination under White supremacy. *The coloniality of gender thus unveils what I am calling "the coloniality of ethics."* At stake for politicized straight-identified men of color in adopting a decolonial ethics is the way to create solidarity within and across communities of color that builds toward social and institutional transformation.

WHY ETHICS?

Although understanding the coloniality of ethics is a necessary step in resisting complicity with the coloniality of gender in one's antiracist commitments, the next step is to chart avenues toward liberation that encompass all members of (post)colonized communities. Lugones offers us a map to reveal both the coloniality of ethics and the "ethics of decoloniality." I cautiously use the term *ethics* in relation to Lugones's work given the modern/colonial philosophical conceptions of this field of study. Modern ethics, whether expressed via ethical theories such as deontological theory, utilitarianism, neo-sentimentalism, or social contract theory, does not address how the legacy of colonialism operates in contemporary society, let alone how it shapes its own history as a field of philosophical investigation.[5] Nevertheless, I use it because it creates bridges to the work of other thinkers who recognize that antiracist struggles demand a transformation of personal and communal values. To be clear, Lugones herself does not use the language of ethics to conceptualize resistance. However, her emphasis on praxical thinking brings into focus how the creation and sustainment of intersubjective relations is a necessary node of political resistance. Praxical thinking is attentive to the complexities of oppression that are hidden by the logic of domination. It is this emphasis on conscious, flesh and blood interactions with others in the context of oppression that I wish to call forth by using the term *ethics*. Drawing on Lugones's theories and her idea of praxis, I wish to retain and expand on the conception of ethics in elaborating a decolonial ethics.

We need to recognize that resistance to oppression requires a transformation of the ethical perceptions of ourselves and of one another that undoes the coloniality of gender. Lugones underscores this need in her understanding of decolonization as a process of liberation from colonial cognitive mechanisms: "How do we practice with each other engaging in dialogue at the colonial difference? How do we know when we are doing it?" (TDF 755). She offers a way to think of the practice of liberation as open-ended and created by one's way of life with, and among, survivors of colonization. Decolonial ethics elaborates a way of life that confronts, resists, and yet is separate from coloniality at the fleshy level of daily embodied relations and interactions. It is not based on universalizing ways of thinking, nor is it normative or prescriptive; instead, it is critically heuristic, characterized by three connected cognitive practices. First, decolonial ethics entails making sense of and thinking from, what Lugones calls, the "anti-structure" (SAS 60). The anti-structure is the living social space not comprehended by the coloniality of power. Second, thinking within the anti-structure requires a streetwalker's/*callejera*'s sensibility of the palpable frictions between hegemonic and nondominant senses of social reality and of one's self (TSC 222). A decolonial ethics finds its hermeneutic footing in this streetwalking awareness that exists in tension with dominant normative structures. Third, a decolonial ethics does not pivot on the individual(ist) self and the illusion of individualist modern agency. Rather, it gives attention to "active subjectivity," a type of subjectivity that emerges through and from nondominant socialities that enable collective action against institutionalized oppression (TSC 211). Taken together, these elements serve to propel a decolonial ethics.

Men of color may glimpse in mainstream ethics the possibility of adopting a clear moral standing that promises a solid conceptual foundation in an immoral racist world. In so doing, modern ethics emphasizes a moral autonomy that makes it possible to imagine oneself as a moral hero struggling against irrational social evils. Because of its assumption of solitary self-discipline, modern ethics makes it difficult to conceptualize and to create social transformation that does not depend on abstract individualism. In the context of coloniality, however, the colonized cannot wield individual action with any effective and enduring consequence in the struggle against oppression. Decolonial ethics responds to this limit in modern ethics by addressing the structural dimensions of oppression that expose personhood itself as a racial and gendered fiction. In this regard, decolonial ethics makes clear the need to forge solidarity and foregrounds the embodied social interactions that constitute the point where supportive connections are built. Building solidarity with nonheterosexual people and women of color, rather than inhabiting the abstraction of modern moral autonomy, offers an opening for antiracist men of color to resist internalized oppression and cultivate a new way toward self-love (personal and communal) delinked from the logic of domination.

THE COLONIALITY OF ETHICS

Ethical projects against racism take many forms. Some argue racism is a betrayal of ethics, and thus antiracist work requires the fair adherence to moral principles (Zack 2011). Other antiracist theorists criticize dominant forms of ethics by arguing that these frameworks already contain racialized presuppositions that maintain and naturalize social inequalities (Mills 1998). Interrogating the ethical motivations and perceptions of the politics of antiracism, especially where carried out by politicized straight-identified men of color, can serve to foreground, confront, and offer ways to resist the indifference of men of color toward the violence directed at women of color.

As Charles Mills underscores, many discussions regarding racism usually dismiss ethics as secondary to, or derivative of, the politics and economics of racial classification (1998). While Chicana/o thought similarly lacks attention to moral philosophy specifically, Chicana/o thinkers have, however, highlighted the importance of intersubjective relations in the process of social transformation (Soldatenko 2009).[6] For the Chicano philosopher Patrick Carey-Herrera, the Chicano Movement shows that "Chicanos have discovered for themselves the meaningfulness of the question, 'What is the basis for morally right and morally wrong action?'" (1983, 154).[7] According to him, Chicanismo, as the philosophy of the movement, suggests an "ethically superior way of living" that has been obscured by Anglo American society (153). In opposition to the values of the dominant culture, a "Chicano Ethic" is grounded in "a metaphysical bond [that] exists among Chicanos in the sense of an inherent condition of brotherhood or family" (150).[8] "Carnalismo," Carey-Herrera explains, "creates a framework of ethical imperatives upon which both theoretical and actual constructs can be tried and tested" (151). The moral life for Mexican Americans would entail the "voluntary submission to the ethical demands inherent to this expanded understanding of Carnalismo" (153). According to Carey-Herrera, the Chicano Ethic does not suggest cultural relativism; rather, "[i]t causes the Chicano to ascend to a higher level of inquiry ... that of universal principles" (154). Carnalismo leads to a value system rooted in the universal principles of "Equality and Dignity" (156). It reveals a universal demand: "The respect and dignity referred to in this case are the humanistic universal imperative, the equality of man" (155). In other words, Carnalismo demands that advocates of the Chicano Movement perceive and act toward each other as persons (rather than as subpersons as in the view of White racism); however, it does not restrict personhood to Mexican Americans only. In the project of

Chicanismo, Carey-Herrera perceives an alternative, but universal, moral philosophy that expands personhood to non-Whites, and thus offers a guide to transform the values of the Mexican American community and, eventually, those of the larger society.

Antiracist ethical projects, such as the one articulated by Carey-Herrera, are nonetheless unwittingly anchored in the *moral structure of modernity*. As a result, they undermine their own anti-oppressive aims. The contradiction of the Chicano Movement was clear to many Chicana feminists. Alma M. García notes: "Many Chicanas, active within every sector of the movement, raised their voices in a collective feminist challenge to the sexism and male domination that they were experiencing within the movimiento ... these Chicanas began to see and experience some of the contradictions of *Chicanismo*, specifically as it applied to women" (1997). While "macho attitudes" are explicit expressions of sexism and male domination, Chabram-Dernersesian notes how these oppressive views are embedded within the discourse itself: "Chicano identity is written with linguistic qualifiers—*o/os*—which subsume the Chicana into a universal ethnic subject that speaks with the masculine instead of the feminine and embodies itself in a Chicano male" (1992, 82). She explains that the effect of the centering of the male Chicano subject is that "the silenced Other, Chicanas/hembras, are thus removed from full-scale participation in the Chicano movement as fully embodied, fully empowered U.S. Mexican female subjects" (83). Chicanas who wished to be treated according to principles of equality and dignity within the Chicano Movement "had to embody themselves as males, adopt traditional family relations, and dwell only on their racial and/or ethnic oppression" (83).[9] In other words, Carnalismo implies machismo. Lugones offers further clarity of how the logic of an antiracist ethics can be rooted within modernity.

In his critique of modernity, Quijano argues it is historically and conceptually inseparable from *coloniality* (2000).[10] The coloniality of power describes the global system of power based on racial stratification. In this system, Quijano points out that "... only European culture is rational, it can contain 'subjects'— the rest are not rational, they cannot be or harbor 'subjects'" (2007, 173). And, where White Europeans are assumed to be modern subjects, Quijano observes that, "certain races are condemned as inferior for not being rational subjects" (2000, 555). In modernity/coloniality, the world system of power established domination over social existence by "Whites" over "Indians," "Negroes," and "Orientals." Although Quijano does not directly address ethics in his discussion of modernity/coloniality, it is clear that ethical concerns were never meant to apply to non-Europeans , as explicitly admitted by modern ethical theorists themselves.[11] Given the modern/colonial paradigm, the only relation that exists between Europeans and non-Europeans is one of domination.[12]

Mills offers a way to understand the effect of coloniality on ethics through his explanation of what he calls *Herrenvolk* morality. Mills describes *Herrenvolk* ethics as "the moral code appropriate to the racially privileged population within a social order simultaneously committed to liberal egalitarianism and racial hierarchy" (1998, 152). The fundamental principle of this moral system is "all persons should be treated equally (by contrast with the morality of feudalism), but the racially inferior are not full persons" (152). Mills points out this principle may be overt or covert, or even denied in a *Herrenvolk* ethics and yet still be operative. The effect can be perceived in how the racial identity of full persons limits their ability to have empathy for those marked as racially inferior, subpersons.

Mills shows how this abstraction of personhood in mainstream ethics can serve to disguise the coloniality of ethics. He points out that the concept of personhood is fundamental in modern ethics. For example, in modern ethics, a person is conceived as a "self-owning appropriator," such as in Lockeanism, or, the person is a "self-directing being," according to Kantianism (152).[13] If we look through the lens of the *Herrenvolk* framework, however, the starting point is not, in fact, an abstract population of equal individuals, but "a population that is, before anything else, racially categorized and of differential moral status" (153). Historically, this population has been divided roughly between Whites and non-Whites. In a *Herrenvolk* ethics, "racialized personhood" is central. Whites are considered full persons, while non-Whites are subpersons. The racial distinction is central to determining whose life has moral value and whose life has less or none at all. In a *Herrenvolk* Kantianism, subpersons are not "rational, self-directing entities" and depend on others (full persons) for guidance. In a *Herrenvolk* Lockeanism, subpersons lack the property of Whiteness, which is necessary in order to possess "full self-ownership, for the ownership of efficient nature-appropriating labor ... and for full entitlement to (ownership of) rights" (154). Non-Whites, lacking Whiteness, are incapable of self-ownership, and thus full personhood. *Herrenvolk* ethics assumes a racial distinction between personhood and subpersonhood in its articulation of abstract personhood. As Mills states, "When one talks in general about abstract persons, then, one is really talking about [Whites]" (153). In this way, modern ethics, as *Herrenvolk* ethics, perpetuates the coloniality of power.[14]

In the context of *Herrenvolk* ethics, Carey-Herrera's articulation of Chicano Ethics is a challenge to the construction of Mexican Americans as subpersons. While he does not view Carnalismo as a striving for Whiteness, it is still a claim for personhood. In his conception of Chicano Ethics, Carey-Herrera does not question the modern conception of personhood. Because he does assume an abstract personhood, he does not recognize how Chicano Ethics parlays into modernity's underlying logic of coloniality. His focus on defending the personhood of Mexican Americans does not allow Carey-Herrera to consider how personhood is not only racialized, but also gendered. As a result, his concept of Chicano Ethics does not and cannot address the problems within Chicano politics identified by Chicana feminists, such as Sosa-Riddell, Moraga, García, Martínez, and Chabram-Dernersesian. Where *Herrenvolk* ethics assumes personhood is White, Carnalismo assumes all Mexican American persons are male (Chican*os*). Lugones brings our attention to how the coloniality of power continues to frame personal and social relations *between and among* the colonized through gender. Gender relations, she argues, are a central mechanism by which systems of domination rooted in colonialism are maintained and perpetuated *within* communities of color.

Instead of assuming personhood as a basic element in social reality, Lugones lets us understand it as a product of social relations. Lugones uses the term *structure* to reference that which shapes the constitution of persons: "Structures construct or constitute persons not just in the sense of giving them a facade, but also in the sense of giving them emotions, beliefs, norms, desires, and intentions that are their own" (SAS 60). These structures construct beings with particular selves by way of specific institutional and societal roles and statuses. They grant personhood "the fiction of effective individual agency" (TSC 210).

In this conception of agency, the successful agent reasons practically in a world of meaning and within social, political, and economic institutions that back him up and form the framework for his forming intentions that are not subservient to the plans of others and that he is able to carry into action unimpeded and as intended (TSC 211). The illusion of personhood is to hide "the institutional setting and the institutional backing of individual potency" (TSC 210). A *moral structure*, as I am using it, produces persons who can assume value to their own lives and thus have moral worth to be respected. The moral structure of modernity valorizes "single authorship, individual responsibility, individual accountability, and self-determination" (TSC 210). It creates a social space that makes visible the value of relationships between the persons it constructs. In doing so, the moral structure of modernity distinguishes between those who have personhood, and those who lack it. Lugones shows us how this moral structure is framed by the coloniality of gender.

Lugones contends that the coloniality of power is inseparable from the heterosexualist gender system.[15] The colonial/modern moral structure is not only racialized but thoroughly gendered. Within modernity, womanhood is identified with European females and femininity is racialized as White. Modern femininity is characterized by the moral values of "sexual purity and passivity" (HGS 203). Where White women are valued within modernity for the sake of reproducing the status of White men, colonized females "were understood as animals in the deep sense of 'without gender,' sexually marked as female, but without the characteristics of femininity" (202). Lugones contends that gender is a necessary condition to being constituted as a person in the logic of the coloniality of power. Those who lack gender are not valued as a person. She writes: "The behaviors of the colonized and their personalities/souls were judged as bestial and thus non-gendered, promiscuous, grotesquely sexual, and sinful" (TDF 743). To be a nongendered being is to be excluded from the realm of personhood. In this manner, the coloniality of gender defines the modern moral structure; it thus reveals the coloniality of ethics. Because women of color do not fit clearly the colonial/modern gender system, their lives do not have moral value. So, where White women are marginalized in the public sphere, women of color are marginalized within the community of persons. The effect of the coloniality of gender is to produce women of color as non-persons. Consequently, for women of color, the coloniality of ethics is "thoroughly violent" (HGS 206).

As Quijano notes, modernity/coloniality constrains the imagination of the colonized.[16] Lugones reveals the logic that limits the ethical imagination of the colonized, particularly of those politicized straight-identified men of color who struggle for moral recognition in the mainstream political culture. Yet it is precisely this desire to be perceived as ethical actors, as rational persons, that seduces antiracist men of color into complicity with the coloniality of power. *This is the contradiction of Chicano Ethics*. Politicized straight-identified men of color accept a gendered identity assumed by the moral structure of modernity as a way to conceive the antiracist as a rational person. Hence, the seduction of fulfilling the role of the modern personhood. The contradiction of Chicano Ethics is its attempt to reject the imposition of subpersonhood by White supremacy while it assimilates nonetheless into the modern/colonial moral structure by claiming personhood, and consequently reproducing the coloniality of ethics.

Lugones allows us to see that mainstream ethics is ultimately based on the history and logic of coloniality. She shows us how modern ethics can serve to perpetuate colonial oppression within communities of color *by* people of color, especially by men of color. Lugones argues:

> We see the gender dichotomy operating normatively in the construction of the social and in the colonial processes of oppressive subjectification. But if we are going to make an-other construction of the self in relation,

we need to bracket the dichotomous human/non-human, colonial, gender system that is constituted by the hierarchical dichotomy man/woman for European colonials + the non-gendered, non-human colonized. (TDF 748–49)

In order to live against White racism, she calls on us to delink from the coloniality of gender, and thus to refuse positioning ourselves within the moral structure of modernity. For politicized straight-identified men of color, it is vital to separate ourselves from the limits of modern ethics in order to decolonize and re-create intersubjective relations that can transform our communities.

DECOLONIZING ETHICS

Recognizing the coloniality of ethics enables us to see how, when politicized men of color adopt the colonial/modern moral structure, this only further reproduces indifference to "the systematic violences inflicted upon women of color" (HGS 188). Modern ethics, by way of its logic of subjectivity and intersubjectivity, as well as its perception of social reality, normalizes the colonial world of White masculine subjectivity and, in doing so devalues the lives of women of color. A politics based in modern ethics can only "affirm rather than reject an oppressive organization of life" (187). Consequently, to refuse the coloniality of ethics makes it more possible "to place ourselves in a position to call each other to reject this gender system as we perform a transformation of communal relations" (189). Lugones, however, does not claim that an alternative moral structure or another formulation of personhood is necessary for this shift in our ethical attitude. Rather, she suggests a decolonial ethical praxis involves a creative and resistant way of thinking and living beyond a moral structure centered on personhood.

In contrast to the concept of the "structure," Lugones describes the *antistructure* as a state where "there are no structural descriptions" (SAS 60–61). It is liminal, "the place in between realities, a gap 'between and betwixt' universes of sense that construe social life and persons differently, an interstice from where one can most clearly stand critically toward different structures" (59). The antistructure is inhabited by living beings that are not totally defined by dominant social categories, and thus who do not stand "with respect to others ... as in a hierarchy" (PIS 60). Based on Lugones's conception, I pose the *moral antistructure* as the liminal space that exists outside of the realm of personhood.

The abstraction of personhood implies a particular epistemic perspective, a viewpoint of society that is distant from embodied interactions. The concept of personhood implies what Lugones calls a "bird's-eye view": a perspective "perched up high, looking at or making up the social from a disengaged position" (TSC 207). The spectator of this perspective, the "strategist," is assumed to be a full person with the rational capacity to view reality as a whole. Framed by this disembodied point of view, the strategist adheres to what Lugones names the "logic of purity," a mode of thinking premised in a "unity underlying multiplicity" (PIS 126). The strategist only recognizes a social reality composed of beings who, like the strategist, possess full personhood.

Instead of the top-down perspective of the "strategist," thinking in the moral anti-structure demands a viewpoint from street level. So, in contrast to the "bird's-eye view" of modern ethics, Lugones suggests a different starting point: "the location of the theorizing subject is from within the midst of impure subjects negotiating life transgressing the categorial understandings of a logic of binaries that renders hard-edged, ossified, exclusive groups, as well as succumbing to the reductions of that logic" (ED 197). A decolonial ethics is informed by the perspective of the streetwalker that can perceive "underneath" the moral structure and sees the "other" side of personhood. This mode of perceiving necessitates what Lugones calls a logic of impurity, or "the logic of curdling": "According to the logic of curdling, the social world is complex and heterogenous and each person is multiple, nonfragmented, embodied" (PIS 127). This logic of impurity is not limited by the boundaries of modern personhood. As such, it makes it possible to perceive that those outside the realm of (White and gendered) personhood do not exist purely as subpersons or non-persons. Lugones tells us: "Impurity grounds the need for an against-the-grain sociality that one is moved to discern, sustain, affirm amid those subjected who harbor the ambition to become nonsubjected subjects" (ED 196). Within the moral structure of modernity, resistance to oppression by so-called subpersons and non-persons "is conceptually disallowed as moral" (TSC 211). In contrast, engagement with decolonial ethics facilitates an understanding of those who undermine or do not conform to the fiction of personhood within the moral anti-structure. Thinking within the moral anti-structure, as a *callejera*, social reality is "a tense, contested terrain" because one can see the dynamic effect that the conflict between oppression and resistance has in producing social reality (ED 200).

For decolonial ethics, the moral structure and the moral anti-structure both exist. Lugones explains that this requires the development of a "duplicitous perception" in order to simultaneously recognize the activities both within and outside the realm of personhood (TSC 225). Such a mode of perception allows for the understanding of "subpersons" and "non-persons" as resistors. She emphasizes: "The streetwalker theorist keeps both logics in interpretation but valorizes the logic of resistance as she inhabits differentiated geographies carrying with others contestatory meanings to praxical completion" (TSC 218). So, rather than focusing on personhood, decolonial ethical praxis focuses on the intersubjective phenomenon where intentions and meaning are generated. Through relational practices, resistant values—values that work against the coloniality of power—become discernible. The perspective of *la callejera* allows for making sense of the values of resistance generated by social practices and relations take place underneath the moral structure—values not necessarily articulated or understood in terms of personhood.

These resistant values are not necessarily articulated by individual persons, but emerge from concrete relational practices. In contrast to the modern ethical idea of personhood, Lugones points out the idea of "active subjectivity." She describes it as "alive in the activity of dispersed intending in complex, heterogeneous collectivities, within and between worlds of complex sense" (TSC 217). Active subjectivity is an embodied, collective movement of resistant energies that inhabits in the moral anti-structure. For a decolonial ethics, active subjectivity is the source for values of resistance generated underneath the abstract realm of personhood. Decolonial ethical praxis involves striving to perceive, move with, and amplify these values toward a transformation of the oppressive situation. With the sensibility of the streetwalker /*la callejera*, decolonial ethics operates as "a tactical strategic practice" (TSC 222). Lugones explains the tactical strategic practice is one in which "one places, takes up, follows, aids, resistant emancipatory intentions in the midst of active, resisting subjects who are indispensable to each other if their intending is to inform their social reality" (TSC 224). A tactical strategic practice is attuned to the immediate context as well as the wider fields of power where these intersubjective practices are located. By engaging in this practice, the decolonial ethicist participates in a socially creative process in which collective relationships, rather than individual persons, generate resistant values from practices that work against/in spite of/within mainstream political culture.

By moving beyond the moral structure based on personhood, decolonial ethics suggests a way to resist White supremacy without succumbing to the hegemony of the gender dichotomy, and the accompanying perpetuation of violence against women of color. As discussed previously, the logic of coloniality links personhood to gender identity; that is, in order to be a person, one must be a "man" or a "woman." In a modern ethics of antiracism, women of color must be assimilated into the moral structure of modernity. However, if a politicized man of color relies on the concept of personhood to formulate an ethic-politics of antiracism, it can have the effect of limiting it to heteropatriarchal norms and marginalizing those folks of color whose resistance to racism does not fit or exceeds those norms. Lugones writes: "If we only weave man and woman into the very fabric that constitutes the self in relation to resisting, we erase the resistance itself" (TDF 749). Linking resistance to gender identity can have the effect of obscuring the moral anti-structure. So, first of all, masculinity is not elemental to resistance in a decolonial ethics; insofar as masculinity is tied to personhood, it can actually be an obstacle because an ethics of decolonial resistance depends on its decentering of personhood in viewing fellow resistors. And, if, second of all, straight-identified men of color want to undo White supremacy, then their resistance to sexism cannot be reduced to the terms of "gender equality," as it is formulated within the dominant moral structure, but they must give attention to and move with the resistant values of nonheterosexual people and women of color that evade the colonial/modern gender system. For politicized men of color confronting White racism, to thoughtfully inhabit the moral anti-structure would offer a manner by which working against violence against women of color can become a premise for an antiracist politics. Through the cultivation of resistant values the active subjectivity can grow into an intentional community against oppression. By forging an "impure community," the oppressive situation can be transformed (IC, C). To engage in decolonial ethics is to see both the life oppressed in the moral structure and the resistant life in the moral anti-structure. In resistance to the coloniality of ethics, Lugones suggests conceptual conditions that abandon the colonial/modern gender system. In contrast to a modern ethics that pivots on the notion of personhood, a decolonial ethics searches to create impure communities through the generation of resistant values by active subjectivity.

TOWARD A DECOLONIAL ETHICS

Since antiracist politics assumes a moral view in its struggle against White supremacy, it is vital for us, politicized men of color, to consider the ethics that frames our politics. When Chicanos accept heteropatriarchal norms for an ethical stance, this has the effect of reinforcing the oppression of Chicanas as well as nonheterosexual members of the community. In her essay "History and the Politics of Violence Against Women," Antonia I. Castañeda writes:

> The legacy of the Americas is violence and exploitation based on sex, gender, race, sexuality, class, culture, and physical condition—based on the power and privilege to exploit and oppress others that each of those

elements confer on us.... Where do each of us stand on each of these interlocking elements? I would ask each of us to interrogate ourselves, our individual gender, sexual, racial, and class politics, and our power and privilege in each realm.

We cannot change the last 500 years, but we can change the next 500. We must take personal responsibility to act against rape, sexual violence, racism, sexism, homophobism, classism. Every time we remain silent and do not take a stand against these interlocking evils wherever we encounter them, we become complicitous with them and we reproduce them. (1998, 317–18)

Historically, antiracist politics, including Chicano nationalist politics, has assumed a basis in modern ethics. Such an antiracist politics challenges the person/subperson divide that grounds White supremacy, countering with the claim that such a division does not exist. Carey-Herrera does this in his conception of a Chicano Ethics by expanding the notion of personhood to include Chicanos. However, he never questions the historical paradigm of personhood. Quijano indicates the coloniality of power is embedded within the notion of personhood. As Mills contends, the notion of personhood is theoretically abstract, and historically rooted in Whiteness. The effect of assuming personhood as a basis of antiracist politics is to affirm a White morality and thus be unable to recognize resistance to that morality. Because an antiracist politics presumes a particular ethics, it is necessary for politicized men of color to rethink and enact an ethics delinked from the logic of coloniality.

In understanding how modern ethics is produced by the interlinked racial and gender logics of colonial oppression, Lugones offers a way to think of an ethics of resistance that goes beyond the notion of personhood. Modern personhood is racialized and gendered. The use of personhood not only results in subpersonhood, but can have the effect of turning women of color into nonpersons. Lugones argues personhood is not innate, but is constituted by structures, and its very abstractness obscures violence at the street-level. By offering a way to think outside those structures, she suggests ways to undermine the coloniality of power at the mundane level of daily, embodied relations, and interactions.

In making sense of practices of resistance within complex situations of oppression, Lugones gestures toward a decolonial ethics. Decolonial ethics is not based on universal principles or norms, or on establishing an alternative moral framework. Rather, it is an ethics that exists within and is attentive to praxis. Lugones's decolonial gesture is motivated by making liberation from the logic of domination praxically possible. Rather than attempting to discover or construct a moral structure, decolonial ethics searches for and takes up resistance among the colonized as it already exists.

A decolonial ethics makes clear the necessity of rethinking how we perceive resistance within the context of oppression. The elaboration of a decolonial ethics, Lugones suggests, involves three aspects. The first is inhabiting the antistructure, the social space that is obscured by personhood. Related to living in the anti-structure is thinking from the anti-structure, which requires a viewpoint that does not begin from abstraction. From the perspective of the streetwalker, what becomes perceptible is active subjectivity and the intentionality that emerges through the relationships of a collectivity. It is through attention to this active subjectivity that one can discern the values of the praxis of resistance, values that are not predefined or conceptualized in modern ethics. A decolonial ethical praxis means endeavoring to think and live in the moral anti-structure.

Lugones challenges us, politicized straight-identified men of color, to (re-)consider how our focus on fighting oppression is based on a collusion with the colonial/modern system. In this chapter, I have attempted to show how this collusion emerges among men of color in community-based movements against White supremacy, in part through the seduction of personhood into modern ethics. Modern ethics leaves the coloniality of gender undisturbed. A decolonial ethics is an invitation to reflect on how we act, think, and live in the context of multiple colonial oppressions. In order to think and perceive resistance to oppression, Lugones argues, it is necessary to live, move, and think within the moral anti-structure. This requires the decolonial ethical agent to trespass through the map of oppression hidden by the dominant moral structure.[17] Modern ethics, as an attempted source for oppositional struggle for justice, prevents the oppressed from recognizing differential resistance within their own community. Accordingly, modern ethics inserts the logic of the colonizer into the relations of the colonized. Where the adherence to modern ethics is a commitment to self-colonization, a decolonial ethics can show us how to create an alternative ethical sense that lives beyond the limits of heterosexualism, and how to learn to love ourselves in a new way.

NOTES

1. In this chapter, I capitalize the term *White* to emphasize "Whiteness" as an ideology that is distinct, though not separate, from the racial description of individuals.

2. I owe much to the work of Anzaldúa (1987), Moraga (2000), Trujillo (1998), Córdova et al. (1990), García (1997), and Sandoval (2000) in my own intellectual development as a Chicano theorist committed to decolonizing feminist principles.

3. In the rest of this chapter, I use the term *modern ethics* to refer to *modernist ethics*, a moral philosophy embedded within modernity.

4. See Hoagland (1988). In her work, Hoagland provides a thorough criticism of "modern patriarchal ethics."

5. See LaFollette (2000) for an overview of these different schools of thought. In his work *Blackness Visible: Essays on Philosophy and Race* (1998), Charles W. Mills argues that the racist legacy of colonialism is generally unacknowledged in mainstream philosophical discourses. He remarks that "race barely exists" for "mainstream First World political philosophy" (1998, 97). I believe the same can be said for mainstream First World moral philosophy.

6. Soldatenko argues that the future of Chicano thought must include an "ethical turn."

7. Patrick Carey-Herrera elaborates on the argument first put forward by Elihu Carranza (1978). I will focus on Carey-Herrera's interpretation for this essay.

8. In his work, Carey-Herrera uses the term *Chicano* to refer to all members of the Mexican American community, assuming the masculine as representative of all genders. In the rest of this section, I will show the limits of this gendered conceptualization for an antiracist ethics.

9. See also Rodríguez (2009). Rodríguez makes the argument "that the connection between the trope of the family and Chicano cultural nationalism holds much more symbolic (and material) currency than tracing nationalist roots and routes to the phantasmatic geography of Aztlán" (29).

10. Coloniality characterizes the relations of power that condition the existences of both the colonizers and the colonized (and both of their descendants) on the global scale. While Western thinkers conceive of modernity as an autonomous phenomenon, uniquely generated by Europe, he argues that such a portrayal neglects the role of colonization of the "New World" as well as of Africa and Asia in its production. In fact, he argues, modernity/coloniality originated at the point of the formation of "Europe" (and the "West") as a geo-political identity that "discovered" "America" (itself created as a geo-political identity). According to Quijano, modernity/coloniality articulates a Eurocentric rationality that expresses the demands of a "First World" capitalism, affecting all aspects of global society.

11. See Eze (1997) for a brief overview of some major modern philosophers' views of non-Europeans, such as David Hume, Immanuel Kant, Thomas Jefferson, and G.W. Hegel. In his essay, "On the Treatment of Barbarous Nations," John Stuart Mill writes: "To suppose that the same international customs, and the same rules of international morality, can obtain between one civilized nation and another, and between civilized nations and barbarians, is a grave error, and one which no statesman can fall into... In the first place, the rules of ordinary international morality imply reciprocity. But barbarians will not reciprocate. They cannot be depended on for observing any rules. Their minds are not capable of so great an effort, nor their will sufficiently under the influence of distant motives. In the next place, nations which are still barbarous have not got beyond the period during which it is likely to be for their benefit that they should be conquered and held in subjection by foreigners" (1874, 252–53).

12. Maldonado-Torres (2008) argues that modernity established an "ethics of war" between Europeans and non-Europeans.

13. Mills does not include utilitarianism since personhood is not a necessary element, as it is for the moral philosophies of Locke and Kant. However, as the quotation in note 14 shows, the Utilitarian J.S. Mill did not consider "barbarians" to have full personhood equal to those of "civilized nations."

14. Mills makes a distinction between a "symbiosis" view and a "multiple traditions" view of U.S. political culture. The symbiosis view understands Whiteness and classical liberalism as inseparable, while the multiple traditions view claims that these two aspects of U.S. political culture are separate—though sometimes mutually supportive, but sometimes in conflict. While it is beyond the scope of this essay, I think a decolonial perspective maintains that the symbiosis view is true, and that an oppositional view must be gathered from non-Occidentalist histories (located in the exterior of Whiteness and classical liberalism).

15. Citing the work of Oyèrónkẹ́ Oyěwùmí and Paula Gunn Allen, Lugones argues that heterosexualism did not exist in non-European societies before European colonialism. The imposition of heterosexualism up-ended preexisting social relationships within indigenous familial, communal, and political structures. Lugones argues that this gender system is an instrument of colonialism as much as are those of race and class.

16. Quijano writes: "[I]n spite of the fact that political colonialism has been eliminated, the relationship between the European—also called 'Western'—culture, and the others continues to be one of colonial domination. It is not only a matter of the subordination of the other cultures to the European, in an external relation; we have also to do with a colonization of the other cultures,

albeit in differing intensities and depths. This relationship consists, in the first place, of a colonization of the imagination of the dominated; that is, it acts in the interior of that imagination, in a sense, it is part of it" (2007, 169).

17. Lugones offers the image of the map of oppression, "a map that has been drawn by power in its many guises and directions and where there is a spot for you" (IP 8). See also this book's chapter 11.

REFERENCES

Anzaldúa, Gloria. 1987. Borderlands/La Frontera: The New Mestiza. San Francisco: Aunt Lute Books.
Carey-Herrera, Patrick. 1983. *Chicanismo: Hypothesis, Thesis and Argument.* Torrance, CA: The Martin Press.
Carranza, Elihu. 1978. *Chicanismo: Philosophical Fragments.* Dubuque, IA: Kendall/Hunt.
Castañeda, Antonia I. 1998. "History and the Politics of Violence Against Women." In *Living Chicana Theory*, edited by Carla Trujillo. Berkeley, CA: Third Women Press, 310–19.
Chabram-Dernersesian, Angie. 1992. "I Throw Punches for My Race, but I Don't Want to Be a Man: Writing Us—Chica-nos (Girl, Us) / Chicanas—into the Movement Script." In Cultural Studies, edited by Lawrence Grossberg, 81-96. New York: Routledge.
Córdova, Teresa, Norma Cantú, Gilberto Cardenas, Juan García, and Christine M. Sierra, eds. 1990. *Chicana Voices: Intersections of Class, Race, and Gender.* Albuquerque: University of New Mexico Press.
Crenshaw, Kimberlé. 1989. "Demarginalizing the Intersection of Race and Sex: A Black Feminist Critique of Antidiscrimination Doctrine:Feminist Theory and Antiracist Politics." *University of Chicago Legal Forum* 140: 139–67.
Eze, Emmanuel Chukwudi, ed. 1997. *Race and the Enlightenment: A Reader.* Malden, MA: Blackwell Publishing.
Hoagland, Sarah Lucia. 1988. *Lesbian Ethics: Toward New Value.* Palo Alto, CA: Institute of Lesbian Studies.
García, Alma M., ed. 1997. *Chicana Feminist Thought: The Basic Historical Writings.* New York: Routledge.
LaFollette, Hugh, ed. 2000. *The Blackwell Guide to Ethical Theory.* Oxford: Blackwell Publishing.
Maldonado-Torres, Nelson. 2008. *Against War: Views from the Underside of Modernity.* Durham, NC: Duke University Press.

Martínez, Elizabeth. 1998. *De Colores Means All of Us: Latina Views for a Multi-Colored Century*. Cambridge, MA: South End Press.

Mill, John Stuart. 2005. *Dissertations and Discussions: Political, Philosophical, and Historical*. Vol. 3. New York: Adamant Media Corporation.

Mills, Charles W. 1998. *Blackness Visible: Essays on Philosophy and Race*. Ithaca, NY: Cornell University Press.

Moraga, Cherríe L. 2000. *Loving in the War Years: lo que nunca pasó por sus labios*. 2nd ed. Cambridge, MA: South End Press.

Quijano, Aníbal. 2000. "Coloniality of Power, Eurocentrism, and Latin America." Translated by Michael Ennis. *Nepantla: Views from South* 1(3): 533–80.

———. 2007. "Coloniality and Modernity/Rationality." *Cultural Studies* 21(2): 168–78.

Rodríguez, Richard T. 2009. *Next of Kin: The Family in Chicano/a Cultural Politics*. Durham, NC: Duke University Press.

Sandoval, Chela. 2000. *Methodology of the Oppressed*. Minneapolis: University of Minnesota Press.

Soldatenko, Michael. 2009. *Chicano Studies: The Genesis of a Discipline*. Tucson: University of Arizona Press.

Sosa-Riddell, Adaljiza. 1974. "Chicanas and El Movimiento." *Aztlán: A Journal of Chicano Studies* 5(1–2): 155–65.

Trujillo, Carla. 1998. *Living Chicana Theory*. Berkeley, CA: Third Women Press.

Zack, Naomi. 2011. *The Ethics and Mores of Race: Equality after the History of Philosophy*. Lanham, MD: Rowman & Littlefield.

Part IV Knowing on the Edge of Worlds and Sense

9 Beyond Benevolent Violence

Trans* of Color, Ornamental Multiculturalism, and the Decolonization of Affect

Pedro J. DiPietro

What does it feel like when you are seen but half-seen? I mean, half-seen not in the way that we all are kind of half-seen, half-there, not quite full reflections of who we understand ourselves to be. Right? Half-seen "that way" wouldn't sting this much. It would be more like a little smudge or a sliver of pain, one more speck in the trail of our vulnerability. What I truly mean is half-understood in the way that makes you feel like there's a pit in your stomach pressing against your lungs and like your armpits are flashing with a rush of heat. Half-understood because the person in front of you wanted to understand you; not fully, fully understand you but understand you nonetheless. I mean, getting to understand you for more than what life has taught them to understand with their own senses. So, between half-understanding you and not fully understanding you, they intended to extend themselves, and you felt like they were reaching out to you, trying to go out of their own world to what lies beyond their reach. That's why, when you end up feeling deserted, the pain feels more piercing and even demoralizing. That's why, over time, it makes you hopeless. So much more because you kind of recognize this response in yourself, "that something" in the way you've been half-seen, half-felt, day in and day out, "that" something that has made you more sensitive, more likely to gingerly get a sense of what someone is about not just to you but to themselves. You kind of feel that this type of sensing of another's world through the limitations of your own senses begins as a visceral response, with the surging of an affect, of a type of openness and permeability that are as much daring as they are risky. It invites you to navigate seeing, sensing, and knowing, and their connections, with all their enticements and dangers, with all the layers of power lines between and across each other. It brings you to confront the failure of half-seeing and half-sensing others and their world. So, would it be possible to turn this visceral response toward an otherwise way of sensing, feeling, and knowing? What would it take to affect the visceral and its unfolding, not from within the limits of your own understanding, of your understanding of yourself and another, but rather from within the openness of an incomplete you and an incomplete me, of a timid and yet pulsating vocation to empathize not in spite of but rather through each other's ineffable differences?

I begin by reflecting on hope and recognition but also on despair and distortion. It is a way of framing the connections between sensing, feeling, and knowing, between yearning to mean well and not fully knowing whether you truly, truly, mean well, between feeling that you might have meant well and being afforded the privilege of ignoring whether your meaning well leaves another well or unwell. Increasingly, political views and intellectual positions get traction by channeling heart-wrenching and emotionally charged validation. Moreover, many expect an almost immediate surge of affective outpouring, right from where our guts pulsate, as confirmation of being down with the right kind of politics. Do our guts speak long enough for us to wonder whether the world is *feeling* all the *good* we mean for them?

The affective turn shows that contemporary *intimate publics* move subjectivities in contradictory ways, at times amplifying the range of political action while at others relegating interpersonal closeness to the domestic sphere (Berlant 2004; Gould 2009). I would like, instead, to direct our attention to the political labor that affect performs under the guise of the visceral, or the not-so-public or not-so-counterpublic orientation of affects. While it is heartwarming to find oneself at the receiving end of visceral validation, its seduction is far more perplexing insofar as it may make us complacent with the practice of dissociating empathic sensibility from power relations.

Foregrounding what María Lugones and Joshua Price theorize as structural monoculturalism and ornamental multiculturalism, this chapter examines global and local sites of affectivity surrounding transing embodiments of color and trans* of color realities.[1] Monocultural and condescending ignorance figure prominently at these sites under the veneer of what I call *benevolent violence*. More puzzling are the benevolent inclinations of so many allies and advocates for trans* justice and acceptance worldwide. As we'll discuss shortly, Lugones and Price warn us about the kind of neoliberal, ornamental, multiculturalism that often provides allies and advocates with that *feel-good* rush even when they refuse to examine their commitments to benevolent violence. Damaging as this type of benevolence might be, the motivation behind it merits further examination. If trans* of color communities, our allies and advocates, truly mean to be accountable for what we don't know about each other, and about each other's understanding of transing phenomena, we have much work ahead of us as we make commitments, radically multicultural commitments, decolonizing and intercultural commitments, to know, sense, and feel otherwise.[2]

In deciphering what type of affect prevents us from engaging each other through decolonizing dispositions, and as a member of trans* of color collectives, I explore the relations between Eurocentrism and white-centered accounts of transgender phenomena, and between ornamental multiculturalism and the affective inclinations it elicits toward trans* of color phenomena. First, I locate affect within Lugones and Price's analysis of ornamental multiculturalism and the ways it relies on the cognitive dispositions of simplicity, certainty, and agreement. Second, I turn to the docuseries *Gaycation* and its affective labor across transnational lgbt counterpublics, their alignment with ornamental multiculturalism, and their attachments to a domain of shared white-centered indignation. Third, I identify the role that synecdoche plays, as modernity's preferred mode of sexual representation, on the benevolent and yet violent acts that *Gaycation* performs in its treatment of India's hijra community. Finally, I seek to expose the implication of lgbt counterpublics in everyday acts of benevolent violence and the scars they leave on trans* of color embodiments.

Lugones and Price analyze cognitive dispositions that feed on monocultural structures in American society at the end of the millennium. Monoculturalism is an operation of cultural domination whereby nondominant culture is simplified, discredited as insignificant, and rendered an ornament (DC 111). Condescension and distortion underwrite any acknowledgment of cultures thus rendered insignificant. They stir a willingness not to know beyond the walls of dominant culture. As both structural and interpersonal, monoculturalism permeates subjectivities. It mutates into ornamental multiculturalism by neutralizing nondominant cultures and giving them the function of ornaments with stable, immutable, and stereotypical contents.

Although they link knowing practices with our emotions or desires, Lugones and Price emphasize the cognitive content of an agency that is radically multicultural (DC). They avoid making assumptions about cultures since they don't submit to the notion that describes cultures as sharing a bridge of similarity; they refuse to translate moments of silence and hesitation into familiar meanings; and they embrace misunderstandings over any rush judgment about cultural (in)competence. In their text, words that enact affective dispositions—such as *feeling*, *emotion*, and *sentiment*—represent a minor cluster of meaning compared to those underscoring cognition—such as *cognitive, recognize, recognition, understand, understanding, know, knowledge,* and *acknowledge*. While they broaden our engagement with cultural practices, they don't fully delve into the domain of affect. The ways we *make sense* of the world also refer back to the ways we emote and give off feelings, especially when members of one cultural terrain meet members of another. At these encounters, we retrieve prior emotions including the sense of self-righteousness that privilege affords to practitioners of monoculturalism and ornamental multiculturalism. What we consider cognitive dispositions also entails physical and psychic attachments. What appears unknown to us may feed into sensations of coldness or desertion characteristic of an affective attachment such as fear. An indefatigable sense of anticipation over what might feel uncertain may equally contribute to a learned behavior such as ignorance. Sensing, feeling, and knowing are not as discreet as we may think. Practitioners of monoculturalism and ornamental multiculturalism consent to learning nothing as long as they get to keep their grip on the forces they fear, or the forces that pose resistance to being controlled or possessed.

Lugones and Price examine the lack of ease that is intrinsic to negotiating life as members of nondominant cultures. Remaining numb to the suffering of members of nondominant cultures fits into the monocultural structure of privilege and ease. In their account of coming to awareness of structural monoculturalism and ornamental multiculturalism, Lugones and Price evoke the plasticity of affect and the routes it offers toward intercultural dynamics. For Price, who is socialized into white cisgender masculinity, to disengage from interlocking systems of privilege entails the practice of interactive and dialogical defamiliarization, of becoming indignant toward the cognitive enticements attached to cultural domination (DC 113–16; see also ch. 10, this volume). In the case of Lugones, who is socialized into accepting the marginalization of Latina/o gender-nonconforming communities, disengaging from this damaging environment requires a dialogical affirmation of her duplicity in the face of being reduced to ornamental existence (110–13; see also WT). This ontological plurality may feel puzzling even when it pushes the minoritized self to a constant search for resistant company, for those who break ranks with ornamental multiculturalism.[3] Lugones and Price imply that the intercultural labor that they perform, across the map of cultural domination, doesn't operate as the bridge between each other's sense of indignation. They exclude the typical impulse to claim that they each know what the other is feeling, or that each can identify with the other's feelings, or that they each feel the same. As they travel to each other's encounter with the affect of becoming indignant, their dispositions raise questions about both cognition and affect since Lugones and Price refuse to rely on simplicity, certainty, and agreement. This chapter turns next to sites where lgbt counterpublics recruit indignation on behalf of white-centered and transnormative projects and to the consideration of the ways this process bears on the circulation of affects toward transing embodiments of color.

AFFECTS, LGBT COUNTERPUBLICS, AND THE POLITICS OF TRANSNORMATIVITY[4]

"Beneath, alongside, and generally *other than* conscious knowing" (Seigworth and Gregg 2010, 1), affects encompass visceral forces in their "transduction" or their mutation in form, shape, or intensity (Bertelsen and Murphie 2010, 140). They pull our attention to the sensual reality that lies between the self and others. Affects arise from this *in-between-ness* that modulates becoming, of relations, forces, capacities, and stillness (Seigworth and Gregg 2010, 1–27). They bring embodiment into being through energetic outpouring for they impinge, attract, gravitate, lean in, halt, clash, subside, and fade (Ahmed 2004, 129). Affects challenge the insulation characteristic of modern notions of a self-determining individual (Lacey 1998, 144). Indeed, affects underscore the more-than-rational connection between selves, the eerie and thin lining of emotions that makes the inside/outside between oneself and others a zone of permeability, of passing through and letting in, of activating histories of openness and rejection, absorption and avulsion.[5] By all appearances, the participants in a classroom may engage in a common task, sit by their desks, and position themselves in a semicircle formation. But the crosscultural dynamics that underlie our learning environments show that shared bodily positions are misleading. Affects communicate various lineups that remain hidden or invisible. As soon as the topic of trans* and transing comes to the fore, affective intensities coalesce into fleeting yet tangible expressions, actualizing layers of cultural asymmetries. With nervous smiles, frowning lines, winking eyes, hunched shoulders, tight grips, gut feelings, and other intensities, the classroom members sense the air getting hard to breathe, chests compressed within body frames, and eyelids at times twitching with impatience.

Organizing with trans* of color populations while creating environments in higher education to engage trans* lives, embodiments, and subjectivities, I am aware that contemporary publics mobilize transnormative affects. Together with increased visibility for trans* identities, *we* consent to rehabilitating notions of transing, from medicalization turning into the dominant technology for transitioning to Caitlyn Jenner having surrogate status for an ultraconservative repressive regime.[6] As a transing person of color myself, I teach a class on transgender theory and politics where we challenge Western-centric dispositions that tend to colonize transing embodiments and subjectivities.[7] Part of the pedagogical challenge is to examine empathy and apathy toward the decolonization of transing realities. The tribulations that I've witnessed convey that focusing on content and critical thinking is insufficient. As it happens with the public sphere in general, sentiments and emotions about trans* phenomena move back and forth between our need to show how much goodwill we have, embarrassment for the little we actually do, and our urge to anticipate the many ways that what *we* feel compares to how trans folks do.

In preparation for our discussion of Gayatri Reddy's *With Respect to Sex* (2005), an ethnography of *hijra* communities in northwestern India, the class I taught searched for videos where hijras spoke in their own words. We located a clip from *Gaycation*, a docuseries that Ellen Page and Ian Daniel co-host for the network Viceland. Page and Daniel set off on a millennial journey to explore lgbtq cultures around the world, presenting in their role of goodwill ambassadors for Western cultures. *Gaycation* involves the audience in the struggles of nonconforming communities, bringing them closer together by inciting visceral responses such as indignation, compassion, rage, sorrow, hope, and dismay. Affects surge through the screen into plights for recognition, acceptance, and respect. Specifically, indignation arises with ambiguity, not quite intelligible but very much felt.

Gaycation's second season goes to India by bridging not only Hindi and English, the former a language that underwent official colonization, but also Western and non-Western worldviews of gender and embodied differences.[8] This episode features members of the country's "lgbtq" community, including "lesbian and bisexual women," "gay nightlife," "queer culture," "transmen," "hijras," and lgbtq rights organizations. The episode reiterates the term *queer* twelve times, *trans* or *transgender* six, *lesbian* six, and finally *gay* a whopping thirty-seven times. By contrast, the episode iterates the word *hijra* only five times, with the caveat that the voice-off employs the word *third-gender* to introduce them. It works as an exploit of sorts, inviting viewers thought to be fluent in lgbtq terminology to lean on the half-familiarity of *third-gender*. Throughout the episode, a pattern of mishearing and dismissing interviewees develops whenever they point to local Hindu and Muslim embodiments without having them fit into the mold of Western lgbtq embodiments.[9]

For a show claiming to learn from social justice tourism, it is paradoxical that *Gaycation* focuses on assimilating what they encounter to the realities of lgbtq marginality familiar to them. They follow the Eurocentered and hegemonic mode of representation of sex and its relation to gender and embodiment. Biopolitics explains the emergence of medico-legal categories within Western institutions, including those concerning sex/gender, and the representational operations they employ (Foucault 2003). While I offer an account of how synecdoche bears on this mode of representation in the next section, I mention it here because its force steers the counterpublic orientation of *Gaycation*'s transnational media platform.

One case in point is an interview with Ashok Row Kavi, the head of The Humsafar Fund. For Kavi, gay identity relays self-affirmation, societal change, and acceptability. He wittingly assumes not only that all histories produce homophobia under a similar guise, or that one history of homophobia stands for all histories of homophobia, but also that gay identification is the best method to break free from this heterosexist system. In assembling local lgbtq advocates such as Kavi, or Parmesh Shahani, who wrote the best-selling *Gay Bombay*, *Gaycation* performs a unique form of colonizing work. It aligns local lgbtq activists with the cohosts through the recognition of each other's advocacy for marginalized lgbtq communities, extending thereby what I describe elsewhere as a global network of counterpublic sentiments (DiPietro 2016). They yield to a model of modern sexual identification that constructs nonconforming gender embodiments as having common historical roots. Global denizens of an imagined lgbtq counterpublic, Kavi and *Gaycation* cohosts feel closer to each other by sharing the experience of being denied dignity. This interview shows Kavi seeking Westernizing recognition with an ironic smirk that Page and Daniel absorb, signaling that all three identify "the conservative" ways of India's Gender Non-Conformity. Kavi takes it further, stating that, "Even today, there's no identity called gay. They say: 'are you *this* way?'" Page and Daniel, and the rest of the audience, partake in the subtle mocking of the *unfamiliar* form "to be *this* way" vis-à-vis "gay."

Not far from the affects that we bring to the classroom, the show mobilizes indignation only to the extent that universalizing notions of dignity secure empathy toward lgbtq counterpublics. In Kavi's normalizing formulation above, "gay" operates as a sociohistorical construct that recruits our consent, on the one hand, to see sexual identification as part and parcel of human dignity—what makes *us* like everyone else—and, on the other, to see our sexual dignity in terms of an implied capability to pronounce, in front of ourselves and others, that variations in sexual identification qualify for membership within the human domain. Thus, Kavi's and *Gaycation*'s counterpublic claims, and their twinned sentiments, arise from an evacuation of non-Western affective history under the guise of shared dignity; that is, an elision of *this way* in India's non-conformity.

Through what affective operations does *Gaycation*'s encounter with hijras colonize the indignation of trans* of color communities, our allies and advocates? What affective intensities does it occlude? Which ones does it cast as the most trodden path? What affective intensities does this episode transact as it delivers the paradoxical effect of (a) providing release for the viewers' indignation, and (b) offering little motivation for the viewers to actively confront their own attachments to ornamental multiculturalism? Answers may lie with the geopolitical dynamics that I describe next within *Gaycation*'s realm of affect and its counterpublic orientation (MP; DiPietro 2015; Price 2001; Scott 1990).

THE PART FOR THE WHOLE: AGREEMENT TO TRANS[F](N)ORM

Studies of homonormativity and transnormativity document Westernizing cognitive practices that domesticate nonconformity (Duggan 2003; DiPietro 2015, 2016; Puar 2007; Snorton and Haritaworn 2013). They posit that lgbt counterpublics pursue white-centered projects and that, in many ways, their agreements about lgbt-led social *transformation* may work as agreements about homo- and *transnormativity*. *Gaycation*'s counterpublic reflexivity recruits: (a) certainty about the content and value of indignation when prompted by transing embodiments across different cultures; (b) simplicity by favoring a Western model of sexual identification and marginalization; and (c) agreement on a common ground that explicates gender and trans* marginalization across the globe.

The show's spotlight on hijras begins with a segment on *6 Pack*, a pop band of six hijra members who hit India's charts with more than twenty-five million *YouTube* views and attained international celebrity status in 2016. *Gaycation* brokers an invitation from one of them, Komal Jagtap, to visit the hijra house where she lives located north of Mumbai. Broadly speaking, hijras have religious-based functions in both Hindu and Muslim communities where, primarily, they confer fertility and prosperity on newlyweds and newborns. Designated cismen at birth, they construct their embodiment after a model of idealized and sacrificial celibacy, including the excision of their penises and testicles and the adoption of ways of dressing and loving characteristic of hetero-identified Indian ciswomen (Reddy 2005, 2; Prieur 2006, 331). More generally, hijras live in community, many times sharing the same precarious dwelling and respecting formalized structures of mentorship and conviviality. Part of a larger network of belonging that hijras call "*kotis*," loosely glossed as "effeminate" cismen or "behavioral not-men," hijras may also make a living from sex work (Reddy 2005, 15). Personhood in the hijra world "[operates] across and within multiple subject positions constituted by the crisscrossing of gender, kinship, class, caste, and religion" (Rogers 2007, 244). One defining trait of hijra personhood is the notion of *izzat* that, within a constellation of honor or respect, gives them legitimacy in front of members of their own community and beyond (see also ch. 5, this volume).

In its portrayal, *Gaycation* pigeonholes hijras into the "third-gender" category of modern sexual identity, of flesh elevated to colonizing universals (Roen

2001, 255–56, 260). Based on a positivist rationalization of reproductive normalcy, the colonial/modern, white supremacist man/woman distinction suppresses alternatives to dimorphism such as Galenic anatomy, among many others.[10] It attains this measure of certainty by following a *synecdochal device*, a way of producing knowledge distinctive of positivist leanings across the sex sciences. Synecdoche is a relation of correspondence where a part represents the whole. In the West, it assists with the definition of sexual boundaries and, as the remainder of this chapter shows, with the definition of affective boundaries within processes through which lgbt counterpublics vie for the recognition of their dignity vis-à-vis non-Western transing embodiments. *Gaycation* employs three instantiations of this synecdochal device to encapsulate hijras' embodiments within an either/or reality of absolute, human-centered, Western-centered, differences.

This hegemonic synecdochal model takes genitalia [a part] to stand for the entirety [the whole] of not only human anatomy but also of social and psychological sexual dimorphism (Bettcher 2012, 320; Laqueur 1990, 20–21; Fausto Sterling 2000, 16–19). Borrowing this device, *Gaycation* calls upon biological determinism to describe hijras within the frame of "neither male nor female." Missing from its portrayal is the intercultural labor that would allow the audience to consider whether hijra embodiments point to realities other than male or female, other than lgbtq biomaterialities that the West designates as variations of male and female. Even when an alternative option such as "third sex" comes into the picture, the notion stabilizes rather than contests a unitary model of binary, male/female, sexed identity. The imposition of this model evacuates uncertainty or nondimorphic biomaterialities.[11] *Gaycation*'s first synecdochal rendering of hijra embodiments *excludes complex, trans* of color, and intersex biomaterialities whose histories contest the supposed crosscultural validity of lgbt embodiments.*

Komal takes an oppositional route when discussing the cohosts' question about hijras' membership within the lgbtq community. With a cut-to-the-chase tone, her claim that hijras "don't participate in that community" and that they "inhabit" (Hindi: *bas-e hain*) *half-male* and *half-female* (Hindi: *adha nar, adhi nari*) convey an ontological status opaque to the Eurocentered two-sex model. If the lgbtq nomenclature of *third sex* violently summons hijras to the man/woman monocultural distinction, Komal's answer indicates instead that hijras underscore a place, a "where we come from," or a set of relations of provenance rather than a state of being. *Gaycation* prescribes the irrelevance of those notions of embodied nonconformity inasmuch as they remain unthinkable and unfamiliar in the West. Hijras' own self-awareness, by contrast, leads us to an otherwise ecology of mattering bodies, such as the Hindu and Muslim incarnations of *izzat* and its recasting of kinship across religiosity, caste, and nation.

As concerns affectivity, why are *we* more inclined to hear the appeals to our shared human compassion in the claims of hijras? If we are truly invested in advancing self-determination for all transing embodiments of color, why do *we* cast a white-centered sense of indignation, of lack of *human* dignity, on hijras' appeals for respect? The answer belongs with *Gaycation*'s pursuit of an affective work that lgbt counterpublics find more conducive to their global fight against discrimination and shame. The show encourages Komal to join this counterpublic strategy since the show conflates empathy toward nonconforming bodily variations with the underlying compassion that *humanity* warrants to conforming and hegemonic bodily variations. In so doing, however, it engages the second instantiation of the Eurocentered *synecdochal device*. It establishes the white supremacist and heterosexualizing man/woman divide as the foundation for dignity and respect, and consequently, for the type of affect they ought to inspire.

This second instantiation of synecdoche draws the following affective correspondence between part and whole. Whenever lgbt counterpublics demand that we empathize with the vulnerable condition of nonconforming biomaterialities such as hijras', we do so to the extent that we heed to the more encompassing source of empathy, the one typically derived from recognizing the absolute humanity socially and historically conferred upon the man/woman divide. Therein lies the contradiction of what Lugones calls "the coloniality of gender" (HGS). In being denied gender, those who underwent colonization come to inhabit a zone of nonbeing defined by lack of dignity/humanity as this is understood within the hegemonic man/woman divide. From outside this zone, empathizing with hijras and other non-Western nonconforming biomaterialities arises from an emotional domain where *the human* remains lodged, where the very possibility of a benevolent sentiment lies with elevating hijras to the ground of the human. Through this second instantiation of synecdoche, *hijras and other non-Western nonconforming biomaterialities collapse into objects of benevolent ignorance.*

Gaycation follows a global politics of benevolent ignorance, a type of forgetfulness that results from more than slightly misled fuzzy intentions. Cohosts and audience actively participate in availing the counterpublic sphere with this emoting disposition. Moreover, they look for sociohistorical cues and they rearrange them in a secular narrative of modern sexual identification. The show takes an atavistic approach by painting hijras as one of "the oldest recorded third-gender communities in the world, dating back to Hindu scriptures."

According to *Gaycation*'s atavistic gaze, Hindu history contained the principles of equality and respect that contemporary India denies hijras. It submits that a Hindu past extended to them the type of equality that lgbtq communities in the West demand today and that, at least at the level of the law, they have successfully obtained. Little matters to *Gaycation* that the notion of *izzat* across hijras' social life endows equality and respect with spiritual and nonsecular contents. *Gaycation*, thus, delivers the third instantiation of synecdoche. If India's social rules harm hijras' sense of dignity, arousing indignation among lgbt counterpublics, *Gaycation* responds by couching monocultural ignorance in the benevolent act of claiming respect for the humanity of trans* of color embodiments. The show takes an aspect, or part, of the notion of respect, namely its modern and secular register, to represent the entirety of all potential relations between personhood, dignity, and honor. The markings that indigenous understandings of honor and respect infuse into communal, rather than personal, accounts of *izzat* among hijras exclude them from the man/woman divide. When tradition shows that hijras receive remuneration for dancing and singing at ceremonies (Hindi: *badhai*), *Gaycation* neglects any connection between this practice and the success that *6 Pack* achieves or the personal respect and communal honor it inspires. In sum, this third instantiation of synecdoche *distorts hijras' realities by narrowing respect and indignation to a Westernizing economy of sexual mores.*

In the interview with Komal's community, a few hijras tear up recounting their families' rejection. The segment halts with sentiments that can't be transferred from a subaltern to a colonizing tongue. Dismissed are Komal's references to an elder or grandmother (Hindi: *Mujra Nani*) who apparently took them in and whom the members of this hijras' house follow.[12] The audience receives not only English captions but also a Westernizing worldview when the subtitles introduce this grandmother. An English-speaking viewer would totally miss the reality of religious kin that *Mujra Nani* invokes among hijras. The segment instead builds on the typical sentiments attached to the rejection one may experience when our own families deny us self-determination. Were *Gaycation* to maintain dissonance between the West and postcolonial cultures or non-Western legacies, between blood and religious kinship, members of lgbtq counterpublics may encounter the less-trodden path that Lugones and Price propose in their praxis of radical multiculturalism, the path of intercultural humility, defamiliarization, and ontological confusion.

With synecdoche at play, *Gaycation* seeks a common good fitting of global lgbtq counterpublics. Monoculturalism operates at a global scale by dismissing spiritual, nonsecular, and decolonizing sites of hijras' agency and embodiment. Their realities across religion, caste, and nation are not "to be investigated or resolved, but rather [...] set aside in an act of simplification in the direction of one [Western] culture" (DC 122). This is ever more evident when the audience hears Page meditate on how easy it can be "to [...] not look at yourself or look at where you come from." Laziness makes Page swiftly forget her own suggestion. *Gaycation* provides her, and subsequently, the audience, with the psychic intensities of both benevolence and self-righteousness.

BENEVOLENT VIOLENCE

Cohosts Page and Daniel stress the pain they feel when they witness the marginalization of their interviewees. Despite pausing in utter shock and staring in disbelief, they shelter themselves behind the distance between them and the object of their empathy. Even when experiencing sensations that pull them closer to their interviewees, they fail to listen to the many registers of indignation in their voices and lives. They are consumed by a benevolent sentiment that prompts them to express discontent and indignation about their vulnerable interviewees who, in turn, remain at a loss whenever they try to express their own frustrations with lgbt counterpublic affects.

Colonizing legacies provide a foundation for the benevolence that *Gaycation* foregrounds. Becoming indignant works within a larger affective infrastructure that I am calling benevolent violence. At the transfer points between sensing, feeling, and knowing, benevolent violence actualizes certainty, simplicity, and agreement. Benevolent violence operates as both affective attachment and disposition. *As attachment, it entices the practitioners of ornamental multiculturalism toward self-righteousness.* It takes the form of "I pity you, I *must* feel pity." While these practitioners may give off compassionate energy, its unfolding into pity rests on the violation of another's way of seeing, thinking, feeling, and presenting to the world. Arrogance creates the conditions of ignorance for such vicious intrusion. *As disposition, benevolent violence provides the practitioners of ornamental multiculturalism, including white-centered trans* activists, advocates, and their allies, with the most trodden path for affectivity, from an imagined correspondence between those practitioners and the recipient of their pity to the arrogant replacement of the latter by the former.* This disposition adopts the form of "You feel *like I do* and, thus, my feelings stand for yours."

Not unlike the synecdochal shift from Galenic to modern sexed differentiation, becoming indignant while violently benevolent inscribes an *isomorphic* correspondence between affects with *similar* forms but contrasting intensities. Komal's hijra community becomes indignant as a way of affecting their broader environment, negotiating what to do and how to act across caste, religion, and nation. Page and Daniel, instead, become indignant about hijras' plight by assuming crosscultural familiarity and validity among nonconforming embodiments. As we see next, lgbtq counterpublics and their affective intensities inform many other publics and their interactions with transing embodiments of color.

SCARRING FROM BENEVOLENT VIOLENCE

Zev Al-Walid's "Pilgrimage" narrates a "movement from woman to man," from "a farewell trip" on a journey to visit "the Almighty in female garb" to gaining insight on "how to be a Muslim man" (2010, 261–67). *Pilgrimage* aptly conveys the liminal possibilities of unsettled departures and arrivals for biomateriality: (a) those found within the domain of "hormone replacement therapy" or men "with bilateral chest scars, men with breasts, short men with hips" (262); and (b) those associated with a feminist framework that sees multiple oppressions as inseparable and that enables us to see Al-Walid's self-presentation not just as *trans* but rather as "trans and queer and brown and Muslim" (266). Al-Walid's pilgrimage intensifies the tension between synecdochal, westernizing, accounts of *trans* and the complex, liminal, and diasporic carnalities of transing beyond lgbt embodiments.

A pilgrimage, as an encounter with the otherworldly, signals ritualized passages into mattering and embodiment. If at first Al-Walid's story aligns with typical narratives of trans self-discovery (Prosser 1998), the affective tone of the text migrates from the lived experience of transitioning to that of occupying gender spaces that are paradoxically nonconforming and typical. His narrative looks for auspicious and inauspicious signs for trans* of color embodiment: "[t]he women's entrance of the mosque," a walk "out from [his] hotel room in a state of ihram, or ritual purity," and a few years down the road the act of removing "more than just the outer layer of [his] clothing to be seen as [something other] than a rather unremarkable looking stocky guy" (262–63). Through these signs, trans* of color subjectivity and embodiment come into being in the visceral terrain where two or more subjects connect. But more than signs, they materialize pressure points, minute tiny beads whose very mass depends on the position and weight of each other. Affects operate in this agentic fashion, laying grids of energetic relay, feeding off one another. Al-Walid's own transing embodiment lives at that pressure point between self-realization and indignation, between, on the one hand, the hope of finding other trans-identified Muslim men among the pilgrims and, on the other, "a pang of loneliness" on the way to the mosque, at its women's entrance, or inside it when he can't but to follow the dress code of ciswomen.

In his journey, Al-Walid focuses on vulnerability and transing every time he stands before immigration checkpoints, their racializing biotechnologies and criminalizing of non-Western religions. Often a source of anxiety, his gender presentation prompts suspicion at international borders due mainly to "traveling with a woman's documents," "being brown-skinned, or simply for having Arabic writing in [his] passport" (263). While he tempers this account by acknowledging the privileges he has—e.g.: graduate degree, career, comfortable housing—the person that *he* is "does not legally exist and cannot exist given the law in [his] country of citizenship [Saudi Arabia]" (266–67).

In the post-9/11 environment, immigration agents see with suspicion what Al-Walid does and how he presents. They don't know whether he is impersonating a person of the opposite sex/gender, perpetrating a terrorist act, or employing poor judgment and hence failing at living in the gender he presents. When entering Canada, tensions ensue between Al-Walid and an immigration supervisor. First, the officer apologizes for having to ask a question involving "any mistakes" in Al-Walid's passport (265). Second, upon Al-Walid's self-identification as "transsexual," and after him conceding that his country of origin still "[has] some work to do on making appropriate accommodations for people who transition from one gender to another," the officer praises Canada for providing, in contrast to Saudi Arabia, *more advanced* legislation (265). Third, the officer adds unsolicited assessment of Al-Walid's transitioning by stating that, to legally change gender identity in Canada, where it is permitted, "[*he*'d] have to at least *try* to be a woman first" (265). Fourth, Al-Walid feels forced to clarify that he is "a transsexual man [who] had been born female" and, thus, is not trying to be a *woman*.

At that interaction, both benevolence and indignation shape the material possibilities of transing. The officer swivels between rehearsed stiffness and suspecting politeness. She recognizes that gender biomateriality lies with the most intimate domain of personhood. A beginning of empathic intensity arises, and it is probably felt by Al-Walid whose very transing project will be assessed in the few minutes it takes to get admission at a checkpoint. The supervisor anticipates that the question leaves scars on the recipients. "Sorry" may express empathy for Al-Walid's circumstances but, when used by this supervisor, it operates as condescension, a coating of affected and mitigating regret for the shame that the intrusion inflects on Al-Walid.

Benevolence underwrites the officer's mitigating gesture. It authorizes and authenticates her scrutiny over what transgender and transsexuals are not, cannot, or might not be.[13] It also deploys synecdoche as the most-trodden path for a form of colonizing, monocultural, ornamentally multicultural, and counterpublic empathy. Feeling sorry for Al-Walid tethers the officer, a practitioner of ornamental multiculturalism, to transgender embodiments as the recipients of pity. Through this benevolent gesture, the officer comforts her own sense of self, of coming to do what she feels is right. The excitement, perhaps, at making another feel at ease, ends up transfigured into self-righteousness. Paradoxical as it might be, her misplaced empathy issues from the affectivity and reflexivity that lgbtq counterpublics circulate.

Momentarily, the visceral and not quite conscious deployment of synecdoche attains proximity between Al-Walid and the officer. It comes at the price of slipping into counterpublic trans-coherence [all cultures including India and Saudi Arabia have third-genders and lgbtq populations]. "[S]he could contain herself no longer" before scrutinizing his intimacy, couching this violent affront under a compassionate sentiment toward lgbtq counterpublics (Al-Walid 2010, 265). It is with a gesture of "extravagant cleavage" that the officer underlines that Al-Walid presents as incoherent and unfamiliar (265). Al-Walid probably shrank his lungs in disgust but, at the same time, with an acute understanding of the impossibility of talking back, of the risks he might have faced if he had protested the officer's and, by extension, the world's damaging expectation over trans* embodiments and their (dis)ability to pass as cis.

That Al-Walid delivers a jaw-dropping reaction to the officer's blatant misrecognition of his transing is to be dismissed. In the manner that *Gaycation* recruits indignation on behalf of lgbtq counterpublics, the border officer safeguards the role the West plays in endorsing lgbtq freedoms. The moment of affective proximity, albeit painful, damaging, and violent, creates dilemmas for Al-Walid. Becoming indignant for the lack of lgbtq legislation in Saudi Arabia allows the officer to *see* Al-Walid's plight, to feel one's personhood questioned in the experience of another. Recognizing each other's implication by the affect of becoming indignant overlaps, however, with the officer's disposition toward certainty, simplicity, and agreement. Her benevolence, when cast upon Al-Walid, places her with ease at the center of a society that is both structurally monocultural and ornamentally multicultural. Well-meaning indignation without checking one's complicity with colonial legacies often results in an impoverished account of trans* phenomena.

The affective, cognitive, and moral damage that benevolent violence inflicts renders indignation into monocultural resource but, most important, it leaves bleeding wounds in its recipient. Studying benevolent violence toward transing embodiments of color makes visible the *trans*phobic* and racist tenets of mainstream and counterpublic lgbtq activisms (Snorton and Haritaworn 2013). In its globalizing dissemination, white-centered transnormative affect, both as attachment and disposition, enacts benevolent violence. It works through synecdoche: first, casting modern sexual identities as nonprovincial and as placeholders of all nonconforming biomaterialities; second, establishing the provincial, Westernizing, white-supremacist notion of human dignity attached to the man/woman divide as *the* source of empathy for all plights about respect that come with non-Western, gender-nonconforming, collectives; and third, imposing modern and secular notions of respect that lgbt counterpublics infuse into their demands for equality over notions of honor, respect, and acceptance that trans* of color communities mobilize from within non-Western and spiritually-rich histories. In sum, benevolent violence deploys synecdoche and it operates as the denial of intercultural sensing, feeling, and knowing.

White-centered empathy makes room for benevolence to arise. Such as the cohosts of *Gaycation* do, lgbt counterpublics and their practicing of ornamental multiculturalism intensify affective attachments to colonizing violence. Despite *meaning well*, they exhibit an almost unshakeable faith in certainty, simplicity, and agreement. The scars that benevolent violence leaves on trans* of color communities make visible the affective labor that white-centered lgbt counterpublics circulate. Ultimately, undoing benevolent violence requires more than wishing well to those one cannot, might not, and will not listen to. It begins with the desire to enrich each other's souls. It begins with decolonizing your guts once and for all.

NOTES

1. Used with an asterisk, *trans** involves many different identities within the ecologies of embodied differences that the word "transing" attempts to capture among gendered spaces (Ryan 2014; Stryker, Currah, and Moore 2008).

2. As a decolonial alternative to critical pedagogy, interculturality fosters horizontal relationality among all cultures through "a political process, practice and project of fundamental structural and institutional transformation, including of [the] state" and its epistemic roots (Walsh 2015, 12).

3. Lugones and Price update their study of contemporary cultural dynamics that combine ornamental multiculturalism with faith in national unity at the expense of any difference (FU).

4. In extending Lugones and Price's radical multiculturalism to focus in on the inseparability of feeling and knowing, I move away from the pervasive rationalist lineage across theories of publics and counterpublics (Fraser 1997). While queer and queer of color critiques see artful engines for nonnormative futures

in counterpublicity (Muñoz 1999, 2009; Warner 2005), they fail to recognize meaning-making possibilities when oppositional subjectivities rupture the social with infrapolitical activity (MP).

5. However, Lugones and Price do convey that many members of nondominant cultures live in anguish and despair, fearing to be absorbed and impoverished by monocultural practitioners.

6. At the time of this writing, there are at least ten shows on TV focusing on transing lives: *Becoming Us* (ABC), *Better Things* (FX), *Big Freedia: Queen of Bounce* (Fuse), *I am Cait* (E!), *I am Jazz* (TLC), *Lost in Transition* (TLC), *Orange is the New Black* (Netflix), *RuPaul's Drag Race* (Logo), *Sense 8* (Netflix), *Strut* (Oxygen), *Transparent* (Amazon Video), and *Transcendent* (Fuse).

7. I taught this iteration of this class in fall 2016 at Syracuse University. There were sixteen students enrolled; among them, most identified as white ciswomen, 37 percent as students of color, two as transgender or gender variant, and one as gay. No student of color presented other than as a ciswoman.

8. Ruth Vanita, however, insists on the importance of following speech for the work it performs in each context and without creating more anxiety about colonial power than what it's due (2001). Vanita thinks about the Indian public sphere circulating terms such as *gay* and *lesbian* since the 1980s. They have currency because Indians are using them. Vanita doesn't make the connection between language and social ontology that proponents of the coloniality of gender pursue.

9. For an introduction to hijras vis-à-vis Western categories, see Gramling and Dutta (2016).

10. There are alternatives. On the Afrodiasporic ontology of embodiments, see Wekker (2006) and Strongman (2008).

11. On February 2018, *the New York Times* reports the case of a new species of crayfish whose recent genetic mutation allows them to clone themselves. The report relies on the binary between "normalcy" and "mutation" to describe them as a "mutant" species. Against scientific evidence of nondimorphic reproduction, Westernizing and dichotomizing views continue to frame sexed differences in specialized media.

12. I thank Dr. Himika Bhattacharya for her interlocution on matters of translation between Hindi and English. While I traveled in India for about eight months in my twenties, I do not have technical training in Hindi. Captions provided by *Gaycation* lead most viewers to understand that the grandmother is a ciswoman instead of a hijra elder.

13. See also Lugones on intersexuality (HGS).

REFERENCES

Al-Walid, Zev. 2010. "Pilgrimage." In *Gender Outlaws: The Next Generation*, edited by Kate Bornstein and S. Bear Bergman, 261–67. Berkeley: Seal Press.

Ahmed, Sara. 2004. "Affective Economies." *Social Text* 22(2): 117–39.

Berlant, Lauren, ed. 2004. *Compassion: The Culture and Politics of an Emotion*. New York: Routledge.

Bertelsen, Lone, and Andrew Murphie. 2010. "An Ethics of Everyday Infinities and Powers: Félix Guattari on Affect and the Refrain." In *The Affect Theory Reader*, edited by Melissa Gregg and Gregory J. Seigworth, 1–27. Durham, NC: Duke University Press.

Bettcher, Talia Mae. 2012. "Full-Frontal Morality: The Naked Truth about Gender." *Hypatia* 27 (2): 319–37.

DiPietro, Pedro. 2015. "Decolonizing *travesti* Space in Buenos Aires: Race, Sexuality, and Sideways Relationality." In *Gender, Place, and Culture* 23(5): 677–93.

———. 2016. "Of *Huachafería*, *Así*, and *M'e Mati*: Decolonizing Transing Methodologies." In *TSQ: Transgender Studies Quarterly* 2(4): 67–76.

Duggan, Lisa. 2003. *The Twilight of Equality?* Boston: Beacon Press Books.

Fausto-Sterling, Anne. 2000. *Sexing the Body: Gender Politics and the Construction of Sexuality*. New York: Basic Books.

Foucault, Michel. 2003. *Society Must Be Defended*. New York: Picador.

Fraser, Nancy. 1997. *Justice Interruptus: Critical Reflections on the Postsocialist Condition*. New York: Routledge.

Gould, Deborah. 2009. *Moving Politics: Emotion and Act Up's Fight Against AIDS*. Chicago: The University of Chicago Press.

Gramling, D., and Aniruddha Dutta. 2016. "Introduction." *Transgender Studies Quarterly* 3(3–4): 333–56.

Lacey, Nicola. 1998. *Unspeakable Subjects: Feminist Essays in Legal and Social Theory*. London: Bloomsbury.

Laqueur, Thomas. 1990. *Making Sex. Body and Gender from the Greeks to Freud*. Cambridge, MA: Harvard University Press.

Muñoz, José Esteban. 1999. *Disidentifications: Queers of Color and the Performance of Politics*. Minneapolis: University of Minnesota Press.

———. 2009. *Cruising Utopia: The Then and There of Queer Futurity*. New York: New York University Press.

Page, Ellen (director). 2016. "India." *Gaycation*, Season 2, Episode 3. Viceland TV.
Price, Joshua. 2001. "Violence Against Prostitutes and a Re-Evaluation of the Counterpublic Sphere." *Genders* 34.
Prieur, Annick. 2006. Review of *With Respect to Sex: Negotiating* Hijra *Identity in South India* by Gayatri Reddy, *American Journal of Sociology* 112(1): 331–33.
Prosser, Jay. 1998. *Second Skins: The Body Narratives of Transsexuality.* New York: Columbia University Press.
Puar, Jasbir. 2007. *Terrorist Assemblages: Homonationalism in Queer Times.* Durham, NC: Duke University Press.
Reddy, Gayatri. 2005. *With Respect to Sex: Negotiating* Hijra *Identity in South India.* Chicago: The University of Chicago Press.
Roen, Katrina. 2001. "Trangender Theory and Embodiment: The Risk of Racial Marginalization." *Journal of Gender Studies* 10(3): 253–63.
Rogers, Martyn. 2007. Review of *With Respect to Sex: Negotiating* Hijra *Identity in South India* by Gayatri Reddy, *The Journal of the Royal Anthropological Institute* 13(1): 244–45.
Ryan, Hugh. 2014. "What Does Trans* Mean, and Where Did It Come From?" *Slate*, January 10. www.slate.com/blogs/outward/2014/01/10/trans_what_does_it_mean_and_where_did_it_come_from.html
Scott, James. 1990. *Domination and the Arts of Resistance: Hidden Transcripts.* New Haven, CT: Yale University Press.
Seigworth, Gregory J., and Melissa Gregg. 2010. "An Inventory of Shimmers." In *The Affect Theory Reader*, edited by Melissa Gregg and Gregory J. Seigworth, 1–27. Durham, NC: Duke University Press.
Shahani, Parmesh. 2008. *Gay Bombay: Globalization, Love and (Be)longing in Contemporary India.* New Delhi: Sage Publications.
Snorton, C. Riley, and Jin Haritaworn. 2013. "Trans Necropolitics: A Transnational Reflection on Violence, Death, and the Trans of Color Afterlife." In *Transgender Studies Reader 2*, edited by Susan Stryker and Aren Aizura, 66–76. New York: Routledge.
Strongman, Roberto. 2008. "Transcorporeality in Voudou." *Haitian Studies* 14(2): 4–29.
Stryker, Susan, Paisley Currah, and Lisa Jean Moore. 2008. "Introduction: Trans-, Trans, or Transgender?" *WSQ: Women's Studies Quarterly* 36(3–4): 11–22.
Vanita, Ruth. 2001. *Queering India: Same-Sex Love and Eroticism in Indian Culture and Society.* New York: Routledge.

Walsh, Catherine. 2015. "Decolonial Pedagogies Walking and Asking: Notes to Paulo Freire from AbyaYala." *International Journal of Lifelong Education* 34(1): 9–21.

Warner, Michael. 2005. *Publics and Counterpublics.* Brooklyn: Zone Books.

Wekker, Gloria. 2006. *The Politics of Passion: Women's Sexual Culture in the AfroSurinamese Diaspora.* New York: Columbia University Press.

10 Travel to Death-Worlds

Joshua M. Price

We are sitting in the cramped living room of a second-floor walkup. A young man is telling me what happened to him at the jail. I have never met him before. His companion, another young man dressed similarly in loose jeans and a long-sleeved shirt, keeps coming in and going out of the room. They apparently have several dogs in the next room, all of them pit bulls. I know this because each time the friend comes in, he brings in a different fully grown dog on a tight metal chain. Each dog pulls and twists at the chain by turning its neck and trying to jump, in that muscular, pugnacious pit-bull way that makes them seem so aggressive and terrifying. Other dogs bark in the next room. The ritual is odd—bringing dog after angry dog into the room singly and without saying anything. Although I don't know this man, and although he does not look at me or give me any reason to feel any warmth, I instinctively trust him at least enough to believe that he will take care of my well-being, and so the dogs do not intimidate me at all; to the contrary, I have a desire to reach out and pet each one as it pulls at its chain. The presence of these dogs distracts the young man from his narrative. He also keeps getting cell phone calls and text messages, as does his friend. At length, the young man leaves the room for a few minutes, accompanying his friend into the kitchen (or whatever it is), and then he comes back, re-centers himself in his story and continues his narrative.

"I was in the jail when my appendix burst. I was in my cell. The pain was unbelievable. I was sitting there and I could hardly move. I was able to tell a guard but I could tell he didn't really believe me. He told me I have to go to medical [the medical unit]. *But I couldn't walk. I was doubled over in pain. I was able to make it in a wheelchair. I only saw a nurse at first. All they gave me was Pepto-Bismol. Pepto-Bismol! I was like that for days. I couldn't do anything. Eventually, I was able to see a doctor and he told them that this was serious and they sent me to an outside hospital. They told me I was lucky, that I could have died. Man, that pain was the worst of my life. I pled guilty just to get out of that place."*

The man tells his story plainly and succinctly. He is not exactly perfunctory, but neither does he dwell on the story. He is not particularly expressive emotionally.

Some people burst into tears, or break off their stories. Some become enraged, as if tapping into their experiences taps into the frustration they felt. He does not seem to be looking for sympathy or understanding. On the other hand, he is taking the time to tell me the story. His account of administrative neglect and indifference is consistent with several dozen other people who have told me stories of languishing, sick in their cells at the county jail, or suffering from strained ligaments, abscesses, or even open wounds, including head wounds.

I feel I need to respond somehow to the story. I try employing the usual linguistic machinery to express sympathy, but my attempts fall flat. He looks back at me blankly. At length I thank him, I give him my contact information and encourage him to call me again if he'd like to tell me more, but I already know that he won't call. "OK," he says, without looking at me, already making the transition back to his daily activities. I never see him again.

To live under modern forms of colonial domination, Achille Mbembe has argued, is to experience a permanent condition of being in pain. The pain is a consequence of the social organization: "fortified structures, military posts, and roadblocks everywhere; buildings that bring back painful memories of humiliation, interrogations, and beatings" (Mbembe 2003, 39). Modern forms of colonial domination generate what he calls "death-worlds," "new and unique forms of social existence in which vast populations are subjected to conditions of life conferring upon them the status of living dead" (40). Under these conditions, death and freedom "are irrevocably interwoven" (38).

The colonized live a condition of perpetual war, with all the violence and chaos that this implies. The condition is racialized. "In the racial/colonial world, the 'hell' of war becomes a condition that defines the reality of racialized selves," posits Nelson Maldonado-Torres (2008, 218). He calls those confined to the other side the *damnés de la terre* (condemned of the earth), drawing on Frantz Fanon's famous formulation (2007). Maldonado-Torres sees the *damnés* as dispensable or disposable.

Arguably, however, the *damnés*' living the hell of war are crucial to the rest of the society in at least two ways. First, in their very abjectness, they confer on those in the dominant culture—the rest of us—the status of the human (I have more to say about this below; also see Hartman 1997; Povinelli 2011, 1–45). Second, the *damnés* are important in material terms. Those with social power in particular often have acquired it, or inherited it, by appropriating the labor and life substance of the colonized.

As a result, although not everyone inhabits a death-world, everyone is touched by death-worlds, and may even benefit from them. However, one of the common illusions for those of us who live outside of death-worlds is that our lives are unconnected to those who live in a condition of living death. "Your high independence only reveals the immeasurable distance between us," Frederick Douglass declaimed bitterly, addressing himself presumably to white people (1852). But as he knew better than anyone, high independence is a delusion and depends on self-deception.

What, on the other hand, is the experience of inhabiting a death-world? The experiences are not uniform, of course. W.E.B. Du Bois serves as a good point of departure, even though he frames it in binary terms. Late in his career, he described African Americans as a people entombed in a cave, shunted aside and hindered in their development, but who try to gain recognition of their condition from the "passing world."

> The passing throng does not even turn its head, or if it does, glances curiously and walks on. It gradually penetrates the minds of the prisoners that the people passing do not hear; that some thick sheet of invisible but horribly tangible plate glass is between them and the world. (Du Bois 2014, 66)

For those who are part of the passing throng or passing world (and I guess I figure in that number), delivering oneself from the self-deception of independence and separation requires not only listening to the entombed souls and recognizing our connection, but also entering their perception of the world. It requires travel to death-worlds.

INCARCERATION AS A DEATH-WORLD

Du Bois employs "prisoners" as a rhetorical conceit for racial difference. But let's take the term *prisoners* literally. If your life is touched directly by the penitentiary (if you or a loved one has been incarcerated), then the connection to that death-world is concrete and vivid. If not, you nevertheless know, even if only as an abstract idea or as a niggling sensation at the edge of your consciousness that people in prisons and jails throughout the United States are being forced to undergo extreme isolation, exposure to systematic and systemic racism, transphobia, sexual assault, along with occasional beatings, daily cavity searches, and other chronic and pervasive forms of debasement.

The modern penitentiary thus epitomizes the hell of a death-world. People who are confined to a jail or prison stand strangely distant from the rest of the society and the world community. They suffer chronic pain, humiliation, and a peculiar kind of separation from others that impresses on them that they are alone and vulnerable (Price 2015). The concertina wire, sally ports, and high fences mark a visible line. But invisible lines are there as well. Even though it feels a world away, I know that from my university office, I can drive a short ten minutes to find people at our county jail undergoing constant brutalization and cruel treatment.

JAIL RESEARCH

Since 2004, I have directed various community-based projects to monitor health care practices at the Broome County Jail, in Central New York State. I first directed a monitoring project under the auspices of our local branch of the NAACP (2004–2007). Our monitoring work centered on interviewing people incarcerated at the jail. They or their relatives would contact the NAACP, who turned over the contact information to me, and I went, often accompanied by my students, and presented our NAACP credentials to the jail staff to be admitted for a "noncontact" visit through heavy glass. Since the focus is health, and the health care is poor, many incarcerated people we interviewed were in pain. Eventually, we began to interview formerly incarcerated people on their experiences at the jail. This is how I met the young man I described at the beginning of this chapter.

TRAVEL TO DEATH-WORLDS

How does one cross through the glass plate to the imprisoned souls on the other side? In this case, the glass plate is literal and figurative, visible and invisible. María Lugones has provided a framework to think about how and why to cross such a distance and the possible social benefits, as well as the risks (WT). World-travel in the case of crossing from one side of the prison wall to the other implies crossing lines of gender, race, and class difference, as well as ability, where those lines mark social hierarchy.

Before we go further, an account of "worlds": Lugones eschews fixed, closed definitions. Nevertheless, she characterizes several of its attributes in negative and positive terms. A "world" in her sense is not a utopia, nor simply a subjective worldview. "It has to be inhabited at present by some flesh and blood people..." (WT 87). It can be a society "given a nondominant or resistant construction.... It may be a construction of a tiny portion of a particular society. It may be incomplete" (87). One can travel between different worlds and one can (and usually does) inhabit several worlds at the same time (88). "Traveling" between worlds also has a special, technical sense. It refers to changing one's identity: "The shift from being one person to being a different person is what I call traveling. This shift may not be willful or even conscious, and one may be completely unaware of being different in a different 'world,' and may not recognize that one is in a different 'world'" (89). Lugones concedes that this may be ontologically problematic, but insists (and this is one of the criteria) that it be true to experience (89).

This raises methodological questions for the activist-anthropologist. In the course of our research, I received accounts of people's experiences in jail and prison in verbal form, through interviews. The interviews were often conducted in a chaotic setting (in a jail visiting room, for example, or a homeless shelter, or even in the company of snarling pit bulls), and the accounts were a brief sliver of a person's life that they told to a white stranger. How do I travel to another's world based on a brief oral fragment from a person whom I have just met and may never see again?

METHODS, MOTIVATION, AND THE POLITICS OF EMPATHY

It is a common gesture, engendered by identity politics, for someone like me, a white, cisgender man who has never been incarcerated, to say that he could never understand the suffering experienced by subaltern people, in this case the experience of incarceration. But is this really true? Or does that merely let me off the hook? Who knows what I will come to know and understand? Can I shift or transform to become a person who does understand? And although it appears to be safer and more truthful to be humble about the possibilities of understanding another, are there not perils in making the gulf so total and irreversible?

For the purposes at hand, I am only interested in exploring travel to death-worlds as a possible form of political engagement. Based on available evidence, sympathy or empathy alone is not sufficient to motivate a person to political engagement. But what about that world-travel that leads a person to engage in changing the conditions that cause the suffering or pain? What are the conditions or qualities of understanding another's pain or suffering that are politically motivating?

In this spirit of full disclosure, I should say that this idea was not mine originally. After finals one semester, one of my undergraduate students, a psychology major, emailed me with news that surprised me. Having studied me all semester, she announced her diagnosis: Asperger's Syndrome. She had obviously spent a great deal of time brooding on the subject. She was happy to have reached this conclusion, she wrote me, and it made her feel tenderness toward me, since her son also had Asperger's.

At the time, I shrugged off her comment as just another weirdly brazen misstep by an undergraduate. Honestly, I am not sure what she meant, and one can go crazy trying to parse the thinking of some students. In using a ready-made term from psychology, she certainly was not world-traveling to *my* world. But her email set me down a line of thinking about whether I am able to apprehend other people's emotional tonalities as real as my own. Maybe she had divined something about my character that I kept well hidden, including from myself. I had already wondered about my ability to commiserate in a deep way with the people who were telling me such horrific stories about the jail.

I suspect that most people who know me well think of me as a sympathetic or caring person. I am unmoved by others/I am an empathetic person. In Lugones's vocabulary, I might speculate that in different worlds I have these different characteristics. Or perhaps my friends have been taken in by the external display. I simply ape the gestures and sounds of sympathy. I have learned, in other words, the choreography of acceptable responses to others' suffering or expression of grief, stress, or anguish, but I am not able to take it on empathetically. This is how it often feels experientially: I understand intellectually that others are in pain, that they are suffering, and it is on that basis that I act.

I have devoted my political and intellectual life to documenting others' pain (Price 2012, 2015). It seems curious, not to mention obscene and thoroughly terrifying, as James Agee pointed out long ago, to pry into the intimacy of one group of human beings and then parade their nakedness, disadvantage, and humiliation before another group (Agee and Evans 2001, 6); to do so in the name of critical research and political liberation can sometimes serve more as a salve for the conscience of a researcher than as sufficient moral justification. My student's assessment thus led me to try and take inventory of my possible motivations. If I am emotionally stunted, for example, then maybe I have undertaken solidarity work with the incarcerated as a response to an abstract principle I hold, a slogan like "social justice." Or perhaps I do it for baser reasons—pity, or even as a way of avoiding middle-class ennui and boredom. Maybe I plunge myself into this work not out of solidarity but indeed for reasons quite nearly the opposite: revitalizing myself (either psychically or professionally) through ruthless intellectual exploitation of the poor. If this is so, then, to paraphrase Slavoj Žižek, writing about the incarcerated is a cynical way to try and get ahead in my career as I try and titillate an academic or nonacademic audience with stories of blighted lives and true crime.

Intellectual and political arrogance of this sort seems inconsistent with empathy. But perhaps they are related. It can be arrogant to think one understands another. It is parasitic to use any knowledge gained through empathy (or false empathy) for my own ends. Deciding whether I can feel genuine sympathy and whether I am treating people instrumentally seem like hard questions to answer purely through introspection (phenomenologically).

JAIL'S LONELY TORTURES

Placing my biographical and psychological idiosyncrasies aside (although I will come back to them), the project of ending death-worlds generates these kinds of questions about motivation and methodology, including epistemological and ethical questions of solidarity (Levinas 2001, 228; 1969; 1998, 99–124; Gutiérrez 1988; Maldonado-Torres 2008, 2011).[1] Here I will frame them in the real time of concrete human interaction.

> It's a Friday at the jail. 8:30 in the morning. It's been an exhausting week but I make myself go to observe one of my interns conduct an interview because she asked me. She has a much more informal style than I. I am ambivalent about this. I am concerned that she is taking license, not finding out enough about the imprisoned women's situation, not enough about whether she sees patterns of discriminatory treatment. My intern tends to give too much advice, and I worry it is patronizing. On the other hand, she seems to have a much easier rapport with the women at the jail and so maybe my suspicions are not justified.
>
> The woman who comes in is new to both of us. She has a Latino surname. Her skin is pale and almost translucent. Her hair is such a colorless white that at first I think she is a person with albinism. She communicates a pink vulnerability. She is thin boned, small, and looks weary. "I have a fused lumbar and a narrowed spinal column. I was supposed to have spinal surgery at the end of the month at [a local hospital]," but now she will be unable to because she is serving a short-term sentence. "How bad is your pain on a scale of one to ten?" my intern asks her. In the afternoon, it is about a twelve, she says, with her pinched smile. She was at a residential drug treatment center in Pennsylvania, but she left early because she was being sexually harassed and fondled by staff members. After she got out, she kept trying to check into another clinic, but she was not successful and she started using [drugs] again, and landed in jail with a ninety-day sentence. Several of the women we interview this

morning complain that the heat has been turned off in the jail and they are all freezing. This woman tells us that the acute cold, the first frost of the upstate fall, has entered her bones. "Maybe I should have just stayed at the clinic," she muses, and endured sixteen days more of sexual harassment, "because then I wouldn't be in the jail for ninety days now, cold, missing my surgery, and facing eviction for me and my dogs." Then she bursts into tears. Her shoulders sag, her posture weakens, and she seems to fold in on herself, and that gives me the uncanny sensation that she is melting in front of me. I shift uncomfortably. My intern asks if she has any other complaints. "Well, I was supposed to have all my teeth removed. I have eleven teeth left in my mouth. They are all rotten and infected, but they won't do that for me, either." "Can you eat?" my intern asks. "Kind of," she responds with that weak smile.

The memory of this woman haunts me. I sometimes wonder whether she serves as a shameful psychic keystone for our society. Do we celebrate our cruel freedom through contrast? William James thought few of us would accept a world where "millions [are] kept permanently happy on the one simple condition that a certain lost soul on the far-off edge of things should lead a life of lonely torture" (1891, 333; also see Povinelli 2011, 1–45; Le Guin 2004). How hideous it would be if this were the bargain that we have implicitly accepted. I hope this is not the deal. I want to believe it is unnecessary to warehouse millions in steel cages. But this woman and the situation she is forced to live raises the specter that her degradation and that of other incarcerated people makes us savor our freedom and happiness.

Let's explore this psychosocial relationship in more depth. To do so, let's return to my student's diagnosis that I have Asperger's. It is easy to dismiss it as sophomoric. Instead, I will zero in on my limited ability to feel real sympathy for or identify deeply with others.

WHITE SELF-REGARD AND THE BODILESS RESEARCHER

Two interrelated pillars hold up the subject/subject distance. The first pillar is what Patricia Williams once called white self-regard. She explains: "Very little in our language or culture encourages looking at others as parts of ourselves" (1991, 62). "'When you talk to someone you establish a relationship.' Such a self-concept is a way of experiencing the other, of ritualistically sharing the other's essence and cherishing it. In our culture, seeing and feeling the dimension of harm done by separating self from other requires somewhat more work"(62; also see Rafael 2000, 19–51). Williams sees white people constructing a self-concept as if it were (as if we were) untouched by, as separate from, the Other. I study the Other, but they do not know me. They do not touch me. Their understanding of me does not change my theorizing.

That construction of selfhood fits how the sociologist comes to live the fiction of being bodiless, the precondition of assuming a posture of omniscient knower, above the fray, looking down at social phenomena from a bird's-eye view. I was trained to separate my scholarship from my body. Feminist intellectuals have long pointed out how social science training engenders this separation. In Dorothy Smith's influential contribution, the body of the male sociologist, attended to and serviced by subordinates, is able to be rendered in the sociologist's theorizing as if it didn't matter, as if he could transcend his body (1974). The male sociologist is maintained in that illusion. In retrospect, it is particularly the *white* male, or the white, able-bodied male, who is maintained in that illusion.

In fact, it is that social location marked by race, class, and gender that is particularly relevant in my case. The social organization renders white people feeling untouched by social interaction, on the one hand, and on the other, leaves the sociologist free to think of himself as bodiless, floating above. Two parts of my life, inhabiting the subjectivity of a white person and my training as a social scientist, work together to bolster a separation.

JAIL INTERVIEWS

I remember the first interview I conducted with students. Before us, on the other side of plate glass, was an elderly man. His relatives had contacted the NAACP for help. Though he seemed glad to speak to us about his situation, he seemed a bit disoriented. He sat uncomfortably in a plastic seat opposite us, looking very alone. He lost the thread of the conversation a few times. One student, Tommy, asked him how long he'd been in the jail. "Let me see." A pause. "Well, you know I really couldn't tell you." His words hung in the air. The other student, Ayesha, proceeded tentatively with the questions on the sheet we had prepared. "How many times have you been held at the jail?" He looked off, beyond us. "I am not really sure…" His voice trailed off. We asked him what his experience had been of the medical attention at the jail. He told us that he had been refused his heart medication when he had arrived late at the medical unit. "When was that?" He couldn't say.

My students seemed a little taken aback. Before we went in for the interview, they had been excited but also a little intimidated by the prospect of the jail and meeting a real prisoner face to face. Now they seemed struck by how helpless and vulnerable the man seemed, at least that is what they told me later, in the jail's parking lot. One of the students, a young white man, had been extraordinarily cordial and polite to him. That seemed to underscore the defenselessness of the man. What purpose could this serve? I wondered. Here is how my students rendered that first interview:

> Subject also claims that on one occasion his scheduled four o'clock insulin shot was not administered until 6:30 and he feared he would go into shock. When asked if he had filed a complaint about this or other treatment he had received, subject said that it usually takes a week or more for a grievance officer to contact the plaintiff and the officers seem not to care either, according to the subject. He claims this forms an aura of apathy about the prospects of enacting change by complaining.
>
> Finally, subject contends that in his opinion African American inmates are discriminated against in the jail and that the white inmates receive preferential treatment. He points to the example mentioned previously and claims he has witnessed many more.
>
> On a follow-up visit with the subject on 10/26/2004, T. found that the subject had no further medical complaints since the interview and actually stated that the jail staff as a whole was treating him much better in the intervening time period. Subject stated there were no repercussions from the guards or medical staff or administrators for participating in the interview.

This gentleman died several months later, immediately after being released from the jail. As I re-read these lines, written by undergraduates from one of my classes, several things stand out. First, the routine indignities and petty mistreatment did not amount to causing his subsequent death directly in some demonstrable, immediate, and clear way. Nevertheless, the treatment he reported—and especially that he was in jail in the first place—may well have hastened his death (Gilmore 2007, 28).

A second quality I note is the quasi-clinical language used by my students. The plain, emotionally toned-down style they instinctively adopted no doubt reflects their attempt to appear sober and dispassionate. But I knew they were discombobulated, angry, and upset. The document they produced is shorn of all of that. What really mattered, after all, was a fair description of what they witnessed and what he said, not their reaction. Exposing hidden violence in all its banal, chronic, and mundane coloration may have been the most effective tactic.

The social repression of the reality of suffering throughout all our towns, villages, and cities, the expansive hostility that lies throughout and at root in the society, is reflected in its social invisibility. Some would say we repress and deny the memories—the actualities—of injustice (Cohen 2001). As bleak as it sounds, this might itself be too hopeful a reading. The psychology might be less complex: everyday violence has become invisible in plain view; it has become banal and quotidian as people grow accustomed to it (Scheper-Hughes and Bourgois 2003, 19). Ordinary people, as part of their professional and bureaucratic lives, participate in the violence.

I go and pick up Monique, one of my students, at the pre-arranged street corner. We are going to interview a woman in the Johnson projects. When we get there, I give the person's name to a few of the residents and ask for the apartment. When we find the right door and knock, we are invited in by a voice deep in the interior. We enter and a large woman waves us into her bedroom while she gives a small child an activity to do in another room. She then follows us in. She is visibly disabled. We perch on stools near her bed as she tells us of her intake at the jail. She was forced to strip and shower before a gauntlet of male and female guards. As she concludes her account, she starts to cry. The sexual humiliation here interlocks with the classism, ableism, and the racism in concrete ways.

We continue with our questions, and I venture to ask her if she'd like to join our research team, a suggestion she takes in thoughtfully. She eventually calms a bit and begins to talk with us more generally about jail conditions. She refers us to several gay men she knows who were jeered by guards. She'll check with them and then give us their contact information.

Toward the end of the interview, as we gather up our things to leave, and since we are within hearing of her grandchildren in the small apartment, she writes "HIV+" on a scrap of paper and hands it to me, and then looks at me dead in the eye. Then she brightens and she tells us that she distributes condoms in the projects. Lots of young people stop by, she says with a wry smile, and so she's always up on the gossip. I make a mental note; it is good to be connected to people who know what's going on. As we leave, she reaches over and jovially hands me a large bag of condoms to take with me "to distribute to your students." I accept the bag to be courteous, but my first thought is that it would be inappropriate for me to distribute them in my classes. Then I wonder if I am just being prudish.

The guards found it delightful to demean her. They liked poking fun at a large, naked, black woman with missing limbs, whom they forced to strip and take a shower. The guards' reaction reflects a larger social delight, it seems to me. From a certain mainstream and widespread perspective, holding up incarcerated women for ridicule and for titillation is fodder for popular tastes and late night talk shows. It is crucial because the amused contempt for vulnerable, naked incarcerated women—disproportionately women of color—is the cultural backdrop of humiliation.

Up until now, I have focused on the methodological and ethical challenges for someone coming from the dominant class to world-travel to the death-worlds of the incarcerated. But those who occupy death-worlds travel to other death-worlds as well. Indeed, this probably happens more often. A formerly incarcerated man told us in an interview:

> As I was being booked into the county jail, I saw this guy and I don't even know his name. He is completely naked and there is urine and blood and he is totally out of his mind. He's on PCP or something and he is in a cell. I mean a little glassed-in cage where the police desk is right there where they can watch this guy. And he was bent totally, he is handcuffed and the cuffs were cutting him and you could tell he was on something. Maybe LSD or PCP or something. Instead of giving him something to knock him out, they just laughed at this guy, or something. So I said to them, "He is still a human being, man." "Mind your business" [was the correction officers' only reply]. That's like, I'll never forget that, man. It's still in my mind and I'm still angry about that shit because it happens all the time. But when you see it and you're that close to it, you'll never forget… (Fieldnotes 2006)

"Mind your business," implies disavowing the other and yielding instead to the inhumanity around him, and thus upholding the distance. This man remembers his own sense of self of that moment, the sense of solidarity denied, frustrated, and blocked.

A decent society is one whose institutions do not humiliate anyone, the philosopher Avishai Margalit has argued (1998). But as I have come to see it, a society can be both decent and indecent. It is a decent society to those it counts as full citizens, and it is indecent to the social dead, to those who are the refuse of the society. This combination can be confounding. To world-travel from a position of privilege and comfort is to live a decency that is simultaneously, schizophrenically, the worst sort of indecency. Through travel to death-worlds, one can see and live vividly the indecency while seeing that other, crucially linked world, that appears clean and safe.

Empathetic understanding, long rejected in anthropology since the interpretive turn in the early 1970s (Geertz 1973), can be given a new gloss. First, the empathetic project could occur not with the ambition of mastery, not with the psychic projection of oneself into the skin of another, especially when this risks the colonization of a subordinate's subjectivity, as of old. Instead, it could be undertaken as transforming a subject position, based on the external manifestation of a person's subjectivity in language. Marilyn Frye once wrote that knowledge is, above all, a question of attention (1983). Attention precedes world-travel.

Karen Wenzel was a fifty-two-year-old white woman who took the first class I ever taught, when I was little more than half her age. She was finishing her BA after having worked odd jobs for most of her life. Wenzel had also survived horrendous violence and sexual torture from her partner. For her final project in my undergraduate methods class, she conducted a series of interviews with a battered woman she had met, a woman she very much identified with. She would meet the woman at a laundromat, the only place the woman could go to be free from her batterer, even if only temporarily. They shared stories of how to hustle brief respite from an abuser. After Wenzel finished her cycle of interviews, she wrote up this woman's life story. Before turning it in to me, she brought her essay to the woman who read it and, to Wenzel's astonishment, signed it and asked Wenzel to retain a copy, "especially if he kills me," the woman remarked, handing back the signed essay. As Wenzel drove home, she realized that what for her was an "ethnographic exchange" was, from the standpoint of the battered woman, a canny method to prepare a quasi-legal written document that testified to the abuse. In her paper, Wenzel provided two accounts of her research. On the one hand, she framed her work as an ethnography of battering. On the other, Wenzel pointed to that which ethnography fails to name, cannot but fail to name: how this ethnographic description looked (and functioned) from the perspective of the battered woman. Wenzel had identified with this woman. But she identified with her so strongly that she came to see herself as this woman saw her—not as sharing an identity (that is how Wenzel felt initially), but as precisely an other, a witness (Price 2001).

Karen Wenzel's story of world-travel can be contrasted with a distance that we usually uphold, a distance that maintains social hierarchies and a stable sense of self.

> I am on the Shortline bus from Binghamton, in Central New York, coming down to New York City. Shortline buses are full of people who are between jobs, many of the people are lost, lonely, but there are also

lots of students who live along the Eastern corridor. Next to me is a young white woman, an undergraduate at an Ivy League college not far from Binghamton. She tells me she is going to be a school teacher. She is from Long Island. She loves her mother, her father, her sisters, and she is going home to stay with them. "Where do you want to teach when you graduate?" "I wouldn't teach at a school that wasn't upper-class or upper-middle-class. So, I'll probably teach at a place like the one near where I live on Long Island. I wouldn't know how to teach other kinds of kids. Kids of different cultures." "But if everyone thought this way," I say, "then aren't we doomed to Apartheid?" She does not know what to do with this and looks at me quizzically. I try a more basic question. "Why can't you teach elsewhere?" "Because I might get raped. I had a friend who did Teach for America and she had to be escorted to her car every day after she was threatened with rape by a student."[2] As we pull in to the Port Authority in Manhattan she gets a phone call on her cell. She takes the call and talks to the person as she gets off without saying goodbye. I realize that she has not seen me at all.

So, this seems to be a crucial clue, too—this woman fears being raped by a phantom-future elementary school student rapist. That fear has been created and toked.

The war on women is endemic, and rape is one of men's prevalent tactics in the war. The fear of rape is justified in general. And her fears are real. Nevertheless, and I say this gingerly, I am not sure that what she fears is real, since she seems to fear difference. Statistically, rape survivors often know their attackers. Thus, her fear may be misplaced—or more accurately displaced—onto the wrong people—unknown elementary school kids. Is she also a victim of her own fears? As a question of social organization at the point of race, others may have to steer clear of her and her ghastly fears of adolescent kid rapists outside of her neighborhood.

This is just one case and I do not want to blow it out of proportion, or blame women for their fears. It serves simply to illustrate that we have organized our society in some ways around fears, including phantom fears. Her fears join others and through some implicit dystopian calculus, through some terrible bureaucratic illogic, land a large group of people in jail, in prison, or in other forms of misery. Fears like hers organize the war on terror and the war on drugs. A theory of world-travel might consider developing criteria to evaluate whether another's fears are justified. More generally, we need to think about the social consequences of planning our society around fears and specters and real things. Lugones once said to me that a basic political problem is misunderstanding which spaces are dangerous and which are safe.

"I am scared," the woman tells us at the jail. "I am scared." She pauses and looks at us searchingly. She shows us her pinky finger, monstrously swollen. "The swelling is starting to go down my arm. I don't know what to do about it." Noelle, my intern, acts clinical and uses some medical words, but I know it's an act. Neither of us knows what to do.

When I am talking of people in jail or prison who are suffering, dying, in pain, made desperate by the random mistreatment and endless delays and waiting, I do not mean to paint them as just innocent victims, though, I should quickly add, many of them have not committed any crime more serious than being poor. A state of denial is not a state of innocence (Cohen 2001). And we certainly do not become innocent or good by insisting on it, by cleaving to it, despite all the evidence.

I pose to my students an exercise based on the work of Anna Deveare Smith (1998): What inhibits them from imitating other people? They say they do not imitate others because they want people to be happy and they are worried that copying them will make them feel humiliated. But it is not that. They appropriate and appropriate and appropriate. The English they speak, the clothes they wear, their taste in music, their most intimate and deadly desires, are inherited, copied from, and influenced by the cultural production of African Americans, Latinos, Asians and Asian Americans, Native Americans, and others. But I also sometimes fear that they—all of us—are largely indifferent to the happiness of others.

LIVING IN PAIN

About a decade ago, I started having a persistent pain behind my right brow. It lasted for months. Eventually, I came to worry that it was a tumor. Besides the discomfort and its inconvenience, this was worrisome because my father and a younger brother had just been through bouts with cancer, and I felt bad burdening my already emotionally taxed family, especially my mother who had been stalwart in simultaneously chaperoning her husband and youngest son through hell, with yet another cancer case among the inner circle.

Nothing so colorful as cancer, a neurologist with a gentle manner wryly informed me. He diagnosed me as suffering from daily migraines. This was such a weird thing, developing migraines after writing so much with, and hence spending so much time with, María Lugones since she is in chronic pain, especially due to migraines. I wondered if the migraines were some kind of sympathetic reaction. Without having heard my theory, some friends of mine clearly thought the headaches were psychological—displaced anxiety, for example, or stress—rather than physiological, an excess of a cerebral chemical, a misfiring nerve, or some wayward signal in some suburban lobe in my brain whose off-switch had broken down or was in ill-repair. Other friends thought they had the perfect cure ("alternative" medication, as it's usually called) and would recommend boiling all kinds of herbs and confecting potions. The chronic pain sufferer learns patience and forbearance.

Before I got migraines, once in a while I would ask María if she was in pain. Yes, she would say, almost invariably. Very occasionally, her eyes would widen and say, "No, today there is no pain!" This was cause to celebrate. In a quiet moment, María observed that most people soon tire of hearing about pain, and thus one is better off keeping it to oneself. It's difficult for others, those who are not in pain, to live with the understanding that the person they are interacting with is in pain in a more-or-less constant way. The knowledge disappears from view.

My pain is not attributable to colonial domination. Nonetheless, I have gained some insight in how others are not particularly moved to alleviate even the superficial conditions that engender more discomfort for me. And if they do, I am less interested in their subjective state and much more interested in the concrete modifications (not speaking so loudly, allowing me to sit in a darkened room, or that rare commodity, a shoulder massage).

On that note, and at the risk of reaffirming my austere emotional landscape, I have an impulse to conclude that solidarity work can be best measured by *actions*, not sentiment, and not fellow-feeling. The problems associated with prisons and jails require practical solutions such as decarceration.

But if "action" is the measure, then what is new here? What is new about an emotionally stunted white man who wonders if he can really empathize with others? Whose emotional life is semi-opaque, even to himself? A man who thinks pragmatic change is more important than empathy?

When I visit a person in jail, I see only a thin shard of a life: jagged, fragmentary, and piercing. In many cases, I will never see the person again. I usually do not have any basis to understand the world from their eyes in any deep way, or to know them as the person they are; I do not know in any profound or detailed way how I appear in their eyes. Given the fleeting nature of the interaction, I distrust any reading I have of the situation; more generally, I doubt my ability to travel to death-worlds. The practical focus on "action" and objective change to jail conditions is a substitute. The practical focus is also because I have come to distrust those who would probe another's subjectivity without any other goal or purpose than the voyeuristic or academic.

But focusing on practice and action to the exclusion of trying to apprehend the subjective contours of death-worlds is only my first impulse. World-travel does not and should not have mastery of another's subjectivity as a goal. This is particularly true in the narrows of the brief encounter. The inquisitive disposition, the wonder, the attempt to grasp the unfathomable—how this person sees me, how I can grapple with that perception—can confront, if not dismantle, the self-regard, and the illusion of bodilessness people like me sometimes have. Instead, this disposition, this wonder, can hearken to a kind of journey, or attempted crossing, that leaves one, if not apprehending the other, then at least salubriously off-balance and uncertain.

Considering the philosophies of subaltern people who social scientists usually treat as if they are receptacles of unrefined data engenders a self-consciousness (Gwaltney 1993). Absorbing those philosophies, those ways of thinking, being, and feeling, is potentially transformative of one's social location. Traveling to another's death-world puts at risk a restricted, narrow sense of self. This can be unmooring. But the risk is also the benefit.

One benefit is learning anew how we are entangled with one another, sometimes in irreversibly complicated ways. The lives we lead are not independent of each other, and the differences between us are not absolute. Social indifference and false independence denies the entanglement and represses how the prisoner's suffering, pain, and humiliation seem to offer some curious psychic balm, or perhaps it is an affective counterpoint, against which the dominant culture implicitly measures the beauty of our lives, the depth of our friendships, the moral postures we strike.

We are incomplete beings; the incompleteness can be masked through an arrogance that is so deeply ingrained that it does not even know itself as arrogance. Or it can be engaged, if not resolved. If we are connected, then to fail to world-travel to and through death-worlds, or to do something like world-travel, to recognize and reckon with the relationship, is not just a moral failure, it is a political failure.

World-travel to death-worlds means chipping away at a racial, class, and colonial divide that is also deeply gendered. The ongoing conditions of colonialism, as they are embodied in the carceral state, speak to a certain set of human relationships. We destroy those conditions, to paraphrase Gustav Landauer by forging other relationships (2010, 214).

NOTES

I would like to thank the editors of this collection, Pedro DiPietro, Jennifer McWeeny, and Shireen Roshanravan for their crucial comments and suggestions. I would also like to mark my appreciation for María Lugones, who has been a substantial influence on my thinking over the course of these many years. I of course take responsibility for any errors in the chapter.

1. Some of the subtlest formulations of this cluster of problems, and the most compelling responses, have been in theology and theologically oriented texts. Gustavo Gutiérrez, for example, in his influential *A Theology of Liberation*, reinterprets the story of the Good Samaritan and gives the ethical agent a more active role. The neighbor is "not he whom I find in my path, but rather he in whose path I place myself, he whom I approach and actively seek" (1988). The ethical agent seeks out injustice and pain in order to act in a neighborly way. In *Totality and Infinity* (1969), Emmanuel Levinas confronts this problem of ethical responsibility in order to refute the dehumanization of the Holocaust. Drawing on Levinas and Lugones, Maldonado-Torres has proposed a decolonial attitude against colonial dehumanization (2011). These worthy considerations emerge from a moral conviction and a philosophical commitment to solidarity with the other, the *damnés* (Maldonado-Torres 2008).

2. She also may be casting her own firsthand experience into a third-person narrative as some survivors may do. I thank Jennifer McWeeny for pointing out this possibility.

REFERENCES

Agee, James, and Walker Evans. 2001. *Let Us Now Praise Famous Men.* New York: Houghton Mifflin.

Cohen, Stanley. 2001. *States of Denial: Knowing about Atrocities and Suffering.* Malden, MA: Polity Press.

Douglass, Frederick. 1852. "Oration, Delivered in Corinthian Hall, Rochester, By Frederick Douglass, July 5th, 1852." Rochester, NY: Lee, Mann & Co. www.lib.rochester.edu/index.cfm?PAGE=2945. Accessed January, 2015.

Du Bois, W.E.B. 2014. *Dusk of Dawn: An Essay toward an Autobiography of a Race Concept.* Oxford: Oxford University Press.

Fanon, Frantz. 2007. *The Wretched of the Earth.* Translated by Richard Philcox. New York: Grove Press.

Frye, Marilyn. 1983. "On Being White." In *The Politics of Reality: Essays in Feminist Theory*, 110–21. Freedom, CA: The Crossing Press.

Geertz, Clifford. 1973. *The Interpretation of Cultures*. New York: Basic Books.
Gilmore, Ruth. 2007. *Golden Gulag: Prisons, Surplus, Crisis, and Opposition in Globalizing California*. Berkeley, CA: University of California Press.
Gutiérrez, Gustavo. 1988. *A Theology of Liberation: History, Politics, and Salvation*. Translated by Caridad Inda. Maryknoll, NY: Orbis Books.
Gwaltney, John. 1993. *Drylongso: A Self-Portrait of Black America*. New York: New Press.
Hartman, Saidiya. 1997. *Scenes of Subjection: Terror, Slavery and Self-Making in Nineteenth-Century America*. Oxford: Oxford University Press.
James, William. 1891. "The Moral Philosopher and the Moral Life." *International Journal of Ethics* 1: 330–54.
Landauer, Gustav. 2010. "Weak Statesmen, Weaker People!" In *Revolution and Other Writings: A Political Reader*, edited by Gabriel Kuhn, 213–14. Oakland, CA: PM Press.
Le Guin, Ursula K. 2004. "The Ones Who Walk Away from Omelas." In *The Wind's Twelve Quarters*, 254–62. New York: William Morrow.
Levinas, Emmanuel. 1969. *Totality and Infinity: An Essay on Exteriority*. Translated by Alphonso Lingis. Pittsburgh, PA: Duquesne University Press.
———. 1998. *Otherwise Than Being: Or Beyond Essence*. Translated by Alphonso Lingis. Pittsburgh, PA: Duquesne University Press.
———. 2001. *Is It Righteous To Be?* Palo Alto, CA: Stanford University Press.
Maldonado-Torres, Nelson. 2011. "Thinking through the Decolonial Turn: Post-continental Interventions in Theory, Philosophy, and Critique—An Introduction." *Transmodernity* 1(2): 1–11.
———. 2008. *Against War: Views from the Underside of Modernity*. Durham, NC: Duke University Press.
Margalit, Avishai. 1998. *The Decent Society*. Cambridge, MA: Harvard University Press.
Mbembe, Achille. 2003. "Necropolitics." Translated by Louise Meintjes. *Public Culture* 15(1): 11–40.
Povinelli, Elizabeth. 2011. *Economies of Abandonment: Social Belonging and Endurance in Late Liberalism*. Durham, NC: Duke University Press.
Price, Joshua. 2001. "Hacia una contra-historia de antropología." *Política y Sociedad* 38: 229–43.
———. 2012. *Structural Violence*. Albany: State University of New York Press.
———. 2015. *Prison and Social Death*. New Brunswick, NJ: Rutgers University Press.
Rafael, Vicente. 2000. *White Love and Other Events in Filipino History*. Durham, NC: Duke University Press.

Scheper-Hughes, Nancy, and Philipe Bourgois, eds. 2003. *Violence in War and Peace.* Malden, MA: Blackwell.

Smith, Anna Deveare. 1998. *Fires in the Mirror: Crown Heights, Brooklyn and Other Identities.* New York: Dramatists Play Services.

Smith, Dorothy E. 1974. "Women's Perspective as a Radical Critique of Sociology." *Sociological Inquiry* 44(1): 7–13.

Williams, Patricia. 1991. *The Alchemy of Race and Rights.* Cambridge, MA: Harvard University Press.

Part V *Hablando Cara a Cara*

11 Deep Coalition and Popular Education Praxis

Cricket Keating

> Coalition is always the horizon that rearranges both our possibilities and the conditions of our possibilities.
> —María Lugones, Preface to *Pilgrimages*/Peregrinajes: *Theorizing Coalition against Multiple Oppressions*

Central to María Lugones's political philosophy and praxis is a deep commitment to popular education, a mode of political organizing that challenges the dichotomy between theory and practice as well as the division between "organizers" and "organized." As an approach to social change, popular education emphasizes the importance of opening up movement-building and decision-making processes so as to include people's often undervalued and overlooked experiences, forms of knowledge, and perspectives. Although Lugones is most well known for her foundational work in feminist philosophy, Women of Color feminisms, and decolonial politics, Lugones's work has been pivotal to the contemporary development of the theory and practice of popular education as well. In particular, this chapter explores Lugones's work with the popular education collective *la Escuela Popular Norteña* (EPN) in developing a distinctly coalitional approach to popular education, one that takes up the complex interlocking of oppressions based on race, culture, class, gender, sexuality, age, and ability in people's lives, towards the building of what she calls "deep coalition."

Deep coalition, in Lugones's framing, are those coalitions that go beyond short-term interest-based alliances and challenge us to align our own self-understandings, interests, and goals with other oppressed groups (IP 26). For Lugones, we come together in deep coalition not only to pool our collective resources in the fight against oppression, but also, and perhaps more powerfully in terms of long-lasting change, to transform our relationships with each other. Such an approach to coalition highlights the ways that our own understandings and potential enactments of our lives are deeply tied to one another and to the meanings that we create together, as well as the ways that the transformation of our relationships with one another has the potential to ground deep social change. Exploring ways to motivate, practice, and sustain this transformation constitutes the focus of much of Lugones's work, both in her writing and in her political engagement with people. In her praxis, she has long worked with others to build anti-hierarchical spaces where power can be interrogated through collective analysis and living differently can be practiced, even within institutions and settings that are often extremely hierarchical. In doing so, her work both draws on and points to a new direction in popular education praxis.

BUILDING A COALITIONAL APPROACH TO POPULAR EDUCATION

Popular education is a mode of political and educational praxis that grows out of critiques of hierarchical and top-down approaches to political organizing and education. As an approach to education geared to liberation, popular education pivots on a process of people developing critical consciousness and analysis through collective critique and visioning. One of the central tenets of popular education theory and practice is that oppressed people have knowledge and experience that can serve as important grounds for political change and social transformation. In the words of popular educator Geoff Bryce, "popular education is experience based and action-oriented, bringing people at the grassroots together for dialogue in a non-hierarchical setting, enabling them to analyze the conditions in which they live and to develop plans for collective action based on their own values and perceived needs" (Escuela Popular Norteña 1994).

Popular education has its roots in struggles for social change in the Americas. Two of its most influential theorist-practitioners are Paulo Freire from Brazil and Myles Horton from the United States. Work inspired by their writing and organizing has been pivotal in many struggles for liberation. For example, learning circles and *comunidades de base* growing out of Freire's theories of education have played important roles in Latin American liberation movements (Freire 2000). In addition, the Highlander Folk School, founded by Horton in Tennessee, produced many of the South's union organizers in the 1930s as well as some of the leading organizations of the Civil Rights Movement, including the Citizenship Schools and the Student Non-violent Coordinating Committee (Horton 1997).

Inspired by the work of Freire, and in conversation with Horton and others at Highlander, Lugones, Geoff Bryce, and Sylvia Rodriguez founded EPN in 1990 as a "school for political education at the grassroots, focused on the liberation of Latinos from poverty, violence, and cultural extermination"

(EPN Mission Statement). The three had been working together for many years in Valdez, a small rural Hispano community in Northern New Mexico with a long history of struggle around issues of land, water, and cultural survival. Among other community political work, they worked with Valdeños on successfully blocking the development of condominiums on the valley floor in a sustained community protest that became known as the "Valdez Condo War." Since 1990, EPN has developed popular education programs in Valdez and in Chicano, *Mexicano*, Central American, Puerto Rican, Caribbean, and mixed communities, both urban and rural, across the United States. Some of the themes the collective has worked on include colonization, internalized oppression, homophobia, the interlocking of oppressions, community economic development, participatory research, community health care, political video, micro-radio, community art, ethics for communities in struggle, alternative schooling, violence against women, linguistic and cultural resistance, and tools for building movement. This work has taken several forms, including one- to two-week-long intensive residential *encuentros*; developing popular education materials and workshops for organizations such as Incite!: Women, Gender Non-Conforming, and Trans People of Color Against Violence and Critical Resistance; and designing thematic workshops for various community settings.

By emphasizing the importance of addressing multiple oppressions, EPN's work differs in several respects from traditional approaches to popular education. For example, while traditional formulations of popular education praxis often cast the division between oppressors and oppressed as a dichotomous one, such that some people are understood as the "oppressed" and others as the "oppressors," EPN's coalitional approach to popular education theorizing and practice takes up the complexity of people's relationship to multiple systems of oppression. Given this complexity, the lines between oppressor and oppressed often shift, such that people are positioned as oppressed in some contexts and along some lines of power and as oppressors in others. Taking up this complexity in a popular education situation means that one cannot assume a homogeneity of interests among oppressed communities (and thus presuppose a singularity of oppositional practice that could be applicable or translatable to all its members). Instead, a coalitional approach to popular education highlights the heterogeneity of people's positioning in relationship to power, and underscores the interlocking, intersecting, and intermeshing of multiple forms of oppression in people's lives (see this book's chapter 4).

Further, rather than presuming that a shared experience of oppression provides the impetus for political solidarity and collective action, a coalitional approach emphasizes that the experience of oppression and resistance is highly contextual and varies depending on one's positioning in terms of race, class, gender, age, sexuality, ability, nationality, ethnicity, and other nodes of power. Instead of looking for commonalities in experiences across contexts, a coalitional approach to popular education is grounded in a collective process of learning about each other's varied contexts and resistant practices and then thinking together about how to connect these practices so as to better sustain and amplify their effects in challenging oppressive conditions. As Lugones explains, popular education spaces in this approach can be:

> defamiliarizing environments where one's experiences acquire a diversity of "readings." These readings expose the differences in power and privilege among the learners as barriers to possible understanding and to collective action authored by all learners for their collective benefits.... In these environments, popular education proceeds to create new possibilities that are firmly rooted in these re-readings of experiences, [that] arise from conflict, and [that] do not erase the complexity of styles, needs, values of learners. (Escuela Popular Norteña 1994)

Indeed, rather than treating difference as something to be ignored, oversimplified, or overcome, this coalitional approach to popular education takes up people's multiple positioning as extremely generative grounds for developing a collective understanding of the many ways that people resist oppression in their everyday lives.

Lugones, often in collaboration with other collective EPN members, designed more than 15 popular education workshops in her work with EPN. These workshops, like so much of Lugones's work, ask people to reflect upon their own and each other's lives in ways that highlight rather than downplay difference and complexity. The workshops themselves create spaces for people to learn and practice new ways of being and of interacting with each other toward the goal of deep coalition. In the workshops, people come together in collective dialogue in order to learn 1) to recognize and appreciate each other's resistant strategies across a wide variety of contexts 2) to back up each other's resistant practices as well as link them to their own across different contexts and lines of power 3) to treat each other well in the context of different modes of oppression.

LEARNING TO SEE RESISTANCE

One of the crucial components of building deep coalitional solidarity is developing an eye for the ways that we resist oppressive power relations in our everyday lives. Such resistance can be enacted in public and on a large scale, but it is most often enacted in everyday modes of being and relating. This everyday resistance is often quite hard to see or recognize for two reasons: first, becuase those enacting the resistance might want the resistance to stay hidden in order for it to be successful; and second, because those in power often have a stake in resistance not being recognized as such.[1] In Lugones's words, "resistance hardly ever has a straightforward public presence. It is rather duplicitous, ambiguous, even devious. But it is also almost always masked and hidden by structures of meaning that countenance and constitute domination" (PP x). Given these conditions under which resistance is so often hidden, a particular challenge for building deep coalition is learning to see each other's modes of resistance, including one's own, in oppressive situations. A coalitional approach to popular education involves creating dialogic situations in which people develop an understanding of their own and other's strategies for challenging oppressive logics, interactions, relationships, and institutions in their everyday lives.

EPN's *The Map of Oppression* is a workshop geared toward generating collective dialogue and insight about such everyday resistance (Lugones, n.d.). In order to do so, the workshop asks people to draw a map reflecting the ways the spaces in their lives have been shaped by those in power in society. In particular, the workshop asks people to draw lines on their map that indicate where they are allowed, enticed, or forced to go and where they are forbidden or discouraged from going. This kind of prompt—one that encourages people to analyze the power relations that mark their situations—is very much in the tradition of popular education. In traditional forms of popular education, the group might move from an analysis of the oppressive ways in which space is organized by the powers that be directly into a collective conversation about how the participants might work together to challenge this oppression. In EPN's approach, however, the workshop takes a different tack: after analyzing the oppressive power relations illustrated in their maps, the participants next turn attention to the ways that they resist such power in their everyday lives. The workshop *The Map of Oppression* asks that people take another look at the maps, this time with a different lens, a magnifying glass that shows

> how we are when we are following our own hearts and wills in resistance to the interests of those in power. It shows you how we are when we are trying to do and be self-determining and good to ourselves.... With it you see that we're not just quiet and tired, but mischievous, energetic, active, creative. (Lugones, n.d., 2)

In the workshop, people share stories of what they uncover about their lives and their communities when they look at their map through this magnifying glass.

The *Politicizing the Everyday* workshop also focuses on the process of developing a sense of one's own and others' resistances (Beltré et al. 1999). In order to do so, the workshop draws on a traditional popular education approach: the use of a code (a photo, a word, a drawing, an object) as a catalyst for the collective analysis of power relations.[2] In one iteration of the workshop, for example, the code presented was a conservative electoral campaign advertisement showing a picture of a tattooed Latino man locked up in jail on one side and a picture of a young Latina girl on the other side. Below the picture, a caption read: "Where do you want violent criminals? Here or Here?" The first exercise of the workshop asked participants to analyze the code in terms of what message was being conveyed. In their analysis of the campaign advertisement, for example, the workshop participants observed that the image drew on and perpetuated stereotypes of Latino men as violent and dangerous, and was geared toward generating support for the prison industrial complex among Latinos as well as Anglos by positioning the young Latina girl as vulnerable to violence.

Next, the workshop asked the participants to reflect upon their own experiences of seeing the advertisement. For many, the ad was upsetting because it brought to mind people they knew and loved who had been or were in jail. For others, it reminded them of ways that they had been harassed or targeted by police. Others noted that the picture of the young girl brought up memories of their own experiences of violence when they were young. In their discussions, the participants both explored what was problematic in the scenario and also located themselves in the discussion. Both these moves—reading power as well as situating oneself in relation to power—are crucial in popular education. Rather than highlighting only one primary line of oppression, the workshop asked participants to pay close attention to the multiple lines of racialized, gendered, and classed power that could be seen at play in the code. For example, in addition to analyzing the racist message the advertisement conveyed, they also noted that the picture of the little girl was stereotyping young Latinas as vulnerable and in need of protection by the state.

After decoding the power relations they saw embedded in the political advertisement, the participants next were asked to look for resistances. For example, they noticed that the man in the ad had tattoos and that while the ad seemed to imply that this was an indication that he was dangerous, the participants noted that tattoos are often themselves a form of resistance. One person said that she thought it was resistant that everyone saw through the oppressive message behind the ad and that they recognized and were critical of the stereotypes of Latinos that were being used in it. Others discussed ways that they resisted violence against women and girls that didn't depend on the state, but rather on networks of familial and community support. Another pointed out that the very act of listening and learning from each other in the workshop was deeply resistant.

Complex Unity is an EPN workshop that focuses on the importance of building movements against violence against women of color that challenge the notion that unity is built on sameness. As the workshop notes, "the need for unity comes from the realization that struggling against violence must be a collective project, but collectivity is reduced to sameness" (Beltré et al., n.d., 1). In contrast, the workshop calls for "a unity that is creative, that shows our connections in an empowering light, a unity that makes us imaginative, strong, that takes advantage of what each one brings to the struggle against violence because of our differences. We need a unity that is complex" (1). As a starting point in building this complex unity, the workshop focuses on ways that people have resisted gender-based violence. The workshop's aim is not only to illuminate and encourage particular resistant acts, but also to find each person's "resistant self" that has desires, intentions, and motivations that move against such violence, often even while in the midst of it (Beltré et al., n.d.,1). In order to direct attention to that self, the facilitators of the workshop ask participants (including the facilitators themselves) to share a time when they encountered violence and to think about ways in which they resisted the harm being done to them. Participants are asked to "find the self that resisted in the situation of violence, the self that didn't just accept that everything that was happening was good, fitting, or what you deserved, what you should accept" (Beltré et al., n.d., 2). The workshop suggests that when trying to find this self:

> don't think about what you could have done, or what you would do, but about what you did that was not what you were supposed to do, feel, believe in a situation where part of the violence is being told what to do, what to say, what to believe, what to be. That's her, the one who in some way or another, big or small, hidden or for all to see, said "no." (2)

As a way of both representing and honoring these resistant selves, the workshop asks the participants to build an altar that contains "both things that remind you of the violence in the situation but also of what helped you to negotiate the situation, anything that helped you not to accept the situation as good and what you deserved" (2). One altar, for example, had a bottle of beer that signified the role alcohol played in the violent situation, and also a key that she had made without her girlfriend's knowledge that would help her escape to a neighbor's house if she needed a place to go in the middle of the night.

All three of these workshops have as their central focus people's everyday resistance to power in their lives. In EPN's framing, coalitional political movement is built from an intersubjective recognition of such resistance. Such a move is in keeping with traditional popular education's emphasis on the importance of people's experience of, and knowledge about, oppression, but moves it even deeper: it assumes that people also have valuable experience in resisting that oppression. This resistance, of course, is often obscured by power. In Lugones's words: "As the understanding of our own resistance is heavily veiled by the strategist's plans, and by the deployment of his power and authority, it is important to clear the air so that to be able both to understand the space where we are actively resisting as worldly—*mundano*, an emancipatory, complexly voiced sense of 'public'—and to take up its possibilities" (TSC 210). These three workshops are geared to be spaces where these possibilities can be taken up.

BUILDING COALITION: LINKING RESISTANT SELVES

In addition to working to see, understand, and value the ways that people resist multiple forms of oppression, another key component of a coalitional approach to popular education is generating collective analysis about ways that people's resistances might connect to one another and how people might support and back up each other's different resistant practices. For example, the workshop *Coalition: Linking Contexts of Resistance* is geared toward forging "enduring, changing, and complex coalitions among people who are subjected to and resist different oppressions ... [by] developing isolated resistances into collective and diverse resistances towards emancipation" (Graciano et al., n.d., 1). The workshop emphasizes that coming together in coalition is an active process that requires two crucial steps: getting to know each other as resistors and working to build connections among our resistances (1).

Toward getting to know each other as resistors, *Coalition*, like *The Map of Oppression* and *Complex Unity* workshops, asks participants both to share and listen to accounts of instances in which they resisted oppression. This workshop emphasizes the process of learning about another's resistance; in it, groups closely analyze resistance in terms of the context in which the resistance takes place, the resistor's intentions, and the relationship of the resistance to various structures of oppression. In particular, participants are asked to pay careful attention to the oppressive structures that "backed your oppressor and made his/her behavior acceptable, condonable, ordinary, invisible, and made your own objections not able to be voiced, unintelligible, not actionable in court, etc."

(Graciano et al., n.d., 7). They also look closely for ways that a specific resistance may collude with or reinforce one structure of oppression while also working to subvert another. As the workshop explains: "[A] certain activity, for example, may be liberatory in gender terms but racially, it colludes with oppression. A situation may resist class divisions, but it reinstates ageist assumptions" (7). In doing so, the workshop encourages participants to develop an eye for the complexity of resistance in a situation of interlocked oppressions as well as the way that power relations structure which actions and intentions can be readily seen and those that are made more difficult to countenance.

Next, participants analyze ways that they could connect to each other's resistant practices across their different contexts, and work to amplify and help sustain them. The guiding question of this moment in the workshop is, "What does the protagonist need to keep herself or himself alive as a resistor?" As the workshop explains, "this question is not just about validating the act as a resistant act . . . it is also a question of understanding that act as one step in a life of resistance to and under oppression" (8). In other words, the workshop asks participants to move beyond thinking of a particular resistant act and think about what it might mean to live *a life* of resistance to oppressive structures. How can we become companions in resistance to each other? That is, how can we back up, encourage, and sustain each other in moving our lives in a resistant direction? What changes in our own lives would we have to make in order to make such a commitment to each other? The workshop asks participants to consider these questions as they take up the challenge of forging coalition together, examining ways that such a commitment to each other might require a "rethinking of our analyses of oppressions," a "redistribution of our political energies," and an alteration "of the paths we cross in everyday life" (9).

The *Complex Unity* workshop also follows a logic that moves from developing an understanding of people's resistances in the face of violence to connecting and linking these resistances. The workshop underscores that the very act of sharing one's own, and listening to others', stories of violence and resistance is a tremendously important move toward solidarity, especially given the many different forces that keep people silent about interpersonal violence. The act of sharing our stories of resistance is itself valorized as an act of coalition, in that in hearing each other's stories one might begin to think of one's own resistance as linked to others, without erasing the differences between the forms that these resistances might take (2). Indeed, the workshop asks people to listen to each other very carefully, without presupposing that they know what each other's resistance could or should be. As the workshop explains:

> Keep yourself open to what she [the resistor] is saying. You are trying to understand her, well enough to speak to her and to be her companion in struggle. Avoid thinking "I know just what you mean, the same thing happened to me" and also avoid thinking "that doesn't make any sense." We are trying to recover together things that may be very difficult to understand, things for which society makes no space as part of the harm done to us. Ask her questions trying to keep the conversation going and trying to understand even if there is much that you don't quite understand yet: give her room! Maybe there is a little detail you noticed and if you ask her more about it, she will tell you and that will help understanding and help becoming closer. (2–3)

Complex Unity concludes with each person making a liberatory gift to be put on another person's altar in the room. This gift is something tangible; it is "a token of our understanding and commitment to her well-being and to joining in struggle together" (3). The gift, in the workshop's framing, represents a transformation of our resistant selves in a coalitional vein, toward "growing as women in struggle that are open to hear what is not already in us, what we may have imagined" (3).

Several of EPN's workshops are geared toward generating conversation and engagement about the barriers that keep communities isolated and fragmented from each other. *The Map of Oppression* workshop, for example, asks people to draw "roads" to other oppressed communities on the maps they created and think about both the possibilities and difficulties of traveling along these roads. In response to this prompt, one woman explained that what makes her road to others so difficult to travel is that "I don't have any time. I have to take care of my children and work all day serving tables at the restaurant. I haven't got the time to go anywhere other than the places that are obligatory" (3). This woman's example speaks to the ways that oppressive systems (in this instance, the gendered division of labor and the structure of the American workday) create conditions in which it is very hard to seek each other out in and for solidarity. One straight man explained that he has difficulty traveling along roads that lead to nonstraight people because "I am revolted by seeing men kissing or embracing each other." Another man living in a predominantly Mexican neighborhood said that what makes his road to Puerto Rican neighborhoods difficult is his perception that "the Puerto Ricans don't want us in their neighborhoods" (3). These second two examples speak to the ways that negative evaluations and perceptions fostered by the dominant culture work as barriers toward building deep coalition with each other.

As participants consider a variety of barriers, the workshop asks them to imagine themselves walking on those rough roads toward other oppressed people on the map, bringing liberatory gifts to each other. These gifts, in the framing of *The Map of Oppression*, are "things you have learned that go against what the powerful want from you that work in undermining their power" (Lugones, n.d., 4). For example, one woman shared that her gift to others on her map was teaching Spanish to her kids, and speaking it at home so they "grow up proud of their culture" (4). Another woman's gift to her family was modeling resistance to gendered roles in the family: "Everyone in my family expects me to do everything for them and I tell them that they are going to do their own wash" (4). In conceiving of her refusal to do the laundry, a refusal to be taken for granted, as a gift, she was turning the dominant framing of housework as a gendered duty or as an act of love for the family on its head: the resistant gift was *not* to do the laundry so as to model moving against such demands.

Coalitional solidarity can sometimes be blocked by issue-based politics grounded in self-interest. Indeed, a dominant conception of "political work" in the United States is that people come together on an issue that affects them personally. One of EPN's workshops, *Fragmentation: A Workshop on the Political Uses of Popular Education* (Lugones, n.d.), takes up this problem directly. In its overview of fragmentation as a problem, the workshop notes that, often, when one is doing political work, it seems that "no one cares about what your group is doing except for people who are directly affected by the problems your work addresses" (3). It suggests that the problem is partly rooted in the fact that grassroots political organizing in the United States is so often grounded in an appeal to self-interest. Such organizing "defines the issues and the group very narrowly and a hostility or indifference is cultivated or simply allowed to foster with respect to other issues and other groups" (3). Organizations working on particular issues, such as police brutality, violence against women, or LGBTQ rights, often work in isolation from one another, with little sustained analysis of each other's struggles (3).[3] Given this mode of doing political work, the conditions in which coalition can be formed are limited, occurring only when the self-interests of different groups coincide. Further, these kinds of coalitions are often short-lived, ending when a particular goal or outcome is reached. This is especially true when group interest is conceived in a monolithic way, without considering the deep heterogeneity of groups along lines of class, race, sexuality, age, nationality, language, gender, and ability.

Indeed, in contemporary politics in the United States, deep coalitional solidarity is tremendously difficult even in the midst of grassroots political movement. Popular education in a deep coalitional vein works to change this direction in political culture by asking, in the words of the *Fragmentation* workshop, "What keeps us from each other? What do we know about each other? Who fed us that information? How can we get to know each other better? What can we bring to the meeting in terms of knowledge of resistance?" (3).

TOWARD RESISTANT RELATIONALITY

A central aspect of the coalitional approach to popular education is close collective attention to the issue of how people treat each other within communities and in everyday relationships, with the aim of fostering new and better ways of treating each other in the face of homophobic, racist, sexist, and economic oppressions. Such an approach draws on popular education's tradition of highlighting the importance of transforming our everyday modes and practices of relating to one another. For Freire, for example, undercutting hierarchies between teachers and students in classrooms and elsewhere holds the possibility of deeply transforming our social and political life. In Tennessee, Highlander challenged segregation and Jim Crow laws in the South in the 1950s and 1960s by establishing the school as an integrated space where blacks and whites ate, lived, talked, and thought together in a non-hierarchical space (Horton 1998, 134). EPN shares with this popular education tradition a commitment to such resistant relationality and to creating environments in which non-hierarchical relationships can be enacted and sustained. While popular education in the Freirian and Highlander traditions primarily emphasizes fostering non-hierarchical relationships *between* groups and communities (for example, between teachers and students in Freire's case and between blacks and whites in the Highlander model), a coalitional approach to popular education addresses how to foster transformational relationships *within* communities complexly shaped by multiple lines of power.

Exemplifying this approach, the *Un Nuevo Camino* workshop begins with the assertion that "communities are only as strong as the relationships that we build with each other" (Lugones and Benfield, n.d., 1). The workshop proceeds by asking people to discuss the question, "What is it to treat another person well?" At one iteration of the workshop that took place with Latinas in the Pilsen neighborhood in Chicago, participants responded to this question with a wide range of thoughts and insights. Some focused on the importance of challenging hierarchy in relationships as a component of strong relationships, with responses such as "he or she treats me as an equal"; "we share responsibilities everywhere: taking care of the children, in the house, doing politics, on the job";

and "he or she asks for my opinion and takes it seriously." Other responses highlight the importance of care, appreciation, and fun in being treated well: "He or she treats me to little things, like bringing me a cup of coffee"; "We take care of each other in ways that are not demeaning"; "We do not take each other for granted. We appreciate each other and what each one of us does"; "We have fun together, we are playful and know how to relax with each other" (2). Also, for some, being treated well meant that there was space to be different, as well as space to change. As one participant explained:

> When someone treats me well, I can explore, experiment, and change without fear of the relationship ending. That we both change is a part of the relationship, for example, I can go to school to get my High School diploma or for other studies; [t]here is room for agreement and disagreement between us. There is room and enough trust that we can criticize each other in a well-meaning way, instead of not saying anything when we see what appears to us as a mistake. (2)

Finally, people noted that being treated well means not being oppressed or abused. After discussing what it means to be treated well, the *Nuevo Camino* workshop moves to collective analysis of ways that participants are actually treated in their lives, as well as to the consequences of being treated well and being treated poorly. For example, several people mentioned that their husbands did not help out with responsibilities at home, which meant that they were solely responsible for all the housework and the childcare. Further, they talked about being seen as people who take care of other people and not people with their own individual needs. Others discussed not being listened to or being controlled, battered, and abused (2–3). As one participant noted: "When we compare how Latinas are treated in our community with what we believe it is to treat someone well, the situation seems very sad. There is such a great difference!" (4).

The workshop also explores the impact on people's lives of being treated well or being treated badly. When a person is treated poorly, in the words of the workshop, one may become "someone who lacks self-respect, a person accustomed to take beatings and insults or someone who is destructive of herself or those who have less power than her" (4). Further, one may become less creative, accustomed to obeying orders, or constantly angry. In contrast, the workshop notes that being respected, appreciated, and treated well often leads people to be more creative in their lives. Under these relational conditions, "life becomes something good and happy, worth living. One feels active, a person with dignity. One takes care of oneself and one's ideas, growth, health, physical appearance because one has self-respect and one is appreciated. One thinks of nice things to do" (3).

In the workshop, participants, most of whom were members of community organizations, considered what it would look like if their community organizations directed political energy to working toward strong and caring relationships among its members. For most groups, it would mean a significant shift in political direction. Reflecting on his popular education work, Myles Horton writes: "I believed in changing society by first changing individuals, so that they could then struggle to bring about social changes" (1997, 184). In EPN's workshop, the emphasis is on exploring what it might take to transform relationships so as to effect social change. Structures of sexism, racism, homophobia, and economic oppression, among others, have conditioned us to treat each other badly; the work of becoming companions in resistance requires that we need to unlearn this training and practice treating each other well.

AFFIRMING AND ACTIVATING OUR TRANSFORMATIVE CAPACITIES

Key to the praxis of popular education is a rejection of top-down modes of political analysis or movement-building. In focusing on people's resistance to oppressive ways of being, these EPN workshops work against the tendency in much political organizing to provide the "answers." Indeed, by conceiving of movement toward social change as grounded in people's everyday acts of resistance and leaving the concept of resistance open ended, participants can take it up in ways that make sense to their own lives and situations. For example, instead of explaining what "resistance" might mean, the workshops give concrete and extremely varied examples of things that other people have identified about their own resistant ways of being.

In EPN, Lugones and the other collective members worked to develop a coalitional approach to popular education grounded in sustained and radical rethinking and a redoing of our relationships with one another. This approach pivots on the possibility of learning to see and appreciate ways that people resist inequitable power relations, even if these resistances might seem mundane, nonpolitical, or even criminal. Further, the approach invites us to think closely about the specificity of each other's lives and contexts, and to look for ways we might keep each other's resistant selves company, a company that can encourage, amplify, and sustain the possibility of deep and lasting social change. Finally, such an approach entails figuring out ways to treat each other well in our relationships and communities in the face of oppressive institutions and structures that would have us do otherwise.

Although this chapter has focused on the workshop setting as a place to learn and practice a coalitional approach to popular education, the practice is by no means restricted to such settings. Indeed, it is in our everyday lives—in our conversations, in our work with each other in a variety of settings, in our relationships—that such resistant companionship is lived. Popular education is a mode of political engagement that takes up the tremendous cultural and political power of collective analysis and turns us toward each other rather than to movement leaders for the possibility of change; coalitional popular education in particular turns us toward each other in a way that takes up the complexity of our lives and our communities and affirms the transformative capacity of our resistant practices.

NOTES

1. See Scott (1990) and Kelley (1996) for more on the politics of everyday resistance. In *Wild Garden*, Dian Marino calls such resistant practices "cracks in consent" (1998, 22). Those in the dominant position often want to downplay these cracks.

2. Paulo Freire, for example, discusses the use of codes as a tool for collective analysis in *Pedagogy of the Oppressed* (2000).

3. For example, the work of the violence against women movement and the movement against police brutality often work and have worked in isolation—and sometimes at odds—from and with one another. One of the important interventions of the Incite! Women, Gender Non-Conforming, and Trans People of Color Against Violence collective has been to link these two organizing efforts (Incite! Women of Color Against Violence 2006).

REFERENCES

Beltré, Mildred, Cricket Keating, Laura DuMond Kerr, María Lugones, Rafael Mutis, Joshua Price, and Julia Schiavone Camacho. 1999. *Politicizing the Everyday*. Workshop prepared for the Escuela Popular Norteña.

Beltré, Mildred, Maria Benfield, Julia Schiavone Camacho, Laura DuMond Kerr, Aurelia Flores, Marta Garcia, Sarah Hoagland, Gladys Jiménez-Muñoz, Cricket Keating, Suzanne LaGrande, María Lugones, Rudiah Primariantari. n.d. *Complex Unity*. Workshop prepared for the Escuela Popular Norteña. EPN archives, Valdez, NM.

Escuela Popular Norteña. n.d. *Mission Statement*. EPN archives, Valdez, NM.

Escuela Popular Norteña. 1994. *Popular Education Seminar Overview*. EPN archives, Valdez, NM.

———. 1998. *Complex Unity.* Workshop prepared for the Escuela Popular Norteña. EPN archives, Valdez, NM.

Freire, Paulo. 2000. *Pedagogy of the Oppressed.* New York: Bloomsbury.

Graciano, Hector, María Lugones, Joshua Price, and Ricardo Santos. n.d. *Coalition: Linking Contexts of Resistance.* Workshop prepared for the Escuela Popular Norteña. EPN archives, Valdez, NM.

Horton, Myles, with Judith Kohl and Herbert Kohl. 1997. *The Long Haul: An Autobiography.* New York: Teachers College Press.

Incite! Women of Color Against Violence. 2006. *The Color of Violence: Incite! Anthology.* Boston: South End Press.

Kelley, Robin D.G. 1996. *Race Rebels: Culture, Politics, and the Black Working Class.* New York: The Free Press.

Lugones, María. n.d. *The Map of Oppression: A Workshop on the Creation of Liberatory Awareness.* Workshop prepared for the Escuela Popular Norteña. EPN archives, Valdez, NM.

Lugones, María, and Dalida María Benfield. n.d. *Un Nuevo Camino.* Workshop prepared for the Escuela Popular Norteña. EPN archives, Valdez, NM.

Lugones, María, Hector Graciano, Joshua Price, and Ricardo Santos. n.d. *Fragmentation: A Workshop on the Political Uses of Popular Education.* Workshop prepared for the Escuela Popular Norteña. EPN archives, Valdez, NM.

Marino, Dian. 1998. *The Wild Garden: Art, Education, and the Culture of Resistance.* Toronto: Between the Lines Press.

Scott, James. 1990. *Domination and the Arts of Resistance: Hidden Transcripts.* New Haven, CT: Yale University Press.

12 Walking Illegitimately

A *Cachapera/Tortillera* and a Dyke

Sarah Lucia Hoagland

Thinking about structural relationality between U.S. feminists, about what happens when two marginalized others meet, in particular U.S. white women and U.S. women of color. My focus is not about possibly well-meaning attempts to gain acknowledgment or relief for self and/or others in dominant institutions. I am interested in how we, who are marginalized in particular ways and privileged in others, meet *each other*.

I am interested in ways we animate or resist animating dominant logic with regard to *each other*, how we come to see *each other* through difference and negotiate various means of engaging, how we build complex connections, at least in significant measures, away from dominant framings, how we enact our relationality and develop community. Do we walk legitimately, finding each other along state-sanctioned discourses and structures, reading each other through dominant interpellations even while chanting inclusivity? Or will we travel illegitimately? And what facilitates this?

It was choosing the label "dyke" that sent me looking for others, going into other worlds, finding the lesbians: in bars, at concerts, on the softball field, at music festivals, at feminist bookstores, international feminist book fairs, at the Midwest Society for Women in Philosophy, at coffeehouses, political actions, through lesbian feminist rags, underground collectives, organizing wimmin-only events, seeking one another, drawn to each other, our desire leading us to spaces where we found respect, developed friendship, created networks, and made new meaning. It was a process of opening to the possibility of female friendship and of loving women that 1970s feminism nourished. Lesbian activism made and makes pockets in time and space. All of this took, and still takes, me into other worlds, rethinking "home," making it possible to encounter and meet others I was never meant to meet—all of this leading me to engaging, screwing up, learning, screwing up, loving. Seeking and finding the lesbians, taking me to spaces off institutionally structured paths, walking illegitimately.

Over the years, María Lugones's activism, theorizing, and companionship have fertilized my efforts, my engagements, and my understandings. Her theorizing is deeply embedded in and fed by her activism as she refuses the theory/practice, town/gown binaries. She takes up conceptual offerings and inhabits them, practices them in community. Her critiques build on and shift focus. Her creations are enabled by, and explored, developed, and grounded in praxis. Hers is not academic work for scholarly debate but paradigm shifting, imaginative, challenging work helpful in resisting absorption into, erasure by, or appropriation by monocultural heteropatriarchal racist sexist colonial neoliberal society. Hers is a way of doing philosophy, being in conversation, a way of loving.

I met María at the Midwest Society for Women in Philosophy (SWIP) in the early 1980s. For many years this was created to be a space where many of us developed our thinking, bringing ideas to each other rather than imagining work for mainstream philosophy. Midwest SWIP at the time was a biannual gathering where lesbian and heterosexual feminist philosophers were developing community and generating ways of thinking fertilized by radical feminism and lesbian separatism.[1] It was a community that benefitted from and promoted participation by nonacademic community members. And with one exception, there were no concurrent sessions; we gathered as a group to engage.

At that time, Midwest SWIP created two caucuses: a Woman of Color Caucus that María formed and, with the help of Jackie Anderson, sustained for many years. It gave women of color, both community and academic, a place to present their work to each other without white women present, making possible creative and experimental thinking in new directions. This took place during the Midwest SWIP program proper—the only concurrent session we had. This practice made blaringly clear to us white women some of the consequences of the loss of women of color's presence, for not only would we not be able to hear those papers, we would not have the benefit of their comments on the concurrent paper. An uncomfortable, critical lesson.

The other caucus, a Lesbian Caucus, formed after one heterosexual woman complained about a SWIP program being dominated by lesbians' papers. In reality, only three papers out of twelve were by lesbians. Other than pointing this out, we were left speechless. But at the next gathering, several lesbians were furious. As a result, we realized we needed a meeting time at each conference so we could check in with each other and strategize about problems before taking them before the conference as a whole. (Both caucuses would bring reports to the business meeting.) This developed into a place to take up lesbian community matters, and María and Jackie often brought critical issues we all worked on. Blearily, we held these meetings at eight in the morning, before the program began at nine.

When I first met María, and we talked and talked, I gave her a spare journal I had with me to write down her thoughts as she struggled with ideas swirling in her head needing expression. She later told me that around this time she had set herself to embrace lesbian separatism as it seemed very attractive from all of us embedded in it at Midwest SWIP (Joyce Trebilcott, Anne Waters, Jeffner Allen, Julien Murphey, Claudia Card, Marilyn Frye, Amber Katherine, Jackie Anderson, Anne Leighton, Christa Lebens, Annie Courtney, myself and others), but subsequently found she could not. And she began taking up what she found valuable while shifting focus for what she found problematic.

Separatism. It's about power. It's about rupture of normalcy, it's about control over access, but most importantly, it's about animating disjunctive vortexes of meaning, about the creation or affirmation or maintenance of values and habits distinct from what passes as common sense. In a Black- or Latina/o-centered space, the centrality of whiteness dissolves. Zora Neal Hurston's separatism was in part to keep Black children from absorbing white supremacist value and hatred. Critics argue one can never separate from culture, that to think so is to deceive oneself. Yes, but even if some worlds of sense are not completely separate, incommensurate, from the dominant frame of meaning, this does not mean they operate from the same logic and grounding premises. It is colonial arrogance and epistemic laziness to imagine, declare all meaning limited to dominant/hegemonic logic.

Lesbian separatism is not about safety from men, it is not adhering to rigid rules, not about purism—or it undermines itself when it pretends to be. It is about what Marilyn Frye and Carolyn Schafer call lesbian connection. Imaginations, and hence development of possibilities, are able to move in distinct directions through collective activist process. That's why I chose separatism. Bottom line.

However, María rightly notes that for lesbians of color, separating can support goals of white supremacy, and she addresses complexities of lesbian pluralism (HL). Moreover, for María, the work necessarily involves engaging men as well as women in Latina/o and other communities of color, addressing, for example, questions of authenticity and horizontal hostility as well as violence against women (BP). María is not challenging separatism (or nationalism) by insisting we struggle within the frame of dominant meaning (or assimilate). It is the move to purity she challenges. And practices of both separatism and nationalism have been guilty of that (PIS).

However, separatist movements, though flawed, have been central in creating and maintaining distinct collective grounds of meaning. Actually, many of the standard challenges to separatism emerge from a veiled division between socialist and anarchist sensibilities and politics. Significantly, critiques from women of color of white feminist work concern white feminist reliance on the state, what they call carceral feminism, for the state exercises with impunity very different practices toward women of color. While María found she could not walk a separatist path, her notion of ontological plurality travels sympathetic and complimentary illegitimate anarchist paths. And as our paths crossed and recrossed, our imaginations flourished.

My interest in *Lesbian Ethics* lay in separating from dominant logic and culture, moving toward new value that promotes lesbian community, enacting agency under oppression, challenging constructions of female agency, challenging the logic of control, and moving away from the individualism of modern Western ethics and its destruction of community. Moral agency under oppression involves the ability to go on under oppression and create meaning through our living. "It is not *because* we are free and moral agents that we are able to make moral choices; rather, it is *because* we make choices, choose from among alternatives, act in the face of limits, that we declare ourselves to be moral beings" (Hoagland 1988, 231).

One of María's early creations that fertilized my thinking, "Playfulness, 'World'-Traveling, and Loving Perception," engages Marilyn Frye's analysis of male arrogance: everything is either for him or against him. Marilyn's analysis certainly spoke to my experience. Even as a child I found women of my mother's generation dissolving into men, acting like little girls around them, deeply offending my sensibilities. And Marilyn continued: the mark of a voluntary association is that one can survive displeasing the other. The one who loves is not selfless, but she also knows the independence of the other, where one's self leaves off and the other begins (Frye 1983). Yes, I thought.

However, María found something lacking here: understanding love as just independence misses complexity in our relationality. María notes that white women remain independent, untouched, and without a sense of loss when women of color are not present. She states: "I am incomplete and unreal without other women. I am profoundly dependent on others without having to be their subordinate, their slave, their servant" (WT). Understanding this untouched independence as a failure of love was part of the lesson we gained at Midwest SWIP as the Women of Color Caucus met separately.

But finding and loving each other does not mean we have simply divested ourselves of dominant values in our interactions. María's work on the Trickster, along with that of Anne Cameron (1981) and Anne Leighton (personal communication circa 1982), was key in *Lesbian Ethics* to my letting go of duty as the moniker of ethics, and as a means of challenging each other. For regardless of admonitions to duty with regard to racism, standard means of dismissing challenges to racism continue to thrive. With few exceptions, duty doesn't work, and guilt doesn't foster community. As Jackie Anderson remarks: "White lesbians feel at home with whiteness. There isn't any automatic identification with marginalized peoples of other cultures. Where whites are at home in other places, others are no longer at home" (personal communication circa 2010). The Trickster is one way of unsettling this failure of love.

From my early work, part of enacting agency under oppression involves learning to demystify dominant narratives of resistant behavior so we can meet each other outside hegemonic performances, re-cognize resistances, and engage through other dimensions. I developed my sabotage thesis questioning slave stereotypes: docile, childlike, clumsy, lazy, and I came to realize the very behavior, such as breaking a tool, that supports white supremacist narratives of slaves as inept are themselves indications of slave resistance, sabotage. The Trickster, though not acknowledged in dominant Anglo culture, is at work here. And I began challenging constructions of femininity, asking what would *count* as resistance to domination—women's resistance, slave resistance, Jewish resistance during the Holocaust, and coming to realize that within hegemony the answer was "nothing." For example, the very behaviors, facts, that contribute to the feminine stereotype and dismissal of women actually indicate women's discontent and resistance, sabotage—from the "fluffy-headed" housewife who sends raw eggs in her husband's lunch box all the way to the wife who burns her husband to death as he sleeps.

One Thanksgiving, María invited Claudia Card and me to her parents' home in Buenos Aires. Later she told me this story: When she was young, her mother used to tell lies. Her father would ask something like, "Where is the salt?" and her mother would say it was in the kitchen when it wasn't in the kitchen, it was in the dining room. María used to get very angry at her father and brothers for letting her mother get away with this. But they would simply reply, "Oh, that's just your mother, dear." Thinking about my notions of sabotage and agency under oppression, she went back home one time and after talking with her mother about many things, finally asked her, "Why did you lie?" In that moment her mother was able to answer: "I was making sure no one was listening to me." And in that moment María saw a dimension of her mother as well as her self that she had not seen before, saw her mother as one if oppressed, also resisting. A Trickster.

In talking about her failure of love toward her mother, María argues that loving her mother "required that I see with her eyes, that I go into my mother's 'world,' that I see both of us as we are constructed in her 'world'… only then could I see at all how meaning could arise fully between us" (WT 86). Only then could she meet her mother outside the Argentinean patriarchal construction of her.

Seeing resistance is critical to meeting outside dominant logic.

However, while taking up my concept of agency under oppression, María shifted focus, noting that the modern Western concept of "agency" presupposes the myth of autonomy (the powerful have enormous collectivities backing them up). Analyzing the Aristotelian practical syllogism that ends in action, she began developing her concept "active subjectivity" by raising the question of forming nonsubservient intentions which are regularly rendered nonsense in dominant logic (TSC). Engaging the work of Gloria Anzaldúa, María explores the possibilities of resistance of the borderdweller who is a subject and is active, but is not an agent, not one who can successfully carry intention into action (HL, WGS). Active subjectivity allows us to re-cognize the ways intentions work in different logics, different worlds of meaning, opening the possibility of understanding as resistant, possibly sabotage, what appears as inactivity, disengagement, or nonsense in hegemonic logic. Seeing our intentional meaning reduced to nonsense made many of us aware of the fragility of sense. And think about the Trickster.

Active subjectivity is not abstraction; it emerges from within concrete complex messy contexts, not utopian ones, and we begin to comprehend how our possibilities are framed and how we take them up in relation to others. All this took me into María's work on ontological pluralism, and a conception of multiplicity distinct from the Anglo European postmodern unified subject who is understood as fragmented by oppressive structures.

Multiplicity, ontological plurality. I remember arguing with María, my back figuratively and literally against a wall, at my first EPN (Escuela Popular Norteña) *encuentro*, not being able to fathom anything but a singular self ("What, then of memory," I asked. And she answered, "it's important, to remember who we are in different worlds"). I could not let go of a singular self, one torn/rendered by the reason/emotion split, despite my own work on sabotage and resistance. She, most graciously, helped to end the argument by saying, "Then we just disagree about that." And I stopped feeling I had to defend what I understood to be my ground of sense/meaning.

Later I talked about this at our lesbian collective gathering, Institute of Lesbian Studies (ILS), and Michal Brody responded: The idea that we are different in essence in different contexts is familiar, even our cores are context-dependent. This is familiar in a Jewish context, a certain chameleonness. The notion of the immutability of core identity, or of the impermeability of identity (I am who I am regardless of where I am located) focuses on the individual as the primary social unit rather than a larger molecule. She laughed, "This idea is very protestant" (personal communication circa 2004).

One head of Women's Studies struggled and fought and risked her job promoting the program, challenging the administration. Obtaining funding for a Women of Color film series, she brought in innovative and radical women of color films, producing a powerful film series. Subsequently she discovered that the women students of color were angry at her, and she threw up defenses. She understood herself to be a revolutionary, taking risks and fighting the good fight, which she certainly was. But in the process she had not worked collectively with the women of color students (originally many women's studies programs—following the activism that birthed them—were collectively organized among students, staff, and faculty). So regardless of the fact that the students liked and gained much from the films she chose for them, they saw her as another part of the white power structure. Which she was. More importantly, she was *both:* she was both a revolutionary and part of the system. Unfortunately, she could not handle the complexity and shut down.

As María argues, our subjectivity changes as we become subject to local jurisdiction, to the practices and understanding of non-mainstream collectivities in concrete contexts. Working to avoid being subject to local jurisdiction is a practice we are trained in by imperialist culture. It defines our sovereignty and hence is the basis of our freedom.

But we form and are formed by our histories and our relations and engagements, which is to say, if we inhabit more than one world, we are multiply formed and forming. We are subordinate and resistant and oppressive, *really.* We white women are, *really*, subordinated women. And we are, *really*, resisting women. And we are, *really*, colonizing women. One can be both a fluffy-headed housewife *and* a saboteur *and* a colonist. Actually, in this culture, many of us often *are* exactly that.

This is not the fragmentation that presupposes a unified self—this is about multiple selves. As María notes, fragmentation is cognizized as a variety of oppressors' needs, beliefs, desires, inhabiting multiple categories constructed of dominant agendas—a Black woman disappeared between (white-dominated) feminism and (male-dominated) civil rights struggles. Fragmentation glosses interactions, intersections, crossroads, it disappears liminal spaces, borderlands, and it obscures the ease with which categories institutionally facilitate strategies of divide and conquer. Most importantly, it disappears resistances.

This order of things makes it almost impossible for a *cachapera/tortillera* and a dyke to engage in complex relationality. Do we both meet as women, as lesbians? As ethnic grounding comes in, are we necessarily at odds? Certainly, we choose to struggle to undermine dominant interpellations of "woman" or "lesbian" or "Latino," but developing unity through sameness animates and does not undermine the fragmentation.

It was Audre Lorde who challenged radical feminism on organizing through sameness rather than difference (Lorde 1984). She and her lover tried to leave difference outside the relationship—they were just two gay girls. But there was the fact that she was Black and her lover was white. There was also the fact that her lover had had a nervous breakdown and received shock treatments, and Audre had not (Lorde 1982, 203–4). All this was left outside the relationship, outside the love.

On first encountering Jackie Anderson, I gained a great lesson. In the late 1970s on campus, more than one Black lesbian came to me for validation not available at that time in their home community. I was describing to Jackie how I was challenging some of what was going on, including challenging some of the Black faculty. I saw myself as revolutionary, fighting the good fight. After I described two incidents, Jackie looked at me and said, "You're one of those white girls, who, when everything is going along ok, comes in and just stirs things up." Not the response I was expecting, and I nursed my wounded ego. But one day I stopped, realizing "I *am* one of those white girls, that's what I do." Coming to see myself through Jackie's eyes gave me a more solid sense of who I was than the unified self I'd been trained to imagine had to fight the good fight. And it made it possible to better strategize.

Working toward common ground necessitates organizing through difference: conditions we face, struggles we have (and have not) engaged in, what we have learned to navigate and how it affects others in this complicated process of negotiating structures of power.[2] This statement is not an invitation to academic debate, to an academic world of meaning—it is about moving to a liminal place that frees up the imagination.

María's work on resistant subjectivity developed as she explored pluralist spaces where structural meaning is destabilized. She first explored the limen, where one finds oneself without institutional description, thinking about Malcolm X and pilgrimages, where king walks alongside peasant. Subsequently she took up Gloria Anzaldúa's borderlands, spaces in constant transition, yielding a Mestiza consciousness and requiring a tolerance for ambiguity. In *Borderlands*, Gloria talks of intimate terrorism, and *la facultad*: "It is anything that breaks into one's everyday mode of perception that causes a break in one's defenses and resistance, anything that takes from one's habitual grounding, causes the depths to open up, causes a shift in perception" (Anzaldúa 1987, 39). This is particularly possible in consciousness raising and practices of popular education.

Popular Education. Somewhere in the 1980s I participated in a popular education workshop María conducted in Chicago. She drew out our knowledges and understandings, shifting our consciousness. For example, she asked us to "[n]ame one spot on the map of oppression you occupy and something about it you bring to the liberatory process" (this included privileged and oppressed spots) and "[n]ame a survival skill you've learned and something about it you bring to the liberatory process." I used what I learned in developing workshops I conducted in tandem with lesbian community talks I gave, asking each participant to "[n]ame something about yourself that changes as a result of identifying as a lesbian." I developed related workshops in my ethics classes about resistance and giving each other backup. This work energizes, enables us to see into the social, concretely, at street level, to see relationally (TSC).

In the 1990s, Jackie Anderson, Anne Leighton, and I began a collective called the Institute of Lesbian Studies (ILS)[3] after holding backyard summer gatherings for two years to bring Black lesbians and white lesbian separatists together to dialogue. Over the years, ILS has been through various permutations. Currently we gather once a month and have biannual three-day retreats, taking up various questions and issues.

In 1995, María invited me to an *encuentro* of the Escuela Popular Norteña (EPN) because of my work with *Lesbian Ethics*, along with popular educators from very different communities. EPN was founded in 1988 by María and Geoff Bryce, both of whom had trained at the Highlander School. During the 1990s, EPN was a popular education school, a grassroots collective directing its work to Latino communities, designing and conducting workshops and *encuentros* in Valdez, New Mexico, bringing activists from Latino communities to work around critical issues to take back to their communities. The collective was a mixed group of popular educators from specific communities and included women and men, lesbian, gay, and straight, Latino and Anglo.[4] I was invited, as a community worker and separatist, and was respected as such. I went, grateful for the invitation.

Here collective members were animating vibrant spaces as we found ourselves reflected in different worlds of sense, spaces that were not about safety and comfort but respect and possibility. When one is expecting safety and comfort, *cachaperas/tortilleras* and dykes are not going to meet beyond superficial levels. This *encuentro* deepened my intuitions of *Lesbian Ethics*. For those concerned with social justice, we can struggle to develop the skills to meet each other as well as others in unfamiliar geographies, spatialities, and without boomerang perception, *without* translation, particularly translation into hegemonic sense. What I found theorized and practiced at the *encuentro* was a lifeline. I joined the collective the next year.

The collective would meet for a week before the *encuentro*, finalizing workshops, cooking and freezing food for everyone, preparing accommodations. The *encuentro* itself would last a week, as we worked with invitadas/os on matters central to their community activism. The collective continued to meet for the week after to assess the *encuentro*, discussing what worked and what went wrong and why, beginning preparations for the next year. Over the years, EPN developed popular education workshops for activists, working on violence against women, particularly Latina women, on *jotería*, on harm free zones (where calling the cops is not the first response, or even the second or third), on resistant negotiation, on complex unity, and on politicizing the everyday (PRE).

Violence against women. What does it mean to think and act *with*? As María notes, this is particularly difficult within progressive social institutions (TSC 230). As Lesbians and Women of Color have articulated, many of our efforts have been compromised through our struggles against violence—turning to the state and organized police, legal, and medical forces.[5] We went from grassroots collective action to helping facilitate state intervention.

In Chicago, this began in the late 1970s as underground feminist collectives, helping women and children escape abusive males, found they could not use private homes even temporarily because when the husband/boyfriend, perhaps following her back from work, discovered the safehouse, he beat up both women. So the activists needed a separate location, for which they needed money, and subsequently for which they needed understanding lawyers and sympathetic cops. Underground action persisted (one night posters went up all over one area of Chicago announcing a curfew on all men after six in the evening, and regularly locations were spray painted where a woman had been raped, and Take Back the Night Marches were held without permits marching in "red light" districts and engaging women). But efforts to provide safety became more and more institutionalized (including eventual cooperation with state agencies such as INS and ICE), with degree-holding professionals developing formulaic workshops whereby women were told what they felt and how to understand themselves, and lesbian volunteers being told to stay in the closet—no collective consciousness raising here. María challenged the move away from popular education, away from women participating in developing their own understandings, analyses, goals.

EPN's Complex Unity workshop involves revisiting situations in which we found ourselves in the midst of violence and making an *altar* of *cositas* that helped us get through the situation. The workshop helps each participant find her voice and re-cognize her resistances (even in just saying to herself, "I don't like this"). It offers strategies for participants to attend women in very different situations, having a place of speaking and hearing that does not require making perfect sense. And it positions participants to create and develop strategies and support in the event of future violence.

As María argues, the business of the dominant frame of meaning is to foreclose all meaning outside its logic by rendering it nonsense, crazy, meaningless. But looking again at sabotage, traveling to different worlds at the *encuentros*, learning to critically make sense of others' resistances outside dominant logic ... there are many, many critical things happening not countenanced by dominant logic. The streetwalker hangs out in places where she can discover different logics, where the dominant frame of common senses crumbles, where she is off center and awkward and so alert, constantly, in an ever-changing field of activity, where her skills at pattern detection increase exponentially, where things never settle into take-it-for-grantedness (TSC).

It is here where a *cachapera/tortillera* and a dyke have a chance to meet, engage other dimensions, and animate conceptual shifts.

But María points to a paradox: even if we nourish a resistant logic with respect to our own marginalization, we may nevertheless approach other others through normalizing, dominant logic (BP). And I come back to the question: What happens when two marginalized others meet?

A big part of the work for me at EPN involved María's distinction between the logic of oppression and the logic of resistance. AnaLouise Keating developed a paper on going back to the Mother for the anthology on Mary Daly that Marilyn Frye and I co-edited (2000). She contrasted four radical lesbian feminists who did so: Gloria Anzaldúa, Audre Lorde, Paula Gunn Allen, and Mary Daly. Gloria, Audre, and Paula located their understanding firmly within their respective traditions, animating a logic of resistance, while Mary, more focused on a logic of oppression, universalized. Her work, along with that of Gloria, Audre, and Paula, certainly facilitated much resistant thinking. However, the effect of Mary's universalizing was that the unacknowledged grounding of her work in Anglo-European tradition erased other traditions, so while highly resistant, it was also colonizing.

I remember María at my home one time in rage that Mary's resistant work had thereby erased her. The exclusion was not a matter of saying someone like María wasn't in Mary's mind, wasn't one of the women she was speaking to and about. Quite the opposite: the exclusion lay in the implication that María *was* included. For that inclusion brings María into Mary's tradition of struggle and resistance while erasing María's own history and struggles, resistances fertilized within a distinct context.

Early on, when I read Audre's and Gloria's and Paula's writing, I was inspired. I did not imagine I was to fit myself into these stories; instead I found myself invited to search for my own back-to-the-mother tradition that fertilized me. The strategic work, then, becomes developing the ability, the skill, to engage local histories without animating colonial practices and colonial identities.

Directing our attention to intersections of language, territoriality, and sociality, María takes up Mary Daly's *Wickedary* (1987) as an explicit performance of linguistic resistance and transgression together with another text of linguistic resistance *El Libro de Caló* (2005), a dictionary of Pachuco slang, which contests territory and disrupts Anglicity, destabilizing colonial relations (WC). Inhabiting both dictionaries, María rejects a bilingual's temptation to translate. Seeking, instead, unmediated communication, conversation which speakers must struggle for, fashioned through lived connections, she laments the impossibility of a "wicked caló." Because the *Wickedary* does not take to the streets but stakes its domain in the Background, *Wickedary* gossips have no way of meeting Caló *marimachas* who, while needing to contest the limits of *El Libro de Caló*, nevertheless must take up its spatial, decolonial, emphasis. And so María reaches for an everyday vocabulary that simultaneously contests both patriarchies and colonialism, a territory where *marimachas* and gossips meet and converse, where *cachaperas* and dykes meet and converse (WC).

Hers is a continuing struggle to get to the root of why men of color as well as why white women both continue to ignore women of color, particularly the violences against women of color. And so she began developing her analysis of the heterosexual colonial/modern gender system and its construction of colonial and colonized genders. And María opened my world to Latin American Decolonial Theorists such as Aníbal Quijano, Walter Mignolo, and Enrique Dussel, as well as Rodolfo Kusch, Édouard Glissant, and Paget Henry.

Addressing the sado-ritual syndrome in relation to Europe that Mary Daly (1978) articulates, and analyzing the Anglo-European bourgeois construction of gender, Silvia Federici argues that the European witch hunts were terrorist acts against peasant women, attacking outspoken women central to community life, wresting away control of production and restricting women's possibilities for survival (2004). With the development of capitalism, women were removed from the public as a force, deskilled, and privatized in men's houses. Significantly, these were attacks not just on women, but on peasant *communities* through the undermining of women's collective public authority. As María argues, the discourse of gender we have today is a product of this, of Anglo-European Modernity.

A related attack on community was central to the Anglo-European colonial project that began in 1492 with the Spaniards. These attacks were also designed to destroy communities, existing systems of organization, languages, economies, knowledge, history, spirituality. However, those colonized and enslaved were never meant to assume bourgeois white gender identities. Indios and slaves were sexed and raped but not gendered. María argues that the resulting gender productions in colonized territories were critically different from those within Anglo-European communities.

Thus she names a "light" side and "dark" side of the colonial/modern gender system in order to re-cognize the extent of the practice of colonization in disintegrating communal relations, egalitarian relations, ritual thinking, collective decision-making and authority, and economies—a framing for both women and men of color as not-women and not-men (HGS). And it is central to white women's and lesbian present-day failures of love in regard to women of color.

This analysis is critical in raising consciousness about how what has been inherited from this history affects current practices and strategies. Thus the work of men of color in relation to violence against women of color is located in the dark side of the colonial/modern gender system and is distinct from the work of white women. María's concern in terms of present-day men of color is explored by theorists such as Manuel Chávez Jr.

Regarding white women, U.S. feminist projects, primarily grounded in white culture, including globalizing projects, typically address and challenge the form of gender that applies only to the light side of the colonial/modern gender system. Indeed, many U.S. white feminist academics deploy "gender" as a means of *reading* other cultures when working to find common cause. But instead, this reads them as less evolved, backward in time, as if women of color have no distinct resistant culture, epistemology, spirituality, economy, and can only be saved by Anglo-European women's U.S. imperial cultural productions (TDF).

That is, deploying gender in this way is a colonial move, for the naming is not a simple denotation, not an empirically decidable question, it is an interpellating, translating, into Western semiotics and practices. Such work thereby delineates the possibilities and limitations available, for example, equal rights or a room of one's own. This is a deploying of Anglo European possibilities and limitations to the erasure of other, for example Indigenous possibilities and limitations, thus reanimating colonial identities (Hoagland 2010).

At the Lesbian Caucus of Midwest SWIP, María raised the question of many lesbians of color not being able to come out in their home communities, together with the fact that many white lesbians don't go into Latina/o or Black communities even though these are public spaces. Moreover, even when we find separate spaces to gather, unless organized by lesbians of color, we are grounded in white cultural logic. For example, coming out, as María and Jackie have noted, tends to be a white lesbian and gay rite of passage, not so much in communities of color. This is one bit behind Jackie's initial challenge to me about stirring things up on campus back in 1979.

And this brings me to María's critique of "community" in *Lesbian Ethics*. She argued that lesbian communities, while forming everywhere lesbians gather, remained an abstraction in my work because I was not taking up the journeys lesbians travel in order to come together, the histories and struggles from our respective home traditions (HL).

I felt the depth of the ontological dimension of multiplicity and lesbian pluralism as well as the significance of the concrete journeys or paths lesbians take as María articulates: "La tortillera exists en la comunidad only as a pervert. Perversion constitutes her and marks her as outside of countenanced relationality" (DP 174). Moving into the Lesbian Movement, *la tortillera* becomes a Latina/Lesbian; thus fragmented, she embodies an absence of relation (DP, HL).

"Lesbian" is a relational concept. For many of us, lesbians of color and white, we've gained grounding in lesbian living, moving (not institutionalized Movement), creating community where none existed. But valuing how home communities animate us is critical to addressing the tension between social fragmentation and heterogeneity (HL, ED). For me, community was never about belonging. My longing has always been for possibilities of collectively creating and sustaining new value, about giving life to new meaning that… anything I write here becomes solidified the moment ink touches paper. That's not what it's about. It's about conspiracy, conspiring, breathing together.

When I wrote *Lesbian Ethics*, women loving women was nonsense; lesbians were outcasts; lesbianism was essentially invisible.[6] As Jackie Anderson has remarked more than once about our ILS gatherings, we were never meant to be. María argues that as lesbians are cast out, there are possibilities in the disjunctive space (ED). And when one travels to various lesbians' worlds, for me for example, particular Black lesbian gatherings on the South Side of Chicago, or Latina lesbian gatherings on the West Side, or Jewish lesbian gatherings, possibilities of complex communication and lesbian pluralism emerge (HL, OC). For the concern isn't about "everyone is different and can be themselves, let's include everyone." It's about how we are structured in relation to each other and our active subjectivity in engaging, loving. Our possibilities exist in embedded locations, both ours and others', and involve becoming competent as we enter different logics and meet each other, as a *cachapera/tortillera* and a dyke meet.

Over the years, in interaction with various communities, María's work has developed from thinking about an individual unable to carry a resistant intention into action, to the active oppressing←—→resisting intersubjectivity of individuals, to Women of Color coalitional politics and the intersubjective relationships of oppressed cultures, to approaching Indigenous cosmologies, histories, languages erased by the coloniality of knowledge, and developing decolonial feminism.

She has developed the logic of resistant subjectivity exploring pluralist spaces where structural meaning is destabilized: first the limen, then Gloria Anzaldúa's borderlands, and most recently with Latin American theorists, the fractured spaces of the colonial difference. In all these spaces, imagination breaks from the dominant structure, requiring double and triple consciousness as one navigates multiplicity, ontological pluralism.

Her concern for Women of Color coalitional politics, and more recently, decolonial feminism, puts at center the ability to find resistance and engage in complex communication without transparency or translation. And she continually explores the relation of oppression and the resources we bring to liberation. Me, I keep working on the light side of the colonial/modern gender system where I am located, continuing to work in communal intention (a concept María developed in visiting again the work of Gloria Anzaldúa), resistance, ontological plurality, and coloniality of knowledge.

Speaking alone, I cease to exist. Speaking among others who challenge dominant narratives in conceptually distinct spaces offers the possibility of moving in the everyday in a different logic. What pushes me is what I become engaging you.

Walking illegitimately, a *cachapera/tortillera* and a dyke meet in the realm of analyzing structures and preparing meals, of classes and parties, of gatherings and sharing books, of political struggle and creation of lesbian spaces, a dyke and a *cachapera/tortillera* engaged as colleagues, as compañeras, as friends, as intellectual companions in home communities and in communities we collectively create. And Lesbianing was central to this, for me, going through many changes as we worked against the grain.

Walking illegitimately involves decolonial praxis. It involves recognizing we are incomplete without each other. It involves working to not translate or render each other transparent. It involves complex communication. It involves finding oneself a different person in different spacialities. It involves facing the tensions between us as we go against the grain of social fragmentation, as we work toward coalition. It involves being willing to face the Trickster. It involves being willing to *engage* each other, all without a blueprint, a map, a set of rules, without translation and with many mistakes... and successes.

NOTES

1. The radical lesbian feminism (and radical lesbianism) of my work involves extended conversations with Julia Penelope, Mary Daly, Gloria Anzaldúa, Audre Lorde, Chrystos, Barbara and Beverly Smith, Marilyn Frye, Harriet Desmoines, Catherine Nicholson, Adrienne Rich, Susan Leigh Star, Elana Dykewomon, Alix Dobkin, Naomi Littlebear Morena, Vivienne Louise, Billie Potts, Toni McNaron, Ariane Brunet, Louise Turcotte, Jackie Anderson, Anne Leighton, and a number of others, particularly when we met at various locations, many of which were initially made possible for me by Julia's determination and lesbian networking.

2. Julia Penelope and I strategized several actions, trading off between her skills as a working-class white dyke and mine as a middle-class white dyke.

3. ILS, actually, is the name Jeffner Allen gave to the publishing house she created. Subsequently I took over the book distribution business; but Anne and Jackie and I developed the collective side of it.

4. When I joined, EPN members also included Mildred Beltré, Cricket Keating, Laura Dumond Kerr, Julia Schiavone Camacho, Rafael Mutis, Joshua Price, Rick Santos, Aurelia Flores, Suzanne Lagrande, and, of course María and Geoff. Subsequently others joined: Easa Gonzales, Rocío Restrepo, Nydia Hernandez, Shireen Roshanravan, Rocío Silverio, and Xhercis Méndez.

5. See, in particular, Silliman and Bhattacharjee (2002) and Shah (1997).

6. Today lesbians are again rendered invisible through attacks on lesbian spaces from transideology and a sector of trans activism: for example, lesbians are being de-platformed, womyn-born-womyn space is deemed hateful, butch dykes and radical fairies are being named men and women, respectively—the man/woman binary reified, naturalized, even if divorced from biology. And the light side of gender is reinforced.

REFERENCES

Allen, Paula Gunn. 1986. *The Sacred Hoop: Recovering the Feminine in American Indian Traditions*. Boston: Beacon Press.

Anzaldúa, Gloria. 1987. *Borderlands/La Frontera: The New Mestiza*. San Francisco: Aunt Lute Books.

Cameron, Anne. 1981. *Daughters of Copperwoman*. Vancouver, BC: Press Gang Publishers.

Daly, Mary. 1978. *Gyn/Ecology*. Boston: Beacon Press.

———. 1987. *Webster's New Intergalactic Wickedary of the English Language*. Boston: Beacon Press.

Federici, Silvia. 2004. *Caliban and the Witch: Women, the Body and Primitive Accumulation*. New York: Autonomedia.

Frye, Marilyn. 1983. "In and Out of Harm's Way: Arrogance and Love." In *The Politics of Reality: Essays in Feminist Theory*, 52–83, Trumansburg, NY: The Crossing Press.

Hoagland, Sarah Lucia. 1988. *Lesbian Ethics: Toward New Value*. Chicago: Institute of Lesbian Studies.

———. 2010. "Colonial Practices/Colonial Identities: All the Women Are Still White." In *The Center Must Not Hold: White Women on the Whiteness of Philosophy*, edited by George Yancy, 227–44. Lanham, MD: Rowman & Littlefield.

Keating, AnaLouise. 2000. "Back to the Mother? Feminist Mythmaking with a Difference." In *Feminist Interpretations of Mary Daly*, edited by Sarah Lucia Hoagland and Marilyn Frye, 349–87. University Park, PA: The Pennsylvania State University Press.

Lorde, Audre. 1984. *Sister Outsider*. Trumansburg, NY: Crossing Press.

———. 1982. *Zami: A New Spelling of My Name*. Watertown, MA: Persephone Press.

Polkinhorn, Henry. 2005. *El Libro de Caló: The Dictionary of Chicano Slang*. Northridge, CA: Floricanto Press.

Shah, Sonia, ed. 1997. *Dragon Ladies: Asian American Feminists Breathe Fire*. Boston: South End Press.

Silliman, Jael, and Anannya Bhattacharjee, eds. 2002. *Policing the National Body: Race, Gender, and Criminalization*. Cambridge, MA: South End Press.

13 Carnal Disruptions

Mariana Ortega Interviews María Lugones

Mariana: Thank you for sharing your thoughts and experiences with me. I am deeply appreciative of your work as it provides key contributions to the development of Latina feminism as well as to philosophy in general. *Tanteando* and *tanteando*, you have found and made flexible yet robust structures and practices in your path—world-traveling, active subjectivity, dispersed intentionality, complex communication, deep coalition, decolonial feminism—leading the way to a space of multiple possibilities in which we can, as you quote Margarita Cota Cárdenas, "*abortar los mitos de un solo sentido.*" I ask the following questions so as to get to know you more and disclose more of you and your thought to the reader, a movement of you←→us.

In a recent presentation I heard you discuss how your mother was able to navigate a heteronormative environment and practice resistance within it. I was touched by how you understood the complexity of your mother's actions and went beyond what in your groundbreaking world-traveling essay you describe as an arrogant vision of her. How do you see your mother as resistant even within the constraining environment she occupied? Could you elaborate on the ways in which your mother practiced resistance even within heteropatriarchy?

María: I recovered from my arrogant perception of my mother through a cognitive shift that I could not have performed except for my loving her. My mother was always a painter. Since very young, she painted on the side of the wooden boxes in which the fruit for her parents' shop came. After primary school, she began high school in the Academia de Arte. My grandmother became sick, and she took my mother out of school because art was nothing in her own understanding. My mother became her mother's servant for many years. She made the clothes for everyone, embroidered tablecloths, pillowcases, dresses, and whatever else she was asked to embroider. She also cleaned the house, made her sisters' and mother's beds and, more generally, kept house for them. Her father was also her mother's servant, so they developed a relation of equality and transgression together. They would escape and go to the zoo, or the "*biógrafo*," the old term for theater. She painted every day till she died. In my mind that was my mother's most significant resistance to her situation, both as her mother's daughter and her sister's servant, and to my father's and our, her children's, assumption that she existed to meet our needs, desires, and whims. When I traveled to my mother's "world," I perceived her as a painter, a subject in her painting. It was by centering on my mother as an artist that I could follow her in her everyday resistance to what life placed in her path. I could understand her actions, her words, her gardening, as ways of resistance. My mother created beautiful and complicated flower paths. The flowers of one color would die, and the next color would show. The paths were half-a-block long, intricate, completely her own. She kept her own seeds. She painted with flowers and brushes.

Mariana: Art can help us travel to numerous worlds. It can indeed move a self to be otherwise than what she was meant to be. Art both sustains your mother as resistant and allows her, you, and us other possibilities of being. In addition to seeing resistance through your mother's engagement with art, with color and flowers, were there particular experiences in your early years that were pivotal in the development of philosophical visions that go "against the grain" and away from the "logic of purity"—how did you become an "impure subject"?

María: I learned to pay attention to the miniscule through sight. Looking for holes in the trees where a bird's chicks could be; watching the snakes swallow frogs; following the ants around. You don't see these beings living their lives without having patience and a honing of one's vision onto the ground or the trunk of trees. This visual attentiveness also became an attention to people's gestures, ways of walking, of interacting. Often I would have to shift my vision, because I had the feeling that I had been found watching. My sister invented the word "*bichar*" for looking into the neighbors from the roof of our parents' house in the barrio of Floresta—that is as high as I went watching the peopled world. I learned to read people. In a way, that is why my attention led to resistance. You cannot see resistance from afar. It requires a honing of the senses. I discovered that I was impure. I came to understand what aspects of people made them focus on others as a way of keeping or attaining a prized place among them. We were not comfortable going to the parties to which my father's position would take us. He was the most uncomfortable. The way people dressed, talked, moved their hands, and laughed was accompanied by a sense that they were superior people, that they were better than we were in ways undecipherable by me. Why would they be better when everything about them seemed forced to me, as if they were acting for others and hiding themselves? Ridiculous dresses that I was told were very expensive, risqué ways of talking, an air about them. I did not like, value, or want to become them. And yet, I could see how my mother and father were only valued because my father was brilliant and had attained posts at the university and in the biochemistry industry that were highly regarded. Yet, he, himself, was not respected, not in his ways of moving, talking, sneezing comfortably into his not immaculate handkerchief. We were all impure because we were not white; we came from the country, from poverty or, in my mom's case, from immigrant poverty, lack of education, lack of worldliness.

Mariana: In your own lived theoretico-practical-political pilgrimages described in your work, you walk toward a more embodied, tactile experience of coalition and resistance in such a way that we, your readers, can see the world-traveler's journey toward streetwalking theorizing. The last chapter of *Pilgrimages/Peregrinajes* calls for a cultivation of an "ear and a tongue for multiple lines of meaning." Without wishing to prioritize the visual as the key mode of understanding, could you elaborate on your view of the visual in so far as it connected to the coloniality of power? How do we also cultivate an *eye* for multiple lines of meanings or to what extent do you think the image in its various artistic presentations can disrupt and resist colonizing norms and the grip of modernity? If aesthesis is connected to decoloniality, how do we emancipate our very senses from the standards of beauty formed through the colonization of our very eyes, ears, and tongues? Is an emancipation of our senses a key for decoloniality? Would you comment on artists or works of art that you understand as pointing to or illustrating a decolonial vision?

María: Thinking about aesthesis, I think about the body and permeability and all that permeability allows us to reconceive about the world we live in. So, before going to the visual, I want to tell you how I have taken up "decolonial aesthesis," the decolonial deconstruction of aesthetics that privileges the senses.

Mycelia, fungi, constitute one third of the earth's living beings. They are the oldest living beings. They are more like animals than like plants. They are the mushrooms we eat, in all their enormous variety, the fungal spores that we breathe, the miles-long underground mushrooms that surround the roots of trees, enabling them to get the water they need through their roots and to communicate with other trees in large forests. Mycelia stay in constant molecular communication with their environment, achieving the greatest mass of any organism in the planet. They partner with plants. As spores, they travel and attach themselves to anything moving. Animals, including human beings, breathe them as microbiospora. They form a communicative tree system as they connect trees together. In my view, they are the most clear and astonishing example of the permeability of living things, and rocks, water, as they all carry and are made, in part, by mycelia—sometimes very old mycelia turn to stone. I choose mycelia to think about permeability, because they are not as socially normed as many other organic and inorganic living beings. They exhibit clearly the porosity of our habitat, not just their own permeability. Thus they exhibit the porosity of the habitat itself.

I have been thinking with some tenacity about how to do away with gender and its insidious intromission into all of our lives. The coloniality of gender has been an extremely successful way of harming the possibility of communality in every kind of relation. I am for coalition among women that backs the very possibility of exercising one's communal self.

I feel solitude [*soledad*] as a disintegration of my communality. Sensing, living, one's communal "I" as reduced, as a difficulty to imagine having a communal intention toward liberation, is a spring toward coalitional liberation. The communal self needs company.

I think about the colonized female body crossing into decolonial aesthesis, crossing from being isolated from everything in one's habitat, from one's world, through being "turned" into female animals by coloniality to being a self who is open to her habitat. The racialized female body becomes all sex and labor. Sex: open holes; those holes are her—no other fleshiness makes this body identifiable with her—body energy in her every muscle extracted brutally, moving as a terrorized animal puppet into betraying her aesthesis of connection. The body, in movement like a rigid violated puppet, produces pleasure and ample sustenance for the Man, a power machine closed to any world, without habitat. The Man, the white bourgeois man, tied to, addicted to, power. This body is penetrable but impermeable. It is an animal's body that can be raped without being raped, because it is not rapeable, a body that senses the rapist pleasuring himself in grunts, thrusts, and brutal movements on her flesh without her sensual collaboration. It is a body penetrated, assaulted, reduced, made to bleed and scream, not aroused, not giving, screaming rather than issuing sounds of pleasure, a property-thing forced to move in every form of pain, soul pain, body thing, impermeable, turned tool, weaving wool, washing the clothes of power, breaking fruit from plant without connection, working before dawn till dusk, unceasingly accumulating value for those who make a being without connection.

Thus, she is made to think herself woman, *mujer*, femme, vrouw, or not, always penetrable. No tender, permeable, responsive moving with water, earth, mycelia, trees, seeds, embodied selves—people. She knows that; she senses, touches, feels, recognizes her slow disintegration as she pushes against the white man's bestiality and insatiable greed. We can talk a lot more about the coloniality of embodied female aesthesis. We have; we have talked over and over and over, just to be gagged.

Imagine her, sense her, feel her from the inside, inhabit her in her habitat, be in her connection, sense her as porous, permeable, deeply inside the world connection. No thing, no object here. Every aesthesis is from within a permeable connection. How can she/he live? How can she-he-everything live in the midst of violence? She awakes in her embodied self a double feeling/consciousness of the permeable body, and then to discover, explore, appreciate, engage her permeable body in reciprocity, in an unstable, dynamic balancing.

Permeability is necessarily reciprocal. But it is not just about eroticism and certainly not just about sex (eroticism reduced) but about all *estando en el mundo*. Solitude of having been reduced as a communal self. One always looks for company to feed it, to imagine what can only be imagined when one's communal "I" is healthy.

Thinking of aesthesis brings me back to my disorientation in my childhood with respect to cause and effect and to my paying so much attention to smallness. Also my mother's painted faces, landscapes, particular trees like the *ombú*, are my orientations into visuality, a kind of tact, touching with the eye, in my imagination. I cannot "see" images with my mind's eye. I don't know how it works, what you can see, but I cannot do it. I wish I could remember my brother and mother that way, but I can't. So, I look at pictures. In our place, there was a beautiful, enormous wisteria. When it was in bloom the purple-lilac bunches of flowers hung from a very long trellis. My father said to my mother that the wisteria was going to have to be cut down because the roots were breaking up the patio floor. That night my mother had a dream, and she painted it. Men in suits and overalls are trying to cut the tree. The wisteria defends itself with her branches taking up the men and throwing them in a very large hole. A dark woman with long black hair and fire coming from within her witnesses the plant's resistance. In my mother's painting, I felt the violence in the intention to cut it down.

I have recently discussed a Cuban cinematographer with my student Patrick Crowley, who is writing a dissertation on the Caribbean, focusing on decolonial poetry, theater, and cinema. He is teaching me how to see the cinema, and we have been thinking about what collectivity means in the work of Cuban cinematographer Gloria Rolando. We talked about *Voces para un silencio* and *My Footsteps in Baragua*, as a beginning. He is thinking about collectivity in the work. Rolando says "we would like to be a part of or recreate or to catch the image of the people who don't have a voice for themselves." I said to him that the collectivity is in the maker of poetry, film, theater, painting, and philosophy when it is decolonial. That is my own view. Sometimes the communal is in the present in continuity with the past in a challenge to coloniality; sometimes the communal is the communal doings, beings, imaginings which themselves are tied to the past in ways that are neither linear nor obvious. *Red Roots* by Celia Herrera Rodriguez, *State of Grace: Angels for the Living/Prayers for the Dead* by Kathy Vargas, *Trinity* by Santa Contreras Barraza and the work of Ester Hernández, Carmen Lomas Garza, and Yolanda López. These artists are all Chicanas. Diane Gamboa captures the collectivity but from within. Laura Pérez quotes her as saying "I take on the 'urban warrior' mode when I am on the streets of Los Angeles." In her work, the body is taken from within the collectivity that denies carnal desire, androgyny, sexual excess as deviancy. Contestation is crucial to the community one takes up from the inside. African American and Afro-Latina artists that I think have community inside are Corey Barksdale, Dalida María Benfield, Kara Walker, and Diane Britton Dunham, to name a few. Patricia Hill Collins and Elsa Barkley Brown are African American thinkers who think about the tie between community and freedom, a freedom that is not negative. It is rather about creating, maintaining, being in community. Community, means both actual people together in the flesh, but also those African Americans who have made the ground they walk on, and people in the diaspora. Bernice Johnson Reagon, a historian of Black music, long-time activist, and founder and lead singer of Sweet Honey in the Rock, the a cappella Black women group that has made communal political music, says that Blacks did not have a territory of their own—so culture was their communal territory.

Mariana: I am moved by this intertwining of porosity, permeability, and connection that allows for seeing with all our senses in the midst of a shared world, a world, as you would say, that is long and wide, just as your selves are. I hear you naming a connectedness that is always *a flor de piel*, even when it is deep within the earth. And I think of your important account of coalition, which I consider to be one of the most important contributions on the topic. You are one of the few thinkers that provides what I think is an expanded notion of coalition that is attuned not just to difference but to the difference within difference. You urge us to understand that limens are spaces that those in conditions of marginalization come to occupy from different journeys. To what extent do you think that women of color are engaging in deep coalition, especially at a time in which we have been witness to multiple incidents of brutality and violence against Black men and women, Latinos/as, and other populations of color, but the media highlights the murders of Black men? What obstacles, whether theoretical or practical, do you think currently stand on the way for deep coalitions among U.S. women of color?

María: I would like to begin by saying more about how I understand coalition in relation to coloniality/decoloniality, rather than beginning with the question on the presence of deep coalitions in our present landscape. I have moved from Women of Color feminisms to decolonial feminisms, without losing the thread that ties them together, attempting to keep the substance of Women of Color feminisms and to find my own voice as a decolonial feminist. Many women have adopted both the term *decolonial* as well as what I call "decolonial feminism." I have, of course, been aware of Emma Perez's usage of *decolonial*, which is different from Chela Sandoval's usage, and both their notions of *decolonial* are different from mine. The difference between our uses of *decolonial* is important, because we need to figure how our meanings connect or whether there are discrepancies that we need to address. When I wrote *Pilgrimages*, I did not have a theory of race. I thought about the racial state and understood "racial formation" in Omi and Winant's terms. *Oppression* was the main term for me, and the one I theorized. I came to a theoretical understanding of race that was clear, persuasive, historicized, comprising a matrix of domination that was multifaceted in Aníbal Quijano's "the coloniality of power." What I mean by *decolonial feminism* is tied to what I came to call "the coloniality of gender," which follows Quijano up to the point where our understandings of sex and gender differ. Both of us understand gender as inseparable from race, but I do not think of gender/sex as subsumable to race. I also think that both sex and gender are socially, historically constructed in ways that give rise to "gender systems" rather than to the ahistoricity of patriarchy. I use *gender systems* to name oppressive constructions of women, and sometimes men. *Gender*, as I understand contemporary usage is the name for an oppressed woman in relation to men. This I understand as a problematic usage. When reporters show gender trends in voting, buying, and so on, *gender* does not have the meaning that it has when *gender* is used to name women as oppressed. Women are oppressed in relation to men. Women are inferior and men are superior. This is also simplistic and in much need of critique. Women of color have presented the critique.

It is in the complexities of the possibilities of decoloniality that I think of coalition, because I think the decolonial task of rejecting every bit of modern cosmology, economics, aesthetics, and so on is a task racially oppressed peoples exercise with interestingly different strategies. I think that in many cases Quijano's and Mignolo's word *de-linking* names an important practice of response to and from the oppressive constitution that requires inferiority and which attacks the intimacy of struggle through language, film, symbols, et cetera. I continue to think of the tie between coalition and complex communication, searching for a deep sense of coalition. I also think of people as in historical and cotemporaneous intricate relations, so that no person makes sense alone without history, particularly without a history of relations that takes oppressions into account, including racial and sexual oppression. Human selves are, in this sense, long and wide. A recognition of this complex, relational character of human beings is erased by capitalist, colonial, modernity. Unveiling, unravelling, disentangling, and honoring the complexities of this relationality becomes central to complex communication and to coalitional possibilities. From this position, we can think of communicative utterances as moving through the communicative landscape in a way that makes them incomplete. The incompleteness makes communication uncertain, but open to other responses, other meanings that take up the utterance in another of the meanings that the speaker may or may not intend, for example, emotive meanings, that are not captured in other responses. The uncertainty makes us unwilling to close the communicative circle.

Thinking about coalition with the coloniality of gender in mind gives me a larger understanding of oppression. I have focused on Abya Yala, the name that the Kunas of Panama have given us to replace the colonial "America," including native and Afro populations. I do not think of the United States as outside the possibility of coalition with Afro-Colombians, Afro-Caribbean, Afro-Bolivians, or with the indigenous and mestizo/a population. I emphasize deep coalition because modernity has led to a closing of circles of resistant meaning within fragmentation. This closing is harder to overcome in the United States, though we have seen Mexicanas/os, Blacks, Chicanas/os, Asians march together against the treatment of transnational labor coming to the United States from Mexico, El Salvador, Guatemala, and beyond. But there is not a constant communal impulse to learn from each other and form deeper and more enduring coalitions. Many women of color have theorized and promoted deep coalitions, including Patricia Hill Collins, Chela Sandoval, Audre Lorde,

Bernice Johnson Reagon, and Gloria Anzaldúa. A transversality of relation that searches for the historicity of cotemporaneous socialities is part of what they understand as Women of Color feminisms. What blocks deep coalition, then, becomes clearer: at the level of activism and organizing, men and women of color with a history of coloniality of gender are focused inward, in the remaking of communities against the ravages of imbricated systems of oppression. This blocks the relationality of selves under oppression and, thus, transversality is very difficult to follow. The permeability of the community is hard to see as a source of coalition. It is perceived as a source of danger. There are examples that show that sometimes permeability is activated as in the huge marches all over the country on behalf of those who cross the border as transnational workers.

Mariana: Your 2014 *Hypatia* essay "Reading the Nondiasporic from within Diasporas" is a short meditation about the decolonial move in your pilgrimages, with your turn to decolonial feminism that includes a "shift from US women of color to colonized and enslaved women." Here I see you *rompiendo* "*espejos que nos muestran rotas, despedazadas,*" shattering cracked mirrors that show you and others as fragmented beings. Could you first tell what is your understanding of diasporic and nondiasporic subjects in the United States? What is the status of U.S. Latinas within these categories? How are nondiasporic subjects chopped into many people within a white or Eurocentered paradigm?

María: Many Latinas in the United States immigrated from countries in severe political turmoil without a community to call their own, sometimes without any contacts. You are one of them, so am I, so is Breni Mendoza, and many others. I think of us as nondiasporic precisely because we do not constitute a diaspora and because there is no diaspora in the United States from the societies we come from. In that piece I pursue the difference that makes for those of us who are intellectuals, particularly for those of us who think and write about questions of women and race. Whether or not the U.S. government was instrumental in the violence in "our" countries, the United States has a long history of fragmentation of groups immigrating into the U.S. that will not be processed into whiteness. Not that we wanted to or took steps toward whiteness. Rather, we found ourselves in a society that defined us racially. Groups marked as nonwhite bear animosity to each other as one more of the violences from the oppressing white society—its laws, the *migra*, the police, organized white supremacist groups, lack of jobs, severe exploitation in the worst jobs in the country, inadequate housing, lack of access to education, attempts at erasure of memory, and many other facets of the U.S. racial state, with whiteness and European ways of being and citizenship all being at its core. The groups of which I am thinking, Native American nations, African Americans, Mexicans/Chicanas-os, and Asians, have turned inward in resistance to violence and formed communities with understandings of themselves that not only defy, but are also from a different cloth than the matrix imposed on them. The inward turn is conceived as diasporic in some cases and not in others, but none of those peoples are nondiasporic. Their histories of resistance, creativity, survival, community building, keeping and recovering of memory, creation of new knowledges, and ways of being that are continuous with their past, leave the nondiasporic Latinas out. Our voices are here and there in their creations, but we are not part of their histories, neither as people, intellectuals, or activists. This has been as it should be, but maybe a time for coalition is coming and then we can enter a history not merely of defiance and challenge, but also one of interweavings of creations born of resistance. In our case, this means an unbearable solitude as workers in a nonculture of creative resistance to the coloniality of gender.

I think your Latina Roundtable (Latina/x Feminisms Roundtable-formerly the Roundtable on Latina Feminism) conference is important in getting some of the nondiasporic racialized Latinas together, though you do not restrict it that way.

Mariana: In this meditation on the nondiasporic and the diasporic, I also see you lifting the obsidian mirror to look at your face, the face of a subject. It is this mirror that connects you to your ancestors, to those who have been racialized and to communities indigenous to the Americas. As you point out, "I share with many diasporic U.S. subjects the formation of ourselves as racialized during the first modernity that initiated the modern colonial capitalist system of world power." Quijano teaches us that colonization, modernization, and capitalism work to create a structuring of labor based on race understood as a natural kind. It is within this history of racialization that you find continuity with diasporic subjects. Could you comment on how this continuity can be understood vis-à-vis your view on ontological pluralism or a more general account of pluriversality?

María: The obsidian mirror is an important image I use only with respect to Chicanas and Mesoamericans. Symbols also close circles. The obsidian mirror shows multiplicity while the Andean mirror shows symmetry in opposition. This opposition does not create superiority and inferiority. I know that I cannot search for my ancestors looking into the obsidian mirror as I am not

Mesoamerican or a Chicana shaman. I see my face as devoid of knowledge of my ancestry.

I am racialized emphatically in the United States. Indigenous people in Latin America call each other by their peoples' names. No one in the Andean region said that they were my ancestors, that I was Quechua or Aymara. I did not see my face in them either. In the Patagonia, on the other hand, people include me as Mapuche. Does that make me feel good? It does in a tender, deep way, that goes some way to heal the absence of knowledge about my indigenous ancestors. One woman that people call "*abuela*" said to me: "*Hermana*, why did you go so far away from us? You are Mapuche, maybe also Tehuelche, because you are so tall."

That I am racialized as less is also what motivates me to get that shit off my back. I think that racialization and resistance to racialization provoke a doubling that makes for plural realities. It is this that I share with other racialized people, even those who go through a kind of death in assimilation. It does have a relation to pluralism; I inhabit a doubled reality. The doubling becomes a plurality as we understand our interrelationality as racialized people. Pluriversality is important here as an entanglement of meaning, of cosmologies, of relation.

Mariana: Given that this continuity with diasporic subjects is key to the non-diasporic subjects' coalitional projects, how do you see the reception of your work within Chicana feminism? And more generally, how do you see the relationship between Latina feminism and Chicana feminism?

María: I have done popular education for thirty years among Chicanas/os, Hispanas/os, Latinas/os, including Afro-Latinas/os. This is political work at the grassroots. You begin where people are, and more often than not, people show a direction which you consider and try to see the resistance to and the assimilation into colonization. I have done this work in many places, but my base is in Valdez, New Mexico. There we bought a one-acre piece of land with the hope of one day having a big building where people can come and sleep and a big room for the meetings. The Highlander Folk School is like that. I visit with people and we talk about health issues, land and water issues, the kids, English only. I have come to know the people in Valdez and the surrounding area well. My relation to Chicanas/os, Hispanas/os in New Mexico enabled me to critique my easygoing feminist position. I dropped it. I began rethinking the self and the world as unitary. I wasn't from Valdez, though Valdeños called me "*raza*," and "Mexicana" as in "You don't know how to make tortillas? What kind of

Mexican are you?" People made fun of my English and were respectful of my Spanish. Once, as I was explaining some idea from the EPA (Environmental Protection Agency) in the *Escuelita*, I said "sheet-something." They had me repeat the "sheet" part over and over in great fun. I participated, of course.

I have also done popular education in Chicago. Young people, gay people, Latinas working against violence against women have come to New Mexico for one week of popular education workshops. But it has been the people of Valdez that I think of as my extended fictive kin, even though I know I cannot cross the line and think that I am of the community. I have been with them for thirty years. I do not count the years of sickness. I think people call me *"raza"* because I am *mestiza* and speak Spanish, Spanglish, and New Mexican Spanish. I think it is right that I cannot be of them, belong in the long way of having been overrun by the border in 1848. Though I know we share a colonization in the sixteenth century, so the first colonization that marked us with the coloniality of power is something we share and so *raza* feels like the right "turned around" term that includes me. I am well there. I like talking with people about what matters in a political way that is not pushy. People get tired of me bringing up the politics, but I am OK with that and they are OK with me. When we are in a conflict with government agencies, people like my ability to argue down the opposition and they like that their kids have grown into men and women who have shared in a local history of struggle. I have spent a lot of time with them politically since they were very young.

Chicana feminism is another matter altogether. When I meet Chicana feminism, I meet intellectuals and activists. Many Chicana feminists are both. I carry their words with me deeply in my person and, with some Chicanas, I feel reciprocation and love which I reciprocate. I cannot be Chicana, of course. Do I want to? That is not a sensical question. I miss not having a community in struggle to which I belong, but I think radical nondiasporic Latinas have an important political place in understanding the boundaries of communities and speak to the desirability of keeping them open horizontally. I cannot be a part of the history of Chicana feminism either, but I work for a coalition that has room for isolated racialized non-Eurocentered women. Most important is that we can hear each other, learn each other through each other's words.

Thank you María for your words of flesh and bone.

Afterword

Paula M. L. Moya

I never set out to become a Lugonesian. I have always been suspicious of academics who, by way of claiming their scholarly *bona fides*, announce their intellectual affiliations by identifying as a "Foucauldian" or a "Derridean"—or even by announcing that they are taking a "Freudian" approach to this or that text, this or that problem. I wondered at their theoretical monologism, and even more at how they might see themselves as intellectuals in relation to their chosen intellectual guru—particularly since those intellectuals were usually deceased and had developed their insights in other times and other places, with a disparate set of concerns. And because early in my career I developed an approach to literary texts in relation to which I claimed affiliation with a group of scholars who take a "post-positivist realist" approach to identity and experience, I was not looking for a theoretical home. For all these reasons, it took me some time to fully appreciate how deeply María Lugones's work has shaped my thinking.

I still will not call myself a Lugonesian—both because I retain my post-positivist realist theoretical commitments and affiliations, and also because I dislike critical moves that hail any great thinker as if she had been born fully formed and armed from the belly of *Coatlicue*.[1] Great thinkers always develop their ideas and practices in company with others; individuals might discover the most compelling way to convey a generative principle or a system of thought, but they are never the sole authors of their insights.[2] But despite the fact that I will not identify myself with an eponymous adjective, I cannot deny that Lugones—or, more accurately, the intellectual presence I have construed from reading and rereading her scholarship and from hearing her give numerous presentations—walks with me everywhere I go. María Lugones's influence on me has been profound. Certainly, my students will testify to the frequency with which I urge them to consult one or another essay from *Pilgrimages*/Peregrinajes so that they might incorporate one or more of her key concepts into their own scholarship. My advice in such cases has proven to be productive—my students read her work, incorporate her insights, and their work is much stronger as a result.

It gives me sincere pleasure, then, to celebrate the publication of this excellently conceived and brilliantly executed collection of original essays. In bringing together essays that engage deeply with Lugones as a thinker, teacher, and mentor, Pedro DiPietro, Jennifer McWeeny, and Shireen Roshanravan have compiled a groundbreaking volume. They have assembled an eminent group of scholars—several of whom have longstanding engagements with the strains of thinking and activism that animate Lugones's scholarship—and have provided a scholarly apparatus that will be of enormous help to Lugones scholars, such as the chronologically organized bibliography of her writings and a helpful standardization of abbreviations. But their jointly written introduction and their individual contributions arguably make an even greater impact. In the intricately braided narrative that opens their introduction, DiPietro, McWeeny, and Roshanravan testify eloquently to the profound effect that Lugones has had on each of their lives. They describe her loving and demanding mentorship and tell how she provided them with recognition and the experience of having been faithfully witnessed. They depict her as a model of intellectual bravery and resistance whose transformative scholarship stands on the precipice of social change. They narrate the way her affirmation and encouragement call forth their best selves to forge loving and complex connections with their near others. And they speak of the relief her wisdom brings to them as they learn from her how to faithfully witness their families of origin that still, sometimes, do not fully accept them in their complexity and fullness. Understanding that María Lugones and her scholarship are for these young scholars "like an earthquake to the soul," I genuinely appreciate the care they have taken to compile a book that could "entice others to encounter her thinking, enter into it, and be touched by it" (2).

The volume includes a wide-ranging interview with Lugones by the philosopher Mariana Ortega, herself a leader in the field of Latina feminist theory. It touches on how and why Lugones developed her astute visual attentiveness (important for reading people and perceiving resistance), and touches on Lugones's work on the coloniality of gender. But before the interview, we encounter a diversity of scholarly essays that provide context for the development of her thinking, and that extend her insights into new domains.

Essays that provide context for Lugones's intellectual and personal development include pieces by long-time collaborators Elizabeth Spelman, Sarah Hoagland, and Cricket Keating. Because they trace Lugones's evolution as a thinker, these essays are a valuable resource for newcomers and long-time scholars alike. In chapter 1, "Trash Talks Back," Elizabeth Spelman examines one of Lugones's key terms—*oppression*—in relation to the trope of trash. In so doing, she gives the concept of "oppression" further depth, texture, and sensuousness. Sarah Hoagland's friendship with Lugones dating back to the 1980s when they were both involved in the Society for Women in Philosophy (SWIP) informs "Walking Illegitimately: A *Cachapera/Tortillera* and a Dyke" (chapter 12). By reflecting on how Lugones's philosophical moves affected her own, and by filling in details of the environments from which essays familiar to Lugones's long-time readers emerged, Hoagland pulls back the curtain and makes visible the conditions of possibility for Lugones's system of thought. Explaining that her notion of "agency under oppression" was modified by Lugones into "active subjectivity," Hoagland demonstrates how intellectual engagement can resemble a *pas de deux*, a salsa, a two-step, or (even better) a tango of two thinkers who care deeply about the words and the images they choose to convey the depth, intricacy, and complexity of their embodied ideas. Cricket Keating's contribution, "Deep Coalition and Popular Education Praxis" (chapter 11), operates similarly to contextualize the building up and shaping of Lugones's multilayered intellectual praxis. As a participant in the *Escuela Popular Norteña* (EPN), Keating is admirably positioned to illuminate the notion of deep coalition—the type of activist connection that goes "beyond short-term interest-based alliances" and that challenges us "to align our own self-understandings, interests, and goals with other oppressed groups" (239). Through a description of the different workshops conducted by the EPN over time—workshops inspired by the radical pedagogy of Paulo Freire and the organizing strategies of Myles Horton—Keating gives specificity to Lugones's pedagogical practices.

The other type of essay in the volume carries Lugones's insights into new terrains, effectively testing their viability and range. A good example is Jennifer McWeeny's "Motion Sickness and the Slipperiness of Irish Racialization" (chapter 7). McWeeny provides an historically informed account of a psychological affliction tied to colonization and its aftermath across multiple generations. She movingly describes the "postcolonial stress disorder" that can arise among those whose racialization is easily hidden, and elucidates why people who inherit a sense of racialized shame and inferiority (but whose visage enables them to "pass") might seek out that escape. As long as negative racial associations live on in the world—either in an individual's psyche or in the ideas that others have about that individual's racial group membership—the shame will never simply disappear. By extending Lugones's work into a consideration of Irish racialization, McWeeny provides a superb illustration of Audre Lorde's lesson that the only way out is through. In "Witnessing Faithfully and the Intimate Politics of Queer South Asian Praxis" (chapter 5), Shireen Roshanravan explores her own struggles with her mother's dismay at her queerness to explicate key elements of Lugones's notion of deep coalition. Roshanravan explains that most South Asian worldviews are shaped by a collective ethos such that "individuals are understood as interdependent in the collectivist mission of familial and communal wellbeing" (115), but reminds us that differently positioned people have differential access to diverse worlds of resistant sense-making. Roshanravan then notes that the angst experienced variously by the gay child and the disappointed parent often stems from a shared fear—the very real fear of losing the self-in-community. Emphasizing the importance of "being there" for one another, Roshanravan argues convincingly for the efficacy of approaching resistant family members with the goal of "witnessing faithfully" rather than "seeking acceptance." By exemplifying the activity of "learning to read resistance across worlds of sense," Roshanravan sheds light on the subtlety, complexity, and lovingness of Lugones's commitment to building deep coalitions.

In chapter 9, "Beyond Benevolent Violence: Trans* of Color, Ornamental Multiculturalism, and the Decolonization of Affect," Pedro DiPietro discusses the damages that accrue to people from nondominant cultures when they encounter the well-meaning but ignorant empathy offered to them by dominant-culture people who do not recognize the existence of ontological plurality. Building on work by Joshua Price and Lugones on structural monoculturalism and ornamental multiculturalism, DiPietro narrates two case studies—one involving Indian *hijras* and the other a Muslim trans man. In a sensitively wrought analysis that attends to the synecdochal relations that always structure interactions between people who do not know each other well, DiPietro shows how structural monoculturalism often leads to a "benevolent violence." Other similarly perceptive chapters also push the boundaries of Lugones's theoretical reach. Madina Tlostanova's chapter regarding the second-order colonialism of the Asiatic part of Russia confirms that even when we talk about a lighter and a darker side of modernity, configurations of coloniality never break down into uncomplicated binaries (chapter 6). Finally, Manuel Chávez, Jr.'s chapter on decolonial ethics examines Lugones's contributions to rethinking what it means to transform dominant masculinities among straight-identified Chicano men (chapter 8). Chávez builds on Lugones's core elements in the coloniality of gender, underscoring that nonrelational understandings of the colonial condition within Chicana/o communities tend to erase the multiplicities of worlds and plural selves where what might look like resistant masculinities might be in allegiance with colonial patterns of violence against Chicanas.

I first met María Lugones in October 1995 at a conference at Cornell University that I co-organized with the writer Helena María Viramontes. I was a fifth-year graduate student in the Department of English, and Lugones was one of the keynote speakers.[3] She made a strong impression on me then, and I have followed her peregrinations ever since—through her writings and occasionally in company with her through friends or at conferences. I have absorbed her teachings, occasionally debated her observations, and my thinking advanced exponentially after I reviewed her book *Pilgrimages*/Peregrinajes.[4] Along the way, I have watched brilliant young scholars build on her work as they develop a corpus of decolonial scholarship.[5] The essays in this book prove that Lugones's influence spreads wide; the book itself will ensure that she is recognized for the major thinker and teacher that she is. And so, if I *were* inclined to identify myself with an eponymous adjective, I might well call myself a Lugonesian.

NOTES

1. The reference is to the myth of the birth of the Aztec god of war, Huitzilopochtli. The events related in the story inaugurated Aztec warrior society and affirmed an ideology of male dominance in Tenochtitlán even prior to the arrival of the Spaniards. The story begins with Coatlicue doing penance at Coatepec. As she sweeps the temple, a ball of feathers appears and falls on or touches her. Coatlicue tucks it into her bosom for safekeeping and goes on with her task. When she is finished, she looks for the ball of feathers. But it has disappeared, and she is pregnant. When Coatlicue's daughter, Coyolxauhqui, and her sons, the Centzonuitznaua, find out about this unexpected and shameful pregnancy, they become infuriated and decide to kill their mother. The infant in her womb, who is Huitzilopochtli, hears the commotion, and calls out to his mother that he will protect her. At this point, everyone stops and girds for battle. Then, at the decisive moment, Huitzilopochtli is born and appears fully armed with the fire serpent Xiuhcoatl, with which he strikes his sister: "Then he pierced Coyolxauhqui, and then quickly struck off her head. It stopped there at the edge of Coatepetl. And her body came falling below; it fell breaking to pieces; in various places her arms, her legs, her body each fell" (de Sahagún 4). After Coyolxauhqui's defeat and dismemberment, Huitzilopochtli pursues the Centzonuitznaua until they flee into the southern sky and he remains victorious.

2. Even the great naturalist Charles Darwin rushed to publish his world-shaking book *On the Origin of Species* before Alfred Russel Wallace, with whom Darwin was in communication, could lay claim to what turned out to be a similar theory of evolution.

3. The conference was "El Frente: U.S. Latinas Under Attack and Fighting Back." Lugones was one of six invited keynote speakers alongside philosopher Linda Martín Alcoff, filmmaker Ana María García, playwright and essayist Cherríe Moraga, Yvonne Yarbro Bejarano, and performance artist Ela Troyano.

4. Editors' note: Dr. Moya refers to her review of *Pilgrimages/*Peregrinajes (2006).

5. I have been privileged to teach several of these. In his most recent work, Ernesto Martínez witnesses faithfully his childhood traumas to explore the (de)formation of his sexual subjectivity; Alisa Bierria builds on the concept of active subjectivity to propose a theoretical framework that can account for the problem of racial conflation in the ascribing of "phantom intentions" to Black women's strategic actions; and (although her dissertation is still in progress) Modern Thought and Literature PhD student Luz Jimenez Ruvalcaba is developing herself as a faithful witness to the problem of domestic violence as an outcome of structural violence as represented in the work of 20th- and 21st-century Latinx writers.

REFERENCES

Bierria, Alisa. 2018. *Missing in Action: Agency, Race, & Recognition*. PhD diss., Stanford University.

———. 2014. "Missing in Action: Violence, Power, and Discerning Agency." *Hypatia* 29(1): 129–145.

de Sahagún, Bernardino, Arthur J. Anderson, and Charles E. Dibble. 1982. *Florentine Codex, A General History of the Things of New Spain. Book 3—The Origin of the Gods*. Salt Lake City: University of Utah Press.

Martínez, Ernesto J. 2014. "¿Con Quién, Dónde, y Por Qué Te Dejas?" *Aztlán: A Journal of Chicano Studies* 39(1): 237–46.

———. 2013. *On Making Sense: Queer Race Narratives of Intelligibility*. Stanford, CA: Stanford University Press.

Moya, Paula M. L. 2006. "Review of *Pilgrimages/*Peregrinajes: *Theorizing Coalition Against Multiple Oppressions*." *Hypatia* 21(3): 198–202.

María Lugones
A Chronology

1983

"Have We Got a Theory for You! Feminist Theory, Cultural Imperialism, and the Demand for the 'Women's Voice,'" co-written with Elizabeth V. Spelman. *Women's Studies International Forum* 6: 573–81.
  Reprinted in *Women and Values: Readings in Recent Feminist Philosophy*, edited by Marilyn Pearsall, 19–32. Belmont, CA: Wadsworth, 1998.
  Reprinted in *Feminist Theory: A Reader*, edited by Wendy Kolmar and Frances Bartkowski, 17–29. Columbus, OH: McGraw-Hill, 1999.
  Reprinted in *Philosophy and Gender*, Vol. 1, edited by Cressida Heyes, 165–80. New York: Routledge, 2012.

1984

"Racism and Pedagogy." *Breaking Ground* 6: 38–43.

1987

"Competition, Compassion, and Community: Models for a Feminist Ethos," co-written with Elizabeth V. Spelman. In *Competition: A Feminist Taboo?*, edited by Valerie Miner and Helen Longino, 234–47. New York: Feminist Press.
"Playfulness, 'World'-Traveling, and Loving Perception." *Hypatia* 2(2): 3–19.
  Reprinted in *Women, Knowledge, and Reality: Explorations in Feminist Philosophy*, edited by Ann Garry and Marilyn Pearsall, 419–34. Boston: Unwin Hyman, 1989.
  Reprinted in *Pilgrimages/Peregrinajes: Theorizing Coalition against Multiple Oppressions*, 77–101. Lanham, MD: Rowman & Littlefield, 2003.
  Reprinted in *The Feminist Philosophy Reader*, edited by Alison Bailey and Chris Cuomo, 69–80. Columbus, OH: McGraw Hill, 2008.
  Reprinted in *Philosophy and Gender*, Vol. 3, edited by Cressida Heyes, 179–92. New York: Routledge, 2012.

Translated as "Attitude joueuse, voyage d'un "monde" à d'autres et perception aimante." In *Théories féministes et queers décoloniales: interventions chicanas et latinas états-uniennes*, edited by Paola Bacchetta, Jules Falquet, and Norma Alarcón, 117–39. Paris: Cahiers de CEDREF. 2012.

1990

Common Reading Presentations: On Hunger of Memory by Richard Rodriguez. Carleton College New Student Convocation. Northfield: Carleton College.

"*Hablando Cara a Cara*/Speaking Face to Face: An Exploration of Ethnocentric Racism." In *Making Face, Making Soul*/Haciendo Caras: *Creative and Critical Perspectives by Feminists of Color*, edited by Gloria Anzaldúa, 46–54. San Francisco, CA: Aunt Lute Books.
Reprinted in *Pilgrimages*/Peregrinajes: *Theorizing Coalition against Multiple Oppressions*, 41–51. Lanham, MD: Rowman & Littlefield, 2003.

"Hispaneando y Lesbiando: On Sarah Hoagland's Lesbian Ethics." *Hypatia* 5(3): 138–46.

"Structure/Anti-structure and Agency under Oppression." *Journal of Philosophy* 87(10): 500–7.
Reprinted in *Pilgrimages*/Peregrinajes: *Theorizing Coalition against Multiple Oppressions*, 53–63. Lanham, MD: Rowman & Littlefield, 2003.

1991

"On the Logic of Pluralist Feminism." In *Feminist Ethics*, edited by Claudia Card, 35–44. Lawrence: University Press of Kansas.
Reprinted in *Pilgrimages*/Peregrinajes: *Theorizing Coalition against Multiple Oppressions*, 65–75. Lanham, MD: Rowman & Littlefield, 2003.

1992

"On Borderlands/*La Frontera*: An Interpretive Essay." *Hypatia* 7(4): 31–37.
Reprinted in *Adventures in Lesbian Philosophy*, edited by Claudia Card, 27–33. Bloomington: Indiana University Press, 1994.

"Sisterhood and Friendship as Feminist Models," co-written with Pat Alake Rosezelle. In *The Knowledge Explosion*, edited by Cheris Kramarae and Dale Spender, 406–8. New York: Teachers College Press.

1994

"Purity, Impurity, and Separation." *Signs* 19(2): 458–79.
    Reprinted in *The Feminist Philosophy Reader*, edited by Alison Bailey and Chris Cuomo, 329–44. Columbus, OH: McGraw Hill, 2008.
    Reprinted in *Pilgrimages*/Peregrinajes: *Theorizing Coalition against Multiple Oppressions*, 121–48. Lanham, MD: Rowman & Littlefield, 2003.
    Reprinted in *The Second Signs Reader: Feminist Scholarship, 1983–1996*, edited by Ruth-Ellen B. Joeres and Barbara Laslett, 275–96. Chicago: University of Chicago Press, 1996.
    Translated as "Pureza, Impureza, y Separación." In *Feminismos Literarios*, edited by Neus Carbonell and Meri Torras. Translated by Marta Marín Domine, 235–64. Madrid: Arco, 1999.

1995

"Dominant Culture: *El Deseo por un Alma Pobre* (The Desire for an Impoverished Soul)," co-written with Joshua M. Price. In *Multiculturalism from the Margins*, edited by Dean A. Harris, 103–27. Westport, CT: Bergin & Garvey.

"Hard-to-Handle Anger." In *Overcoming Racism and Sexism*, edited by Linda Bell and David Blumenfeld, 203–17. Lanham, MD: Rowman & Littlefield.
    Reprinted in *Pilgrimages*/Peregrinajes: *Theorizing Coalition against Multiple Oppressions*, 103–18. Lanham, MD: Rowman & Littlefield, 2003.

"Multicultural Cognition." *Phoebe: A Journal of Feminist Theory and Aesthetics* 7(1–2): 23–36.

1997

"Motion, Stasis, and Resistance to Interlocked Oppressions." In *Making Worlds: Gender, Metaphor, Materiality*, edited by Susan Hardy Aiken and Ann E. Brigham, 49–52. Tucson: The University of Arizona Press.

1998

"Community." In *Blackwell Companion to Feminist Philosophy*, edited by Alison Jaggar and Iris Marion Young, 466–74. Malden, MA: Blackwell Publishers.

"*El Pasar Discontinuo de la Cachapera/Tortillera del Barrio a la Barra al Movimiento*/The Discontinuous Passing of the Cachapera/Tortillera from the Barrio to the Bar to the Movement." In *Daring to Be Good: Feminist Essays in Ethico-Politics*, edited by Bat Ami Bar-On and Ann Ferguson, 156–66. New York: Routledge.
    Reprinted in *Pilgrimages*/Peregrinajes*: Theorizing Coalition against Multiple Oppressions*, 167–80. Lanham, MD: Rowman & Littlefield, 2003.

1999

"Tenuous Connections in Impure Communities." *Ethics and the Environment* 4(1): 85–90.

"Towards a Practice of Radical Engagement: EPN's 'Politicizing the Everyday' Workshop," co-written with Mildred Beltré. *Radical Teacher* 56: 13–18.

2000

"Multiculturalism and Publicity." *Hypatia* 15(3): 175–81.

"Wicked Caló: A Matter of Authority of Improper Words." In *Feminist Interpretations of Mary Daly*, edited by Sarah Lucia Hoagland and Marilyn Frye, 246–64. University Park: Pennsylvania State University Press.

2002

"Impure Communities." In *Diversity and Community: An Interdisciplinary Reader*, edited by Philip Anderson, 58–64. Malden, MA: Blackwell.

2003

"The Inseparability of Race, Class, and Gender: Response to Antonia Darder and Rodolfo D. Torres," co-written with Joshua M. Price. *Latino Studies Journal* 1(2): 329–32.

Pilgrimages/Peregrinajes*: Theorizing Coalition against Multiple Oppressions*. Lanham, MD: Rowman & Littlefield.

"Problems of Translation in Postcolonial Thinking," co-written with Joshua M. Price. *Anthropology News* 44(4): 7–9.

2004

"*Encuentros* and *Desencuentros*: Reflections on the LatCrit Gathering in Latin America," co- written with Joshua M. Price. *Florida Journal of International and Comparative Law* 16(3): 743–52.

2005

"From within Germinative Stasis: Creating Active Subjectivity, Resistant Agency." In Entre Mundos/*Among Worlds: New Perspectives on Gloria Anzaldúa*, edited by AnaLouise Keating, 85–100. New York: Palgrave Macmillan.
"Multiculturalismo Radical y Feminismos de Color." *Revista Internacional de Filosofía Política* 25: 61–76.
Translated as "Radical Multiculturalism and Women of Color Feminisms." Translated by María Lugones. *Journal for Cultural and Religious Theory* 13(1): 68–80, 2014.

2006

"On Complex Communication." *Hypatia* 21(3): 75–85.

2007

"Heterosexualism and the Colonial/Modern Gender System." *Hypatia* 22(1): 189–219.
Reprinted in *Philosophy and Gender*, vol. 1, edited by Cressida Heyes, 327–48. New York: Routledge, 2012.
Translated as "Colonialidad y Género." Translated by Pedro DiPietro. *Tabula Rasa* 9 (2008): 73–101.

2008

"Colonialidad y Género," *Tabula Rasa* 9: 73–101.
Reprinted in *Descolonizar la Modernidad, Descolonizar Europa. Un Diálogo Europa-América Latina*, edited by Heriberto Cairo and Ramón Grosfoguel. Madrid: IEPALA, 2010.
Reprinted in *Tejiendo de otro modo: Feminismo, epistemología, y apuestas decoloniales en Abya Yala*, edited by Yuderkys Espinosa Miñoso, Diana

Gómez Correal, and Karina Ochoa Muñoz, 57–74. Cauca, Colombia: Editorial Universidad del Cauca, 2014.

"The Coloniality of Gender." *Worlds & Knowledges Otherwise* 2, no. 2: 1–17.
Reprinted in *The Palgrave Handbook of Gender and Development*, edited by Wendy Harcourt, 13–33. London: Palgrave Macmillan, 2016.

2009

"Cosmology and Gender in Sylvia Marcos's *Taken from the Lips: Gender and Eros in Mesoamerican Religion*s," *The C.L.R. James Journal* 15(1): 283–88.

"Faith in Unity: The Nationalist Erasure of Multiplicity," co-written with Joshua M. Price. In *Constructing the Nation: A Race and Nationalism Reader*, edited by Mariana Ortega and Linda Martín Alcoff, 96–101. Albany: State University of New York Press.

2010

Translation with Joshua M. Price of *Indigenous and Popular Thinking in América* by Rodolfo Kusch. Durham, NC: Duke University Press.

"Toward a Decolonial Feminism." *Hypatia* 25(4): 742–59.

Translated as "Hacia un Feminismo Descolonial." Translated by Gabriela Castellanos. *La Manzana de la Discordia* 2(6): 105–17, 2010.

Translated as "Rumo a um feminismo descolonial." Translated by Juliana Watson and Tatiana Nascimento. *Estudos feministas* 22(3): 935–52, 2014.

2011

"It's All in Having a History: Response to Michael Hames-García's 'Queer Theory Revisited.'" In *Gay Latino Studies: A Reader*, edited by Michael Hames-García and Ernesto Martinez, 46–54. Durham, NC: Duke University Press.

"Methodological Notes toward a Decolonial Feminism." In *Decolonizing Epistemologies: Latina/o Theology and Philosophy*, edited by Ana María Isasí-Díaz and Eduardo Mendieta, 68–86. Bronx, NY: Fordham University Press.

2012

"Interseccionalidad y Feminismo Decolonial" [Intersectionality and Decolonial Feminism]. In *Lugares descoloniales: Espacios de intervención en las*

Américas, edited by Ramón Grosfoguel and Roberto Almanza, 119–24. Bogotá: Editorial de la Pontificia Universidad Javeriana.

"Subjetividad Esclava, Colonialidad de Género, Marginalidad y Opresiones Múltiples" [Slave Subjectivity, Coloniality of Gender, Marginalization and Multiple Oppressions]. In *Pensando los Feminismos en Bolivia*, edited by Patricia Montes, 129–39. La Paz, Bolivia: Fundación Fondo de Emancipación.

"*Milongueando* Macha Homoerotics: Dancing the Tango, Torta Style (A Performative Testimonio)." In *Performing the US Latina and Latino Borderlands*, edited by Arturo J. Aldama, Chela Sandoval, and Peter J. García, 51–56. Bloomington: Indiana University Press.

2014

"Reading the Nondiasporic from within Diasporas." *Hypatia* 29(1): 18–22.

2015

"Hacia metodologías de la decolonialidad" [Toward Decolonizing Methodologies]. In *Conocimientos y Prácticas Políticas*, Vol. 3, edited by Xochitl Leyva Solano, Camila Pascal, Axel Köhler, Hermenegildo Olguín Reza, and María del Refugio Velasco Contreras. Chiapas, México: Cooperativa Editorial Retos.

2016–2019

At work on a manuscript under the title *Decolonial Feminisms*.

"On the Concept of Gender as a Universal in Colonial Methodology." In *Decolonial Feminism in Latin-America: Contributions and Challenges*, edited by Yuderkys Espinosa Miñoso, María Lugones, and Nelson Maldonado-Torres.

At work on *Decolonial Feminism in Latin-America: Contributions and Challenges*, co-edited with Yuderkys Espinosa Miñoso and Nelson Maldonado-Torres.

At work on a co-edited manuscript under the title *Educating for Coalition: Popular Education and Political Praxis*, with Cricket Keating.

Contributors

Anna Carastathis is a postdoctoral researcher in the Department of Social Anthropology at Panteion University in Athens. She received her doctoral degree in philosophy from McGill University and is the author of a monograph, *Intersectionality: Origins, Contestations, Horizons* (2016). Her articles have been published in *Signs*, *Hypatia*, *Feminist Review*, *Women's Studies International Forum*, *Frontiers*, *Australian Critical Race and Whiteness Studies Journal*, and *Philosophy Compass*.

Manuel Chávez Jr. is a lecturer of philosophy at Monmouth University. He is a graduate of the Philosophy, Interpretation, and Culture Program of the State University of New York at Binghamton. His current research interests focus on the intersections of decolonial theory, ethics, and social philosophy.

Pedro J. DiPietro is an assistant professor in the department of women's and gender studies and a member of the Democratizing Knowledge Collective at Syracuse University. They work at the intersection of decolonial feminisms, transgender studies, and women of color thinking. Their work has appeared in journals such as *Gender, Place & Culture* and *Transgender Studies Quarterly*. Prior to joining Syracuse, DiPietro was a Mellon Postdoctoral Fellow in the Humanities in the department of ethnic studies at the University of California, Berkeley. They are currently at work on a manuscript under the title *Sideways Selves: The Decolonizing Politics of Trans* Space across the Américas*.

Sarah Lucia Hoagland is a collective member of the Institute of Lesbian Studies in Chicago since 1992, a collective member of the Escuela Popular Norteña from 1995 to 2005, a Bernard Brommel Distinguished Research Professor, and professor emerita of philosophy, women's studies, and Latino/Latin American studies at Northeastern Illinois University. She is author of *Lesbian Ethics: Toward New Value* (1989) and co-editor of two anthologies constructed to disrupt dismissals and encourage the discussion to continue: *For Lesbians Only: A Separatist Anthology* (1992), and *Feminist Interpretations of Mary Daly* (2000), which she co-edited with Julia Penelope and Marilyn Frye respectively.

Cricket Keating is a co-director of the Escuela Popular Norteña and an associate professor of gender, women, and sexuality studies at the University of Washington. She is the author of *Decolonizing Democracy: Transforming the Social Contract in India* (2011) and a co-author with María Lugones of *Educating for Coalition: Popular Education and Political Praxis* (forthcoming). She has been a collective member of the *Escuela Popular Norteña* since 1992.

María Lugones is co-founder and co-director of the Escuela Popular Norteña and associate professor of Latin American and Caribbean area studies and comparative literature at Binghamton University where she also directs the Center for Philosophy, Interpretation, and Culture. She is the author of *Pilgrimages/Peregrinajes: Theorizing Coalition against Multiple Oppressions* (2003) and the co-translator, with Joshua M. Price, of Rodolfo Kusch's *Indigenous and Popular Thinking in América* (2010). She is currently at work on a monograph on decolonial feminism that develops an intersectional engagement with "decoloniality" and "coloniality" toward a new framework for the study of gender. Among other honors, she was named the recipient of the SWIP (Society for Women in Philosophy) Distinguished Woman Philosopher Award in 2015.

Jennifer McWeeny is associate professor of philosophy at Worcester Polytechnic Institute. She is co-editor with Ashby Butnor of *Asian and Feminist Philosophies in Dialogue: Liberating Traditions* (2014) and her articles have appeared in *Hypatia, Continental Philosophy Review, Chiasmi International,* and *Journal for Critical Animal Studies,* among other venues. McWeeny has served as Executive Secretary for the Eastern Division of the Society for Women in Philosophy (SWIP) and is currently Editor-in-Chief of *Simone de Beauvoir Studies.*

Paula M. L. Moya is professor of English and, by courtesy, of Iberian and Latin American Cultures at Stanford University. Moya is the author of *The Social Imperative: Race, Close Reading, and Contemporary Literary Criticism* (2016) and *Learning from Experience: Minority Identities, Multicultural Struggles* (2002). She has co-edited three collections of original essays including *Doing Race: 21 Essays for the 21st Century* (2010), *Identity Politics Reconsidered* (2006), and *Reclaiming Identity: Realist Theory and the Predicament of Postmodernism* (2000).

Mariana Ortega works on Latina feminisms, phenomenology, philosophy of race, and aesthetics. She is interested in questions of identity and visual representations of race, gender, and sexuality. She is co-editor, with Linda Martín

Alcoff, of *Constructing the Nation: A Race and Nationalism Reader* (2009) and author of *In-Between: Latina Feminist Phenomenology, Multiplicity, and the Self* (2016). She is the founder and director of the Roundtable on Latina Feminism, a forum for Latina and Latin American feminisms.

Joshua M. Price is the author of *Prison and Social Death* (2015) and *Structural Violence: Hidden Brutality in the Lives of Women* (2012). He translated with María Lugones *Indigenous and Popular Thinking in América* by Rodolfo Kusch (2010). He writes on race, gender, colonization, and incarceration. He teaches at Binghamton University.

Shireen M. Roshanravan is associate professor of American ethnic studies at Kansas State University where she teaches courses on women of color feminisms, Asian American perspectives, queer of color critique, and decolonial methodologies. She was founding member and active participant in the local chapter of Binghamton Incite! Women of Color Against Violence and was a member of the Escuela Popular Norteña from 2003 to 2013. Her writings have appeared in *Meridians*, *Hypatia*, and *Works and Days*. She is the co-editor, with Lynn Fujiwara, of *Asian American Feminisms and Women of Color Politics* (2018).

Elizabeth V. Spelman is professor of philosophy and Barbara Richmond 1940 Professor in the Humanities at Smith College. Her scholarly work includes four books: *Inessential Woman: Problems of Exclusion in Feminist Thought* (1988); *Fruits of Sorrow: Framing Our Attention to Suffering* (1997); *Repair: The Impulse to Restore in a Fragile World* (2002); and *Trash Talks: Revelations in the Rubbish* (2016).

(Brena) Yu-Chen Tai is assistant professor of English at National Taiwan Normal University. She received her PhD in women's, gender, and sexuality studies from the Ohio State University. Her dissertation is titled "(W)holistic Feminism: Decolonial Healing in Women of Color Literature." Her research interests include U.S. women of color feminism and literature, Chicana feminism, decolonial thought, and the theorization of healing.

Madina Tlostanova is professor of postcolonial feminisms at Linköping University, Sweden. She was a DAAD visiting professor at the University of Bremen, international guest researcher at Duke University, and visiting researcher at Södertorn University. Her most recent books include

Postcolonialism and Postsocialism in Fiction and Art: Resistance and Re-existence (2017) and *What Does it Mean to be Post-Soviet? Decolonial Art from the Ruins of the Soviet Empire* (2018).

Kelli Zaytoun is professor and graduate studies director in the department of English at Wright State University. Her research and teaching focus on the relationship between subjectivity and narration in multiethnic American texts. Her articles have appeared in *MELUS*, *Contemporary Women's Writing*, *Frontiers*, *NWSA Journal*, *Feminist Teacher*, *El Mundo Zurdo*, and in numerous book publications. She is currently working on a monograph on *la naguala*, the shape-shifter, in the works of Gloria Anzaldúa.

Index

Abya Yala, 21, 24n17, 280
active subjectivity, 10, 12, 47–48, 260, 287; and agency, 10, 79; and Anzaldúa, 55–58; and Black women's strategic actions, 290n5; and coalition, 10, 59, 79; and decolonial ethics, 18, 187–88, 190; as fusion, 54–55; intersubjectivity of, 78–79; and liminality, 18–19, 50, 112, 179; and personhood, 187; and resistance, 10; and selfhood, 48, 59
affectivity, 198; and benevolent violence, 208; and *hijras*, 206; and lgbt counterpublics, 204, 206, 208, 211; and ornamental multiculturalism, 211; and synecdoche, 206
affects, 197–98, 201, 209; plasticity of, 200; and trans*, 201
Agee, James, 222
agency: and active subjectivity, 10, 79; and autonomy, 260; and individualism, 10, 176, 179; and masculinity, 177–78; under oppression, 258, 259, 260, 287; and trash, 40. See also active subjectivity
Alarcón, Norma, 56
Alcoff, Linda Martín, 147, 24n10, 61n1, 171n9, 290n3
Alexander, M. Jacqui, 3, 22, 120n9
Alexander-Floyd, Nikol, 101n1
Allen, Jeffner, 257, 270n3
Allen, Paula Gunn, 192n15, 265–66
ally-ship, 4; among queer diasporic South Asians, 117

Al-Walid, Zev, 209–11. *See also* "Pilgrimage" (Al-Walid)
American Irish. *See* Irish Americans
Anderson, Jackie, 256–63 passim, 268, 270n3
antiracism: of Chicano politics, 175; and coloniality of gender, 178; ethics of, 180, 187–88; and mainstream feminism, 100; and masculinity, 175; and men of color, 175–78, 184; politics of, 175–76; and white supremacy, 176, 188. *See also* racism
anti-structure, 190; and coloniality of power, 179; and liminality, 185; moral, 185–87; and personhood, 185–86. *See also* structure
Anzaldúa, Gloria, 3, 21, 47–48, 260, 265–66; and active subjectivity, 55–58; borderlands theory, 262–63, 269; on *conocimiento*, 55–59, 60; and deep coalition, 281; ego in, 57–58, 62n14; the knower in, 55–58, 59, 60; on language, 80n9; *naguala* in, 48, 56, 57, 58–59, 62n13; on *nepantlera* subjectivity, 56–57, 60; on racism, 5; self, theory of, 48. *See also* Chicana feminism
Aristotle, 62n8, 260

Barkley Brown, Elsa, 278
Barksdale, Corey, 278
Barraza, Santa Contreras, 278
Becker, Alton, 108, 120n12
Bell-Scott, Patricia, 21

303

Beltré, Mildred, 270n4
benevolent violence, 19, 198, 199, 288; in *Gaycation*, 208; and ornamental multiculturalism, 208; scarring of, 209; and synecdoche, 211–12
Benfield, Dalida María, 278
Bhattacharjee, Anannya, 110–12
Bierria, Alisa, 290n5
biopolitics, 202
Black Lives Matter, 4
Blackness, 155
black-white binary, 162; and Irish Americans, 157
body-politics, 127–28; praxis of, 139
borderlands theory, 56, 262–63, 269; and Eurasia, 140–41
borders: and decolonial thinking, 80n2, 137
Britton, Diane, 278
Brody, Michal, 261
Bryce, Geoff, 240, 263, 270n4
Butler, Judith, 136; antirealism of, 24n10

Camacho, Julia Schiavone, 270n4
Cambrensis, Geraldus, 149–50, 166
Cameron, Anne, 259
Carastathis, Anna, 14, 24n11
Card, Claudia, 257, 259
Cárdenas, Margarita Cota, 273
Carnalismo, 180–83; and machismo, 181. *See also* Chicanismo; Chicano politics
Castañeda, Antonia, 188–89
Caucasus, 125, 126; and Eurasian borderlands, 140; gender stereotyping in, 134; and Islam, 133; race in, 131–32, 133; Russian annexation of, 129–30; and whiteness, 131
Center for Interdisciplinary Studies in Philosophy, Interpretation, and Culture, 9; and modernity/coloniality/decoloniality network, 23n7
Central Asia, 126; exploitation of women in, 134–36; and Islam, 133; neo–slavery in, 135–36; and race, 133; Russian colonization of, 129–30, 134–35; and secondary Eurocentrism, 132
Cha, Theresa Hak Kyung, 11, 66; decolonial politics of, 67–68. *See also* Dictée (Cha)
Chabram-Dernersesian, Angie, 181, 183
Chávez, Manuel, Jr., 18, 288
Chicana feminism, 176, 278, 283–84; Chicano movement, critiques of, 181, 183; "decolonial," uses of, 279; and deep coalition, 280–81
Chicano ethics, 182–83, 189, 191n8; and white supremacy, 184
Chicano Movement, 180–83: and coloniality of gender, 176–77; Chicana feminist critiques of, 181, 183; and ethics, 180
Chicano politics: antiracism of, 177; Chingón politics, 177; gender binary of, 175; nationalist, 189, 191n9
Chicanos (cisgender straight–identified): and Carnalismo, 180–83; and heterosexualism, 176–77, 188; and personhood, 189
Choi, Chungmoo, 80n7
Civil Rights Movement, 2, 240, 261
coalition: and active subjectivity, 10, 48, 59; coalitional consciousness, 51–52; and coloniality of gender, 59, 276, 280–82; and complex communication, 56, 105, 280; and decolonial self, 66, 68, 76–79; across difference, 1; and EPN, 249–53; and fragmentation, 249–50; and intersectionality, 54, 90, 127–28; Lugones on, 2–3, 20–21, 99, 239–40, 276, 278, 279,

280–81; and multiplicity, 9, 11, 49, 59; and popular education, 239, 241–42, 246, 249–50, 252; and solidarity, 2; and Women of Color politics, 2, 4, 6–7, 23n6, 168, 269, 279. *See also* deep coalition; self-in-coalition
Coatlicue, 285, 289n1
collectivity, 278
Collins, Patricia Hill, 278, 281
colonialism: anticolonialism, 176; and philosophical discourse, 191n5; U.S., 80n7
coloniality: and anonymity, 70–71; defined, 16, 181, 191n10; and difference, 70; and gender, 15, 176; and men of color, 16, 190; and mimicry, 1; and modernity, 125; power relations of, 191n10; and race, 15–16, 149; and resistance, 65–66, 73; and Russia, 126, 128, 131
coloniality of ethics, 178, 185. *See also* ethics; modern ethics
coloniality of gender, 12, 14–17, 65, 149, 206, 288; and antiracism, 178; and benevolent violence, 206; and Chicana/o community, 288; and Chicano Movement, 176–77; and coalition, 59, 276, 280–82; and decolonial ethics, 190; and decolonial feminism, 17, 59, 279–80; and heteronormativity, 127; and intersectionality of oppression, 12, 75–76; and Ireland, 149; and language, 213n8; and modern ethics, 183–84, 190; and patriarchy, 127; and personhood, 184–85; and racial location, 145; and Russia, 125, 133; and sexual dimorphism, 17; violence of, 8, 21, 288; and whiteness, 145. *See also* colonial/modern gender system

coloniality of power, 16, 65, 149, 279; and antiracist men of color, 184; and anti-structure, 179; and gender, 183, 184; and personhood, 184–85; Quijano on, 16, 149, 175–76, 189; and race hierarchy, 181; and slipperiness, 18, 149, 167; and the visual, 275
colonial/modern gender system, 15–18, 22, 50, 125, 267–69; and Irish American identity, 148; and intermeshed oppressions, 100; and intersectionality, 97; and Irish racialization, 155–56; and race, 131; and Russia, 130, 132–35; white feminist collusion with, 53; and women of color, 184
colonization, 192n16: epistemology of, 125–26, 229, 275; of Ireland, 146, 148–52, 160, 169; of Korea, 11, 67, 70–71, 74; and mestiza identity, 284; and Russia, 129, 133–34; and violence, 192n16
Combahee River Collective (CRC), 12; "A Black Feminist Statement," 4, 22, 88; and interlocking oppressions, 88, 93–94
coming out, 103, 106, 108, 120n8, 268
communality: as challenge to coloniality, 278; and solitude, 276, 277
community: and belonging, 268; of choice, 107, 120n5; of lesbians of color, 268; of place, 107; self in, 120n9
complex communication, 47, 48, 53, 270; and Anzaldúa, 56, 59, 60; and coalition, 76, 280; defined, 53; and fusion, 54; and intersubjectivity, 76; in liminal space, 50; and memory, 75–77; and pluralist feminism, 269; and queer diasporic South Asians, 105–6, 113, 117; and resistance, 75; and selfhood, 48; and subjectivity, 11, 76;

complex communication (cont'd)
and witnessing faithfully, 104, 105; and world-traveling, 75, 76
counterpublics, lgbt, 212n4; and affectivity, 206, 208, 211; and benevolent violence, 199; and human dignity, 203; and indignation, 200, 211; and ornamental multiculturalism, 199, 212; and recognition, 205; and whiteness, centering of, 204. See also *Gaycation*
Courtney, Annie, 257
Crenshaw, Kimberlé, 85, 175–76; on intersectionality, 175; intersectionality, coining of, 13. See also intersectionality
Critical Resistance, 3, 20, 241
Crowley, Patrick, 277–78
curdling, 53; curdle-separation, 91, 93, 96; and intersectionality, 53, 89, 97; logic of, 186; and mestizaje, 41–42, 85, 90, 91; and multiplicity, 90; and purity/impurity, 41–42, 53; and resistance, 98–99

Daly, Mary, 147, 265–66
Daniel, Ian, 202, 203, 208–9
DarkMatter, 103
Davies, John, 150–51
Davis, Angela, 22
death-worlds, 218, 223; prisons as, 219–20, 227–28; world-traveling to, 221–22, 228, 232–33
decolonial ethics, 178–79, 189–90; and active subjectivity, 18, 187; and Chicano masculinity, 188, 288; and curdling, 186; and impurity, 186; and personhood, 186–87; praxis of, 187; and universalism, 179; and white supremacy, 187
decolonial feminism, 53, 126–27, 168, 169, 279; and cognitive liberation, 178–79; and coloniality of gender, 17, 59, 99, 279–80; and decolonization of gender, 126–27, 141; and Irish American identity, 148, 168, 169; of Lugones, 13, 18, 22, 24n14, 65, 99, 137, 279–80
decoloniality, 23n7; ethics of, 178; politics of, 67–68
decolonization: of gender, 126–27, 141; and liberation, 178–79; of self, 65–66. See also decolonial feminism
deep coalition, 3, 18–19, 103, 239, 287, 288; barriers to, 248–49; building of, 9–10; and collaboration, 9; and faithful witnessing, 15, 103, 104, 108; and the global South, 137, 140; Lugones on, 279–81; and modernity, 280; and popular education, 239, 287; and solidarity, 242, 249; and subjectivity, 11; and unconditional love, 118–19; and unity, 9; and world-traveling, 9. See also coalition
dehumanization: and anonymity, 70–71; of Blacks, 151, 155; of Irish, 146, 152–55, 157, 159, 160; of people of color, 148; and colonial/modern gender system, 15, 17, 148; and modernity, 148; and racialization, 111, 146, 160–61; and Russia, 134
Dictée (Cha), 11, 66–76; anonymity in, 74; decolonial self in, 67–68, 76–77; genre of, 66–67; interchangeability in, 74–75; narrative voice of, 67; purity in, 72; subjectivity in, 67–68; whiteness in, 69–70; woman warriors in, 73, 77, 79
difference: and coalition, 1; and coloniality, 70; and EPN, 242; imperial, 128; Lorde on, 262; nondominant, 11, 77–79; and organizing, 262; and radical feminism, 262; recognition of, 55, 60
differential consciousness, 12
DiPietro, Pedro, 19, 286, 288

disengagement, 7–8
Douglas, Mary, 46n13
Douglass, Frederick, 219
Du Bois, W.E.B., 219
Dussel, Enrique, 266
Duttchoudhury, Aparajeeta "Sasha," 105, 117
Dylan, Bob, 35

empathetic understanding, 21, 22, 222, 229
empathy, 222–23; and ontological pluralism, 288; and solidarity, 232
empire: English, 149; Russian, 125–26, 128–31, 133–34, 137
epistemology: decolonial border, 137; epistemic de-linking, 125; epistemic shift, 57, 75; epistemic travel, 113; of modernity/coloniality, 125–26; of Women of Color feminism, 6
EPN (*la Escuela Popular Norteña*), 3, 20, 260, 263–64, 270n4, 287; coalitional approach of, 249–53; and difference, 242; *encuentros*, 21, 241, 260, 263–65; and everyday resistance, 243, 246, 252; founding of, 240–41; liberatory gift, 248–49; and multiple oppressions, 241; popular education programs of, 241; and resistance, 241, 243, 244–46, 252. *See also* popular education
EPN (*la Escuela Popular Norteña*) workshops, 21, 264; *Coalition: Linking Contexts of Resistance*, 246–47; *Complex Unity*, 245, 246, 247–48, 265; *Fragmentation: A Workshop on the Political Uses of Popular Education*, 249–50; *Map of Oppressions*, 243, 246, 248–49; *Politicizing the Everyday*, 244–45; *Un Nuevo Camino*, 250–52
erasure: of Black women, 86, 101n1; and fragmentation, 95, 98, 281; of multiplicity, 9, 88, 91; of the oppressed, 37, 38, 39; and purity, 38; of resistance, 10, 119; and world-traveling, 38
ethics: Chicano, 182–84, 189, 191n8; coloniality of, 178, 185; decolonial, 18, 178–79, 186–90, 288; *Herrenvolk*, 182–83; modern, 176, 177–79, 182–83, 184–85, 190; and racism, 180. *See also* Chicano ethics; decolonial ethics; modern ethics
Eurocentrism: and capitalism, 15, 16; and *Gaycation*, 202; and gender, 176, 178, 202, 205; and modernity/coloniality, 191n10; and Orientalism, 130; Russian, 130–31; as secondary, 132; and synecdoche, 205, 206; and transgender phenomena, 199
exchangeability, 71, 73, 80n4

faithful witnessing, 14–15, 51–52, 61n5, 76, 286; and complex communication, 105; and deep coalition, 103, 104; and Eurocentrism, 108; and queer South Asian practice, 110, 119
Fanon, Frantz, 166, 171n14, 218
Federici, Silvia, 266
femininity: colonial, 130, 132–33; and Orientalism, 133; resistance to, 259; white middle-class, 17, 184
feminisms: and antiracism, 4, 12, 100; Chicana, 181, 183, 283–84; and collaboration, 5–6; and difference, 262; Latina, 273, 283; radical, 256, 262, 270n1; second wave, 52; Western, 126–27, 136. *See also* decolonial feminism; white feminism; Women of Color feminisms
Flores, Aurelia, 270n4
Flynn, Elizabeth Gurley, 157
fractured locus, 67–68; and colonial difference, 269;

fractured locus (cont'd)
    and decolonial feminism, 99;
    in *Dictée*, 76; and interlocking
    oppressions, 88; and liminality,
    72; and ripple imaginary, 77, 79;
    and shadow-subjectivity, 16; and
    streetwalker, 73
fragmentation, 8, 97, 270; and coalition, 249–50; and identity, 101n3; and interlocking oppressions, 92, 93, 95, 96; and multiplicity, 42, 67, 85, 87–88, 90–91, 97; and purity, 68, 90–92, 98–100; and subjectivity, 261–62; and whiteness, 280, 281–82
Freire, Paulo, 240, 250, 253n2, 287
Frost, Elizabeth, 73
Frye, Marilyn, 22, 93, 229, 257, 265, 270n1; on male arrogance, 258
fusion: and active subjectivity, 54–55, 58; and intersectionality, 128; logic of, 50, 53–59 passim, 68, 127–28; as plural, 55; and resistance, 54, 60, 68

Gadamer, Hans-Georg, 37
Gamboa, Diane, 278
garbology, 35
García, Alma M., 181, 183
Garry, Ann, 97
Garza, Carmen Lomas, 278
Gaycation, 202–9; benevolent ignorance of, 206–7; and benevolent violence, 208; counterpublic orientation of, 202–3; *hijras* in, 199, 204–8; indignation in, 203–4, 206, 208, 211; and ornamental multiculturalism, 203–4; synecdoche in, 199, 202, 207–8; third-gender in, 202, 204–6
gender: and class, 129; and coloniality, 15, 176; and coloniality of power, 183, 184; and colonization, 130; decolonization of, 126–27, 141; emergence of concept, 129; and Eurocentrism, 176, 178, 202, 205; heteropatriarchal constructions of, 176; and heterosexuality, 15–16; and humanism, 13; and humanization, 176; and intersectionality, politics of, 13; and nature, 132–33; and race, 96, 129, 279; and racialization, 133. *See also* coloniality of gender
geo-politics, 127–28
Gilley, Brian, 115–16
Gines, Kathryn, 97–98
Glissant, Édouard, 266
Gonzales, Easa, 270n4
Gopinath, Gayatri, 120n1
Gordon, Lewis, 126
Gulati, Sonia, 108–9
Gutiérrez, Gustavo, 234n1

Hames-García, Michael, 24n10
Hartman, Rukie, 105, 117
Heartbeats: The Izzat Project, 105, 115
Heidegger, Martin, 49
Henry, Paget, 266
Hernandez, Ester, 278
Hernandez, Nydia, 270n4
Hernández-Ávila, Inés, 58
heteronormativity, 109; and coloniality of gender, 127
heteropatriarchy: and Chicana/o communities, 188; and family, 109–10; and gender, construction of, 176; and model-minority project, 111, 112; resistance to, 273–74; rhetoric of, 16
heterosexualism, 192n15; and Chicanos, 176–77; in *Gaycation*, 206
heterosexuality: failed, 113–14; and gender, 15–16
Highlander Folk School, 240, 250, 263, 283
hijras, 105–6, 116, 204, 288; agency of, 207–8; and affectivity, 206;

and embodiment, 206; in *Gaycation*, 199, 204–8; kin relations of, 113–14; personhood of, 204; subject formation of, 114
Hoagland, Sarah, 21, 286–87
home: and deep coalition, 9; and language, 80n9; and lesbian activism, 255; and South Asians, 106–7, 111, 120n1; and whiteness, 259
homonormativity, 204
homophobia, 203, 252; and Latina/o community, 4
Horton, Myles, 240, 252, 287
Huizinga, Johan, 37
Hull, Akasha, 22
Hurston, Zora Neale, 257
Hyung Soon Huo, 73–74, 76–77

I Am (film), 108–9
identity: *hijra*, 116; Irish American, 148; slippery, 146; and world-traveling, 221
identity politics, 221
Ignatiev, Noel, 171n3
immediate grasp, 161–70; definition of, 161–62
immigration, 80n6, 146, 152, 169; checkpoints, 73, 210
impurity, 90; and decolonial ethics, 186; logic of, 186; and the oppressed, 42, 43; and resistance, 41–42, 98–99; and separation, 41; and trash, 36, 38, 40; and whiteness, 275. *See also* curdling; purity; purity, logic of
Incite! Women, Gender Non-Conforming and Trans People of Color Against Violence, 3, 20, 241, 253n3
Indigenous peoples: and Abya Yala, 21, 24n17, 280; cosmologies of, 105, 126, 140, 207, 269; of Latin America, 283; movements of, 3, 17, 280; pre-conquest cultures, 169, 192n15; women, 99; of Russia, 129, 139. *See also* Native peoples
Indigenous studies, 19, 20, 21, 24n17
indignation, 202; in *Gaycation*, 203–4, 206, 208, 211; and interculturality, 200; and lgbt counterpublics, 200, 207, 211; and ornamental multiculturalism, 200, 204; in "Pilgrimage," 209, 211; and trans* of color, 203, 209–11; *See also* benevolent violence
individualism, 2; and agency, 10, 14, 58, 176–79, 258; and choice, 105, 110, 112, 117; and modern agency, 65, 179; "self-made man," 10. *See also* modernity
Institute of Lesbian Studies (ILS), 261, 263, 268, 270n3
interculturality, 198, 212n2
intersectionality, 12, 175; and coloniality of gender, 75–76; and colonial/modern gender system, 97; criticisms of, 86–87, 98, 100; and curdling, 53, 89, 97; and fusion, 128; and gender, 13; institutionalization of, 86, 87, 94; and invisibility, 89–90, 96–97; and liminality, 95; logic of, 53–54, 57; and logic of purity, 87, 99; Lugones on, 89–90; and masculinity, 89; and multiple oppressions, 53, 140–41; political, 94–95; post-intersectionality, 86–87, 100; post-post-intersectionality, 87; as provisional concept, 85, 87; and purity, 85–86; and race, 13; representational, 94; and resistance, 89; and social location, 89, 94; structural, 94; and subjectivity, 13–15; and whiteness, 89
intersectionality studies, 86

intersubjectivity: of active subjectivity, 78–79; and complex communication, 76; and interchangeability, 74–75; and recognition, 75; and resistance, 178; and shadow-subjectivity, 159
invisibility: and intersectionality, 89–90, 96–97; and lesbianism, 268; and multiplicity, 98; of privilege, 101n7; of suffering, 227; of violence, 227; of women of color, 12–13, 96–97
Ireland: colonization of, 146, 149–52; and coloniality of gender, 149; famine, 152, 160
Irish: as "begrudged majority," 154; dehumanization of, 148, 152–55, 157, 159; females, 150, 156; indentured servitude of, 151–52; and ontological slipperiness, 149–52, 162–66; and pilgrimage, 169; and post-colonial stress disorder, 145, 160; and primitivism, 150, 151; racialization of, 146, 149–58, 162, 166, 168; women, 148; women, racialization of, 155–56
Irish Americans, 170n1; becoming white, 156–57; in Boston, 158; and colonial/modern gender system, 155–56; and decolonial feminism, 148; racialization of, 155–59, 166, 170n2; and racism, 157, 158; and speaking face to face, 148; subjectivity of, 159–60; and white supremacy, 157
Irishness, 159; and decolonial feminism, 169; and whiteness, 146–48, 151, 156, 158
izzat, 106, 113, 114–15, 204: and autonomy, 115–16; and kinship, 206; redefinition of, 115
Izzat Collective, 105, 106, 114–15

Jacobson, Matthew, 147, 152–53, 156
Jagtap, Komal, 204, 205, 207, 208
James, William, 224
Jenner, Caitlyn, 201
Jihad for Love, 121n11
Johnson, Bernice, 281
Jordan, June, 119
Joyce, James, 147

Kant, Immanuel, 182, 192n13
Katherine, Amber, 257
Kavi, Ashok Row, 203
Keating, AnaLouise, 62n10, 265
Keating, Cricket, 21, 270n4, 286–87; on coalitional consciousness, 51–52
Kerr, Laura Dumond, 270n4
Kim, Hyo, 67
Kingston, Maxine Hong, 80n6
Koegeler-Abdi, Martina, 57
Korea: annexation of, 71; Japanese colonization of, 70–71, 74; and U.S. colonialism, 80n7
Kusch, Rodolfo, 266

Lagrande, Suzanne, 270n4
Landauer, Gustav, 233
language: and coloniality of gender, 213n8; and home, 80n9; Lugones on, 266; nonliteral, 147; and resistance, 74
Latina feminism, 273, 283
Latina Feminism Roundtable, 9, 20
Lebens, Christa, 257
Leighton, Anne, 257, 259, 263, 270n3
lesbian activism, 255
Lesbian Ethics (Hoagland), 258, 259, 263, 264, 268–69
lesbians: of color, 257, 268, 269–70; and community, 268; and home, 255, 259; and invisibility, 268; white, 258–59
lesbian separatism, 256, 257–58; and lesbians of color, 257
Levinas, Emmanuel, 234n1
lgbtq rights: and neoliberalism, 19–20; and white supremacy, 19–20

liberation: and decolonization, 178–79; and education, 240; and multiplicity, 76; and praxis, 189–90
liminality, 61n3, 61n7, 262–63; and active subjectivity, 18–19, 50, 112; and anti-structure, 185; and complex communication, 50, 75; and decolonial self, 68, 72, 78; and incarceration, 19; and intersectionality, 85, 95; and multiplicity, 52–53, 72–73; and *nepantla*, 56, 59, 60; and playfulness, 75; and queer of color theory, 19, 20; and structure, 61n3, 185; and subjectivity, 50, 112
Locke, John, 51, 62n9, 182, 192n13
López, Leonard, 101n3
Lopez, Yolanda, 278
Lorde, Audre, 3, 265–66, 281, 287–88; and deep coalition, 281; on difference, 262. *See also* nondominant difference
Lugones, María: on coalition, 2–3, 20–21, 239–40, 276, 278, 280–81; on decolonial aesthesis, 275–78; decolonial feminism of, 13, 18, 22, 24n14, 65, 99, 137, 279–80; on deep coalition, 280–81; on heterosexualism, 192n15; on intersectionality, 89–90; on language, 266; multiplicity, theory of, 66; on the new mestiza, 55–56; as nondiasporic Latina, 2, 23n2, 282, 284; ontology of, 90; on ornamental multiculturalism, 198–200, 212n3; pluralistic self of, 48–49; on popular education, 283–84; praxical thinking of, 1–2, 3, 20–21, 178, 239–40, 256; on resistance, 274–75; on structural monoculturalism, 198–200; on "worlds," 220–21

Majumdar, Rochona, 109
Makhacheva, Taus, 139–40

Malcolm X, 262
Maldonado-Torres, Nelson, 127, 192n12, 218, 234n1
Margalit, Avishai, 228
marginalization, politics of, 91
Marino, Dian, 253n1
Martínez, Elizabeth, 177, 183
Martínez, Ernesto, 290n5
masculinity: and antiracism, 175; colonial, 130, 132–33; and decolonial ethics, 188; hypermasculinity, 156; and individualist agency, 177–78; and intersectionality, 89; and Russian empire, 134; white, 177. *See also* gender
Mbembe, Achille, 218
McCaffrey, Lawrence J., 158
McClintock, Anne, 148
McDaniel, Nicole, 74
McWeeny, Jennifer, 18, 49, 286, 287–88; on exchangeability, 80n4
Mehta, Brinda, 105
memory, 60; body-memory, 171n14; of the colonized, 72–73; and complex communication, 75–76; of self, 51
Mendoza, Breni, 281
men of color, 175; and antiracism, 175–78, 184; and coloniality, 16, 190; and modern ethics, 179, 185, 188–89; and violence against women of color, 16–18, 180, 266–67, 288; and white supremacy, 188, 190. *See also* women of color
meritocracy, 10
mestiza consciousness, 263
mestizaje, 41–42, 56, 90–91, 97, 284; and subjectivity, 57, 85
Midwest Society for Women in Philosophy (SWIP), 256, 268, 287; Lesbian Caucus, 256–57; Women of Color Caucus, 20–21, 256, 258
Mignolo, Walter, 80n1, 171n5, 266
Mill, John Stuart, 192n11, 192n13

Mills, Charles, 180, 182, 189, 191n5, 192n13
model-minority racial project, 110–12; and Asian daughters, 111–12; and "begrudged majority," 154; and white supremacy, 110–11
modern ethics, 185; and coloniality of gender, 190; and individualism, 179; and men of color, 179, 185, 188–89; and personhood, 182–83; and self-colonization, 177–78; and universalism, 177
modernity: and coloniality, 125; and coloniality of gender, 183–84; and death-worlds, 218–19; and deep coalition, 280; and dehumanization, 148; epistemology of, 125–26; and Eurocentrism, 191n10; and individual(ist) self, 10, 179; moral structure of, 183–84; and Orientalism, 130; and personhood, 189; and racism, 130; and Russia, 130; and sexual identity, 199, 203, 204, 206, 208, 212; Soviet, 140; and tradition, 126–27; Western, 130; and white women, 184; womanhood in, 183–84
Mohanty, Chandra Talpade, 3, 22
monoculturalism: as cultural dominance, 199–200, 213n5; and privilege, 200; structural, 198–200, 211, 288
Moraga, Cherríe, 3, 22, 167, 171n12, 176–77, 183. *See also* Chicana feminism
multiculturalism: radical, 53, 207, 212n4; Soviet, 136
multiculturalism, ornamental, 198, 211, 288; and affectivity, 211; and benevolent violence, 208; and *Gaycation*, 203–4; and indignation, 200, 204; and lgbt counterpublics, 199, 212; Lugones and Price on, 198–200, 212n3; and ontological pluralism, 200; and privilege, 200; and trans* of color phenomena, 199

multiplicity, 22, 90; and categorial seeing, 52; and coalition, 9; of the colonized, 72–73; and curdling, 90; erasure of, 9, 88, 91; and fragmentation, 42, 67, 85, 87–88, 90–91, 97; and invisibility, 98; and liberation, 76; and liminality, 52–53, 72–73; Lugones on, 66; methodology of, 65; and ontological pluralism, 10, 260–61, 269; ontology of, 79; of self, 49, 50, 54–55, 76; of subjectivity, 65–66, 68, 260–61. *See also* curdling; oppression; ontological pluralism
Murphey, Julien, 257
Mutis, Rafael, 270n4
Nagarajan, Mala, 116
Nakshbandi, Bahauddin, 139
Native peoples: and the decolonial, 17; and decolonial feminism, 99; and fractured locus, 72; Native American cosmology, 115; *See also* Indigenous peoples
Ndongo, Donato, 17
Ninh, erin Khuê, 111–12, 114
nondiasporic Latinas, 2, 23n2, 282, 284

O'Connor, Garrett, 160
Omi, Michael, 279
ontological pluralism, 12, 258, 282, 288; and empathy, 288; and multiplicity, 10, 260–61, 269; and ornamental multiculturalism, 200
ontological slipperiness, 18, 147; and coloniality of power, 18, 149, 167; and immediate grasp, 161–63, 164–65, 166; of Irish, 162–66; and Irish history, 149–52;

phenomenology of, 161–67; and racialization, 145–46; as subjectivity, 167–69; and world-traveling, 166
ontology, 7, 54, 125, 127, 213n10; and class, 151; and *hijras*, 205, 213; and intersectionality, 85–87, 90–93, 98; and multiplicity, 49, 65, 79, 90, 221, 268; ontological confusion, 207; ontological othering, 137; and racialization, 145–49, 154, 163, 166–68; and religion, 151; of the self, 49. *See also* ontological pluralism, ontological slipperiness
oppression: agency under, 23n4, 258, 259, 260, 287; and coloniality of gender, 75–76; and fragmentation, 95; interlocking of, 53, 85, 87–91, 92–96, 247–48; intermeshing of, 13, 53, 85–86, 87–91, 92–97, 100; intersectionality of, 53, 75–76; logic of, 32–33, 43, 44n2, 53, 265; and purity, 36, 38–39, 40, 41, 43; racial, 175; and resistance, 31, 32; and solidarity, 241–42; and violence, 37; of women of color, 12, 13
Orientalism: and Eurocentrism, 130; and femininity, 133; and modernity, 130; and Russia, 130–32
Ortega, Mariana, 9, 21, 49–50, 62n9, 286
Oyěwùmí, Oyèrónkẹ́, 192n15

Page, Ellen, 202, 203, 208–9
pain, 218, 231–32; and political engagement, 221; of prisoners, 233
passing-as-if, 168
patriarchy, 111; ahistoricity of, 279; and antiracism, 94; and coloniality of gender, 127; and modernity, 126. *See also* heteropatriarchy; heterosexualism
Pérez, Emma, 279. *See also* Chicana feminism
Pérez, Laura Elisa, 278. See also Chicana feminism
permeability, 197, 201, 261, 275–77
personhood: and active subjectivity, 187; and anti-structure, 185–86; of Chicanos, 189; and coloniality of power, 184–85; and decolonial ethics, 186–87, 189; and gender, 184–85; of *hijras*, 204; and logic of purity, 186; and modernity, 182–83; and moral anti-structure, 185–86; and structure, 183; and whiteness, 154, 182, 183, 189
Peter the Great, 130
phenomenology, 7, 86, 141, 161, 166; of selfhood, 47–51, 58, 61n1; of slipperiness, 161–67
Philosophy, Interpretation and Culture program (PIC), 9, 20, 23n7
pilgrimage, 169
"Pilgrimage" (Al-Walid), 209–11, 288; indignation in, 211; synecdoche in, 210–11, 212
Pilgrimages/Peregrinajes: Theorizing Coalition against Multiple Oppressions (Lugones), 3–4, 31, 47, 239, 285
playfulness, 3, 23n5, 81n11; and erasure, 38; and liminality, 75; and subjectivity, 11; and world-traveling, 11, 137
pluriversality, 127–28, 140, 282–83; and Eurocentrism, 130
popular education, 263; coalitional praxis of, 239, 241–42, 246, 249–50, 252; and deep coalition, 239; Lugones on, 283–84; traditional approaches to, 243, 244; See also EPN (*la Escuela Popular Norteña*)

post-positivist realism, 24n10, 285
praxis: decolonial, 270; of decolonial ethics, 187; and liberation, 189–90; and Lugones, 1–2, 3, 20–21, 169, 178, 239–40, 256; and personal transformation, 19; and social transformation, 19
Price, Joshua, 19, 270n4, 288; on ornamental multiculturalism, 198–200, 212n3; on structural monoculturalism, 198–200
prisoners; death-worlds of, 219–20, 228; humiliation of, 227–28, 233; and pain, 233
prison industrial complex, 244
prisons: as death-worlds, 219–20, 227–28; health care in, 217–18, 220, 225–26
purity: in *Dictée*, 72; and fragmentation, 90–91; and hierarchy, 38; and intersectionality, 85–86; and oppression, 38–39, 40, 41, 43; and resistance, 38–39; and whiteness, 69–70. *See also* impurity
purity, logic of, 72, 85, 98, 274; and fragmentation, 92; and intersectionality, 87, 99; and personhood, 186

"queer" (term): limits of, 105, 116
queer of color critique, 19–20; and counterpublicity, 212n4
queer studies: and counterpublicity, 212n4; and performance, 19
Quijano, Aníbal, 266, 279, 282; anticolonialism of, 176; on coloniality of power, 16, 149, 175–76, 189; on colonization, 192n16; modernity, critique of, 181, 184

race: and Caucasus, 131–32, 133; and Central Asia, 133; and coloniality, 15–16, 149; and coloniality of power, 131; and gender, 96, 129, 279; and humanism, 13; and intersectionality, politics of, 13
racialization: ambiguous, 167; colonial processes of, 160; and dehumanization, 160–61; and gender, 133; of Irish, 146, 149–58, 162, 166, 168; of Irish Americans, 145–48, 149–52, 287; of Irish women, 155–56; and ontological slipperiness, 145–46; resistance to, 283–84; of self, 218
racism: and communication, 5; dismissal of, 159; and ethics, 180; and familial violence, 112; and feminist collaboration, 5; and interdependence, 5; internalized, 175; and Irish Americans, 157, 158; and modernity, 130; in Russia, 131; Russian, 130–31
Rancière, Jacques, 140
Rathje, William, 35
Reagon, Bernice Johnson, 3, 278, 281
recognition: and African Americans, 219; of difference, 55, 60; and intersubjectivity, 75; and lgbt counterpublics, 205; of the oppressed, 32–33; of self, 51
Reddy, Chandra, 120n5
Reddy, Gayatri, 106, 113–14, 116, 202
representation: politics of, 96; and resistance, 95
resistance, 113; and active subjectivity, 10; and coloniality, 65–66; and complex communication, 53, 75; and curdling, 98–99; in deep coalition, 9, 48, 51; and EPN, 241, 243, 244–45, 252; erasure of, 119; ethics of, 189; everyday, 243, 246, 252, 253n1; and fusion, 54, 57, 60, 68; and gender, 188; to heteropatriarchy, 273–74; hidden, 22, 24n16, 243; and impurity, 41–42, 91, 98–99; to interlocking oppressions, 88, 247–48; and intermeshed oppressions,

88; and intersectionality, 89; and intersubjectivity, 178; and language, 74; logic of, 32, 43, 44n2, 265; Lugones on, 274–75; and movement, 169; to oppressions, 20, 31, 32, 51; and racialization, 283–84; and representation, 95; and sabotage, 260; to violence, 245, 247–48, 264, 282; and world-traveling, 11
Restrepo, Rocío, 270n4
Rodriguez, Celia Herrera, 278
Rodriguez, Richard, 191n9
Rodriguez, Sylvia, 240
Roediger, David, 147, 156–57
Rolando, Gloria, 278
Rosaldo, Renato, 39
Roshanravan, Shireen, 14–15, 168, 279n4, 286, 288
Russia: Caucasus annexing of, 129–30; Central Asia, colonization of, 129–30, 134–35; and coloniality of gender, 125; and colonial/modern gender system, 130, 132–35; and colonization, 129–30, 134–35; and empire, 125–26, 128–31, 134, 137; and Eurocentrism, 130–31; and modernity, 130, 140; and Orientalism, 130–32; and racism, 130–31; as second-class, subaltern empire, 125, 128, 133
Ruvalcaba, Luz Jimenez, 290n5

sabotage, 259, 260
same-sex marriage, 109
Sandoval, Chela, 3, 279, 281. *See also* Chicana feminism
Santos, Rick, 270n4
Schafer, Carolyn, 257
Schapov, Afanassy, 129
Scott, James, 24n16
self: abstract, 48, 61n4; communal, 105, 107, 109, 112, 276; in community, 120n9; decolonization of, 65–66; individualist, 10; modern/colonial, 50; multiplicity of, 49, 50, 54–55, 76; as pluralistic, 48, 49, 51; racialization of, 218; recognition of, 51; as unitary, 47
self, decolonial, 66, 77; as coalitional, 66, 68, 76–79; and multiplicity, 77–78
selfhood, 47; and active subjectivity, 48; and complex communication, 48; defined, 61n1; and white self-regard, 224–25
self-in-coalition, 47–49, 54–55, 60–61; and active subjectivity, 59; and logic of fusion, 53; and remembering, 51
separation: curdle-separation, 91, 93; split separation, 91
shadow-subjectivity, 159–61, 166, 168, 171n14; and intersubjectivity, 159
Shahani, Parmesh, 203
Silverio, Rocío, 270n4
Singh, Rajat S., 117
Singh, Raju, 117–18
6 Pack, 204, 207
slipperiness. *See* ontological slipperiness
Smith, Anna Deveare, 231
Smith, Barbara, 3, 22
Smith, Dorothy, 225
social justice, 5, 222, 264; tourism, 202
solidarity, 2, 223; and action, 232; and deep coalition, 242, 249; and empathy, 232; with the incarcerated, 222; and queer diasporic South Asians, 103–4; and shared oppression, 241–42; of U.S. Third World women, 12
Sosa-Riddell, Adaljiza, 176, 183
South Asians, queer diasporic, 103–4, 116; "acceptance" of, 103–5, 107–9, 119, 121n14; ally-ship among, 117; and complex communication, 105–6, 113, 117; familial loss of, 106–8;

South Asians (*cont'd*)
　　and solidarity, 103–4; support groups of, 120n6; transgender, 118
speaking face to face: and Irish American racialization, 148; as practice, 5–9, 20
Spelman, Elizabeth V., 11, 286–87
structure, 48; and anti-structure, 185, 186; and liminality, 61n3, 185; moral, 183; and personhood, 183
subject formation, 3; of *hijras*, 114
subjectivity: and complex communication, 11; and deep coalition, 11; in *Dictée*, 67–68; and fragmentation, 261–62; and hierarchy, 69; and intersectionality, 13–15; of Irish Americans, 159–60; and liminality, 50, 112; modern, 69; and multiplicity, 65–66, 68, 260–61; and ontological slipperiness, 167–69; of the oppressed, 32; and playfulness, 11; resistant, 10, 262, 263, 269; unified, 69; white, 225; white masculine, 185; and world-traveling, 233
subjects: co-constitution of, 13, 14; diasporic, 281–82; legal, 14; liminal, 112
Subranamian, Vega, 105, 116
Sweet Honey in the Rock, 278
sympathy, 224
synecdoche, 205; and affectivity, 206; and benevolent violence, 211–12; in *Gaycation*, 199, 202, 207–8; in "Pilgrimage," 210–11, 212

Tai, (Brena) Yu-Chen, 11
third-gender, 211; in *Gaycation*, 202, 204–6
Third World Liberation movements, 2
This Bridge Called My Back (Moraga and Anzaldúa), 4, 12, 62n10

Tlostanova, Madina, 17–18, 288
trans*, 212n1; and affect, 201; synecdochal accounts of, 209
trans* of color, 198, 201; and embodiment, 209; and indignation, 203, 209–11; South Asians, 118; subjectivity of, 209
transing, 19, 198, 210; and benevolent violence, 211–12; embodiments of color, 198, 200–201, 204–6, 209; in "Pilgrimage," 209–12
transnormativity, 204
trash: being treated as, 33–34, 36, 39–40, 42–44; and purity, 40; semantics of, 33–34, 45n5; talking back of, 34, 35–36, 41
trauma, 56, 106, 127, 290n5; inherited, 160, 166
traveling, 221. See also world-traveling
Trebilcott, Joyce, 257
Trickster, the, 258–59, 270
Turner, Victor, 18, 61n3

universalism: and decolonial ethics, 179; and modern ethics, 177
U.S. Third World women: solidarity, politics of, 12

Vaid-Menon, Alok, 103
Valdez Condo War, 241
Vanita, Ruth, 213n8
Vargas, Kathy, 278
violence: and benevolence, 198, 208–12; of coloniality of gender, 8, 21, 288; and colonization, 54, 133; familial, 112; invisibility of, 227; and men of color, 16–18, 180, 266–67, 288; of oppression, 37; against people of color, 279; resistance to, 245, 247–48, 264, 282; U.S. sponsored, 281; against women, 257; against women of color, 16–18, 175–76, 180, 266–67, 288

Viramontes, Helena María, 289

Walker, Kara, 278
Walter, Bronwen, 145–46, 158
Waters, Anne, 257
Weberman, A.J., 35
Weiland, Christine, 55
Wenzel, Karen, 229
Wester, Michelle Black, 73
Weston, Ka-14th, 113
white feminism, 258, 267; colonial/modern gender system, collusion with, 53; and cultural imperialism, 37
whiteness: and Black/Latina space, 257; and the Caucasus, 131; and "civilization," 148; and coloniality of gender, 145; in *Dictée*, 69–70; and fragmentation, 281–82; as humanness, 166–67; and impurity, 275; and intersectionality, 89; and Irish Americans, 156–57; and Irishness, 146–48, 151, 156, 158; lgbt counterpublics, centering of, 204; and liberalism, 192n13; and model-minority racial project, 111; and multiplicity, 69; and personhood, 154, 182, 183, 189; and purity, 69–70; and violence, 281–82; and womanhood, 183–84
white supremacy, 190; and antiracism, 176, 188; and Chicano ethics, 184; and decolonial ethics, 187; and immediate grasp, 166; and Irish Americans, 157; and lgbtq rights, 19–20; and men of color, 188, 190; and model-minority racial project, 110–11; resistance to, 175; and sabotage, 259; and women of color, 169
"white trash," 45n4
Wiegman, Robyn, 87
Williams, Pat, 224–25
Winant, Howard, 279
woman warriors, 80n6; in *Dictée*, 73, 77, 79
women of color: and colonial/modern gender system, 184; invisibility of, 12–13, 96–97; and Irish Americans, 168; and modernity, 187–88; multiple oppressions of, 13; racial oppression of, 175; violence against, 180
Women of Color feminisms, 23n1, 99, 279; coalitional politics of, 2, 4, 6–7, 23n6, 168, 269; epistemology, 6; and intermeshed oppressions, 85, 86
Women's studies programs, 261
Wong, Shelly Sunn, 67
worlds of sense, 10–11
world-traveling, 9–10, 19, 23n8, 50, 125, 260, 265; and complex communication, 75, 76; to death-worlds, 221, 228, 232–33; and deep coalition, 9; and erasure, 38; and identity, 221; and ontological slipperiness, 166; and performance, 44n3; and playfulness, 11, 137; and political action, 221; and prisons, 220–21; and societal fear, 230–31; and subjectivity, 233

Yerofeyev, Victor, 131
Yu Guan Soon, 70–71, 73–74, 76–77

Zaytoun, Kelli, 11, 18
Žižek, Slavoj, 222

Milton Keynes UK
Ingram Content Group UK Ltd.
UKHW010502150324
439524UK00021B/419